AMERICAN DEMOCRACY PROMOTION

American Democracy Promotion

Impulses, Strategies, and Impacts

EDITED BY

Michael Cox

G. John Ikenberry

and

Takashi Inoguchi

OXFORD

UNIVERSITY PRESS

OXFORD

UNIVERSITY PRESS

Great Clarendon Street, Oxford OX2 6DP

Oxford University Press is a department of the University of Oxford.
It furthers the University's objective of excellence in research, scholarship,
and education by publishing worldwide in

Oxford New York

Auckland Cape Town Dar es Salaam Hong Kong Karachi Kuala Lumpur
Madrid Melbourne Mexico City Nairobi New Delhi Shanghai Taipei Toronto

With offices in

Argentina Austria Brazil Chile Czech Republic France Greece
Guatemala Hungary Italy Japan Poland Portugal Singapore
South Korea Switzerland Thailand Turkey Ukraine Vietnam

Published in the United States
by Oxford University Press Inc., New York

First published 2000
Reprinted 2001, 2002 (twice)

British Library Cataloguing in Publication Data

Data available

Library of Congress Cataloging in Publication Data

American democracy promotion: impulses, strategies, and impacts/
edited by Michael Cox, G. John Ikenberry, and Takashi Inoguchi.
p. cm.
Includes bibliographical references and index.
1. United States - Foreign relations - 1989- .
2. Democracy - United States.
3. Democratization - Government policy - United States.
I. Cox, Michael. II. Ikenberry, G. John. III. Inoguchi, Takashi.
E840.A622   2000   327.73-dc21   00-031351

ISBN 978-0-19-829678-2 (Hbk)
ISBN 978-0-19-924097-5 (Pbk)

Typeset by Hope Services (Abingdon) Ltd.
Printed in Great Britain
on acid-free paper by
Biddles Ltd., King's Lynn, Norfolk

ACKNOWLEDGEMENTS

This volume is the culmination of a study that began life in New York, continued to mature in Tokyo, Washington and London and was finally laid to rest—metaphorically speaking—in Aberystwyth in Wales. Along the way, a large number of debts have been accumulated. Perhaps the greatest is to the sponsors, the Social Science Research Council (SSRC), and the associated MacArthur Programme on International Peace and Security. Though many at the SSRC played their part, including Arun Elhance, Martin Malin, and Mark Shoffner, we should like to pay special tribute to the dedication of Robert Latham—a fine scholar in his own right—without whose encouragement and expertise we would not have been able to complete the job. In this connection, we should also mention Peter Katzenstein, Lynn Eden, Lawrie Freedman, Atul Kohli, Jack Snyder, Frank von Hippel and Philip Tetlock, all of whom made their own distinct contributions to the project. Next, we should like to extend a warm word of gratitude to the various scholars who gathered in Japan in September 1996 to discuss the SSRC proposal in more detail. Here, we should particularly like to thank Fumiaki Kubo, Bruce Russett and Davis Bobrow. Bruce and Davis also attended the follow-up conference in Washington held at the Carnegie Endowment in Washington in January 1998. Many of the papers presented there appear in revised form in this book, but others also contributed to what turned out to be a memorable two-day gathering— notably Doug Brinkley, Leszek Buszynski, Ali Mazrui, Alexandre Nikitine, and Quansheng Zhao. We should also wish to record our gratitude to the Carnegie for being such admirable hosts.

Of course, all good things have to come to an end, and this one came to a most fortunate conclusion when Oxford University Press agreed to publish. We should especially like to express our thanks to Christiane Seitz of Aberystwyth for working on the manuscript and compiling the index, Michael James for his excellent copy-editing, Amanda Watkins for pushing the manuscript along at a critical stage, and Dominic Byatt—one of the more patient and dynamic members of the OUP team—who encouraged the editors at a crucial moment. All three editors also owe more than a passing debt to their home institutions; so we would like to express our thanks as well to the United Nations University, the University of Tokyo, the Christopher Browne Center for International Politics at the University of Pennsylvania, and the Department of International Politics in the University of Wales, Aberystwyth. We should, however, wish to extend a special word of gratitude to Steve Smith. As a member of the SSRC team, he helped launch the project in the first place. He then acted as informal liaison between the SSRC and the editors. And he supported the extensive work done in turning the various papers into a book back in Wales. We hope he feels that it was all worthwhile.

Finally, all big books accumulate debts of a more personal nature and the three editors would therefore like to dedicate this study to those who have supported them in more ways than words can express: their respective partners, Fiona Stephen, Lidia Ikenberry and Kuniko Inoguchi.

Michael Cox, G. John Ikenberry and Takashi Inoguchi.

January 2000

CONTENTS

LIST OF CONTRIBUTORS

Michael Cox is a Professor in the Department of International Politics in the University of Wales, Aberystwyth. He is editor of the *Review of International Studies* and has been an Associate Research Fellow at the Royal Institute of International Affairs in London since 1994. His most recent publications include *US Foreign Policy After the Cold War: Superpower without a Mission?* (1995), *Rethinking the Soviet Collapse: Sovietology, the Death of Communism and the New Russia* (1998) and (with Ken Booth and Tim Dunne) *The Eighty Years' Crisis: International Relations, 1919–1999* (1998) and *The Interregnum: Controversies in World Politics, 1989–1999* (1999). In 2000, Professor Cox will also be publishing *E. H. Carr: A Critical Appraisal*, and a study co-edited with Adrian Guelke and Fiona Stephen, *A Farewell to Arms? From 'Long War' to 'Long Peace' in Northern Ireland*.

G. John Ikenberry is Professor of Political Science at the University of Pennsylvania, where he is Director of the Christopher Browne Center for International Politics. He is also a non-resident scholar at the Brookings Institution and a book editor for *Foreign Affairs*. He is the author of several books including *After Victory: Institutions, Strategic Restraint and the Rebuilding of Order After Major Wars* (2000).

Takashi Inoguchi formerly Senior Vice-Rector of the United Nations University, is Professor of Political Science at the Institute of Oriental Culture in the University of Tokyo. His most recent publications include *Global Change: 4* and *Japanese Essay* (2000) *Japan's Foreign Policy Today* (2000).

Thomas Carothers is Vice-President for Global Policy at the Carnegie Endowment for Peace in Washington. A one-time adviser to the US government, his published work includes *In the Name of Democracy: US Policy Towards Latin America in the Reagan Era* (1991) and *Aiding Democracy Abroad: The Learning Curve* (1999).

Michael Doyle is Professor of Politics and International Affairs at Princeton University, where he is also Director of the Center of International Studies and editor of *World Politics*. Author of several books, his most recent is *Ways of War and Peace: Realism, Liberalism and Socialism* (1998).

Barry Gills teaches in the Department of Politics at the University of Newcastle and has published widely on international political economy. His books include (with J. Rocamora) *Low Intensity Democracy: Political Power in the New World Order* (1993) and (with A. G. Frank) *The World System: Five Hundred Years or Five Thousand?* (1996).

Ole Holsti is George V. Allen Professor of International Affairs at Duke University. An expert of public opinion, he is the author of many books including *Public Opinion and American Foreign Policy* (1996).

Henry Nau served in the US government and is now Professor of Political Science at the Elliott School of International Affairs, the George Washington University. His published work to date includes, among other things, *The Myth of America's Decline* (1990) and *Trade and Security: US Policies at Cross-Purposes* (1995).

Jason Ralph teaches in the Department of Politics and International Studies at the University of Leeds. He specializes on security issues, US foreign policy and US-Russian relations. His most recent book is *Beyond the Security Dilemma: Ending America's Cold War* (2000).

William I. Robinson, formerly of the University of Tennessee, now teaches sociology at the New Mexico State University. Among his publications is *Promoting Polyarchy: Globalization, US Intervention and Hegemony* (1996).

Peter Rutland teaches in the Department of Government at Wesleyan University. A long-term student of Soviet and post-Soviet affairs, his books include *The Myth of the Plan* (1984) and *The Politics of Economic Stagnation in the Soviet Union* (1993).

Randall Schweller teaches in the Department of Political Science at the Ohio State University. His most recent volume is *Deadly Imbalances: Tripolarity and Hitler's Strategy of World Conquest* (1998).

Steve Smith is a Professor in the Department of International Politics in the University of Wales, Aberystwyth. He is co-author (with Martin Hollis) of *Explaining and Understanding International Relations* (1990) and (with Ken Booth) of *International Relations Theory Today* (1995).

Tony Smith is Cornelia M. Jackson Professor of Political Science at Tufts University. He has published widely, including *America's Mission: The United States and the Worldwide Struggle for Democracy in the Twentieth Century* (1994) and *One Nation Divisible? Ethnic Groups and Foreign Policy* (2000).

Georg Sørensen is a Professor of Political Science in the University of Aarhus. His most recent books are *Democracy and Democratization* (1998) and (with Robert Jackson) *Introduction to International Relations* (1999).

LIST OF FIGURES

LIST OF TABLES

Introduction

MICHAEL COX, G. JOHN IKENBERRY and TAKASHI INOGUCHI

NO introductory text to the study of politics is ever complete without the standard definitional question being asked: so what is politics? Depending on the author, the answer is never quite the same; none the less, it is remarkable how frequently analysts of different theoretical persuasions usually end up repeating the same old favourite that in some timeless sense politics has always been about the unequal distribution of power, or, to use Laswell's phrase, about 'who gets what, when, and how'. The more adventurous, of course, might turn to Machiavelli or even Mill, Marx or Weber, but they appear only to confirm the 'truth' that politics is little more than the competitive struggle for power conducted among those at the top who care little for ideals, and even less for the comfort of their fellow citizens.

Now while such brutal realism has a long and, some would say, honourable pedigree stretching back to the Greeks and the great historian Thucydides, any understanding of politics that ignored the part played by ideas in the making of the modern world—and in particular the idea of democracy—is liable to be a very partial one indeed. Many historians in fact would contend that at least one way of thinking about political life since the late eighteenth century is as an ongoing struggle between those wishing to expand the boundaries of freedom and those seeking to contain it. Certainly, in most countries, even that celebrated home of constitutional liberty, Great Britain, democracy was not something that gradually evolved and matured some time after the Napoleonic Wars, but was, rather, a political aspiration that had to be fought for against those who sought to control, manipulate and often retard what they saw as this most dangerous of political deviations. Regarded by its enemies—including most nineteenth-century liberals—as a threat to stable order and the institution of private property, democracy had few friends in high places.[1] And even those who did not view democracy in such apocalyptic terms still saw it as the short end of a wedge that would lead, over time, to that most dreaded of all popular afflictions: Americanization! One might even suggest that one of the hidden, and still understudied, themes of nineteenth-century politics is the extent to which negative images of American democracy

[1] See Michael Bentley, *Politics Without Democracy, 1815–1914: Perception and Preoccupation in British Government* (1984; London: Fontana Press, 1996).

were deployed by elites across the European continent to try to justify their continued rule.[2]

Democracy was thus no 'natural' phenomenon but a highly contested concept that divided nations by pitting class against class, men against women, and white people against those they controlled, whether in the slave plantations of the deep South or the colonies of Asia and Africa. But politics, as we have also been told, never stops at the water's edge, and many of the great battles in the international arena mirrored those taking place within the boundaries of the nation-state. America's fight for independence, the various struggles conducted against absolutism in Europe before 1914, the fight to defeat the Axis, and the several wars of national liberation after 1945 were all in their various fashions inspired by a larger set of political values. It is easy to be cynical about motives, but men and women, and countries as well, have to have a political faith, and increasingly in the modern world that faith has come to be based upon the now self-evident truth that democracy, however defined, is not only ethically preferable but increasingly the only legitimate means by which we can manage our political affairs effectively.[3]

The apparently irresistible rise of democracy has generated a vast literature, one that shows no sign of drying up as scholars attempt to come to terms with the three great waves of democratization that swept the world in the last quarter of the twentieth century. It is not the only issue to have excited political scientists, yet democracy as a form of government has clearly dominated 'the political science literature' since the mid-1970s.[4] In the process, more traditional concerns about the political theory of democracy have been supplemented by a series of new concerns. These have ranged far and wide, but have focused on a number of key issues including the underlying reasons for the spread of democracy,[5] the connection (if any) between inequality, democracy and economic development,[6] the ways and means by which the new democracies have become consolidated,[7] the different forms that democracy has taken as it has fanned out from its core original areas,[8] and the complex rela-

---

[2] 'What influence may help us to prevent the English people from becoming, with the growth of democracy, Americanized?', asked the English educationalist Matthew Arnold in 1861. Cited in W. H. G. Armytage, *Four Hundred Years of English Education* (Cambridge: Cambridge University Press, 1964), p. 137.

[3] Some writers insist argue that modern democracy is an unfamiliar and uncomfortable system of governance for non-western peoples. See Katherine Fierlbeck, *Globalizing Democracy: Power, Legitimacy and the Interpretation of Democratic Ideas* (Manchester: Manchester University Press, 1998).

[4] Quoted in J. J. van Wyk and Mary C. Custy, *Contemporary Democracy: A Bibliography of Periodical Literature, 1974–1994* (Washington, DC: Congressional Quarterly Inc. 1999), p. ix. This useful collection lists nearly 8,000 articles on democracy published in the English language.

[5] Samuel Huntington, *The Third Wave: Democratization in the Late Twentieth Century* (Norman: University of Oklahoma Press, 1991).

[6] Manus I. Mildarsky (ed.), *Inequality, Democracy, and Economic Development* (Cambridge: Cambridge University Press, 1997).

[7] See Larry Diamond, *Developing Democracy: Toward Consolidation* (Baltimore: The John Hopkins University Press, 1999).

[8] See Larry Diamond, Mark Plattner, Yun-han Chu, and Hung-mao-Tien (eds), *Consolidating the Third Wave Democracies*, 2 vols (Baltimore: The John Hopkins University Press, 1997).

tionship between that most over-studied of modern phenomena—globalization—and national democratic control of the political process.[9]

Of course, the new literature has not just celebrated democracy as a political form. It has also explored its many contradictions. One of these has been the shallow character of the democratic process in a number of the more recently 'liberated' countries,[10] a theme that has been discussed at some length, particularly by those authors interested in Latin America and the old Communist systems in transition.[11] There is also the much larger problem of the often tense, rarely straightforward relationship between the market and democracy. The question here can be posed quite simply: does the market foster democracy, or, alternatively, does it (as some claim) weaken or even undermine its effective operation ?[12] Finally, there is the issue of democracy itself. Democracy might well have become the political gold standard of the late twentieth century, having swept all opponents aside.[13] Yet within the great bastions of advanced world, all is not well: participation is on the decline, cynicism about the political process has never been higher, and money appears to have become the most important political commodity of all. Democracy may have established itself as the norm,[14] but, as Jean Elshtain has noted, it is faltering not flourishing, and nowhere more obviously than in the great bastion of the free world: the United States.[15] Whether we define this as a crisis or not is a moot pint.[16] The fact remains that democracy appears to have triumphed at precisely the same time when tendencies towards social disintegration and widespread voter alienation are undercutting meaningful political life for the overwhelming majority of people.[17]

Unfortunately, the exponential growth in democracy studies in political science has not been matched by an equally significant body of work by students of international relations or American foreign policy; and if political scientists might legitimately be accused of a failure to relate the dynamics of

---

[9] For two essays assessing the thesis that globalization makes 'national' democracy redundant, see Linda Weiss, 'Globalization and the Myth of the Powerless State', *New Left Review*, 225 (1997), pp. 3–27, and Peter Evans, 'The Eclipse of the State: Reflections on Stateness in an era of Globalization', *World Politics*, 50 (1997), pp. 171–200.

[10] See for example Larry Diamond, 'Is the Third Wave Over?', *Journal of Democracy*, 7/3 (1988), pp. 20–38; Terry Lynn Karl, 'Dilemmas of Democratisation in Latin America', *Comparative Politics*, 23/1 (1990), pp. 1–21; and Alex Hadenius (ed.), *Democracy's Victory and Crisis* (Cambridge: Cambridge University Press, 1997).

[11] See for example Scott Mainwaring and Timothy R. Scully (eds), *Building Democratic Institutions: Party Systems in Latin America* (Stanford: Stanford University Press, 1995), and Harry Eckstein, William M. Reisinger, Eric Hoffmann, and Frederick J. Fleron, *Can Democracy Take Root in Post-Soviet Russia?* (Oxford: Rowman & Littlefield, 1998).

[12] See Ellen M. Wood, *Democracy Against Capitalism: Renewing Historical Materialism* (Cambridge: Cambridge University Press, 1995).

[13] See Ian Schapiro, *Democracy's Place* (Ithaca and London: Cornell University Press, 1996), p. 3.

[14] See David Held, *Democracy and the Global Order* (Cambridge: Polity Press, 1995), p. 3.

[15] Jean Bethke Elshtain, *Democracy on Trial* (New York: Basic Books, 1995), especially pp. 1–36.

[16] Manuel Castells, *The Information Age: Economy, Society and Culture. Volume II: The Power of Identity* (Oxford: Blackwell, 1999), pp. 342–53.

[17] See April Carter and Geoffrey Stokes (eds), *Liberal Democracy and its Critics* (Cambridge: Polity Press, 1998).

democratization to larger changes in the world system,[18] scholars in international politics might be attacked with equal force for ignoring democracy. Even the so-called democratic peace thesis—first articulated by Michael Doyle in 1983—did not excite much intellectual debate initially: it was only after the collapse of communism that commentators began to discuss its merits and policy implications.[19] More remarkable still has been the silence until recently about the role played by the United States.[20] There are studies galore of American foreign policy in the modern epoch, but until Tony Smith's challenging volume on democracy promotion (published in 1994) there had been no serious academic study of the subject. Not surprisingly, this led Smith in the same book to ask the obvious question, why 'given the abundant literature analysing the character of democracy on the one hand and the nature of American foreign policy on the other' has so little been written on the problem?[21] At least three answers might be suggested here.

The first relates to the intellectual prejudices of different scholars, and in particular the refusal by realists and radicals alike to take claims about American democracy promotion seriously: radicals because they do not think the US has actually promoted the cause of political freedom, and realists because they do not think it is America's job to do so.[22] Then there is the obvious problem of the cold war. Though fought under the banner of democracy, after 1947 America's principal objective was not to promote political freedom but to contain the Soviet Union, and in the rough and tough world of the cold war policymakers tended to judge their friends not by their liberal credentials but by their loyalty to the larger cause of anti-communism. Finally, while many policymakers may have endorsed democracy in theory, in practice many like Acheson and Kissinger tended to prefer order to freedom, stability to choice, and thus did not overly concern themselves with the political complexion of certain rather unsavoury regimes.[23] This partly reflected their own hierarchical view of the world. But it was also a response to the unpredictabil-

---

[18] See for example the discussion in Tatu Vanhnen, *Prospects of Democracy: A Study of 172 Countries* (London and New York: Routledge, 1997), especially pp. 10–26.

[19] The most influential empirical study that teased out the policy implications of the democratic peace was Bruce Russett's important *Grasping the Democratic Peace: Principles for a Democratic World* (Princeton: Princeton University Press, 1993).

[20] For two recent empirical studies of US democracy promotion efforts, see Marc Peceny, *Democracy at the Point of Bayonets* (Pennsylvania: The Pennsylvania State University Press, 1999) and Joanne Gowa, *Building Bridges or Democracies Abroad? U.S. Foreign Policy after the Cold War* (Princeton: Princeton University Press, 2000).

[21] See Tony Smith, *America's Mission: The United States and the Worldwide Struggle for Democracy in the Twentieth Century* (New Jersey, Princeton University Press, 1994), p. 346.

[22] The classic radical case is made by Noam Chomsky in 'Market Democracy in a Neoliberal Order', Davie Lecture (University of Cape Town, May 1997). A powerful realist perspective is advanced by John L. Harper, 'The Dream of the Democratic Peace', *Foreign Affairs*, 76/3 (1997), pp. 117–21.

[23] After meeting the Portuguese dictator Salazar in early 1950, Dean Acheson concluded that, while 'a convinced libertarian—particularly a foreign one—could understandably disapprove of Salazar', he did not; and he doubted whether 'Plato would have done so' either! See Dean Acheson, *Present At The Creation: My Years at the State Department* (New York: W. W. Norton, 1969), p. 628.

ity of politics in the post-war period.[24] In an era of turmoil and revolution, where one could not be certain that elections or the exercise of self-determination would always lead to outcomes favourable to American inter-ests, it seemed safer—or so many policymakers felt—to ally oneself with elites one could trust rather than the masses whom one could not.[25]

The collapse of old cold war certainties, in the context of an ever-expanding number of countries calling themselves democratic, clearly makes the study of democracy promotion more interesting and exciting. It also makes it more rel-evant given the higher priority now accorded the policy by US policymakers.[26] Not that we have to be believe what they say, or even assume that everybody in the US now subscribes to the idea. There are many, in fact, who continue to have their doubts about the wisdom of democracy promotion as an object-ive.[27] That said, it is almost impossible to ignore the important shift that has taken place, one that has pushed the issue much higher up the American for-eign policy agenda over the past few years.

But why precisely has democracy promotion assumed greater importance since the end of the cold war, aside from the more short-term one that Clinton decided to make it a political issue in his bid to win the presidency in 1992?[28] One reason, obviously, is that democracy promotion has rather neatly filled the missionary gap left behind by the collapse of international communism.[29] All great powers require a 'big idea' and democratic enlargement, it would seem, has become America's in the post-cold war era. The decision to elevate democracy promotion has also made it possible for the US to square the circle between its behaviour abroad and its attachment to democratic norms at home. Some would even maintain that democracy promotion not only gives full expression to the nation's deeper democratic identity, but also helps bind it together by reconnecting it with core historical traditions.[30] Lastly, the

[24] See William O. Walker III, 'Melvyn Leffler, Ideology and American Foreign Policy', *Diplomatic History*, 20/4 (1996), p. 669.

[25] This security-based analysis can be found, for example, in Stephen Krasner, *Defending the National Interest: Raw Materials Investments and U.S. Foreign Policy* (Princeton: Princeton University Press, 1978) and Stephen Walt, *The Origins of Alliances* (Ithaca, NY: Cornell University Press, 1987). For a concrete example of American support for dictatorship, see Eric Paul Roorda, *The Dictator Next Door: The Good Neighbor Policy and the Trujillo Regime in the Dominican Republic, 1930–1945* (Durham and London: Duke University Press, 1998).

[26] On the origins of 'democratic enlargement' as a policy, see Douglas Brinkley, 'Democratic Enlargement: The Clinton Doctrine', *Foreign Policy*, 106 (1997), pp. 111–27.

[27] See for example Robert W. Tucker, 'The Triumph of Wilsonianism?', *World Policy Journal*, 10/4 (1993/94), pp. 83–99, and Fareed Zakaria, 'Internationalism as a Way of Life', *World Policy Journal*, 12/2 (1995), pp. 59–61. See the useful discussion in Christopher Layne and Sean M. Lynn Jones, *Should America Promote Democracy?* (Cambridge, MA: MIT Press, 1998).

[28] At a number of points during the 1992 presidential campaign, Clinton accused Bush of being soft on dictators and dictatorships and of not appearing to be 'at home in the mainstream pro-demo-cracy mainstream of American foreign policy'. See *Clinton on Foreign Policy* (London: United States Information Service, n.d), p. 45.

[29] On the search for a new American mission since the end of the cold war, see Michael Cox, *US Foreign Policy after the Cold War: Superpower Without a Mission?* (London: Pinter/Royal Institute of International Affairs, 1995).

[30] On the importance of rooting American foreign policy in the American democratic tradition, see Rick Travis, 'The Promotion of Democracy at the End of the Twentieth Century: A New Polestar

renewed stress on democracy promotion has, in part, been a response to discussions in the academic community.[31] Previously, influential commentators like Kennan could easily dismiss the idea as mere moralism, arguing that in the 'real world' such high-minded idealism was not only of little practical utility but likely to lead the United States into dangerous crusades.[32] By the 1990s, this viewpoint came under serious and sustained attack by those who refused to accept the apparently neat conceptual distinction between ideals and interests. Such a division, it was now argued, was not just intellectually dubious but did not actually serve America's purposes. After all, if democracies did not go to war with each other—as many now seemed to believe—then the US clearly had a vested interest in making the world safe for democracy. If moreover 'free markets and democracy formed a symbiotic and reciprocal relationship that produced free, stable and prosperous societies', and that 'both produced benefits for the United States' (to quote one US official), it made even more sense to support the cause of political freedom around the world. It was not just the right thing to do: it was the smart thing to do as well.[33]

The complex relationship between ideals and interests is one we shall be exploring at length in this volume. It is a discussion we cannot avoid: one might even go so far as to suggest that it lies at the heart of the contemporary debate about American foreign policy. It is also a discussion that has so far been falsely polarized between those who apparently favour the policy of democracy promotion because it is seen as being ethical, and others who oppose it in the name of a higher realism. This is not only methodologically unsatisfying, but ignores the obvious historical point that most realists have frequently been dreamers and utopians (witness the obvious case of E. H. Carr), while so-called 'idealists' have often turned out to be rather tough-minded individuals.[34] Take the case of that much-berated moral crusader, Woodrow Wilson. Wilson, we know, talked a great deal about the power of ideas in world politics. However, he was never squeamish when it came to using American force abroad: he did so in fact on no fewer than seven occasions between 1914 and 1918.[35] Nor was his call for a democratic peace motivated by ideals alone. As a number of historians have shown, Wilson advanced his Fourteen Points for many reasons, but one, obviously, was a shrewd appreciation that liberal democracy was the best antidote to Bolshevism and reaction in a world turned upside down by global war. Even his support for

for American Foreign Policy?', in James M. Scott (ed.), *After the End: Making U. S. Foreign Policy in the Post-Cold War World* (Durham: Duke University Press, 1998), pp. 253–4.

[31] This debate is neatly summed up by Steve Chan, 'In Search of Democratic Peace: Problems and Promise', *Mershon International Studies Review*, 41 (1997), pp. 59–91.

[32] See George Kennan, *American Diplomacy, 1900-1950* (Chicago: University of Chicago Press, 1958).

[33] Quote from Travis, 'The Promotion of Democracy at the End of the Twentieth Century', p. 253. The national interest case for promoting democracy is made by Strobe Talbott in his 'Democracy and the National Interest', *Foreign Affairs*, 74/6 (1996), pp. 47–63.

[34] See E. H. Carr, *The Twenty Years' Crisis*, 2nd edn (New York: Harper & Row, 1946).

[35] See Frederick Calhoun, *Power and Principle: Armed Intervention in Wilsonian Foreign Policy* (Kent: Kent State University Press, 1986).

self-determination was as much a strategic ploy as a moral demand. As the record reveals, the ultimate purpose of the slogan was not to free all nations, but rather to undermine the remaining empires on the European continent and win America friends in eastern and central Europe. Wilson understood, even if his later realist critics did not, the power of values and norms in international relations.[36]

This volume seeks to untangle the theoretical and historical issues that are at stake in the American pursuit of democracy worldwide, and it seeks to do this by asking three large questions. In the first section it looks at the fundamental terms of the debate, and examines the contested concepts of democracy, power and ideals: and the broad question it seeks to answer is: to what extent does classical political theory help us unravel the more practical issues posed by democracy and democracy promotion? The following two sections examine the strategy, logic, and politics of the American pursuit of world-wide democracy. Here we pose the question: what are the political and strategic impulses that lie behind the American experience with democracy promotion? In the final section, the book looks at the impacts and legacies of American democracy promotion and asks: how has American advancement of democracy been experienced, how have countries and regions been influenced by American efforts, and how influential have such efforts been?

Democracy Promotion: A Contested Notion

For one of the most debated foreign policy questions, it is remarkable how little agreement there seems to be about the meaning of American democracy promotion in practice. Thus, while some analysts view it as an unnecessary intrusion into the otherwise normal conduct of diplomatic relations—a position still championed by Henry Kissinger[37]—others regard it as part of a practical strategy designed to advance American national interests.[38] More cynical observers see it as a mere facade designed to mask the hard edge of American hegemony; quite a few, however, dismiss it almost completely as being of very minor importance in understanding the deeper sources of American conduct in world affairs.[39] There is even a strand of thinking which seems to feel that the promotion of democracy is a form of Western arrogance, stemming from the quite false assumption that a concept of human rights born under one set of conditions has universal meaning and could and should be applied to

---

[36] For an excellent short guide to these issues see Lawrence E. Gelfhand, 'Where Ideals Confront Self-Interest: Wilsonian Foreign Policy', *Diplomatic History*, 18/1 (1994), pp. 125–3.

[37] See Henry Kissinger, 'Reality and illusion about the Chinese', *Independent* (18 October 1999).

[38] For a national interest perspective see Talbott, 'Democracy and the National Interest', pp. 47–63.

[39] For a sceptical discussion of democracy promotion in general, see Gorm Rye Olsen, 'Europe and the Promotion of Democracy in Post-Cold War Africa: How Serious Is Europe and for What Reason?', *African Affairs*, 97/388 (1998), pp. 343–68.

other, very different, cultures.[40] And so the debate goes on, pitting one school of thought against another, proving (if proof were ever needed) that there are as many views about democracy promotion as there are perhaps ideological perspectives.

In the opening section of the book we bring together three leading writers to explore some of these issues in detail. We begin with an essay by Michael Doyle, whose name has come to be closely associated with the renewal of modern interest in Kant and Kant's views on the so-called liberal peace. Doyle here broadens the discussion considerably by seeking to situate the current policy debate about democracy promotion within a careful reading of both liberal and realist traditions. As Doyle makes clear, there is more than one type of liberalism and more than one form of realism, and to reduce either to a single essence only does damage to what are, in effect, two very complex traditions. Liberals he broadly divides into three: Lockeans, commercial pacifists (Adam Smith and Joseph Schumpeter), and liberal republicans or internationalists—in effect the followers of Kant. All three need to be understood before we can unravel the complex relationship between the idea of what is generically known as the 'liberal peace' and liberalism as a theoretical discourse. But it is Kant who has assumed centre stage in the modern debate about peace and war, and though Kantian insights, according to Doyle, do not unlock all doors, his theory appears to be both necessary and sufficient to explain why liberal democracies do not go to war with each other. The twist in the Kantian tail, of course, is that while Kant helps us understand why liberal states are peace-prone towards each other, he also shows why they are particularly war-prone towards states that are not, and by so doing provides us with a sound theoretical guide to the great conflicts of the twentieth century.

But Doyle is not uncritical of liberalism or those who argue that democracy always leads to peaceful relations between states. As he points out, majority rule alone, without the presence of associated traditions of individual rights, can fuel nationalism and autarky and thereby undermine the cosmopolitan basis of peaceful and interdependent relations. Nor is he dismissive of the insights furnished by classical realists, notably Thucydides, Machiavelli, Hobbes, and Rousseau. Their pessimism about the war-prone character of interstate relations may not be acceptable to most liberals, past or present. On the other hand, their views cannot be lightly dismissed; and while liberalism might better explain the long periods of peace among liberal states in ways that realism cannot, realist insights about diplomacy and the balance of power can still account for certain aspects of international stability. Realism may be flawed, but it is by no means irrelevant.

The more systematic case for realism is made in typically robust fashion by Randall Schweller. Like Doyle before him, Schweller paints a complex picture of realism and distinguishes carefully between three branches stemming from the same intellectual tree: Waltzian structural realism which views all talk of a

---

[40] See Miyume Tanji and Stephanie Lawson, ' "Democratic Peace" and "Asian Democracy": A Universalist-Particularist Tension', *Alternatives*, 22 (1997), pp. 135–55.

democratic peace as both theoretically dubious and politically dangerous, neo-classical realism which sees some merit in the argument, and motivational realism which accepts that states which are transparent and open are likely to behave differently from those which are not. That, at least, is the 'good news' coming from the realist camp. The 'bad news' is that this still does not mean that the creation of a democratic zone will lead to perpetual peace as liberals suggest and many US foreign policymakers assume. Democracy might be able to ameliorate the three causes of war identified by Hobbes—diffidence, competition and glory—but it cannot eliminate them completely. The fundamental causes of conflict and war thus remain intact, and do so precisely because they cannot be transcended.

The other bit of 'bad news' relates to the uneven distribution of scarce resources in an ever-changing world economy where there are clear winners and losers. Naturally enough, the winners like the United States favour peace. However, not everybody is a winner, and those who stand outside the golden circle of satisfied powers are never likely to be content with their lot. This is the true 'Achilles heel' of the democratic peace thesis, according to Schweller. Furthermore, it is just not true that the development and spread of capitalism automatically fosters good relations between states. This particular notion—first articulated just before World War I by Karl Kautsky and Norman Angell—has not only been refuted by modern history, but ignores the simple fact that even under the most propitious of circumstances states will always compete for positional goods. Nor is it the case that capitalism automatically leads to democracy. This is another liberal myth. As Schweller points out, capitalism can coexist with a multiplicity of political forms: basically, what it 'needs' is not democracy but stability, and this can just as easily be provided by repressive polities like China as it can by liberal ones like the United States.

If Schweller provides us with much food for thought, then so too does Steve Smith. Having travelled the long intellectual road from foreign policy analysis to post-positivist theory, Smith is perhaps well equipped to interrogate the empirical and theoretical claims of those who support democracy promotion as a foreign policy objective, and does so from a broadly radical, Foucauldian perspective. Smith does not oppose democracy or America's right to promote it. What he does question however is the extent to which the United States has ever really practised what it has preached. The record until very recently has been far more patchy than apologists claim, he believes. Indeed, in places like Latin America, the American mission has been less politically liberal than hegemonic, and more likely to bolster forces of political reaction than enlightenment. This was true before the cold war began and remained true well into the 1980s. To suggest otherwise, Smith argues, simply flies in the face of the historical evidence.

But if Smith is sceptical about America's commitment to democracy promotion, he is equally critical about the form of democracy the US has chosen to promote: democracy, he notes, is a many-splendoured political phenomenon, but America in his opinion has chosen—and continues to choose—to export only one particularly narrow version of it, especially to the Third World. Smith also wonders about the extent to which US promotional efforts have been subordinated to its larger and more important economic goals; moreover, the US, he feels, constantly undermines its own limited efforts by advancing a neo-liberal economic agenda that reduces the scope of popular participation while entrenching the position of local elites. Yet this is not how American policymakers—or most American academics for that matter—see things; which brings Smith to his central theoretical claim: that the contemporary debate about democracy promotion rests upon a prior political move that separates economics from politics. This makes it possible for otherwise fair-minded people to discuss the issue of democracy promotion in isolation from an assessment of material interests. Not only does this render the debate somewhat abstract, but means that most analysts are unable, or unwilling, to ask the most important questions of all about American 'truth claims' that its global mission is to make the world safe for democracy.

Democracy Promotion as American 'Grand Strategy?'

The second part of the book looks at the 'grand strategy' of American democracy promotion, and the discussion begins with a wide-ranging survey by Tony Smith, who elaborates upon the concept of 'national security liberalism'. A close examination of the historical record, he believes, reveals that democracy promotion has been understood by American foreign policy officials over the decades as more than just a cover story designed to obscure the United States' real purpose in the world. Based upon a relatively sophisticated set of ideas about the relationship between democratic forms and global order, the US, he insists, has had a 'mission' for a very long time to promote democracy. It has not always been able to do this consistently; occasionally it has been impelled to subordinate its larger ambition to other considerations. None the less, the fact that American presidents as far apart in time and viewpoint as Woodrow Wilson and Ronald Reagan have pursued the policy would point to a remarkable continuity in outlook. It would also suggest that those who have championed democracy promotion since the end of the cold war have been a good deal less innovative than they or their critics have implied.

Democracy promotion has thus been a defining characteristic of American foreign policy for the greater part of the twentieth century. Honed in the first instance as a means of countering European imperialism and later given even sharper definition in the struggle against fascism and communism, it was no mere talisman but the cutting edge of the United States' rise to world-power status. The fact that it also gave expression to America's own values and ideals gave it an even more powerful purchase on the political imagination. Yet in spite of this, the US still has to beware the dangers of using it too aggressively or excessively; and Smith warns against an over-enthusiastic adoption of it as a tool of foreign policy. Many forces in the world remain deeply resistant and hostile to American-style liberalism, and to assume that American power can overcome these is to inflate what the US can do. There are many measures the United States can take to make a political difference. But to assume that it can reshape the international system in its own image is both naive and dangerous. The US, therefore, has to understand the limits of its power. If it fails to do so, it could very easily get involved in the same quixotic crusades that cost it so dear during the cold war.

This general argument about America's grand strategy is further developed by G. John Ikenberry. Ikenberry's main thesis—similar in many ways to that advanced by Tony Smith—is that the American preoccupation with democracy promotion must be seen as part of a larger American way of thinking about the sources of a stable, peaceful and prosperous international order. To a large degree this outlook was rooted in America's own experience as the first new nation; but it was also the outcome of a long engagement US policymakers had with the crisis in the international system in the inter-war period. From this they drew important lessons, the most important one perhaps being that global order and American national security were most effectively advanced not by denying liberalism and democracy but by practising it. This idea in turn was based on four associated arguments: democratic states together can establish peaceful order through cooperation; trade and economic openness promote liberal democracy; economic interdependence creates vested interests in favour of stable and continuous relations; and international institutions shape and constrain interstate conflict. Obscured by the strategic stand-off with the Soviet Union, not to mention the dominance of realism in the international relations community, only now are we beginning to appreciate the central role played by this larger vision in the making of US foreign policy in the cold war, and now in the post-cold war era.

In his contribution, Henry Nau—a former policymaker from the 1980s— begins by reiterating what many others in this volume insist upon: that we can seriously appreciate the security logic of democracy promotion only if we move beyond the simple, and simple-minded, idea that the history of American foreign policy is best appreciated in terms of two opposed traditions, idealism and realism. This apparently neat conceptual distinction, he feels, hinders rather than helps us assess the impact of democratic values on America's international relations. It also assumes we can separate the domestic from the international. But as Nau points out, every country behaves abroad, at least in part, on the basis of its self-image, and any analysis that omits to mention this is likely to be flawed. This is not to deny the importance of power. That would be plainly absurd. Rather, it is to suggest that the way Americans perceive themselves and look back upon their own history—in short, the identity they have—is likely to affect and shape the way the United States exercises its influence in the world.

With this in mind Nau goes on to explore the different facets of American democracy promotion and the impact the policy has had on a highly complex international system. This very complexity, he notes, means there is not, and nor should there be, one version of democracy promotion but several. In a world made up advanced capitalist democracies, developing countries, and states that were once communist, it could not be otherwise. Americans must also be sensitive to the fact that their efforts are likely to be regarded differently in different parts of the world. Hence, it has to be careful not to pursue the policy of democracy promotion too aggressively or without regard to local conditions. Democracy promotion is certainly a worthwhile endeavour; but the US has to be cautious and prudent and not infuse its democracy promotion programmes with either moral fervour or exaggerated claims about its likely impact on other systems with a very different character to its own.

The Domestic Politics of Democracy Promotion

The point of departure for the third section of the book is the well-known nostrum that in the United States all politics is domestic politics, and that if one wants to understand the dynamics of democracy promotion as a foreign policy objective one has to look in some detail at America itself as a special, even 'exceptional' type of country. This is true in at least two very obvious senses, according to the four essays assembled here.

It is true firstly in the historic sense: America was, as de Tocqueville pointed out in the early nineteenth century, an experiment in democracy that worked especially well; so well, in fact, that many, if not most, Americans saw and continue to see their own form of democracy as a shining example for others to follow.[41] Created in an age of enlightenment and dedicated to the proposition that all people are born free with inalienable rights, it would be odd indeed if the character of the American system did not impinge on the conduct of US foreign policy. It has impinged, though, in a second, more direct way. US policymakers, it has often been noted, do not operate in a vacuum. On the contrary, they are quite literally forced by the very dynamics of the US political process to take account of different domestic constituencies, many of them keen either to shape the policy of the United States towards a particular country (witness the impact of the Polish-American community upon US policy towards Poland) or (in the case of Northern Ireland) towards a particular conflict. Whether we should celebrate or decry this, the fact remains that public opinion in a highly accessible system like America's, where even the Constitution—to quote Corwin—invites different actors to struggle for the control of foreign policy, is bound to shape the way that policy is made.[42]

This point is made with great empirical clarity by Ole Holsti in his discussion of the impact of public opinion upon American democracy promotion after the cold war. What he shows is as revealing as it is reassuring to those of a realist persuasion who believe that America's commitment to democracy

---

[41] Alexander de Tocqueville, *Democracy in America* (1835; London: Oxford University Press, 1946).
[42] Edward S. Corwin, *The President: Office and Powers* (New York: New York University Press, 1940), p. 200.

promotion is both wrong-headed and unlikely to succeed. Based upon detailed study of recent US opinion polls, Holsti points to what he terms an 'apparent paradox'. On the one hand, the conditions for promoting democracy in the world have probably never been better. On the other, there is now less popular support for such a policy amongst the American public than there has been for many years. The reasons for this, he argues, are complex and arise from a combination of post-cold war prudence, a latter-day form of American isolationism and sheer cynicism. Whatever the deeper causes, this mood, he feels, is likely to last for the foreseeable future; and policymakers who try to resist it will find themselves in great difficulty. As Holsti notes in a sober conclusion, 'leaders who propose to place expansion of democracy at or near the top of the country's post-cold war foreign policy agenda surely cannot count on a powerful groundswell of support from either the general public or opinion leaders'.

But even if those advocating the policy are likely to have a hard time selling democracy promotion to an increasingly sceptical American public, one should not underestimate the seriousness with which policymakers have come to regard it as a strategy. In fact, as the experienced observer Tom Carothers points out, the policy was used to great effect in the last years of the cold war by Ronald Reagan, ironically, as it turned out, one of the great Wilsonians of the last 80 years; and what Reagan used against the Soviet Union his successors have deployed in their quest to build a new post-cold war order. But as Carothers notes in a detailed analysis, while billions of dollars have been invested by the US, this has not always paid the sort of dividends that policymakers might have hoped for: partly because democracy is more than just a set of formal procedures and cannot be imposed on systems where there are few democratic norms, and partly because Americans themselves seem to have some difficulty in understanding that democracy can take several different forms and need not always have a 'made in the US' sign stamped on it to be authentic. In this sense, the real problem is not so much political cynicism on the part of the US or fear of popular democracy abroad—a charge often levelled against policymakers by more radical critics—but a failure by those directly involved in the process to recognize that democracy comes in various shapes and sizes. Indeed, Carothers makes the critically important point that while many of those involved in US democracy aid programmes are well-meaning people, most are 'surprisingly unaware of the different institutional forms in other established democracies', and, confusing American democracy with liberal democracy itself, 'promote a form of democracy that is over-specific' and 'may not apply in other countries, even countries they may fully intend to be democratic'.

If cultural insensitivity is one charge that might be levelled against those promoting democracy on behalf of the United States, another has been an inclination to promote distinctly low-level forms of democracy that seem to be better suited to protect the interests of local and global elites than to empower ordinary people. In his chapter, Jason Ralph engages in a very direct and critical way with this argument. He does not dismiss it out of hand; nevertheless, he feels it is far too simple. Democracy promotion, he argues, is a complex phenomenon, and if we are to appreciate its complexity we have to transcend the notion that foreign policy is merely a reflection of American corporate power. It is wholly unlikely, he argues, that a strategy which advanced the interests only of a fairly narrow group would command support at home. A tension remains however, but it is not between the interests of a specific elite and the expansion of freedom worldwide, but between the broader economic programme favoured by the United States and the basic human needs of millions of people around the world. This is the real dilemma and the only way it will be overcome is when the US promotes a different—hopefully more social democratic—economic agenda. In this sense, the real task facing the United States is not so much political as economic, and, until it abandons its current attachment to a particular set of rather narrow economic objectives, there is always going to be a very real contradiction between its proclaimed desire to expand democracy and its aim of promoting neo-liberal solutions to the world's economic problems.

The relationship between America's economic goals and its political aspirations is explored in more detail by Michael Cox in his discussion of the Clinton administration's foreign policy. Building upon the simple but self-evident truth that in order to critique Clinton we first have to understand why his administration privileged democracy promotion as a goal, Cox suggests that far from being a Wilsonian idealist—itself a problematic term—Clinton always viewed the promotion of democracy as a pragmatic strategy designed to enhance US influence. He was never interested in what he termed 'missions'; indeed, at an early stage he made it quite clear that the pursuit of political freedom abroad would neither be unconditional nor allowed to upset key alliances with authoritarian regimes. In his view, moreover, there was no necessary conflict between global order, market economics and democracy promotion. All three were intimately connected and formed part of an integrated world view. Thus order, understood here to mean the absence of war, presupposed democratic forms; democracy in turn could not be built without markets; but without democracy there was little chance of creating legitimate market-based economic systems.

If Cox perhaps sees more coherence in Clinton's world view than many of his erstwhile critics, he does not deny there were inconsistencies in the Clinton approach. It would be odd if there were none. However, what he seeks to challenge is what he regards as the rather facile notion that democracy promotion was either a mere moral add-on dreamed up by an administration desperate to find a purpose for itself in the post-cold war period, or a piece of ideological clothing easily dispensed with when it got in the way of other, more important, foreign policy goals. As Cox notes, democracy promotion was no veneer but a central part of Clinton's larger strategy to create a stable space within which the US could operate more effectively; and while there were always tensions between Clinton's political ambitions abroad and his foreign economic objectives, his administration actually saw a very clear connection between the two. In fact, far from seeing economics and politics as contradictory, it viewed democracy promotion as one way amongst many of advancing America's new economic agenda in an increasingly integrated, global market system. In this it may have been wrong-headed, cynical even. But it was never as inconsistent and or as naive as its opponents seemed to assume.

US Democracy Promotion in Practice

The rhetoric of the Clinton administration has, of course, to be set against the impact that United States democracy promotion has had on different regions and countries around the world; and perhaps no country has been as important to the United States since the collapse of Soviet power as post-communist Russia itself. How the US has fared here is critically evaluated by Peter Rutland. An experienced observer of the Russian scene, Rutland is no apologist for the old system or opponent of the market. Yet he can see few virtues in what has come to pass in Russia. The causes of the failed transition are many, he agrees. But the West cannot escape its fair share of the blame. It was especially foolish to demand the impossible and to believe one could construct a viable capitalism and American-style democracy together—the so-called 'market democracy paradigm'—on the fragments left behind by Soviet communism. This was 'panglossian complacency' of the highest order and was bound to end in tears. Put bluntly, Russia simply could not bear the weight that the West placed upon it. It also asked far too much of the deeply flawed Russian President who was left 'carrying out the dual role of a Russian George Washington and Adam Smith.' In the end, his somewhat feeble efforts to build one prop of the new Russian order—formal democracy—made it possible for those opposed to the other—the market—to compromise his game plan. Russia in this sense did not fail democracy: democracy failed Russia.

If Russia was America's number one security issue after the cold war, Asia-Pacific was perhaps its most difficult challenge. A region of immense cultural diversity, political tension, and economic dynamism with a deep sense of its own tragic history, there was and remains no simple political formula that one could have adopted to deal with Asia-Pacific as a whole. Nor, as Takashi Inoguchi points out, did it make a great deal of difference that the United States had been a player in Asia-Pacific for the better part of a century or more. Familiarity, after all, can sometimes breed contempt, and while few in the region view the US in this way—it is far too powerful and important for that to happen—many are deeply suspicious of its political intentions and worry that an overly confident America freed of the burdens and discipline of the cold war will seek to undermine what has come to be defined by many elites in the area as Asian values.

But, as Inoguchi notes, to understand the impact of US democracy promotion efforts it is vital to examine what he terms the three different 'frameworks' or 'legacies' that now shape the American outlook on the world: the Westphalian, the anti-Utopian and the Philadelphian. The first might readily be defined as classically realist and assumes that the international system is made up of competing states whose internal political forms are of little concern to the US; the second not only takes for granted the idea of conflict but insists we are now moving into an epoch of civilizational clashes; and the last—and most optimistic—framework is essentially liberal in orientation and has come very much to the fore since the end of the cold war. All three coexist, according to Inoguchi, in a very uneasy way and vie with each other to determine US foreign policy in Asia-Pacific. At heart, however, the United States remains or would prefer to be a 'Philadelphian actor' seeking to promote human rights and democratic values. This, however, is where the conflict has arisen, and for the foreseeable future the tension between American desires and regional realities will be one of the factors determining the shape of Asia-Pacific.

The Danish political scientist, Georg Sørensen, moves the discussion about democracy promotion from Asia-Pacific to Africa. In a critical yet balanced assessment of Western efforts, Sørensen's main point is that the euphoria that accompanied early moves towards democratization in Africa has now petered out—or, as he puts it rather more bluntly, 'a large number of countries' appear to be 'stuck in the initial phases of democratic transition'. The situation is not entirely hopeless, however, and although 'there are no prospects for any substantial democratic progress', no comprehensive 'setback for democracy is on the cards' either. But the West in general and the US in particular should not be complacent. Nor should they escape legitimate criticism. Indeed, they can be attacked on at least three substantial grounds, according to Sørensen: of failing to appreciate the role of nationalism and political community; of placing too much faith in economic and political liberalism; and of supporting elite-dominated democracies. And even if it is true that democracy can only be learned and not taught, the experience of Africa suggests that Western countries—including the United States—would do well to rethink some of their political practices.

If Sørensen is critical of the West, Bill Robinson and Barry Gills are damning; and in two complementary chapters they conclude the volume by seeking to show a clear and close connection between US economic goals and its promotion of what Robinson prefers to call 'polyarchy' and Gills 'low intensity democracy'. Their thesis is as provocative as it is challenging, and for this reason, no doubt, will be questioned by more mainstream writers. For several decades the United States, they point out, ranked democracy promotion very low on its list of foreign policy priorities in continents like Latin America. Only with the passing of the revolutionary threat in the late 1980s and the perceived need for structural economic change did it decide to support some degree of political reform. But it did not do so because it favoured pluralism in principle, but because it viewed some form of limited democracy as the most effective means of fostering stability in countries experiencing painful integration into the world capitalist system. To this extent democracy was not a political end in itself but rather a political means to achieve a desired economic objective. Yet history has not come to an end, they maintain: the consequences of globalization will in time throw up new social forces that cannot be contained within the political framework currently favoured by the United States. At that point, America will face its most severe test of the post-cold war period: either to support those elites opposed to genuine democracy or to stand behind the ordinary people pressing for a more open society. And how it responds to this critical choice could be every bit as important as any it has taken in the twentieth century—or will take in the twenty-first.

Thus we come full circle and return to the ever-present problem of how a great power like the United States both intervenes in the world and manages the complex demands made upon it by the international system at large. There are clearly no easy choices and probably no neat and perfectly symmetrical outcomes either, in spite of the end of the cold war. Indeed, far from clarifying America's international role, the collapse of communism appears to have made life a good deal more complicated for policymakers. Hence the oft-repeated charge that the US has become a superpower without a mission. Yet this apparent lack of purpose should not mislead us into thinking the US has no objectives at all; and, as this volume seeks to demonstrate, one of these increasingly is a desire to promote its own version of democracy. Of course, the policy should not be viewed in isolation from other objectives. That would be one-sided. Nor should our attempt to discuss the policy be seen as providing an intellectual gloss on what the United States does in the world system. That would be ethically indefensible. But we still need to explain and understand the phenomenon: why it has assumed greater prominence over the past few years, where it fits within the larger foreign policy tradition, how it relates to other key goals, why it is pursued so aggressively in certain situations and not in others, and whether or not the policy is likely to be pursued over the long term. Perhaps the sooner scholars of international relations and contemporary American foreign policy can discuss these issues without being accused of either naivety or apologetics, the sooner they can begin have a mature and open debate about the particular—and increasingly important—part played by democracy promotion in US international affairs.

I

US Democracy Promotion
in Theory

1

Peace, Liberty, and Democracy: Realists and Liberals Contest a Legacy

MICHAEL DOYLE

PROMOTING freedom will produce peace, we have often been told. In a speech before the British parliament in June 1982, US President Reagan proclaimed that governments founded on a respect for individual liberty exercise 'restraint' and 'peaceful intentions' in their foreign policy. He then announced a 'crusade for freedom' and a 'campaign for democratic development'.[1] President Bush, similarly, on 1 October 1990, in an address before the United Nations General Assembly, declared: 'Calls for democracy and human rights are being reborn everywhere. And these calls are an expression of support for the values enshrined in the Charter. They encourage our hopes for a more stable, more peaceful, more prosperous world.'[2] In a United Nations Address ('Pax Universalis', 23 September 1991), he stated equally unequivocally: 'As democracy flourishes, so does the opportunity for a third historical breakthrough: international cooperation' (the first two were individual enterprise and international trade). And, perhaps most consequentially, the President justified the large cuts in US tactical nuclear forces as a product of the decline in hostility that stemmed from the survival of democratic forces in the USSR after the 1991 coup. President Clinton continued this tradition, making 'democratic enlargement' the doctrinal centrepiece of his administration's foreign policy. Liberals and democrats have made similar claims elsewhere and before, but the international promotion of democracy has long been a special feature of US foreign policy.[3] Few other liberal great powers have their identity so clearly defined by their principles—principles that have translated into a national grand strategy.

This essay draws on parts of *Ways of War and Peace* (New York: Norton, 1997). It has benefited from discussions held at the Carnegie Endowment in January 1998 that were sponsored by the SSRC, and from the suggestions of the editors.

[1] President Reagan's speech is printed in the *New York Times* (9 June 1982).
[2] Reagan earlier announced as a 'plain truth: the day of the dictator is over. The people's right to democracy must not be denied' (*Deptartment of State Bulletin*, June 1989).
[3] The essays by Tony Smith, John Ikenberry and Henry Nau—the second section of this volume—illustrate this connection.

In making these claims, US presidents and liberal politicians joined a long list of liberal theorists (and propagandists) and echoed an old argument: the aggressive instincts of authoritarian leaders and totalitarian ruling parties make for war. A modest version of this view led the authors of the US Constitution to entrust Congress, rather than the president, with the power to declare war. A more fiery American revolutionary, Thomas Paine, in 1791 proclaimed: 'Monarchical sovereignty, the enemy of mankind, and the source of misery, is abolished; and sovereignty is restored to its natural and original place, the nation. . . . Were this the case throughout Europe, the cause of war would be taken away.'[4]

Liberal states, the argument runs, founded on such principles as equality before the law, free speech and other civil liberties, private property, and elected representation are fundamentally against war. When the citizens who bear the burdens of war elect their governments, wars become impossible. Furthermore, citizens appreciate that the benefits of trade can be enjoyed only under conditions of peace. Thus the very existence of liberal states, such as the US, Japan, and the European democracies, makes for peace. These are large claims and they are, not surprisingly, disputed by the realists—as well as by most socialists. Realists contest the connection between peace and liberalism and the alleged monopolization of peace, liberty and democracy by the liberals. Realists have described a state of war that could be mitigated, but not overcome, short of a world Leviathan. But some of those mitigations involve extensive periods of at least partial peace. Some realists also lay a claim to liberty and democracy, without assuming they will have a pacific impact. Some glory in liberty (Machiavelli) and others cleave to democracy (Thucydides and Rousseau).

In this section, Randall Schweller affirms the continuing relevance of realist motivations for war and Steve Smith raises doubt about the depth of the liberal commitment to democracy. But liberals differ too. Only the pacific liberals (Schumpeter, and in lesser ways other commercial liberals) make the strongest claim. Both Lockean and Kantian liberals are more limited and circumspect. Some liberals, on the other hand, are sceptical of a general liberal peace and of liberalism's responsibility for it. There are at least three distinct theoretical traditions of liberalism, attributable to three theorists. The first is John Locke, the great founder of modern liberal individualism, who together with the later utilitarian, Jeremy Bentham, provided the liberal foundations of international law.[5] A philosopher of liberty, Locke assumed that liberal states would remain in a state of near-war. The second is Joseph Schumpeter and other commercialists,[6] including modern globalists who envisage global

---

[4] Thomas Paine, *The Rights of Man*, in *Complete Writings*, ed. E. Foner (New York: Oxford University Press, 1995), vol. 1, p. 342.

[5] John Locke, *Second Treatise* in *Two Treatises on Government*, ed. Peter Laslett (New York: Cambridge University Press, 1988) and Jeremy Bentham, *Plan for a Universal and Perpetual Peace*, Grotius Society Publications No. 6 (London: Sweet and Maxwell, 1927).

[6] Joseph Schumpeter, 'The Sociology of Imperialism', in *Imperialism and Social Classes* (New York: Harper, 1950) and Michael Doyle, *Ways of War and Peace* (New York: W.W. Norton, 1997), Ch. 7.

accommodation as marketplaces replacing 'war-places'.[7] They form the roots of the liberal pacifism that American presidents and other liberal politicians have frequently invoked. Immanuel Kant, a liberal republican who called us to a demanding internationalism that institutes peace among fellow liberal republics, is the third.[8] He argued that the liberal peace would be limited to fellow liberals, that a dangerous state of war would prevail outside the liberal peace, and that some of that danger must be attributed to liberal aggressiveness.

Realism, Liberalism and International Theory

Realism

Thucydides, the classic founder of realism, developed its core insights. None of the traditional moral norms linking individuals across state boundaries had regular effect, he argued. Interstate relations existed in a condition where war is always possible—a state of war such as that 'hard school of danger' he described that persisted between Athens and Sparta during the 'peace' that preceded the actual outbreak of hostilities.[9] To Thucydides, as to later realists, international anarchy precluded the effective escape from the dreary history of war and conflict that was the consequence of competition under anarchy. The 'truest cause' of the great war between Athens and Sparta—the real reason that made it 'inevitable'—'was the growth of Athenian power and the fear which this caused in Sparta'.[10] States, therefore, had to preserve their security independently.

But, unlike many later realists, Thucydides did not think that states were the only significant actors in international politics. Individuals, such as Alcibiades, played important and sometimes independent roles in the determination of the course of international events. Nor did he think that state interests can or should be defined solely in terms of the rational pursuit of power, or of any other abstract or structurally determined model of political behaviour that reduces the variety of ends ('security, honour, and self-interest') or the significance of differing polities that have characterized the political determination of policy. His work is also a great democratic tragedy, in which Athenian democracy, at the beginning a source of immense strength,

---

[7] Among the recent contributions is Thomas Friedman's lightly argued McDonaldization thesis. Global commerce overwhelms the passions of violent conflict; and, wherever there are McDonald's hamburger outlets (sited by rational market reliability criteria), there no war shall occur. See his *The Lexus and the Olive Tree* (New York: Farrar Strauss & Giroux, 1999) pp. 195–217. Similar arguments in their own times were made at the turn of the twentieth century by John Hobson and Norman Angell who explained, just prior to World War I, how industrial commerce removed the sources of international conflict.

[8] Immanuel Kant, *Perpetual Peace*, in *Kant's Political Writings*, ed. Hans Reiss, trans. H. B. Nisbet (Cambridge: Cambridge University Press, 1970).

[9] Thucydides, *History of the Peloponnesian War*, translated by Rex Warner, introduction by M. I . Finley (Harmondsworth: Penguin, 1954), p. 46.

[10] Thucydides, *History of the Peloponnesian War*, p. 49.

becomes by the end—when corrupted—an albatross whose factionalism provokes imprudent aggression (against Sicily) and civil war.

The modern realists have differentiated his heritage. Modern realism's philosophical foundations lie in Machiavelli, Hobbes, and Rousseau. Machiavelli inaugurated an emphasis on the fundamental sources of the realist state of war in individual human beings. Hobbes refined the structural model of the international system. Rousseau most closely followed the complex heritage of Thucydides, while highlighting the powerful effects of domestic constitutional differences.

Modern fundamentalism as defined by Machiavelli characterizes all social interaction as rooted in mankind's psychological and material needs that result in a drive for power.[11] State behaviour, like all social behaviour from the family through all other organizations, can thus best be understood as a reconstruction of interest-oriented, power-seeking activity.[12] The struggle for power changes form but not substance when we move from a consideration of domestic to international politics. The drive for power produces the state of war.

The fundamentalist accepts the anarchy assumption of all realists, but questions the extent of the differentiation between domestic and interstate politics. This means, on the one hand, that fundamentalists leave open whether the state should be assumed to be a rational unitary actor. On the other hand, fundamentalists specify both the means and preferences—both power—left open to variation by the Thucydidean core of classical realism. Rooted in human nature itself, the drive for power leaves statesmen no choice other than power politics. Power, moreover, is translatable. Its pursuit in one endeavour readily translates into resources available for others as—according to Machiavelli— 'good arms make good laws'.[13] But 'good laws' also make for 'good arms', for liberty, Machiavelli also notes, is one of the key means through which leaders mobilize the energy of the population for security, glory and expansion.[14] Peace, if possible, is a product of empire, as was claimed in their times by the *Pax Romana*, the *Pax Britannica*, and the *Pax Americana*.

Hobbesian structuralism also explains the state of war.[15] Like most of the other forms of realism, structuralism assumes international anarchy and the predominance of state actors. But modern structuralists—like Hobbes—also assume that state actors are 'functionally similar units' differing in capabilities but not ends, as Kenneth Waltz notes in the *Theory of International Politics*.[16]

[11] Hans Morgenthau, *Politics Among Nations* (New York, Knopf, 1967), p. 4.

[12] Morgenthau, *Politics Among Nations*, p. 32.

[13] Niccolo Machiavelli, *The Prince*, trans. Harvey Mansfield (Chicago: Chicago University Press, 1985), p. 48.

[14] Niccolo Machiavelli, *The Discourses*, trans. Leslie Walker (Harmondsworth: Penguin, 1970), book 2, ch. 2.

[15] Thomas Hobbes, *Leviathan* (1651; New York: Penguin, 1980).

[16] K. Waltz, *Theory of International Politics* (Reading, MA: Addison Wesley, 1979), pp. 96–7.

Unitary rational process, translatability of power resources, and a strong preference for power as a means to security form a necessary part of the model.[17] But unlike fundamentalists, structuralists see these features not as variables derived from assumptions about human nature or social organization, but as derivations from the structure itself. State behaviour is homogenized—made rational and power seeking—through competition and socialization.[18] Only the rational and power-seeking will survive the competition to dominate and thus teach their rivals.

Specific structural inferences, such as the hypothesized stability of bipolar world,[19] the instability of multipolarity, and the weaknesses of transnational restraints are deduced from the model, once one specifies the number and capabilities of the states that compose the system. These structures allow for significant periods of peace. Hobbesian statesmen have a duty to try to achieve peace for the sake of the security of their state. They are likely to have some success, it is argued, during periods such as the cold war, when bipolar stability and robust deterrence—such as that offered by nuclear weapons capable of second-strike deterrence—reinforce prudence.

Rousseau's realist constitutionalism, like all forms of realism, portrays a world-view or explanation of interstate politics as a 'state of war'.[20] This view, common to a number of writers in the contemporary field, assumes nothing about the rationality of all states, their pursuit of power or the 'national interest', or the way they set their various goals.[21] Indeed, it assumes that the processes and preferences of states vary and are open to choice influenced by both domestic and interstate considerations. This choice includes moral choices, but it assumes that ethical choices cannot be categorical or absolute—that is, that they must necessarily depend upon a prior consideration of strategic security. Given the lack of international security, states seeking to maintain their independence must provide for their own security and this calls for an attention to relative power. The dominant inference of complex realism is the continuity of the state of war. But this allows for strategies to preserve islands of peace, such as those that Rousseau advocated for Corsica,

[17] Robert Keohane, *Neorealism and its Critics* (New York: Columbia University Press, 1986), p. 172.

[18] Waltz, *Theory of International Politics*, p. 75. The structural determination depends, we need to add, on the systemic interaction being sufficiently intense to select very efficiently for appropriate behaviour, such as would be observed under the economist's model of perfect competition. See the valuable discussion in Keohane, *Neorealism and its Critics*, pp. 171–5.

[19] Bipolarity—the economist's 'bilateral monopoly'—may, however, strain against the assumption of perfect competition.

[20] J.-J. Rousseau, 'State of War', trans. Grace Roosevelt, in *Reading Rousseau in the Nuclear Age* (Philadelphia: Temple University Press, 1990).

[21] For example, this view appears to describe Arnold Wolfers, *Discord and Collaboration* (Baltimore: Johns Hopkins, 1962), especially Chs 1, 2, and 4; Raymond Aron's *Peace and War* (New York: Praeger, 1968); Kenneth Waltz's *Man, the State and War* (New York: Columbia University Press, 1959) ('anarchy is the framework of world politics' but the 'forces that determine policy' are located within the nation [p. 238]); his *Theory of International Politics* (Reading, MA: Addison Wesley, 1979) on the other hand is structuralist); Stanley Hoffmann's 'Theory and International Relations', in Stanley Hoffman, *State of War* (New York: Praeger, 1965), especially pp.15-17, in addition to Martin Wight, *Power Politics* (Leicester: Leicester University Press, 1978) and a number other scholars of the field. It also follows John Vasquez's basic description of realism in *The Power of Power Politics* (New Brunswick: Rutgers University Press, 1983), p. 28).

whose simple economy and geographical isolation might reduce both its temptations toward expansion and its attraction to other expansionist powers.

Why do the separate strands all arrive at a state of war? What makes them all realist? Comparing Machiavelli, Hobbes and Rousseau, it appears that whatever the differences in their views of man and the nature of domestic politics, all agree that the prince or state either does or should command all force (Machiavelli and Hobbes) or command all loyalty (Rousseau). Differences in states and personal values are then contained by their similar degree of authority. There is thus no room for other loyalties and other interests to acquire sufficient strength to transform relations among states. They remain in a state of war.

The core of realism—to simplify—thus portrayed world politics as a 'state of war' among all states and societies, which is a condition in which war was regarded as a continuous possibility in which each state had to regard every other state as presenting the possibility of this threat. This state of war persisted for several reasons. First, relations among states were anarchic in that they lacked a global state. Trade, cultural contact, even institutions and international law could exist under anarchy, but none altered its anarchic and war-like character.

Second, states were independent units that could be treated as strategic units. The variations in state structure range from the abstractly unitary sovereign rationality of Hobbes to the ideally unitary moral rationality of the general will and sociologically diverse non-ideal states of Rousseau, to the rational princes and imperial republics of Machiavelli, to the diverse states of Thucydidean Greece. Despite the variation, each conceptualizes the ideal state—prince, people as a whole, senate, or assembly—as having a monopoly of effective or legitimate power. Not all state authority was legitimate. Rousseau clearly thought monarchies were not. But even if not legitimate, the states that could play a role in international politics were at least effective. (If they were not, the state collapsed or collaborated and became subject to another state, thereby ending anarchy, substituting hierarchy.)

Third, some of these states sought to expand, others merely to survive. None was prepared to engage in long-term accommodation or cooperation.

Fourth, the perception that some societies would have good reasons to want to expand, that the sovereignty similarity of all states made them functionally similar egoists, and the fact that the international system itself lacked a global sovereign: all together, though in various combinations for each theorist, made rational states at least fear each other. They feared each other even if they were not inclined to aggress on each other because they could not be sure that their neighbour was not prepared to aggress on them. Each was in a state of war, which we call a security dilemma. The result was that all international goods have only relative value. They are relative because, as Hobbes opined, 'clubs are trumps'. Games are all zero-sum at the maximum extent. No good has absolute value if some other state can seize it by force. Every good has to be measured first by the extent to which it contributes to security in a world where only self-help secures one's existence. Within an alliance absolute values can be appreciated, but only because they contribute to the relative superiority of the alliance over a rival alliance. And alliances are easy to break.

Liberalism

Liberalism has complicated implications for international relations theory. Defined by the centrality of individual rights, private property, and representative government, it is a domestic theory. Realism, on the other hand, is an international theory, defined by the centrality of the state of war. There appears to be no simple theoretical integration of the two. Realist theory would be falsely portrayed, indeed caricatured, if it were 'domesticized' by limiting it to authoritarian or totalitarian domestic politics or even purely unitary states. Correspondingly, liberal theory too would be caricatured if it were 'internationalized' by limiting it to assertions about the natural harmony of world politics. Some realists are totalitarian; Hobbes justified authoritarian states. Some are democratic communitarians, as was Rousseau and, though less systematically, Thucydides. Machiavelli was a republican realist. Some liberals are homogeneously pacific, such as Bentham or Cobden or Schumpeter. Others, such as John Stuart Mill, justified imperialism under some circumstances and intervention under others. No simplification well represents the actual philosophical and historical richness of their world-views.

Instead, for the sake of expanding our analysis of the range of world politics, we need a conception of world political liberalism that identifies what is special about the international relations of liberal states, but that neither caricatures nor whitewashes them. World-views align themselves on spectrums; they do not fall into neat boxes. We should be looking for a world politics in which liberal individualism makes a difference: in which the good of individuals has moral weight against the good of the state or the nation. From the other side, we should be looking for a world politics in which the state of war is not the general characteristic of international relations (or individualism might not be making a difference, or adding something to realism). In order to make sure that we have not created a vicious circle of cause and effect, we will then need to make sure that our theories are disconfirmable and that we are able to account for theoretical parameters by distinguishing our liberals from their philosophic cousins, the near-liberals. We will need to do this by accounting for differences in both causes and effects.

Liberals are, indeed, different. World politics for them, rather than being a relatively homogeneous state of war, is at the minimum a heterogeneous state of peace and war, and might become a state of global peace in which the expectation of war disappears. If more than one liberal society coexists in the international system, then—rather than having a security rationale governing all interaction, as it must for realists in a state of war—other criteria of policy come into play. Liberals explain how societies can compete to become rich, glorious, healthy, cultured, all without expecting to have to resolve their competition through war. Formal and informal institutions such as international organization and law take on a greater role in competition with the warriors and diplomats who dominate the realist stage,[22] for several reasons.

First, despite international anarchy, meaning the absence of a global government, states are inherently different 'units', differentiated among other factors by how they relate to individual human rights. So liberals distinguish liberal from non-liberal societies, republican from autocratic or totalitarian states, capitalist from communist, fascist, and corporatist economies. Differences in international behaviour then reflect these differences in institutions, interests and ideas.

Second, the aims of the state, as do the aims of the individual, go beyond 'security, honour and interest' to the protection and promotion of individual rights.

Third, for liberals, states behave differently and are not homogenized by the international system either by being competed out of existence or socialized into structural strategies. Some liberals argue that liberal states are inherently respectful of international law. Others argue that liberal states are inherently peaceful, while authoritarians are inherently aggressive. And still others argue that liberals are peaceful, but only toward each other.

Fourth, liberals agree with the realists that states exist under anarchy, but their anarchy is different. Rather than being driven into relative contests, zero-sum games, their contest is a positive- or negative-sum game. They can win or lose together. A failure to inform may undermine coordination when liberals are seeking compatible goals. In more competitive situations, a failure to trust may undermine cooperation when each would prefer at least one alternative to a failure to cooperate. This is because their security dilemma can be solved by stable accommodation. They can come to appreciate that the existence of other liberal states constitutes no threat and instead constitutes an opportunity for mutually beneficial trade and—when needed—alliance against non-liberal states.

Liberals thus differ from the realists. But they also differ from each other, and they do so in systematic ways. Each of the liberal theorists, like the realists, must make some assumptions about international structure, domestic society, and human nature—Kenneth Waltz's three images.[23] Liberals pay more attention to domestic structures and individual differences than do realists. They all think that the international system, or Third Image, has less than an overriding influence and so distinguish themselves from not only structural realists but also from almost all realists. Still, compared to each other we can identify First Image Lockean (human nature), Second Image Commercial (society), and Third Image Kantian (international system) liberals.

---

[22] Aron, *Peace and War*, Ch. 1, identifies the centrality of the two for international politics, as realism. Transnational complexity, though under the label of complex realism, is well-described by Joseph Nye and Robert Keohane in *Power and Interdependence* (Boston: Little Brown, 1989).
[23] Waltz, *Man, the State and War*.

Locke's international system, like Hobbes's, is anarchic. His state is based on representation and ultimately on consent; while Hobbes's is indifferent to these matters as long as the state is sovereign. Locke's citizens, like Hobbes's, are rational independent individuals. The difference then lies in the import-ance Locke attributed to the duties to protect life, liberty, and property that Locke thought accompanied citizens' rights to the same. It is these duties that lead just commonwealths to maintain peace with each other, provided, that is, their natural partiality and the poorly institutionalized character of world politics do not overcome their duties to accommodate. Locke thus por-trayed an international condition of troubled peace, only one step removed from the realist state of war and one fraught with 'inconveniences' that could degenerate into war through the combined effects of bias, partiality, and the absence of a regular and objective system of adjudication and enforcement. There is much Hobbesian rational unitary egoism in the Lockean 'federative power', with its pursuit of 'national advantage'. In troubling times, Lockean international 'inconveniences' might well approach a nearly general state of war. But we also see one crucial difference. Lockean statespersons, like his cit-izens, are governed by the duties of natural law: life, liberty, and property. Lockean states, then, are distinguished, if Locke is correct, by a commitment to mutual trust under the law. In the bargaining literature, trust is crucial for stable agreements, and all rational egoistic bargainers will want to cultivate a reputation for it.[24] But Lockean bargainers, to take a further step, are commit-ted to it by nature (or God).[25]

The commercial pacifists—a second tradition of liberal scholarship—focus on the pacifying international effects of markets and commercial capitalism. The tradition that Albert Hirschman has called *doux commerce* (soothing com-merce) originates in the eighteenth-century attack on the realist doctrine of relative economic power then advocated by the mercantilists, who drew on the fundamental insights of Machiavelli, Hobbes and other realist theorists of war and peace.[26] Although the commercial liberals such as Smith and Schumpeter argued that representative government contributed to peace—when the citizens who bear the burdens of war elect their governments, wars become impossible—for them, the deeper cause of peace was commerce. Democracies had been more than war-prone in history. Thucydides' story of democratic Athens was familiar to all with a classical education. Passions could wreak havoc among democrats, too. What was new was manufacturing and commerce: capitalism. Paine, the radical American democrat, announced, 'If commerce were permitted to act to the universal extent it is capable, it would

[24] Philip Heymann, 'The Problem of Coordination: Bargaining and Rules,' *Harvard Law Review*, 86/5 (1973), pp. 797-877, develops these points.

[25] See the seminal essay by John Dunn, 'The Concept of Trust in the Politics of John Locke', in Richard Rorty (ed.), *Philosophy in History* (Cambridge: Cambridge University Press, 1984).

[26] Albert Hirschman, 'Rival Interpretations of Market Society: Civilizing, Destructive or Feeble', *Journal of Economic Literature*, 20 (1982), pp. 1463–84. For another example of this tradition see Montesquieu, *Spirit of the Laws* I, book 20, Ch. 1. For a discussion of Montesquieu's ideas, see Stephen Rosow, 'Commerce, Power and Justice: Montesquieu on International Politics', *The Review of Politics*, 46/3 (1984), pp. 346–67.

extirpate the system of war.'[27] Paine built on and contributed to a growing recognition, systematically developed by Enlightenment philosophers, of a powerful insight: war does not pay for commercial manufacturing societies. The great Scottish philosopher-economist Adam Smith articulated that view most comprehensively. The twentieth-century Austrian economist, Joseph Schumpeter, extended it into a general theory of capitalist pacification.

Both Hobbes and Schumpeter regard the international system as anarchic. Both regard their citizens as individualistic, rational, and egoistic, and usually materialistic. But Schumpeter sees the combination of democracy and capitalism as opening up a revolutionary transformation of domestic state and social structure. These societies are as self-interestedly, deterministically pacific as Hobbes's Leviathans are bellicist. Hobbesian Leviathans, after all, are merely Hobbesian individuals writ large, with all their individual competitiveness and egoism. Schumpeter's state is a structured whole, distinct from its parts, transformed as it were by an 'invisible hand'—to borrow the classic commercial metaphor from Adam Smith. Market capitalism and democratic majoritarianism make individual material egoism and competitiveness into social pacifism. Markets make for collective solutions—equilibrium prices—separate from those of individual producers who seek to sell dear and individual consumers who seek to buy cheap. Majorities constitute a combined interest of the 50 per cent plus one or the median voter constructed through log-rolling and least common denominators that are different, too, from individual interests. Democratic capitalism means free trade and a peaceful foreign policy simply because they are, he claims, the first-best solutions for rational majorities in capitalist societies. This is the heart of the contemporary enthusiasm, expressed by many liberal politicians, for global democratization and capitalism as the inevitable and pacific routes to peace at the 'end of history'.[28]

First and Second Image Liberals also differ from each other. Schumpeter makes the peace, which is a duty of the Lockean liberal statesman, into the structured outcome of capitalist democracy. Both highlight for us powerful elements of liberal world politics. But if there is a long state of peace between liberal republics, Locke offers us a weak explanation for it. (How do they avoid partiality and bias so regularly in these relations?) He also misses the persistent state of war between liberals and non-liberals. (Why are the liberals so regularly more partial here?) Schumpeter misses the liberal sources of war with non-liberals, unless we should blame all these wars on the non-liberals.

Kant and the liberal internationalists try to fill these gaps as they illustrate for us the larger potential of the liberal tradition. Kant's *Perpetual Peace* offers a coherent explanation of two important regularities in world politics: the tendencies of liberal states simultaneously to be peace-prone in their relations

---

[27] Thomas Paine, *Rights of Man* (1791; New York: Oxford University Press, 1995), ch. 5.

[28] More sophisticated than it has often been portrayed is Francis Fukuyama's argument in the 'End of History', *The National Interest*, 16 (1989), pp. 3–18. Making related arguments about the end of war is John Mueller, *Retreat from Doomsday* (New York: Basic Books, 1989) and Rudolph Rummel, 'Libertarianism and International Violence,' *Journal Of Conflict Resolution*, 27/1 (1983), pp. 27–71.

with each other and unusually war-prone in their relations with non-liberal states. Republican representation, liberal respect, and transnational interdependence—to re-phrase Kant's three 'definitive articles' of the hypothetical peace treaty he asked states to sign—thus can be seen as three necessary and, together, sufficient causes of the two regularities taken together. Thus, no single constitutional, international, or cosmopolitan source is alone sufficient, but together—and only together—they plausibly connect the characteristics of liberal polities and economies with sustained liberal peace. Alliances founded on mutual strategic interest among liberal and non-liberal states have been broken, economic ties between liberal and non-liberal states have proven fragile, but the political bonds of liberal rights and interests have proven a remarkably firm foundation for mutual non-aggression. A separate peace exists among liberal states.

But in their relations with non-liberal states, liberal states have not escaped from the insecurity caused by anarchy in the world political system considered as a whole. Moreover, the very constitutional restraint, international respect for individual rights, and shared commercial interests that establish grounds for peace among liberal states establish grounds for additional conflict irrespective of actual threats to national security in relations between liberal and non-liberal societies. And in their relations with all states, liberal states have not solved the problems of international cooperation and competition. Liberal publics can become absorbed in domestic issues, and international liberal respect does not preclude trade rivalries or guarantee far-sighted collective solutions to international security and welfare.

Kant's theory held that a stable expectation of peace among states would be achieved once three conditions were met. Together they constitute a liberal republic. We can rephrase them as:

(1) representative, republican government, which includes an elected legislative, separation of powers and the rule of law. Kant argued that together those institutional features lead to caution because the government is responsible to its citizens. This, however, does not guarantee peace;

(2) a principled respect for non-discriminatory human rights. This should produce a commitment to respect the rights of fellow liberal republics—because they represent free citizens, who as individuals have rights that deserve our respect—and a suspicion of non-republics—because if those governments cannot trust their own citizens, what should lead us to trust them?;[29] and

(3) social and economic interdependence. Trade and social interaction generally engender a mix of conflict and cooperation. Liberalism produces special material incentives for cooperation. Among fellow liberals

---

[29] The individual subjects of autocracies, of course, do not lose their rights. It's just that the autocrats cannot claim legitimately to speak for their subjects. Subjects retain basic human rights, such as the rights of non-combatants in war. The terror bombing of civilians—as in the bombings of Dresden, Tokyo, Hiroshima and Nagasaki—constitute, in this view, violations of these rights and of liberal principles and demonstrate weaknesses of liberal models in these cases.

interdependence should not be subject to security-motivated restrictions and, consequently, tends to be more varied, less dependent on single issues and less subject to single conflicts.[30]

Kant suggested that each was necessary and together they were sufficient to establish a secure expectation of peace. The first principle specifies representative government responsible to the majority; the second and third specify the majority's ends and interests. Together, the three generate an expectation of peaceful accommodation among fellow liberals and hostility toward non-liberals.

Thus, far from being identical, liberals can be distinguished: we can identify Locke as a First Image liberal, who contributes an elaboration of human rights and consequent international duties. Schumpeter and the other commercial pacifists, Second Image liberals, focus on the effects of variations in domestic society, economy, and state structure. Kant, a Third Image liberal, tells us about the interaction of states, that is, about the effects of dyads and systems, about the genesis of a 'pacific union' of liberal states.

Peace, Liberty, Democracy

Liberalism lays a special claim to what world politics is (can be): a state of peace. It also claims a special property right in what shapes the politics of liberal states: liberty and democracy. But how special is the liberal peace? Can it be equally well explained by realist concerns, such as the balance of power? And how can we reconcile Machiavelli's love of liberty and Thucydides' and Rousseau's commitments to democracy with the liberals' claim to their ownership? Or, why should liberty and democracy produce war in the hands and minds of the realists and peace in the hands and minds of the liberals?

Peace

Are liberal principles and institutions the true source of the peace among liberal states? Neither realist theories of the balance of power nor Marxist theories of capitalist foreign policy account well for long periods of peace among states of a similar constitutional regime. Dispositional democratic theories or commercial capitalist theories or purely rational egoist theories explain, at best, the peace, which is only half of the liberal tradition that also includes the state of war with non-liberals: imprudent vehemence and supine complaisance. Each can account for some of the effects; none accounts for them con-

---

[30] These three points are all developed above in Michael Doyle, 'Kant, Liberal Legacies and Foreign Affairs', *Philosophy and Public Affairs*, 12/34 (1983), pp. 205–54, 323–53. For the debate on the empirical tendency of democracies to remain at peace with each other, see the valuable collection by Michael Brown, Sean Lynn-Jones, and Steven Miller (eds), *Debating the Democratic Peace* (Cambridge: MIT Press, 1996), that includes essays by Bruce Russett and John Owen and critiques by Henry Farber, Joanne Gowa, and David Spiro and others.

sidered together. Kant's theory, on the other hand, appears to be both necessary and sufficient to explain the liberal peace.

Realists hold that the effects of differing domestic regimes—whether liberal or not—are overridden by the state of war under which all states live. Hobbes does not bother to distinguish between 'some council or one man' when he discusses the sovereign. Differing domestic regimes do affect the quantity of resources available to the state and the quality of its morale. But the ends that shape policy are determined for the realist by the fundamental quest for power that shapes all politics or the competitive structure of the international system.

At the level of the strategic decision-maker, realists could argue that a liberal peace could be merely the outcome of prudent diplomacy. Indeed, some, including Hobbes, have argued that sovereigns have a natural duty not to act against 'the reasons of peace'.[31] Individuals established—that is, should establish—a sovereign to escape from the brutalities of the state of nature, the war of all against all, that follows from competition for scarce goods, scrambles for prestige, and fear of another's attack when there is no sovereign to provide for lawful acquisition or regularized social conduct or personal security. 'Dominions were constituted for peace's sake, and peace was sought for safety's sake'; the natural duty of the sovereign is therefore the safety of the people. Yet, for the Hobbesian, prudent policy cannot be an enforceable right of citizens because sovereigns, who remain in the state of nature with respect to their subjects and other sovereigns, cannot themselves be subjects.

The condition of the international system for Hobbesians remains, moreover, a state of war. Prudence can be enhanced by deterring technologies, transparency, geography, and a variety of other factors in complex games of chicken—as we saw in the discussion of Hobbesian realism. Military technologies changed from offensive to defensive and from distinguishable to indistinguishable, yet the pacific union persisted and persisted only among liberal states. Moreover, even the 'clearest' technical messages appear subject to garbling. The pre-1914 period, which objectively represented a triumph of the distinguishable defence—machine guns, barbed wire, trench warfare—over the offensive, subjectively, as Jervis notes, was a period which appeared to military leaders to place exceptional premiums on the offensive and thus on preemptive war.[32]

Safety also enjoins a prudent policy of forewarning (spying) and of forearming oneself to increase security against other sovereigns who, lacking any assurance that you are not taking these measures, also take them. Safety also requires (morally) taking actions 'whatsoever shall seem to conduce to the lessening of the power of foreigners whom they [the sovereign] suspect,

---

[31] Thomas Hobbes, *Leviathan* (1651; New York: Penguin, 1980), p. 186.

[32] Hobbes, *Leviathan*, pp. 186–210, 212. Jervis examines incentives for cooperation, not the existence or sources of peace. Robert Jervis, 'Cooperation Under the Security Dilemma', *World Politics*, 30/1 (1978), pp. 167–214.

whether by slight or force'.[33] If preventive wars are prudent, the realists' prudence obviously cannot account for more than a century and a half of peace among independent liberal states, many of which have crowded one another in the centre of Europe.

Distance or weakness can sometimes make states peaceful, simply because they lack the opportunity to engage in war. In Africa, distance and weak states have made wars seem prohibitively expensive, and a political culture that valued post-colonial independence almost above all else took the prestige out of conquest. Together, they seem to have produced a strong tendency toward interstate peace in the post-war period. Civil strife, on the other hand, has been frequent. Interstate wars have occurred: Tanzania invaded Uganda in 1979, Ethiopia has clashed with Somalia, and subversion and support for guerrillas was prevalent in the long-running confrontation between front-line states and apartheid South Africa. Nigeria and other West African states are now intervening in Liberia and Sierra Leone—with the full endorsement of the United Nations. There has also recently developed extensive international intervention—overt and covert—in the Congo (former Zaire). But until recently and compared with early modern Europe—and twentieth-century Europe, too—Africa in the post-war era has been an oasis of peace.[34] Much of Latin America—with a similar handful of exceptions—has benefited from an equivalent discrediting of war.[35] But this is not an explanation of the peace among liberals, among the most wealthy and powerful states in the international system and whose peace has survived through periods when imperial conquest was both regular and prestigious.

Raymond Aron has identified three other types of prudential interstate peace consequent upon the structure of the international system: empire, hegemony, and equilibrium.[36] An empire generally succeeds in creating an internal peace, but this is not an explanation of peace among independent liberal states. Hegemony can create peace by overawing potential rivals. Although far from perfect and certainly precarious, United States hegemony, as Aron notes, might account for the interstate peace in South America in the post-war period during the height of the cold war. However, the liberal peace cannot be attributed merely to effective international policing by a predominant hegemon—Britain in the nineteenth century, the United States in the post-war period. Even though a hegemon might well have an interest in enforcing a peace for the sake of commerce or investments or as a means of enhancing its prestige or security; hegemons such as seventeenth-century France were not peace-enforcing, and the liberal peace persisted in the 1920s and 1930s when international society lacked a predominant hegemonic power. This explanation overestimates both British and American hegemonic

---

[33] Hobbes, 'De Cive', *The English Works of Thomas Hobbes*, (London: J. Bohn, 1841), vol. 2, p. 171.

[34] Robert Jackson, *Quasi-States: Sovereignty, International Relations, and the Third World* (Cambridge: Cambridge University Press, 1990).

[35] Arie Kacowicz, 'Explaining Zones of Peace: Democracies as Satisfied Powers', *Journal of Peace Research*, 32/3 (1995), pp. 265–76.

[36] Raymond Aron, *Peace and War* (New York: Praeger, 1968), pp. 151–4.

control. Neither Britain nor the United States was able to prever challenges to its interests—colonial competition in the nineteenth [Middle East diplomacy and conflicts over trading with the enemy in t[war period. Where then was the capacity to prevent all armed conflicts between liberal regimes, many of which were remote and others strategically or economically insignificant? Liberal hegemony and leadership are important, but they are neither necessary nor sufficient to explain a liberal peace.

Peace through equilibrium—the multipolar classical balance of power or the bipolar cold war—also draws upon prudential sources of peace. An awareness of the likelihood that aggressive attempts at hegemony will generate international opposition should, it is argued, deter these aggressive wars. But bipolar stability discourages polar or superpower wars, not proxy or small-power wars. And multipolar balancing of power also encourages warfare to seize, for example, territory for strategic depth against a rival expanding its power from internal growth. Neither readily accounts for general peace or for the liberal peace.

Thus, realist theories can account for aspects of certain periods of international stability. But neither the logic of the balance of power, nor that of international hegemony, nor that of ultra-imperialist cooperation explains the separate peace maintained for more than 150 years among states sharing one particular form of governance: liberal principles and institutions.

Most liberal theorists have also offered inadequate guidance in understanding the exceptional nature of liberal pacification. Lockeans (First Image liberals) acknowledge that purely ideological or normative commitments seem insufficient to account for the peace. Statesman seem to need some institutional guarantee beyond a normative commitment to international rights in order to regularize a state of peace. Representative government seems to be what it takes to lock in the solidaristic sentiments of international law (extensive economic interdependence may also help). Second Image liberals have argued that democratic states would be inherently peaceful simply and solely because in these states citizens rule the polity and bear the costs of wars. Unlike monarchs, citizens are not able to indulge their aggressive passions and have the consequences suffered by someone else.[37] Smith saw a strong tendency for manufacturing states to be peaceable. Schumpeter argued that laissez-faire capitalism contains an inherent tendency toward rationalism, and that, since war is irrational, liberal capitalisms will be pacifistic. Others still,

---

[37] The incompatibility of democracy and war was classically asserted by Paine in *The Rights of Man*. See also the citations on the 'democratic peace' in Brown *et al.* (eds), *Debating the Democratic Peace*, and a set of case studies edited by Mirius Elmand, *Paths to Peace* (Cambridge, MA: MIT Press, 1997). Randall Schweller, 'Domestic Structure and Preventive War', *World Politics*, 44 (1992), pp. 235–69, finds some evidence to support the view that democratic hegemons do not engage in preventive wars. And Carol Ember, Melvin Ember, and Bruce Russett, in 'Peace Between Participatory Polities,' *World Politics*, 44 (1992), pp. 573–99, find that pacification is also evident in certain pre-industrial tribal societies. David Lake revives this type of argument in 'Powerful Pacifists', *American Political Science Review*, 86/1 (1992), pp. 24–37. Discovering that democracies are both non-aggressive and 'powerful', he suggests that rational egoism parsimoniously accounts for a democratic peace. What might this argument make of Thucydidean (Athenian) imperialism?

such as Montesquieu, claim that 'commerce is the cure for the most destruct-ive prejudices', and 'Peace is the natural effect of trade'.[38] While these devel-opments can help account for aspects of the liberal peace, they do not explain the fact that liberal states are peaceful only in relations with other liberal states.

Liberty

The liberals were not the first philosophers to conceive of the value of human liberty or equality. What makes a liberal a liberal is making *equal, non-discriminatory liberty* the centre of one's political philosophy. What makes for international liberal theory is an exploration of the significance of that choice for world politics. Machiavelli, for example, gloried in the freedom of the cit-izens of his republics. It was what made Rome strong. But, for Machiavelli, liberty is a means to an end: the glory, the imperial glory, of the republics he envisaged. So Thomas Macaulay, the great nineteenth century liberal histo-rian, in his *Essays* remarked on Machiavelli's special and, for him and other liberals, dangerous communitarianism:

The good of the body, distinct from the good of the members, and sometimes hardly compatible with the good of the members, seems to be the one object which he proposes to himself. Of all political fallacies, this has perhaps had the widest and most mischiev-ous operation.

Locke is different (and differently dangerous). Locke says of all men:

. . . he and the rest of all mankind are one Community, make up one society distinct from all other creatures. And were it not for the corruption and viciousness of degener-ate Men, there would be no need for any other; no necessity that Men should separate from this great and natural Community, and by positive agreements combine into smaller and divided associations.[39]

He did not mean that states should be abolished, or that national security was no longer a prime duty of statesmanship. Both were necessary and thus human beings acquired special loyalties and duties to their states. He just meant that mankind itself was a community, greater in an important sense than Rome or any other single republic. Our understanding of the whole of mankind was what allowed us to understand our rights and thereby gave to us all a set of duties.

Locke is a bridge to the realists in that he too saw the dangers of world pol-itics, including the possibility of slipping from a state of peace to a state of war in the foreign relations of any state, whether liberal or not. The 'federative power' closely resembles the canonical unitary rational actor. Partiality, biased adjudication, weak enforcement all lay close to the state of peace liberals should maintain and thus occasioned a need for constant preparedness and

---

[38] This literature is surveyed and analysed by Albert Hirschman, 'Rival Interpretations of Market Society'.

[39] Locke, *Second Treatise*, para. 128.

strategic game-playing. Statesmen, moreover, should pursue national 'advantage'. But their advantage is tempered or fenced by human rights. Competition, glory, and fear will, as they did for Thucydides and Hobbes, shape foreign policy, because world politics is a troubled peace. But they do so, should do so, and will do so for authentic liberals, only to the extent they are compatible with a respect for the life, liberty, and property that gives the liberal states authority at home.

Democracy

Nor were the liberals the first to conceive of the value of democracy, as either a means or an end. Indeed, for two millennia between Thucydides and Machiavelli, democracy was the great imperial model of government. But in the modern liberal version it becomes the great engine of peace. Thucydides, Rousseau, Kant, and Schumpeter are all advocates—and theorists—of popular, or democratic, or representative republican government. Yet they expect democratic foreign relations to be—variously—imperialist, isolationist, internationalist, and pacific. How can we explain their differences and understand the multiple legacies of democratic foreign affairs ?

The pattern of expected foreign relations of democratic states that they offer us can be seen in Table 1.1. Thucydides' democratic imperialism, Rousseau's democratic isolationism, Kant's liberal internationalism, and Schumpeter's liberal pacifism rest on fundamentally different views on the nature of man, the state, and international relations.

Let us examine the theorists pair-wise.

Table 1.1. Foreign Relations of Democratic States

	Peace	War	Imperialism
With democracies	Schumpeter, Kant	Rousseau, Thucydides	Thucydides
With non-democracies	Schumpeter	Rousseau, Thucydides, Kant	Thucydides, Kant

Schumpeter and Kant.   Schumpeter's man is rationalized, individualized, and democratized. He is also homogenized, pursuing material interests 'monistically'. Since his material interests lie in peaceful trade, he and the democratic state that he and his fellow citizens control are pacifistic. Schumpeter's 'materialistic monism' leaves little room for non-economic objectives, whether espoused by states or by individuals. His states, moreover, are the same. The political life of individuals seems to have been homogenized at the same time as the individuals were 'rationalized, individualized, and democratized'. Citizens, capitalists and workers, rural and urban, seek material welfare. Schumpeter presumes that no one seems to want to rule. He also presumes that no one is prepared to take those measures—such as stirring up foreign quarrels to preserve a domestic ruling coalition—that enhance one's political power, despite detrimental effects on mass welfare. Just as ideal domestic politics are homogenized, so world politics, too, is homogenized. Materially monistic and democratically capitalist, all states evolve toward free trade and liberty together. Countries differently constituted seem to disappear from Schumpeter's analysis. 'Civilized nations' govern 'culturally backward regions'.

Unlike Schumpeter's capitalist democracies, Kant's constitutional democracies—including our own—remain in a state of war with non-republics. Liberal republics see themselves as threatened by aggression from non-republics that are not constrained by representation. Liberal politicians often fail in their categorical moral duties and stir up foreign quarrels with non-liberal states as a way of enhancing their own domestic power. And even though wars often cost more than the economic return they generate, liberal republics also are prepared to protect and promote—sometimes forcibly—democracy, private property, and the rights of individuals in other countries against non-republics which, because they do not authentically represent the rights of individuals, have no rights to non-interference. These wars may liberate oppressed individuals abroad; they also can generate enormous suffering.

Thucydides and Rousseau.   Thucydides' citizens, unlike Schumpeter's, are splendidly diverse in their goals, both at home and abroad. Their characters are shaped in varying proportions by courage, ambition, fear, profit, caution, glory, and patriotism. Although they are equal before the law and all citizens have a right to vote, their circumstances greatly differ, divided as they are among rich and poor, urban and rural. Internationally, their states are driven by fear, honour, and self-advantage. States, too, are radically unequal in size, resources, and power. Such a people and such a state find imperialism useful, feasible, and valued. In a dangerous world, empire adds to the security, profit, and glory of the powerful majority, even if not of all the citizens. The demos makes naval power effective and cheap.

Rousseau's citizens, too, are equal, rational and free. But, going beyond legal equality, social and economic equality distinguishes them from Thucydides' Athenians. 'Particular wills', such as the ones that drove the Athenians to Sicily, would yield to the 'general will'—the rational, national, general interest—which Thucydides (Pericles) had defined as precluding further imperial expansion. The exploitation of non-citizens in the empire—the source of so much national revenue—also would be unacceptable in a Rousseauian republic that demanded that all men be free, ruling and being ruled on an equal basis. This obviously precludes slavery. It also requires that every other form of political rule that did not give an equal voice to all affected had to be excluded from a free democracy, which is why Rousseau's democracy had to be small. Nor, lastly, would Rousseau allow the extensive commerce that both made empire valued and feasible. The Rousseauian democracy was free, independent, and isolationist.

Rousseau and Kant.   Kant's citizens, like Rousseau's, are free, politically equal, and rational. The Kantian state is thus governed publicly according to law, as a republic. Kant's constitutional democracy thus also solves the problem of governing equals. But his citizens are different in two respects. They retain their individuality, whether they are the 'rational devils' he says that we egoists often find ourselves to be, or the ethical agents, treating other individuals as ends rather than as means, that we can and should become. And they retain their diversity in economic and social circumstance. Given this diversity Kantian republics ideally are experiments in how:

To organize a group of rational beings who demand general laws for their survival, but of whom each inclines toward exempting himself, and to establish their constitution in such a way that, in spite of the fact that their private attitudes are opposed, these private attitudes mutually impede each other in such a manner that their public behavior is the same as if they did not have such evil attitudes. [40]

Like Rousseau's direct democracy, Kant's constitutional democracy exercises democratic caution in the interest of the majority. But unlike Rousseau's general will, Kant's republics are capable of appreciating the moral equality of all individuals. The Rousseauian citizen cedes all rights to his fellow citizens, retaining only the right to equal consideration. In order to be completely self-determining, Rousseau requires that there be no limit but equality on the sovereignty and authority of the general will. The resulting communitarianism is intense: every aspect of culture, morality, and social life is subject to the creation and the re-creation of the national citizenry. The tendency to enhance domestic consciousness through external hostility and what Rousseau calls *amour propre* would be correspondingly high. Just as individuality disappears into collective consciousness, so too does an appreciation of the international rights of foreign republics. These international rights of republics derive from our ability to reconstruct in our imagination the act of representation of foreign individuals, who are our moral equals. Kant appears to think that the general will, which Rousseau thinks can be realized only within the community, can be intuited by each individual as the Categorical Imperative. Rousseau's democracy, for the sake of intensifying national identity, limits our identification to fellow citizens.

This imaginative act of Kantian cosmopolitan identification benefits from the institutional process of republican government. Constitutionally divided powers among the executive, legislature, and the judiciary require public deliberation and sometimes compromise and thereby mitigate the effect of particular passions or hasty judgment. Rousseau's direct democracy, while

---

[40] Kant, *Perpetual Peace*, p. 453. And for a comparative discussion of the political foundations of Kant's ideas see Judith Shklar, *Ordinary Vices* (Cambridge, MA: Harvard University Press, 1984).

deliberative, appears to slight the value of republican delay. Moreover, for the sake of equality and autonomy, Rousseau's democracy precludes the private ties of commerce and social interaction across borders that lead to both domestic diversity and transnational solidarity. These material ties sustain the transnational, or cosmopolitan, identity of individuals with each other that serves as the foundation of international respect, which in turn is the source of the spirit of international law that requires tolerance and peace among fellow constitutional democracies—while exacerbating conflict between constitutional democracies and all other states.

Rousseau shares with Kant democratic rationality. Rousseau, however, excludes both the moral individualism and the social pluralism that provide the foundations for Kant's 'international' and 'cosmopolitan' laws, and thereby precludes the liberal peace.

Comparing Thucydides and Rousseau, on the one hand, with Kant and Schumpeter, on the other, we can say that whatever the differences in their special views of man and the nature of domestic politics, the first two agree that the *polis* or state either does or should command all force and command all loyalty. Differences among actual states and personal values are then contained by their similar degree of national authority. There is thus no room for the individualism and domestic diversity that Kant finds is at the root of the transnational loyalties and transnational interests that make a democratic peace. Nor is there room for the simple transnational materialism Schumpeter sees as governing the interests of pacific democratic majorities. The democracies of Thucydides and Rousseau remain in a state of war.

To the extent that these theoretical distinctions tap the actual range of diversity in the development of contemporary democracies, they offer us some useful warnings about the international implications of the current trend toward democratization. While majority rule may be a necessary condition of a state of peace, it is not a sufficient condition. Autarky and nationalism can undermine democratic peace. To establish peace among themselves, democracies must also define individual rights in such a way that the cosmopolitan rights of all mankind are entailed in the moral foundations of the rights of domestic citizens. And they must allow the material ties of transnational society to flourish among themselves.

These are, needless to say, daunting challenges for really existing liberal republics. As this volume illustrates, actual practice often has fallen short in its relations with vulnerable societies in the developing world and in conflicts with powerful competitors among the non-liberal great powers. More remarkable, however, is the tentative but apparently real peace established among liberal republics where, despite numerous potential conflicts over territory, trade, and prestige, a peace has held and holds them together.

2

US Democracy Promotion: Realist Reflections

RANDALL L. SCHWELLER

M Y role in this edited volume is that of the 'evil' realist, spreading not democracy and sunshine but, much like the purveyors of darkness in the 1920s cult cartoon, 'The Sunshine Makers', forecasts of gloom and doom.[1] The job of the evil realist—I prefer sober, cynical, pessimistic realist—is a dirty one to be sure, but someone has to do it. Seasoned realists, like major league baseball umpires, eventually become inured to the occasional hisses, boos, and laughter from the gallery; the really hardened ones learn to enjoy it. As the thick-skinned Robert Gilpin observes, no one loves a political realist—we think bad thoughts, such as 'refus[ing] to believe that, with the defeat of the Soviet Union and the end of the cold war, the liberal millennium of democracy, unfettered markets, and peace is upon us'.[2] But while all self-described realists are somewhat sceptical of the democratic-peace proposition, some are more likely to dismiss it than are others.[3]

Strict Waltzian structural realists, such as Christopher Layne and John Mearsheimer, view the 'democratic peace' as little more than a misleading statistical artefact and warn that a US foreign policy built on the promotion of democracy will lead to a dangerous complacency about future great power challengers, 'disastrous military interventions abroad, strategic overextension, and the relative decline of American power'.[4] In contrast, neoclassical realists, who believe that domestic factors and intentions as well as capabilities shape

---

[1] I was contacted about participating in the edited volume and the conference by Michael Cox, who playfully suggested that he was looking for an 'evil' realist and I would be perfect for the role. It is not the first time that I have been called an 'evil' realist. See Michael Spirtas, 'A House Divided: Tragedy and Evil in Realist Theory', *Security Studies*, 5/3 (1996), pp. 395–400.

[2] Robert G. Gilpin, 'No One Loves a Political Realist', *Security Studies*, 5/3 (1996), p. 3.

[3] For a sophisticated discussion of the various strands of realism, see Michael W. Doyle, *Ways of War and Peace: Realism, Liberalism, and Socialism* (New York: W. W. Norton, 1997), Chs 1–5.

[4] Christopher Layne, 'Kant or Cant: The Myth of the Democratic Peace', in Michael E. Brown, Sean M. Lynn-Jones, and Steven E. Miller (eds), *The Peril of Anarchy: Contemporary Realism and International Security* (Cambridge, MA: The MIT Press, 1995), p. 329. See also, John J. Mearsheimer, 'Back to the Future: Instability in Europe After the Cold War', in Michael Brown *et al.* (eds), *The Peril of Anarchy*, pp. 121–4.

states' foreign policy, see some merit in the democratic peace argument.[5] Because, according to this realist school, threat does not inhere in power alone,[6] the relative distribution of capabilities among states is less important than assessments of others' intentions in determining how states interact with each other. Whether, for instance, a state balances against or bandwagons with a more powerful neighbour depends, *inter alia*, on whether it believes that the latter will use its power advantage to threaten, coerce, manipulate, and destroy it or, conversely, to enable, reassure, and enrich it.[7]

Along these lines, a new school of motivational realists[8] has emerged to challenge the structural and defensive realist view of international politics as a tragedy—one driven by states' search for security in an anarchic world of fear and uncertainty. Instead, motivational realists characterize international relations in terms of 'old style' power politics. Specifically, the binding forces in a system of power politics are competition and conflict among sovereign states, each with a duty not only to defend itself but to augment its power and advance its national interests—by force, if necessary—often at the expense of other states. Given this realist school's emphasis on intentions and goals, the principal benefit of US democracy promotion is the increased transparency of state motivations: 'If a democracy is really a security seeker, the openness of its policy processes will reveal this to the world.'[9] Likewise, if a democracy is not really a security seeker but rather an aggressor, for whatever reason, it will be

---

[5] See Gideon Rose, 'Neoclassical Realism and Theories of Foreign Policy', *World Politics*, 51/1 (1998), pp. 144–72. The list of neoclassical realists includes Fareed Zakaria, William Wohlforth, Thomas Christensen, Melvyn Leffler, Randall Schweller, and Aaron Friedberg; see also John A. Vasquez, 'The Realist Paradigm and Degenerative versus Progressive Research Programs: An Appraisal of Neotraditional Research on Waltz's Balancing Proposition', and the responses by Kenneth Waltz, Thomas Christensen and Jack Snyder, Colin and Miriam Fendius Elman, Randall Schweller, and Stephen Walt, *American Political Science Review*, 91/4 (1997), pp. 899–935.

[6] Stephen M. Walt, *The Origins of Alliances* (Ithaca, NY: Cornell University Press, 1987).

[7] Randall L. Schweller, 'Bandwagoning For Profit: Bringing the Revisionist State Back In', *International Security*, 19/1 (1994), p. 104.

[8] Kydd coined the term 'motivational realist' and calls me a notable exponent of this school of thought. See Andrew Kydd, 'Sheep in Sheep's Clothing: Why Security Seekers Do Not Fight Each Other', *Security Studies*, 7/1 (1997), pp. 114–54; see also Randall L. Schweller, 'Neorealism's Status-Quo Bias: What Security Dilemma?' *Security Studies*, 5/3 (1996), pp. 90–121; Randall L. Schweller, *Deadly Imbalances: Tripolarity and Hitler's Strategy of World Conquest* (New York: Columbia University Press, 1998), especially Chs 1 and 3. The following list of motivational-realist propositions is drawn exclusively from these works: (1) security is not the primary goal of all states—indeed, states, especially great powers, have often placed their security at risk attempting to enhance their power and influence, territory, wealth, etc.; (2) a world of all security seekers would be a perpetually peaceful one; (3) there are many ways that true security seekers can convincingly convey their benign intentions to others; (4) structural realists have overestimated the difficulty of assessing state motivations; in practice, security seekers recognize each other and can screen out aggressors; wars are therefore rarely, if ever, caused by misperception of others' intentions or fears about their future motivations; (5) aggressors, not searchers for security, are at the root of conflict and war; and (6) greedy states bent on aggression in the foreseeable future will be unable to imitate security-seeking states.

[9] Kydd, 'Sheep in Sheep's Clothing', p. 119. Kydd goes on to argue (correctly, in my view) that democratic polities 'cannot help but reveal information about the policy preferences of the actors involved. Elections provide incentives to research voter preferences and disclose candidate preferences, intergovernmental politics provides much information on policymakers' preferences between elections, and even bureaucracies strive to manipulate the policy process by releasing information to the public' (p. 138; also see pp. 129–39).

unable to hide its greedy, non-security aims.[10] More generally, in a world of uncertainty about others' motivations, security seekers value transparency because they need to know others' real motivations and, just as important, they *want* others to recognize their own genuinely benign intentions. Among security seekers, transparency enhances conflict avoidance and reassurance.[11] Inasmuch as the spread of liberal democracy creates shared values, common interests, and, most important, greater transparency of state motivations, it should lower threat perceptions and increase cooperation among such states. As a realist, I have no problem supporting these claims.[12] That's the good news.

The bad news is that extending the democratic zone will not lead to a perpetual peace among nations. This is because the fundamental causes of international conflict will remain, for they cannot be transcended. The spread of democracy promises to dampen potential conflicts but it will not effect a major 'qualitative change' in international politics, which will remain much as it has always been: a struggle for power and influence in a world of, at a minimum, moderate scarcity. Though I am willing to concede the point—though other realists have challenged it—that democracies have not fought each other in the past, I, like Kydd, 'find it perfectly possible that democracies could fight—indeed could fight long and bloody wars against each other—so long as the aims of the populations are in fundamental conflict'.[13]

This chapter addresses several key questions from a realist perspective. Can the extension of democracy overcome Hobbes's three causes of war? Can democracy solve the problems created by the distribution of scarce goods in the absence of political authority? Can the spread of democracy attenuate positional competition and conflict created by growth and status concerns? I conclude that democracy can ameliorate some of the causes of war cited by Hobbes and other realists, but it cannot entirely eliminate them. Moreover, while there is good evidence to support democratic peace theory, the vast

[10] Kydd cleverly captures this crucial point with a wonderfully colourful image: 'We do not need . . . to fear wolves in sheep's clothing. Wolves find sheepskin difficult to wear for long; it is too tight and tends to split at the seams, revealing telltale patches of lupine fur. Sheep, for their part, are pretty good at identifying other sheep. When they are uncertain, they can set up institutions that require all sheep to roll around, scratch their backs on trees, or anything else calculated to remove false overcoats' ('Sheep in Sheep's Clothing', pp. 153–4). For a related point about how satisfied states can convince others of their benign intentions through costly signals, see Schweller, 'Neorealism's Status-Quo Bias', p. 104, where I also point out that 'neorealists have mistakenly conceptualized the security dilemma as a Prisoners' Dilemma (PD) rather than a Stag Hunt . . . When security is the goal, as in the security dilemma, states will seek to succor, not sucker, their neighbors (the CC payoff)'. The logic is straightforward: by resisting the temptation to sucker others, the state demonstrates to all that it is not a greedy expansionist.

[11] Schweller, 'Neorealism's Status-Quo Bias', p. 104.

[12] To admit that democracy can mitigate some of the pernicious effects of anarchy is not inconsistent with realism; after all, Doyle claims that Rousseau 'was and is the democratic Realist' (*Ways of War and Peace*, p. 137). See also Robert G. Kaufman, 'E. H. Carr, Winston Churchill, Reinhold Niebuhr, and Us: The Case for Principled, Prudential, Democratic Realism', *Security Studies*, 5/2 (1995/96), pp. 314–53. At p. 351, Kaufman writes: '[A Churchillian-Niebuhrian realism] recognizes the powerful constraints of international anarchy, without denying, as structural realists erroneously do, the importance of ideology, regime type generally, and liberal democracy particularly'.

[13] Kydd, 'Sheep in Sheep's Clothing', p. 129.

majority of democracies have, until recently, been prosperous, satisfied, fully developed, Western, and insular states. Changes in the values of these critical variables warrant great caution in extending the democratic peace proposition into the future. In the final section, I challenge the conventional wisdom that peace and stability are in the 'global interest' and are intrinsic, universal values, for moral or any other reasons. While global peace and stability may currently serve to advance US national interests, they were not always good for America. The question a realist must raise is: Who wants perpetual peace and why?

A Realist Appraisal of Democratic Peace Theory

If the democratic peace proposition is a law-like generalization, then the following prediction must be true: if every state were democratic, international wars would cease to exist. To disagree with this statement is to conclude that the democratic peace thesis is either incorrect or supplies only a partial corrective to the problems of anarchy and its consequences.[14]

This section evaluates democratic peace theory by applying Hobbes's three causes of war to such a hypothetical 'liberal democratic' world. On the causes of conflict, Hobbes wrote:

All men in the state of nature have a desire and will to hurt, but not preceding from the same cause, neither equally to be condemned. . . . So that in the nature of man, we find three principal causes of quarrel. First, competition; secondly, diffidence; thirdly, glory. The first maketh men invade for gain; the second, for safety; and the third, for reputation.[15]

Let us consider these three causes of conflict to see if the spread of democracy disconfirms Hobbes's judgement of their inevitability.

Diffidence

Distrust plays a special role in Hobbes's argument for the inevitability of war in the state of nature. Because 'even if a *majority* of men were seeking only security'—by implication, a considerable number still desire power for gain and prestige—they too, being unable to distinguish the 'wicked' from the 'righteous', would have to use 'force and wiles', suspecting all others of aggressive motives. In light of the danger of uncertainty and of guessing wrong about others' intentions, individuals who wish to survive must anticipate aggression, act on the assumption of worst-case scenarios, and respond with preemptive attacks. Because, as in a Prisoners' Dilemma, individual rationality produces collective irrationality, conflict and war can be expected to arise even

---

[14] Stephen Walt suggested this logic at the Eleventh Annual Strategy and National Security Conference, sponsored by the John M. Olin Institute for Strategic Studies, Harvard University, 13–15 June 1996, Wianno Club, Cape Cod.

[15] Thomas Hobbes, *Leviathan*, ed. C. B. Macpherson (Baltimore: Penguin, 1985), p. 184.

among individuals (states) who seek nothing more than security and who all prefer peace to war.[16] The common example of this dynamic in international relations is the security dilemma/spiral model of conflict.[17] It is this tragic aspect of conditions under anarchy that animates Waltzian structural realism and its central claim that uncertainty causes war, such that, even when all states seek nothing more than survival, they may be continually disposed to fight one another as a result of their craving for security. How might the spread of democracy affect this situation?

On the one hand, it can be reasonably argued that the spread of democracy is likely to exert a strong dampening effect on diffidence as a cause of war. As mentioned, democracies are highly transparent, making their intentions relatively easy to discern. Moreover, Hobbes believed that individuals in the state of nature *learn* to distrust each other because of the *experience* of their belligerence, not because of an innate and universal distrust of others. Since democracies have rarely, if ever, fought each other, there is no historical reason for such states to anticipate aggression with other democracies. While, according to this logic, one 'bad apple'—that is, a predatory democratic state *vis-à-vis* another democracy—will likely spoil the barrel—that is, force other democracies to engage in 'normal' competitive power politics—so far no such apple has appeared.[18] As long as democracies are seen as pacific, especially in their relations with each other, they can learn to trust each other—and have done so.

But if a history of belligerence causes others to anticipate aggression and pre-empt it, then, if and when all states become democratic, many democratic dyads—particularly contiguous states—will have had a history of rivalry with each other when they were not jointly democratic. If Hobbes's 'diffidence is learned' argument is correct, then the existence of long-standing conflicts among newly democratic states can be expected to override the pacific effect of their common democratic polities. In assessing democracy's likely effect on diffidence as a cause of war, the key question is: will new democratic states have learned that democracies do not fight each other and can therefore be trusted, or will they have learned that their history of rivalry with their now democratic neighbour shows that the latter cannot be trusted?

As I have written elsewhere, I find Hobbes's 'distrust as a cause of war' and the related neorealist 'uncertainty causes war' arguments rather flimsy, both on empirical and theoretical grounds.[19] True security is often a scarce, semi-exclusive resource, particularly when strong, predatory states use their power to make others feel less secure; and power, when it is not recklessly pursued,

[16] For an insightful discussion on this topic, see James D. Fearon, 'Rationalist Explanations For War', *International Organization*, 49/3 (1995), pp. 379–414.

[17] See Robert Jervis, 'Cooperation Under the Security Dilemma', *World Politics*, 30/2 (1978), pp. 167–214; and Charles L. Glaser, 'The Security Dilemma Revisited', *World Politics*, 50/1 (1997), pp. 171–201.

[18] See Alexander Wendt, 'Anarchy Is What States Make of It: The Social Construction of Power Politics', *International Organization*, 46/2 (1992), pp. 407–9; and Schweller, 'Neorealism's Status-Quo Bias', pp. 90–2, 119–21.

[19] See Schweller, 'Neorealism's Status-Quo Bias'.

tends to promote the goal of self-preservation. But security can be commonly enjoyed; and indeed it is most robust when it is universally shared. Among security-seekers, there is no conflict between individual and aggregate benefits. Everyone is made more secure by installing sturdy locks on their doors. Individual benefits of this type add up; that is, the sum of individual actions taken together is positive. This is precisely what is not true for positional goods. What each of us can attain, all cannot. Most individuals, for example, want to occupy 'upper echelon jobs'; but if everyone advances, no one does. The value of a college degree as a means to a superior job declines as more people achieve that level of education. If everyone stands on tiptoe, no one sees better.[20] Likewise, the desire for political power and influence, as Morgenthau suggests, is *positional* in nature and may be limitless in scope:

[T]he desire for power is closely related to [selfishness] but is not identical with it. For the typical goals of selfishness, such as food, shelter, security . . . have an objective relation to the vital needs of the individual . . . The desire for power, on the other hand, concerns itself not with the individual's survival *but with his position among his fellows once his survival has been secured.* Consequently, the selfishness of man has limits; his will to power has none. For while man's vital needs are capable of satisfaction, his lust for power would be satisfied only if the last man became an object of his domination, there being nobody above or beside him, that is, if he became like God.[21]

Driven by a natural, animal-like instinct to acquire power—an *animus dominandi*—and compelled by his environment to compete for scarce resources, '[m]an cannot hope to be good but must be content with being not too evil'.[22]

Neorealists would, no doubt, charge that my claim that security is a positive-sum good overlooks the crucial role of uncertainty and incomplete information in explaining state behaviour under anarchy; that I am too confident in the ability of status-quo states to recognize one another's benign intentions. In response, I do not deny that anarchy creates uncertainty, particularly, as Waltz suggests, under multipolarity. For example, Chamberlain and others misperceived Hitler as a 'normal' German statesman with legitimate and limited pan-German revisionist goals; Stalin refused to believe that Germany would attack the Soviet Union in 1941; and the Kaiser believed that Germany was being encircled. These well-known cases of misperception, however, all involved true aggressors and revisionist states.[23] To disprove the claim that, among status-quo states, security is a positive-sum game and therefore relatively easy to achieve, one has to show examples of wars that resulted from uncertainty when all states sought nothing more than security.

[20] These examples are borrowed from Fred Hirsch, *The Social Limits to Growth* (Cambridge: Harvard University Press, 1976), pp. 3–7.

[21] Hans J. Morgenthau, *Scientific Man vs. Power Politics* (Chicago: The University of Chicago Press, 1946), pp. 192–3 (emphasis added).

[22] Morgenthau, *Scientific Man vs. Power Politics*, p. 192.

[23] In a related point about the causes of World War I, Kydd points out that 'France and Russia certainly did have aggressive nonsecurity-related motivations toward Germany and Austria-Hungary. The French desire to recover Alsace-Lorraine and the Russian desire for hegemony in the Balkans were deeply held and often led to policies that undermined the security of the two countries, as well as that of the central powers' ('Sheep in Sheep's Clothing', p. 149).

To be sure, uncertainty matters under anarchy, but it is not fatal and does not lead to war in the absence of a true aggressor.[24] Uncertainty may explain why a war unfolded the way it did, or why an aggressor went undeterred or under-balanced; but it alone cannot explain the outbreak of war. And indeed, the empirical record strongly supports this position. As Dan Reiter has recently shown, the powder keg explanation of war is more myth than reality: he finds 'only three examples of preemption among the 67 interstate wars between 1816 and 1980'; and in each of these three cases, 'non-preemptive motivations for war were also present'.[25] In *Man, the State, and War*, Waltz, too, argued that, in a world consisting only of security-seekers, there would be no balancing and military competition: 'If all states wanted simply to survive, then none would need to maintain military forces for use in either defensive or offensive action.'[26] But even in such a world—and we may have entered one—primacy and the power to influence others still matter; for as long as there is politics, there will be a struggle over who gets what, when, and how.[27] As Samuel Huntington suggests: 'If power and primacy did not matter, political scientists would have to look for other work.'[28] This brings us to Hobbes's next cause of conflict: competition.

Competition

As Charles Landesman explains: 'Competition consists of two or more individuals desiring the same thing, which they cannot both possess. What prevents them from both enjoying it is that when one enjoys or consumes it, nothing remains for the other—after consumption, the consumed good ceases to exist as a desirable object.'[29] Of the three human motivations causing conflict, Hobbes claimed that 'the most frequent reason why men desire to hurt each other' is not diffidence or glory but rather 'that many men at the same time have an appetite to the same thing; which yet very often they can

---

[24] Schweller, 'Neorealism's Status-Quo Bias'.

[25] Dan Reiter, 'Exploding the Powder Keg Myth: Preemptive Wars Almost Never Happen', *International Security*, 20/2 (1995), pp. 32–3. For more on this point, see Kydd, 'Sheep in Sheep's Clothing', pp. 147–52.

[26] Kenneth N. Waltz, *Man, the State and War: A Theoretical Analysis* (New York: Columbia University Press, 1959), pp. 203–4. Similarly, at p. 227 Waltz said: 'An understanding of the third image makes it clear that the expectation [of perpetual peace] would be justified only if the minimum interest of states in preserving themselves became the maximum interest of all of them—and each could rely fully upon the steadfast adherence to this definition by all of the others.' Later, Waltz changed his mind: 'In an anarchic domain, a state of war exists if all parties lust for power. But so too will a state of war exist if *all states seek only* to ensure their own safety.' Kenneth N. Waltz, 'The Origins of War in Neorealist Theory', in Robert I. Rotberg and Theodore K. Rabb (eds), *The Origin and Prevention of Major Wars* (Cambridge: Cambridge University Press, 1989), p. 44 (emphasis added).

[27] Harold Dwight Lasswell, *Politics: Who Gets What, When, How* (New York: Smith [1936], 1950). The classic statement on social power remains Harold D. Lasswell and Abraham Kaplan, *Power and Society: A Framework for Political Inquiry* (New Haven: Yale University Press, 1950).

[28] Samuel Huntington, 'Why International Primacy Matters', *International Security*, 17/4 (1993), pp. 68–9.

[29] Charles Landesman, 'Reflections on Hobbes: Anarchy and Human Nature', in Peter Caws (ed.), *The Causes of Quarrel: Essays on Peace, War, and Thomas Hobbes* (Boston: Beacon Press, 1989), pp. 144–5.

neither enjoy in common, nor yet divide it; whence it follows that the strongest must have it, and who is strongest must be decided by the sword'.[30] Likewise, the modern-day father of realism, Hans Morgenthau, viewed struggle and competition among individuals as inevitable, since 'What one wants for himself, the other already possesses or wants, too'.[31]

How does democratic peace theory handle competition as a cause of war? In the absence of any political authority whatever, quarrels will inevitably arise over the distribution of scarce goods, whether material or social in nature. If the essential resources of the state of nature are so restricted as to make the selfish alternative the most reasonable one, introducing democratic regimes will not be a solution. Whether or not democratic regimes have truly inculcated the norm of bargaining and compromise, they will not be able to avoid war in this extreme zero-sum world; there is simply no bargaining range for a negotiated settlement. Most worlds, however, are not so nasty and brutish; instead, they are characterized by moderate scarcity. As long as the commonly desired but scarce goods or the specific issues in dispute are divisible and/or not deemed vital to the survival and prosperity of the states concerned, one can reasonably expect jointly democratic dyads to settle their distribution problems peacefully.[32] As Fearon has shown, rational states should have incentives to find negotiated settlements to avoid the costs and risks of war; and feasible bargains must exist, *when the disputed issues are divisible*, that all prefer to war.[33] Fearon claims that all goods are essentially divisible or can be made so through clever political bargaining schemes.

In practice, however, mutually acceptable agreements that all sides prefer to the costs of war are often *not* concluded because states—or other conflict groups—(1) have incentives to misrepresent private information about, among other things, their capabilities and resolve; (2) cannot credibly commit themselves to uphold mutually beneficial agreements they might otherwise reach; or (3) believe that they can improve their welfare only at the expense of others, which locks them into a zero-sum competition for scarce resources.[34] Regarding this last impediment to peaceful resolution of conflicts, the problem is not whether the disputed good is actually divisible or can be made so but rather whether the parties perceive it as such; and in many cases—for example, when the issue is 'who rules?'—a compromise solution is viewed as unacceptable by one or all of the parties. Further, the question itself of what constitutes a divisible good is not a trivial or obvious one. For example, is maritime supremacy a divisible good? The British did not think so: 'Throughout the eighteenth century, Britain never tried seriously to develop a naval part-

---

[30] Hobbes, *Leviathan*, p. 184.   [31] Morgenthau, *Scientific Man vs. Power Politics*, p. 192.
[32] For a brief discussion of the problem of indivisible issues and war, see James D. Fearon, 'Rationalist Explanations For War', *International Organization*, 49/3 (1995), pp. 389–90. Fearon's bargaining model, however, assumes that the issues in dispute are perfectly divisible, such that feasible bargains must exist that rational states will prefer to war.
[33] Fearon, 'Rationalist Explanations For War', pp. 386–90.
[34] The first two points are made by Fearon, 'Rationalist Explanations For War', pp. 390–409.

ner, never encouraged an ally to build up its navy: its objective was to establish naval superiority alone.'[35]

The problem of indivisible scarce goods—apparent or real—is particularly acute for weak, developing states. If and when all states are democratic, some will be poor and dissatisfied with their current condition; some will inhabit a world of extreme scarcity, in which selfish behaviour, non-cooperation, and war are rational. For weak and poor democracies, the problem of securing scarce resources may literally be a matter of life or death; and it will be highly likely that some scarce goods will *jointly* affect their vital national interests, such as security and prosperity. In history, such problems have sometimes been managed by the great powers or a single hegemon assuming the role of sovereign arbiter and deciding who gets what, when, and how. But this situation does not represent a stable, true peace. As Thomas Aquinas, in his *Summa Theologica*, pointed out, peace derives not only from a calm that comes of order—Augustine's *tranquillitas ordinis*—but also from a harmony within the appetites of a single actor:

For there is no real peace where a man comes to an agreement with another not freely and of his own will, but forced into it by fear. In such a case the proper order of things, where both sides come to agreement is not kept but is disturbed by some one bringing fear to bear. This is why Augustine says previously that *peace is the tranquillity of order*, the tranquillity consisting in the fact that all movements of man's appetite are in harmony with each other.[36]

If one cannot imagine—and I cannot—a world in which a complete harmony of interests exists among all states, the extension of democracy throughout the globe will not disconfirm, though it may ameliorate, Hobbes's argument about competition and war.[37]

Glory

For Hobbes, glory is the third cause of war in human nature. Man is innately preoccupied with reputation and possesses a willingness to kill those who undervalue him:

For every man looketh that his companion should value him, at the same rate he sets upon himself: And upon all signes of contempt, or undervaluing, naturally endeavers,

---

[35] Daniel A. Baugh, 'Withdrawing From Europe: Anglo-French Maritime Geopolitics, 1750–1800', *The International History Review*, 20/1 (1998), p. 10.

[36] Thomas Aquinas, as quoted in Peter Henrici, 'Two Types of Philosophical Approach to the Problem of War and Peace', in Caws, *The Causes of Quarrel*, p. 158.

[37] Along these lines, consider the following story of 12 September 1997: 'A war over salmon fishing rights between the United States and Canada in the Pacific Northwest has deteriorated into old-fashioned nationalism: flag-burnings, insults based on national stereotypes and a mild version of gunboat diplomacy.' Timothy Egan, 'Salmon War in Northwest Spurs Wish for Good Fences', *New York Times* (12 September 1997), A1 and A14; quote comes from 'News Summary', A2. If two mature and prosperous democracies with a long tradition of friendly relations can produce what is being called a 'salmon war' (a Seattle newspaper ran the headline 'Let's Take Canada, Eh?'), what confidence can we have that unstable and poor, newly democratic states with a history of enmity with their neighbours will remain at peace with each other?

as far as he dares (which amongst them that have no common power, to keep them quiet, is far enough to make them destroy each other,) to extort a greater value from his contemners, by dommage; and from others, by the example.[38]

The most obvious example of glory as a cause of war in international relations theory is provided by Robert Gilpin's theory of hegemonic war and change.[39] According to the theory, the principal cause of hegemonic wars is a disjunction between the prestige (or reputation for power) in the system and the actual distribution of capabilities. Thus, rising states become dissatisfied and challenge the established order because they perceive themselves to be undervalued; they believe that the distribution of territory, political influence, and governance over the world economy and other institutions does not reflect, and is therefore incommensurate with, their increased power. I will return to the subject of status and prestige concerns as a cause of conflict later in the chapter.

At first glance, it may seem strange to apply glory to international politics as a motivation for war. Yet Thucydides did not explain Athenian imperialism in terms of security and fear—that is, as a response to anarchy and the security dilemma, which was the motivation for Sparta's initiation of the war—but rather in terms of the natural human desire for profit and glory.[40] Noting this, Steven Forde concludes: 'Honor, and profit (i.e., self-interest understood as aggrandizement rather than bare preservation), are necessary to account for [Athenian expansionism]. And these are impulses rooted in human nature, independent of the structural imperatives of international politics.'[41]

Seeming to glorify war, Hegel associated peace with corruption and stagnation; war, he believed, perfected the state and advanced civilizations:

War is not to be regarded as an absolute evil . . . by its agency . . . the ethical health of the peoples is preserved in their indifference to the stabilization of finite institutions; just as the blowing of the winds preserves the sea from foulness which would be the result of a long calm, so also corruption in nations would be the result of prolonged, let alone 'perpetual' peace.[42]

Constant competition among states and their respective modes of social organization serves to advance all domestic institutions by providing a yardstick by which societies can measure their own internal coherence and rationality. For this reason, war has a teleological and beneficial impact on the internal workings of the state and the creation of universal history.

---

[38] Quoted in Landesman, 'Reflections on Hobbes', p. 146.

[39] Robert Gilpin, *War and Change in World Politics* (New York: Cambridge University Press, 1981).

[40] Thucydides, *The Peloponnesian War*, translated by R. Crawley (New York: Random House/ Modern Library, 1982), book 1, pp. 75, 76.

[41] Steven Forde, 'International Realism and the Science of Politics: Thucydides, Machiavelli, and Neorealism', *International Studies Quarterly*, 39/2 (1995), pp. 146, 148.

[42] Quoted in Constance I. Smith, 'Hegel on War', *Journal of the History of Ideas*, 26/2 (1965), p. 282. This passage calls to mind Mancur Olson's views about the negative effects of peace and stability on economic growth. See Mancur Olson, *The Rise and Decline of Nations: Economic Growth, Stagflation, and Social Rigidities* (New Haven: Yale University Press, 1982).

Similarly, the foundation of geopolitics had been laid by Social Darwinism, a creed that preached the singular importance of the 'struggle' itself as the sole mechanism of racial progress and evolution. Social Darwinists asserted that success in conflict, regardless of the intrinsic importance of the actual bone of contention, was all that mattered. 'To shrink or withdraw from a struggle was therefore, if possible, even more fatal to a nation than to be vanquished. It amounted to a public confession of irredeemable decadence.'[43] Seen in this light, states must make war not only for territorial expansion but as an essential—*the* essential—means for glorifying, purifying, and advancing the human race. As a distinguished professor wrote in 1900: 'The path of progress is strewn with the wreck of nations; traces are everywhere to be seen of the hecatombs of inferior races, and of victims who found not the narrow way to the greater perfection. Yet these dead peoples are, in very truth, the stepping stones on which mankind has arisen to the higher intellectual and deeper emotional life of to-day.'[44] Can democracy overcome glory as a motivation for war?

In considering this question we should not forget that Hitler, the most reviled and vocal champion of Social Darwinism in history, was elected to power. Indeed, his failed putsch, his attempt to spearhead a revolution in 1923, convinced him that he must 'achieve power in Germany not through an armed revolution but by acceptable (and, in the broadest sense of the word, democratic) means; not by a dramatic uprising against the state and the social order but by convincing the masses of the German people, reminding them that in their hearts they would know that he was right'.[45] Confirming Tocqueville's dire prediction of a tyranny of the majority peculiar to the coming democratic age, most Germans gave Hitler not only their passive but their active consent.[46] As Ian Kershaw points out: 'Hitler was not a tyrant imposed upon Germany. He was in many respects, until well into the war, a highly popular national leader.'[47]

That said, liberal democratic regimes, while they are no guarantee against glory-through-war seeking leaders, can be expected to bring fewer Hitlers to power than other types of polities. Timing may determine the nature of democracy's effect on glory as a cause of war. During 'normal' times, the values, norms, quality of information, and public debate characteristic of democratic societies—especially, if not only, of liberal ones—all work against the rise to power of demagogues and populists bent on war. During 'hard' times,

---

[43] G. N. Sanderson, 'The European Partition of Africa: Coincidence or Conjuncture?', *The Journal of Imperial and Commonwealth History*, 3/1 (1974), p. 43. See also William L. Langer, *The Diplomacy of Imperialism, 1890–1902*, 2nd edn (New York: Alfred A. Knopf, 1965), pp. 85–96; and Woodruff D. Smith, *Politics and the Sciences of Culture in Germany, 1840–1920* (New York: Oxford University Press, 1991).

[44] Karl Pearson, *National Life from the Standpoint of Science*, p. 64, as quoted in Edward Hallett Carr, *The Twenty Years' Crisis, 1919–1939: An Introduction to the Study of International Relations* (New York: Harper and Row, [1946], 1964), p. 49.

[45] John Lukacs, *The Hitler of History* (New York: Alfred A. Knopf, 1997), p. 83.

[46] Lukacs, *The Hitler of History*, p. 111.

[47] Ian Kershaw, *Hitler: Profile in Power* (London and New York: Longman, 1991), p. 194.

however, democratic institutions and sympathies may result in mobocracy, racist populist nationalism, and the cult of 'the people' as well as the leader. Hitler was partially correct in his belief that it is easier to unite people through common hatred than common love: 'For the liberation of a people more is needed than an economic policy, more than industry: if a people is to become free, it needs pride and willpower, defiance, hate, hate and once again hate.'[48]

Finally, it is should be noted that liberal democracies have not been immune to racism in all its forms, and indeed they have had little problem justifying their not inconsiderable colonial empires in terms of racial superiority. Related to this point, Scott Murray avers: 'Incompatible as they may appear, Cobdenite internationalism and racial and national theories of superior and inferior peoples coexisted comfortably. One would bring "civilization" to the world; the other justified scientifically both the need to perform the task of civilizing and the right of certain powers to carry it out.'[49]

In summary, while a world of only liberal democracies will probably be more peaceful than the current and past worlds, the spread of democratic regimes will not entirely eliminate the causes of conflict and war identified by Hobbes. I reach this conclusion fully recognizing that states possess different properties from those of human beings in the state of nature, and so one must use Hobbes's analogy with due caution. In my view, these very real differences, which Hedley Bull and others have cited, do not in any way stack the deck against the democratic-peace hypothesis in the foregoing analysis, nor do these genuine differences damage or compromise the logic of the preceding arguments.[50]

The Problem of Scarcity and the Prospects of Extending the Zone of Democratic Peace

The Achilles' heel of democratic peace theory is that the history of democratic states has been one of satisfied, prosperous countries that have been far outnumbered by non-democratic ones and have generally enjoyed the surplus security afforded by insularity. When these variables reverse their value, there is far less likelihood that the democratic peace proposition will hold. The reasons for this conclusion are the same as those that realist theory posits: in an anarchic world characterized by scarce material and social resources, states must engage in positional competition for power and influence.

Why should we expect a poor citizenry, many of whom will continue to struggle for subsistence, to be satisfied just because they are living in a democracy? Given the far greater relative importance of scarce material and social

---

[48] Hitler, as quoted in Lukacs, *The Hitler of History*, p. 126.

[49] Scott W. Murray, 'In Pursuit of a Mirage: Robert Morier's Views of Liberal Nationalism and German Unification, 1853–1876', *The International History Review*, 20/1 (1998), p. 42.

[50] Hedley Bull, *The Anarchical Society: A Study of Order in World Politics* (New York: Columbia University Press, 1977), pp. 46–51.

resources for poor states as opposed to wealthy ones, why should not we expect 'resource' wars among today's newly democratic states similar to those historically fought among the great powers? Democratic peace proponents might respond that democracy brings prosperity and peaceful bargaining norms, both of which will solve the traditional problem of scarcity in an anarchic realm. Research shows, however, that the causal direction works in reverse: trade causes prosperity, prosperity promotes—but does not cause—democracy, shared democracy causes peace.[51] More important, global free trade and economic growth are no guarantee of world peace or the extension of democracy; in fact, they can endanger both processes in several ways.

First, free trade reinforces competition, and competition produces losers as well as winners. Fragile democratizing states are under enormous pressure to appease uncompetitive domestic distributional coalitions by adopting protectionist policies at the expense of the general national and cosmopolitan interests in free trade. In other words, there is no reason to expect that developing states will choose free trade and global liberalism over neomercantilist policies; and, indeed, there are good reasons to expect that they will choose the latter.[52] Certainly, the shock-treatment approach to capitalism regardless of social consequences that was adopted by many nations recently liberated from communism placed at risk the fragile democratizing processes under way in these newly autonomous states.

Second, while liberal democracy requires a market economy, capitalism does not require liberal democracy. Benjamin Barber correctly notes:

The stealth rhetoric that assumes capitalist interests are not only compatible with but actively advance democratic ideals, translated into policy, is difficult to reconcile with the international realities of the last fifty years. Market economies have shown a remarkable adaptability and have flourished in many tyrannical states from Chile to South Korea, from Panama to Singapore. Indeed, the state with one of the world's least democratic governments—the People's Republic of China—possesses one of the world's fastest-growing market economies.[53]

Capitalism simply requires a stable political climate and consumers with access to markets. The unstable, even chaotic, conditions characteristic of emerging democracies are scarcely conducive to the development of a thriving market economy. Indeed, the interests of capitalism and democracy—especially the process of democratization—diverge in basic ways: 'On the level of the individual, capitalism seeks consumers susceptible to the shaping of their needs and the manipulation of their wants while democracy needs citizens autonomous in their thoughts and independent in their deliberative

---

[51] See Erich Weede, *Economic Development, Social Order, and World Politics* (Boulder and London: Lynne Rienner, 1996), ch. 8.

[52] See Stephen D. Krasner, *Structural Conflict: The Third World Against Global Liberalism* (Berkeley: University of California Press, 1985).

[53] Benjamin R. Barber, *Jihad vs. McWorld: How Globalism and Tribalism are Reshaping the World* (New York: Ballantine Books, 1996), p. 14.

judgements . . . [C]apitalism wishes to tame anarchic democracy and appears to have little problem tolerating tyranny as long as it secures stability.'[54]

Third, economic growth and integration into the world's economy of developing regions and nations has historically produced wars among these countries. This occurs because increased participation in the global economy accelerates uneven growth, which differentiates the developing countries into major and minor regional powers. Describing how, in South America during the nineteenth century, the process of global integration and uneven growth among the nations of the continent led to conflict, Robert Burr writes:

Nations that could offer good port and distribution facilities, or whose natural resources were coveted, or which offered attractions to capital and immigration, raced ahead to become the predominant powers. A predominant power tended to expand its influence into its own previously neglected lands and beyond into weaker nations where, upon confrontation with a similarly advanced predominant nation, an area of conflict would develop. Predominant powers were at first concerned mainly with regional affairs, but the forces that had created them and others pushed them steadily toward involvement in the affairs of the entire continent.[55]

There are good reasons to expect that these same dynamics that caused successive wars among South American nations will arise in Africa and the developing regions in Asia in the coming century. The processes of integration into the world's economy and uneven development have accelerated dramatically in recent decades. This, combined with the 'post-cold war' relaxation of superpower pressures on developing nations, will have the important effect of allowing these non-European countries to concentrate more strongly and freely on their own regional and continental affairs, and to play power politics in an expanding arena with more vigour than in the past.

Finally, economic growth often exacerbates the condition of material and social scarcity. If 'the Chinese were to drive as many per capita passenger miles as Americans currently do each year', for example, 'it would take only five years to use up all the earth's known energy reserves'.[56] While this is, admittedly, a rather dramatic example of positional competition over scarce goods, it nicely illustrates the point. Let us examine the nature of positional goods and how economic growth intensifies competition over them.

Positional Goods

Positional goods 'are either (1) scarce in some absolute or socially imposed sense or (2) subject to congestion or crowding through more extensive use'.[57] Scarcities, in terms of absolute limitations on consumption opportunities, may arise for three different reasons. First and most familiar is physical scarcity: for example, Rembrandts, antiques, colonies, certain raw materials,

[54] Barber, *Jihad vs. McWorld*, p. 15.
[55] Robert N. Burr, *By Reason or Force: Chile and the Balancing of Power in South America, 1830–1905* (Berkeley and Los Angeles: University of California Press, 1965), p. 9.
[56] Burr, *By Reason or Force*, pp. 37–8.   [57] Hirsch, *Social Limits to Growth*, p. 27.

and so forth. The causal connection between scarce physical resources and interstate conflict is perhaps the oldest theme in international relations theory, especially among realist works. As 'exploitable resources begin to be used up, and opportunities for economic growth decline', Gilpin avers, interstate 'relations become more and more a zero-sum game in which one state's gain is another's loss'.[58] Similarly, the environment-*qua*-security literature finds 'significant causal links between scarcities of renewable resources and violence'.[59]

The other two types of scarcity arise not from physical but from social limits on the absolute supply of particular goods. 'Such social limits exist', Hirsch notes, 'in the sense that an increase in physical availability of these goods or facilities, either in absolute terms or in relation to dimensions such as population or physical space, changes their characteristics in such a way that a given amount of use yields less satisfaction.'[60]

Satisfaction that derives from scarcity itself is called *direct social scarcity*. This common phenomenon is rooted in various psychological motivations, such as envy, pride, or snobbishness. Another form of social scarcity emerges as a by-product of consumption. Hirsch calls this phenomenon *incidental social scarcity* to refer to social limitations that arise among goods valued for their intrinsic qualities independent of the satisfaction or position enjoyed by others that are nonetheless influenced by the consumption or activity of others. The typical manifestation of this type of social scarcity is congestion (or crowding out) in both its physical (traffic, overpopulation) and social (leadership, superior jobs, prestige, title, privilege) forms. An example of incidental social scarcity in global affairs is the increased demand for oil due to the emergence of newly industrialized states; or, more generally, the destruction of the global commons due to overutilization of dwindling resources or the dumping of industrial waste products into common water supplies. Both cases are examples of how growth can produce scarcity and conflict.

Status, Growth, and Positional Conflict

'Status or position', Martin Shubik observed, 'is often more important than wealth or other physical goods'.[61] Status in domestic and international systems is a form of stratification that has been defined and won by many different means throughout the ages. Sociologists commonly recognize that status in domestic societies is achieved in various ways—for example, birth, class, commerce, authority, education, etc.—and that the criteria of status change

---

[58] Robert Gilpin, *War and Change in World Politics* (Cambridge: Cambridge University Press, 1981), pp. 200–1.

[59] Thomas F. Homer-Dixon, Jeffrey H. Boutwell, and George W. Rathjens, 'Environmental Scarcity and Violent Conflict', *Scientific American*, 268/2 (1993), p. 45. For a stinging critique, see Marc A. Levy, 'Is the Environment a National Security Issue?', *International Security*, 20/2 (1995), pp. 35–62.

[60] Hirsch, *Social Limits to Growth*, p. 20.

[61] Martin Shubik, 'Games of Status', *Behavioral Science*, 16/3 (1971), p. 117.

over time and across societies—for example, the amount of land owned, the number of cattle owned, the number of slaves owned, occupation, wealth, reputation of schools attended, etc. Less appreciated by international relations theorists is that status in the international system also varies across time and space.[62] To gain recognition as top dog, states have engaged in all sorts of competitions: competitive acquisitions of sacred relics in ancient Greece, competitive palace-building in the eighteenth century, competitive colonialism and railway building in the nineteenth, and competitive space programmes in the twentieth.[63]

Military success has always been the chief mark of status and prestige. Thus, following R. G. Hawtrey, Robert Gilpin defines prestige as the reputation for power; that is, other countries' subjective calculation of a state's military strength and its willingness to exercise its power.[64] Prestige is the everyday currency of international relations that decides all diplomatic conflicts short of war. For Gilpin especially, the hierarchy of prestige is a 'sticky' social construct that reflects the actual power distribution among the great powers *only* directly after a hegemonic war, when the system is said to be in equilibrium.[65]

In most historical eras, however, prestige and status have not been derived from military strength alone. In the ancient Chinese multi-state system (BC 771–680), for instance, the position of a state in the hierarchy was determined by both its military power and the rank of its ruler: duke, marquis, earl, viscount, or baron.[66] In the Greek city-state system (BC 600–338), the preeminent status of Sparta and Athens was partly a result of their acknowledged leadership of the oligarchic and democratic forces. Similarly, the prestige of the Soviet Union and the United States during the cold war partially derived from their leadership of the two rival ideological camps.

Status concerns are often at the root of conflict. Under positional competition, knowledge of an improvement in B's welfare often causes person A's welfare to decline. In common parlance, this form of envy, which is especially prevalent in affluent societies, is described by the phrase, 'keeping up with the Joneses'. Economists refer to this 'Jones effect' as the 'relative income hypothesis':

Formally this hypothesis states that what matters to a person in a high consumption society is not only his absolute real income, or his command over market goods, but his

---

[62] Morgenthau dealt with this issue in terms of power. See Hans J. Morgenthau, *Politics Among Nations: The Struggle for Power and Peace*, 4th edn (New York: Alfred A. Knopf, 1967), pp. 174–83.

[63] Evan Luard, *Types of International Society* (New York: The Free Press, 1976), p. 207.

[64] R. G. Hawtrey, *Economic Aspects of Sovereignty* (London: Longmans, Green and Co., 1952), p. 65; Robert Gilpin, *War and Change in World Politics* (Cambridge: Cambridge University Press, 1981), p. 31.

[65] Inevitably, however, the system falls into disequilibrium as changes in the actual distribution of capabilities, driven by the law of uneven growth, are not reflected by the hierarchy of prestige, upon which rests the international superstructure of economic, social, territorial, and political relationships. This built-in conflict between prestige and power, which has always been decided by hegemonic war, drives international change. Gilpin, *War and Change*, Ch. 5.

[66] Richard Louis Walker, *The Multi-State System of Ancient China* (Hamden, Conn.: The Shoestring Press, 1953), 26–7. For the importance of prestige to the Ch'un-ch'iu states, see Walker, *The Multi-State System of Ancient China*, pp. 47–8.

position in the income structure of society. In an extreme case, the citizen would choose, for example a 10 per cent increase in his real income provided that the average real income of society remained unchanged rather than a 50 per cent increase in his real income accompanied by a 50 per cent increase in the real income of every one else in society . . . [I]n its more general form—the view that in the affluent society a person's *relative* income also affects his welfare—it is hardly to be controverted. After all, the satisfaction we derive from many objects depends, in varying degrees, both on the extent of their scarcity and on the prestige associated with our ownership of them . . . [T]his Jones Effect . . . can only grow with the general rise in living standards . . .[67]

Thus, in 1985, a clear majority—60 per cent—of Americans, most of whom had been free traders during the 1950s and 1960s, when the United States was at the apex of its economic power, supported the idea of limiting imports even if it meant less choice for Americans.[68] Five years later, in July 1990, a *Wall Street Journal*/NBC News poll 'found that an overwhelming majority (86%) of Americans would prefer a policy of slower growth in both Japan and the United States, over one in which both grew faster, if the latter meant allowing Japan to take the lead economically'[69] To the horror of mainstream economists, it appears that ordinary citizens tend to agree with the words of the English mercantilist, Roger Coke (1675): '[I]f our Treasure were more than our Neighbouring Nations, I did not care whether we had one-fifth part of the Treasure we now have.'[70] The Jones effect also partly explains the proliferation of indigenous arms industries in the Third World and the bias in favour of modern weaponry: 'Advanced weapons—and the capacity to produce them—are coveted not only for their destructive efficiency, but also for their "*symbolic throw weight*".'[71]

Under conditions of anarchy, positional competition *à la* Jones effect is largely driven by the fear of being dominated or even destroyed by others.[72] Here, I am not referring to Hobbes's diffidence argument for war. Rather, I am suggesting that individuals, groups, states, and so forth under anarchy seek the greatest amount of autonomy as is possible; for this reason, *inter alia*, they wish to control others rather than being controlled by them. Precisely because unequal gains can make even friends more domineering or potentially more

[67] E. J. Mishan, *What Political Economy Is All About* (Cambridge: Cambridge University Press, 1982), p. 149.

[68] Findings of 1985 CBS/New York Times poll, as reported in David B. Yoffie, 'Protecting World Markets', in Thomas K. McCraw (ed.), *America Versus Japan* (Boston: Harvard Business School Press, 1986), p. 61.

[69] Michael Mastanduno, 'Do Relative Gains Matter? America's Response to the Japanese Industrial Policy', *International Security*, 16/1 (1991), pp. 73–4.

[70] Quoted in Eli F. Heckscher, *Mercantilism* (London: G. Allen and Unwin, 1935), vol. 2, p. 23.

[71] David Kinsella, 'The Globalization of Arms Production and the Changing Third World Security Context', paper presented at the annual meeting of the International Studies Association, Chicago, 21-5 February 1995, p. 5. The phrase 'symbolic throw weight' appears in Mark C. Suchman and Dana Eyre, 'Military Procurement as Rational Myth: Notes on the Social Construction of Weapons Proliferation', *Sociological Forum*, 7 (1992), pp. 37–161 at 154.

[72] For the security/survival aspect of this motivation, see Joseph M. Grieco, 'Understanding the Problem of International Cooperation: The Limits of Neoliberal Institutionalism and the Future of Realist Theory', in David A. Baldwin (ed.), *Neorealism and Neoliberalism: The Contemporary Debate* (New York: Columbia University Press, 1993), p. 303.

powerful rivals, realists claim that international cooperation is difficult to achieve and even harder to maintain. Fear of domination is also at the root of ethnic group conflict in severely divided societies. Ethnic groups engaged in these particularly bitter, zero-sum struggles want, above all, to make relative gains at the expense of their rivals and not just to improve their lot in absolute terms. On this crucial point, Donald Horowitz writes:

What is sought [by ethnic groups] is not necessarily some absolute value but a value determined by the extent to which it reduces another group's share. Demands are often cast in relative terms, and conflict-reducing proposals that involve expanding the pool of goods available to all groups typically have little appeal. Not 'how many?' but 'what fraction?'—that is the key question. . . . Just as relative group worth is at issue, so is relative power . . . Ethnic conflict is, at bottom, a matter of comparison.[73]

Precisely because ethnic conflict is positional competition, it often intensifies, rather than subsides, as the economic pie expands.

Sometimes the question is not simply 'who gains more?' but rather 'who will dominate whom?' Conflicts of this type are examples of positional conflict *par excellence*: 'Either these conflicts end definitely and abruptly as a result of military action, or they continue in crisis as long as the goal of destruction remains part of the policy of one of the parties.'[74] Given the 'all or nothing' nature of these struggles, economic growth, rather than solving the problem, fuels the fighting by replenishing the combatants' war chests.

Another way that economic growth exacerbates conflict is by shifting aspiration levels from comparisons of current performance with past experience to comparisons with groups that have greater social, economic, and occupational status. Social psychologists use the concept of relative deprivation to explain this phenomenon.

People who once acquiesced in deprived economic conditions because they could visualize no practical alternative now begin to reassess their prospects and possibilities . . . They now compare their present conditions and opportunities with those of other groups who are materially better off than they and ask by what right the others should be so privileged. Perversely, then, as their objective conditions improve, they become more dissatisfied because their aspirations outdistance their achievements.[75]

For this reason, social mobilization, while often seen as a benefit of modernization, tends to foster ethnic strife, particularly when the benefits of modernity such as economic and educational opportunities are unevenly distributed among ethnic groups:[76]

[73] Donald L. Horowitz, *Ethnic Groups in Conflict* (Berkeley, Calif.: University of California Press, 1985), pp. 196–7.

[74] Kenneth N. Waltz, 'Conflict in World Politics', in Steven L. Spiegel and Kenneth N. Waltz, eds., *Conflict in World Politics* (Cambridge, MA: Winthrop, 1971), p. 464.

[75] Milton J. Esman, *Ethnic Politics* (Ithaca and London: Cornell University Press, 1994), p. 236. For relative deprivation theory and ethnic conflict, also see Ted Robert Gurr, *Why Men Rebel* (Princeton: Princeton University Press, 1970), and *Minorities at Risk: A Global View of Ethnopolitical Conflicts* (Washington, DC: US Institute of Peace Press, 1993).

[76] See Robert H. Bates, 'Ethnic Competition and Modernization in Contemporary Africa', *Comparative Political Studies*, 6 (1974), pp. 462–4; Paul R. Brass, 'Ethnicity and Nationality Formation', *Ethnicity*, 3/3 (1976), pp. 225–41.

People's aspirations and expectations change as they are mobilized into the modernizing economy and polity. They come to want, and to demand, more—more goods, more recognition, more power. Significantly, too, the orientation of the mobilized to a common set of rewards and paths to rewards means, in effect, that many people come to desire precisely the same things. Men enter into conflict not because they are different but because they are essentially the same. It is by making men 'more alike,' in the sense of possessing the same wants, that modernization tends to promote conflict.[77]

Likewise, rising states in the international system have historically expressed grievances based on feelings of relative deprivation.[78] Today's China provides a clear example of rapid economic growth producing dissatisfaction and belligerence over its perceived status inconsistency. Lucian Pye observes:

The economic successes of Deng's reforms should have warmed up relations [with the US], making the Chinese more self-confident and at ease with the outside world, less touchy about slights to their sovereignty or perceived meddling in their internal affairs. However, this success has only generated greater tensions and frustrations. The Chinese take seriously the forecast that they will soon have the world's largest economy. They therefore feel that they deserve recognition and respect as a superpower-in-waiting. It is not enough that they are already a permanent member of the United Nations Security Council and one of the five nuclear powers. Somehow all of their accomplishments of the last two decades have not produced as dramatic a change in their international status as they had expected or believe is their due.[79]

Finally, economic growth causes physical and social scarcity through crowding out and congestion. This is the basic logic behind the theory of lateral pressure articulated by Nazli Choucri and Robert North. Their analysis of great-power behaviour between 1870 and 1914 revealed that 'expansionist activities are most likely to be associated with relatively high-capability countries, and to be closely linked with growth in population and advances in technology; and that growth tends to be associated with intense competition among countries for resources and markets, military power, political influence, and prestige'.[80]

In summary, economic growth increases both the demand for and the scarcity of positional goods. Because economic expansion causes aspiration levels to rise and converge, it is impossible for most people, groups, states, and so forth to achieve their goals of greater prestige and status. As a result, they become more dissatisfied with their condition even though their absolute welfare has improved. Thus, the economist E. J. Mishan pessimistically concludes,

---

[77] Robert Melson and Howard Wolpe, 'Modernization and the Politics of Communalism: A Theoretical Perspective', *American Political Science Review*, 64/4 (1970), p. 1114.

[78] Consistent with this argument, Samuel Huntington observes: 'The external expansion of the UK and France, Germany and Japan, the Soviet Union and the United States coincided with phases of intense industrialization and economic development.' Samuel Huntington, 'America's Changing Strategic Interests', *Survival*, 33/1 (1991), p. 12.

[79] Lucian W. Pye, 'China's Quest for Respect', *New York Times* (9 February 1996), A11.

[80] Nazli Choucri and Robert C. North, *Nations In Conflict: National Growth and International Violence* (San Francisco: W. H. Freeman, 1975), p. 28. Also see Nazli Choucri, Robert C. North, and Susumu Yamakage, *The Challenge of Japan Before WWII and After: A Study of National Growth and Expansion* (London: Routledge, 1992).

'the more truth there is in this relative income hypothesis—and one can hardly deny the increasing emphasis on status and income-position in the affluent society—the more futile as a means of increasing social welfare is the official policy of economic growth'.[81]

While there is strong evidence to support democratic peace theory, history has so far provided only a very limited variety and number of mature democratic states. As the qualities of democratic states diversify and their numbers increase significantly, the democratic peace proposition is far less likely to hold in the future. The real acid test for democratic peace theory has yet to come.

One may believe, as I do, that shared democratic institutions and norms do indeed play a pacifying role in disputes among jointly democratic dyads, and still predict that democratic states will go to war with each other in the twenty-first century. The spread of democracy will probably decrease the number and intensity of future interstate wars, but it will not entirely eliminate wars among democracies. This is particularly true for new democracies, which are highly susceptible to wars arising out of internal problems, such as hyper-nationalism, diversionary tactics, death-watch wars, reckless foreign policy strategies caused by competing elites, and domestic disputes over distributional issues. Moreover, as long as international anarchy persists, states will compete for—and sometimes go to war to secure—scarce resources. In this regard, economic growth, far from being a panacea, may exacerbate the condition of scarcity and, in so doing, intensify interstate positional competition. For all these reasons, the current widespread belief that the global spread of democracy offers states a safe exit from the perils of anarchy will likely prove to be mere wishful thinking.

Why Do We Want World Peace and Stability?

Here I should perhaps conclude with two points. First, even if it were clearly shown that the spread of democracy will not produce a more peaceful world—that democracies are in fact more war-prone than non-democratic regimes—the US should still promote democracy abroad simply because it is an intrinsic American value that people be able to decide who governs and how. Second, peace and stability are not necessarily intrinsic values or in the US national interest: it depends on how we value the status quo. For realists as well as Marxists, war is the principal mechanism of international change. To say that we want a world of perpetual peace is to suggest that things should for ever remain essentially as they are. Such a world is not only unattainable—for change is inevitable—but undesirable. Recognizing that there is no general harmony of interests and that morality is the product of power, realists do not confuse the established order with moral good. Instead, satisfied states seek to

---

[81] E. J. Mishan, *Growth: The Price We Pay* (London: Staples Press, 1969), p. 101.

maintain the status-quo order, and dissatisfied states naturally and under-standably try to revise or overthrow it. As Carr put it:

> The statement that it is in the interest of the world as a whole either that the *status quo* should be maintained, or that it should be changed, would be contrary to the facts . . . The utopian assumption that there is a world interest in peace which is identifiable with the interest of each individual nation helped politicians and political writers everywhere to evade the unpalatable fact of a fundamental divergence of interest between nations desirous of maintaining the *status quo* and nations desirous of changing it . . . The fact of divergent interests was [in the 15 years after World War I] disguised and falsified by the platitude of a general desire to avoid conflict.[82]

One hopes that, if forced to choose between peace, on the one hand, and jus-tice and liberty, on the other, Americans will choose the latter as they have consistently done in the past.[83] This is not to suggest that Americans should fight others' wars for them or even offer any material support whatever; that depends on whether a US vital interest is at stake. Rather, it is to say that America, at the very least, should proffer its moral support to the 'just' (in its eyes) side and, more important, that it cannot and should not expect dissatis-fied groups and nations to view war as an illegitimate tool for righting per-ceived injustices.

With respect to the value of peace and stability, it is worth noting that, throughout its history, the United States has prospered mightily from foreign wars. Indeed, America's independence, continental territorial size, and unmatched prosperity have been gained largely as a by-product of others' con-flicts and misfortunes. Now that the US is the undisputed 'top dog' in the world, it naturally champions world peace and stability. Yet, while this desire for peace and stability may be seen—wrongly, in my view—as hypocritical and transparently self-serving, it is hardly surprising. For just as peace, stability, and free trade were the right policies for Great Britain when it was the indus-trially dominant nation in the nineteenth century, these same policies serve America's national interest today. This should not blind us, however, to the fact that peace is tenable only if you leave out the interest of the weak and dis-satisfied, 'who must be driven to the wall, or called in the next world to redress the balance of the present'.[84]

In the end, I suspect that Americans are far more interested in maintaining US global hegemony—which the Clinton administration seemed to believe could be achieved solely by further opening foreign markets to American goods and culture—than they are in the promotion of democracy *per se*.[85] Whether the Congo or Indonesia or Sudan has a democratically elected gov-

---

[82] Carr, *The Twenty Years' Crisis*, p. 53.

[83] On this issue of peace and justice, see Richard K. Betts, 'The Delusion of Impartial Intervention', *Foreign Affairs*, 73/6 (1994), pp. 31–2.

[84] Carr, *The Twenty Years' Crisis*, p. 50.

[85] As Clinton told a gathering of one hundred executives of small and large businesses that are heavily dependent on export markets, new trade deals are 'absolutely critical for our world leader-ship'. David E. Sanger, 'Clinton Seeks Power for Trade Deals Congress Can't Amend', *New York Times* (11 September 1997), A9.

ernment is not a US vital interest. The American public intuitively recognizes the limits of US power and influence in the world; they have little trouble grasping the difference between feasible goals that are worth the costs entailed and counterproductive American meddling in the internal affairs of distant sovereign nations. Thankfully, given America's huge relative power advantage over its nearest competitors and its abundance of surplus security, US leaders enjoy the luxury of foreign-policy experimentation. While I see no evidence either of public support for democracy promotion or that the US can have anything but a marginal impact on this essentially internal process, a continuation of US cheap talk and action about democracy promotion will probably not harm, and may marginally advance, US interests abroad. The financial crisis in east and south-east Asia suggests, however, that simply grafting American ideas on to non-Western civilizations can be a recipe for disaster.

3

US Democracy Promotion: Critical Questions

STEVE SMITH

THIS chapter focuses on a theoretical critique of the assumptions underlying US democracy promotion polices. This is not an easy task, because although I have serious worries about such policies, to criticise them risks easy characterization as being either anti-US or anti-democracy—or both!—and I think I am neither. Having said that, it is probably necessary, in view of the argument that follows, to make explicit at the outset the point that I, too, want to see democracy extended, and certainly prefer it to autocratic regimes. I am not at all a moral relativist on that point; but, in typical social science fashion, I want to insist that the merit of the moral claims about democracy as opposed to other forms of government depend ultimately on exactly what is meant by the term 'democracy'. My underlying worry is that the entire debate about democracy promotion is set up in such a way as to make criticism particularly difficult. Like apple pie, how can anyone be against the expansion of democratic rights to parts of the globe that are currently ruled by despots? My problem is that I do indeed want to criticize aspects of that policy, but not on the grounds of opposing democracy or indeed of opposing the US playing a major role in shaping international society. Rather, I want to voice a set of reservations based upon the form of democracy that is being promoted, and specifically on the relationship between this geopolitical policy and America's geoeconomic policy. Put simply, I think that the latter drives the former, to such an extent that it results in the form of democracy promoted being particularly narrow and thereby suitable for supporting US economic interests.

My reservations apply both to America's historical record and to the role of democracy enlargement as the central theme in the foreign policy of both the first and the second Clinton administrations. With regard to the former, I believe that America's record in promoting democracy is less positive than

I would like to thank my colleagues Steve Hobden and Lucy Taylor for their comments and discussions about this paper. Their expertise in the politics of Central and Latin America helped me considerably. I would also like to thank the participants in the SSRC-sponsored conference, held in Washington in January 1998, and to those who commented on the paper when it was presented at the 1999 International Studies Association conference in Washington. Finally, I would like to thank Michael Cox and John Ikenberry for their comments on the first draft and for their engagement with the ideas expressed in this paper.

Tony Smith claims it to be in his balanced assessment of US policy in the twentieth century.[1] As for the latter, although I agree with many of the qualifications voiced by Douglas Brinkley,[2] I disagree with his claim that the policy uses economics to promote democracy;[3] I see the Clinton administration's policy as more about promoting US economic interests than promoting democracy *per se*. Moreover, I share the scepticism of both Brinkley and Thomas Carothers[4] as to the continuing expansion of democratic enlargement. The 1990s have seen considerable reversals to democratic enlargement, as Carothers[5] shows only too clearly.

So as to set out my stall for all to see, my perspective is Foucauldian, in that I am primarily concerned with the relationship between power and knowledge, and in unearthing the regimes of truth that allow truth claims to be made about democratic enlargement. At base, claims about the desirability of democracy are just that: claims. They are not truths or moral givens, but truth claims or moral preferences, and therefore what matters in assessing them are the rules that determine how such claims and preferences can be evaluated. My central claim is that the debate about the US policy of democracy promotion rests upon a prior political move, masked as an epistemological or methodological one: namely, that of the separation of economics from politics. In other words, I see the debate over democracy promotion as occupying a space demarcated by a prior division between the economic and the political, a space which allows for relationships between the two—such as in how might economic measures support democratic transitions—but which does not allow for the fact that the very separation between the two permits a focus on one in isolation from the other. Thus, democracy equals good, non-democracy equals bad, regardless of the economic context. But what if the political realm is so constrained by the economic as to make democracy, at best, a meaningless ceremonial, and, at worst, a facade? What then is the moral standing of a prior commitment to democracy in such circumstances? I will return to this claim in the concluding section of this chapter, but for now will simply note that a focus on political democracy to the exclusion of a concern with economic or social democracy is a political choice, and a very powerful means of structuring the debate. In this sense, it is the division into politics and economics as separate spheres that both sets up the entire debate and predetermines the answers in favour of enlarging democracy.

I have five related reservations about the US policy of democratic enlargement. I will start with the most specific and move towards the more general.

[1] T. Smith, *America's Mission: The United States and the Worldwide Struggle for Democracy in the Twentieth Century* (Princeton: Princeton University Press, 1994).

[2] D. Brinkley, 'Democratic Enlargement: The Clinton Doctrine', *Foreign Policy*, 106 (1997), pp. 111–27.

[3] Brinkley, 'Democratic Enlargement', p. 125; Smith, *America's Mission*, p. 343.

[4] T. Carothers, 'Democracy and Human Rights: Policy Allies or Rivals?', *The Washington Quarterly*, 17/3 (1994), pp. 109–20; 'Democracy Promotion Under Clinton', *The Washington Quarterly*, 18/4 (1995), pp. 13–25; 'Democracy Without Illusions', *Foreign Affairs*, 76/1 (1997), pp. 85–99; 'Democracy', *Foreign Policy*, 107 (1997), pp. 11–19.

[5] Carothers, 'Democracy Without Illusions'.

The Historical Record

My main worry here is that whereas the debate about democracy promotion seems to assume that the US has had a clear long-standing commitment to such a policy, I see the record as far more complex. Indeed, it can be argued that for many parts of the world the US has not historically stood for the promotion of democracy but instead for resistance to it. The two obvious areas of the world are Latin and Central America, and the Middle East. Of course, there are many examples in other parts of the world—for example, US policy towards Nigeria since 1993—but these two regions of the world seem to support the view that the US has been involved in undermining democratic regimes rather than fostering them. And, crucially, the driver for such a policy in both regions has been US economic interests. It is for these reasons that the US undermined democracy in Chile, Guatemala, and Nicaragua, and it is also why the US continues to support autocratic, and decidedly undemocratic, regimes in the Middle East. The US may well have been justified in its policies towards Saddam Hussein at the time of the Gulf War, but there was a certain paradox about US forces physically protecting and supporting some of the richest and most undemocratic regimes in the world.

The gap between the commitment to the promotion of democracy and the reality of US foreign policy is most evident in the case of Latin and Central America, for whom there must be disbelief at the notion that the US has a long-standing commitment to the promotion of democracy. The entire history of US relations with Latin and Central American countries fails to support the notion that the US has sought to promote democracy. Indeed, the opposite case is strongly supported. There are many examples, but the book by William Robinson[6] has powerfully shown just how actively involved the US was in undermining the Allende regime in Chile and the Sandinista regime in Nicaragua, despite the wishes of the indigenous populations. Interestingly, Robinson points out that US policies towards these countries changed towards the promotion of democracy only when it came to be seen in Washington as a more effective way of furthering US interests. It seems difficult to conclude anything other than that democracy promotion in Latin and Central America has been one tool amongst many in promoting US interests rather than an end in itself in that region.

In my judgement, the US historically supported 'democracy' when this was a useful way of undermining pro-Soviet regimes, but was also equally happy to undermine indigenous democratic regimes when they tilted towards Moscow. Of course, commentators such as Tony Smith know this only too well, and indeed point to it, but none the less there seems to be an underlying assumption that the US has had a mission to promote democracy, as if this was merely an automatic external extension of domestic policy. To my mind, the

---

[6] W. Robinson, *Promoting Polyarchy: Globalization, US Intervention, and Hegemony* (Cambridge: Cambridge University Press, 1996).

record is far more mixed, with the US using democracy promotion as one aspect of its foreign policy, an aspect that was not so much the centrepiece of policy as a tool for furthering US interests. Thus I reject the almost teleological view of the historical record that Tony Smith portrays it as being. Indeed, it could be argued that the evidence in Smith's survey of US democracy promotion supports the opposite interpretation to the one he puts forward. For Smith, the US promotion of democracy has been a reflection of US domestic political culture and debate. Now, whilst he is surely right to argue that realism is inadequate to explain international relations, since it relies on a rational actor analogy borrowed from economics which stresses the international context as central, his account may be said to overestimate the attractions of liberal democracy for many parts of the world, especially when it is accompanied by the dominance of neoliberal economic regimes. As he notes, the expansion of democracy today to some parts of the world is in the US national interest, but unless we are convinced that liberal democracy is indeed applicable to other social and cultural settings then maybe such an expansion may not be in the interests of other populations.

In other words, democracy promotion has not been a goal, let alone *the* goal, of US foreign policy in the twentieth century. At times the US has supported democracy, but at other times it has been more suitable for the US to support local despots because they happened to be rather good at opposing the same 'enemy' as did the US. In the immortal words of Henry Kissinger, commenting on the election of Allende in Chile in June 1970, 'I don't see why we need to stand by and watch a country go communist because of the irresponsibility of its own people'.[7] The US has played a very decisive role in undermining some democratic regimes, and has done so because the external alignment of the states concerned have been far more important than any notion of democracy enhancement being a primary goal of foreign policy. Thus, although there have been clear instances of the US furthering democracy in other countries, this has tended to be in support of more important policy goals.

As far as the Clinton administration's policy is concerned, Thomas Carothers has documented a series of weaknesses that make it difficult to support the administration's contention that the policy was indeed at the centre of US foreign policy, let alone its unifying theme.[8] The main problems he cites are that the pro-democracy rhetoric was overused by the administration; that the emphasis on democracy promotion had the unintended effect of calling attention to America's inconsistencies in this regard; that the policy was based on the mistaken notion that the US could easily affect what happened in other countries, with the result that the US often took credit for democratic transitions that were under way for entirely indigenous reasons; and that the US has tended to place too much hope on an individual leader as equalling democracy's hopes, and on putting in place formal institutions rather than dealing

---

[7] Quoted in Robinson, *Promoting Polyarchy*, p. 146.
[8] Carothers, 'Democracy Promotion Under Clinton', pp. 22–5; 'Democracy Without Illusions', pp. 97–8.

with the much thornier problem of the values necessary to underpin demo-cracy.[9]

In this light, the Clinton administration's focus on democratic enlarge-ment[10] now appears to have been more of an attempt to come up with a 'big idea' or overarching theme for US foreign policy after the cold war than any commitment to democracy enlargement as the centrepiece of actual policy. As the overarching theme for foreign policy it had the advantage of being almost impossible to oppose, since any such opposition could be portrayed as an opposition to democracy itself; and in the post-cold war world such a position had clear connotations of a sympathy to anti-democratic forces such as Islam or communism. My point is simply that I see the Clinton administration's pol-icy on democracy promotion as just as subordinated to US economic interests as were all the earlier overarching themes of US foreign policy. It is also a pol-icy that has been applied to varying extents depending on wider US interests. Note that I am not critical of the subordination of democracy promotion to other foreign policy goals, only that the policy is presented as *the* theme, as *the* dominant goal of US foreign policy, to such an extent that it is presented as the extension of US domestic political values on to the international stage. Indeed, as Michael Cox has argued, one of the main features of the Clinton administration was that it saw little distinction between US foreign and domestic policies: the domestic economy required certain international struc-tures and thus geoeconomics dominated geopolitics. As he writes,

If America's primary purpose was to win the economic race, then how could this be rec-onciled with its historic goal of promoting global democracy? . . . there was bound to be a very real conflict of interest: between promoting American economic objectives on the one hand and supporting the cause of human rights on the other. And one hardly needed a crystal ball to know which one the United States was most likely to sacrifice in an age of geo-economics.[11]

Finally, I am not convinced that it is at all easy for the US to promote demo-cracy in other countries. I think that democracy has to be firmly rooted in the local and very particular conditions of specific states, and that the success of fledgling democracies depends far more on local factors than on anything that the US can or cannot do. In sum, I think that the Clinton administration's commitment to democracy enlargement was more of a public relations ploy than an achievable, and maybe even desirable, goal for US foreign policy.

The Definition of Democracy

One of the main limitations of US democracy promotion is that the policy has been accepted as universally applicable when in fact it is a culturally and

---

[9] Carothers, 'Democracy Promotion Under Clinton', pp. 22–3.

[10] Brinkley, 'Democratic Enlargement'.

[11] M. Cox, *US Foreign Policy after the Cold War: Superpower Without a Mission?* (London: Royal Institute of International Affairs, 1995), p. 37.

historically specific version of what democracy means. As Bikhu Parekh has noted, Western treatments of democracy fail to recognise the 'cultural particularity' of what is really an explicitly liberal understanding of democracy.[12] The literature on US democracy promotion seems to accept a very straightforward definition of what democracy is.[13] Not surprisingly, this version looks a lot like the political system of the US. Indeed, despite all the discussions over how best to present the 'Clinton doctrine' of democratic enlargement, there seems to have been little debate over exactly what counts as a democracy other than to assume that it resembles the US. A similar assumption marked the March 1990 announcement by then Secretary of State, James Baker, that the post-cold war mission of the US was the 'promotion and consolidation of democracy', and that there was little need to spell out its main features, let alone that there could be any real debate over exactly what these main features might be. Tony Smith offers the clearest version of what democracy means: 'free elections contested by freely organized parties under universal suffrage for control of the effective centres of governmental power'.[14]

As Thomas Carothers has succinctly noted:

U.S. officials will make much of the fact that a new constitution has been promulgated in a transitional country rather than examine how the constitution was arrived at or how much it embodies an actual sociopolitical consensus. They will extol an election with little attention to the more complex realities of actual political participation. They will herald a new parliament while knowing little of the actual relations between the parliament and the citizenry. *Supporting democracy too often resembles the application of a preprinted checklist in which the institutional forms of U.S.-style democracy are financed and praised while the more complex and more important realities of political life are ignored.*[15]

This acceptance that there is only one thing called democracy, and that it is exemplified by the US political system, is well illustrated in Francis Fukuyama's infamous 'End of History' thesis.[16] My point is not to add to the criticisms of his argument, only to point out that for Fukuyama liberal democracy appeared to be one thing: 'Democracy . . . is the right held universally by all citizens to have a share of political power, that is, the right of all citizens to vote and participate in politics . . . .. A country is democratic if it grants its people the right to choose their own government through periodic, secret-ballot, multi-party elections, on the basis of universal and equal adult suffrage.'[17] Fukuyama's central claim is that 'a remarkable consensus has developed in the world concerning the legitimacy and viability of liberal democracy'.[18] Fukuyama's work shows very clearly

---

[12] B. Parekh, 'The Cultural Particularity of Liberal Democracy', in David Held (ed.), *Prospects for Democracy: North, South, East, West* (Cambridge: Polity Press, 1993), pp. 156–75.

[13] Smith, *America's Mission*, pp. 13–19; Carothers, 'Democracy', pp. 11–12.

[14] Smith, *America's Mission*, p. 13.

[15] Carothers, 'Democracy Promotion Under Clinton', p. 23; emphasis added.

[16] F. Fukuyama, 'The End of History', *The National Interest*, 16 (1989), pp. 3–18; *The End of History and the Last Man* (New York: Free Press, 1992).

[17] Fukuyama, *The End of History and the Last Man*, p. 43.

[18] Fukuyama, 'The End of History', p. 22.

just how little analysed is the term 'democracy', usually prefaced by the term 'liberal'. There is no need to run through the list of reservations about his definition of 'liberal democracy' as equalling 'democracy'; it will suffice to note that he sees no contradiction between the terms 'liberal' and 'democracy' despite the fact that the clash between the rights of the liberal individual and the duty of democratic governments to limit the freedom of individuals has been the central dispute in democratic theory throughout its history.[19]

The problem, then, is that the debate about democracy enlargement accepts a very specific definition of what democracy is. There are, of course, many different definitions of democracy; David Held's excellent survey of theories of democracy outlines eight distinct models, only one of which is the liberal democratic model adopted by the participants in the US democracy promotion debate.[20] Crucially, Held's work shows just how significant are the schisms between the various forms of liberal democracy, with the result that the US version is only one of a number of powerful contending accounts of how precisely to balance the rights of the individual with the responsibility of government. In view of the argument that I will be advancing below, it is important to note that the US version of liberal democracy comes under very considerable attack from many of the competing versions of democracy. Specifically, it comes under attack from those who want much more of a participatory democracy, and those who stress the limitations of choice available in the kind of Schumpeterian elite democracy found in the US.

Three points follow from this. First, the US literature tends to promote the US version of democracy without any discussion of the criticisms of that version from other liberal democratic theories. Critics would note the main shortcomings of US-style democracy as being: the low turnout at elections—only around 50 per cent for the 1996 presidential election; the low level of participation in political activity by much of the population, especially the economic and racial underclasses; the very limited choices available to citizens within the elite-pluralist system of the US; and the associated socio-economic inequalities, crime levels and societal divisions. And, importantly, it is indeed questionable to accept the view that the US has been a genuine democracy from its founding. Of course, other countries have similar weaknesses, with the UK in particular sharing many of these features, but the point is that US-style democracy is a specific form of democracy, with obvious strengths as well as weaknesses. Its reliance on the formal right to vote masks the narrowness of the political debate that it permits. Yet this version is presented as what democracy really means. It is presented as a truth, not as a normative choice. In short, when the US promotes its form of democracy it is engaged in a political choice, not the furtherance of some foundational true path for humanity; US-style democracy is simply seen as being 'better' than the alternatives. It is for precisely this reason that it matters enormously just how democracy is defined, and why it is very significant that there is no discussion about the

---

[19] D. Held, *Models of Democracy*, 2nd edn (Cambridge: Polity Press, 1996), pp. 278–83.
[20] Held, *Models of Democracy*.

meaning of democracy within the enlargement debate. Viewed in this way, the advocating of democracy gets us immediately into the quagmire of cultural imperialism.

Second, the focus on formal electoral rights masks the necessarily prior debate over what are to be the main values to be promoted by democracy. A fixation with free elections can result in an absence of debate about whether democracy should promote human and political rights; each of these is much more complicated than are questions of electoral procedures, and each raises fundamental issues about the purpose of politics. For example, do all citizens have an equal ability to express views and demands, are they equal before the law, are all individuals accorded recognition as citizens, are rules, norms and rights universal, as well as whether it should further equality? The first of these questions seems particularly problematic for US-style democracy. As Thomas Carothers has pointed out, although many involved in US democracy promotion treat formal democracy and the wider notion of human rights as two sides of the same coin, it can be argued that there are in reality two separate issues, democracy promotion and human rights.[21] He notes five points of difference (summarized crudely: human rights are international legal norms, whereas democracy is a political ideology, and the latter smacks of neo-imperialism; human rights can be seen as more urgent than promoting formal democracy; democracy promotion places far too much stress on formal elections; democracy promotion can often lead to strengthening governing institutions regardless of the fact that these bodies are sometimes involved in human rights abuses; and the funding by the US of indigenous political movements can undermine democracy by linking it to the US government).[22] Although Carothers offers proposals for finding a middle ground between these viewpoints, in my judgement there remains considerable tension between the two perspectives, and the US has tended to ignore the fact that there are very different issues involved, preferring instead to maintain that they are in fact merely aspects of the same policy.

Third, the literature on US democracy promotion seems remarkably short of any discussion of democratic theory outside the US mainstream literature. To be frank, it often reads as if the definition of democracy is uncontested, and that two thousand years of political theory is irrelevant. This may reflect the fact that my reading of the US literature has been partial, but all my efforts to find any analysis of alternative versions of even *liberal* democracy have been unsuccessful. Even in such sophisticated works as those by Tony Smith,[23] Bruce Russett,[24] Francis Fukuyama,[25] and Samuel Huntington,[26] democracy is defined in a very specific and seemingly uncontroversial way. Bruce Russett

---

[21] Carothers, 'Democracy and Human Rights', pp. 109–11.

[22] Carothers, 'Democracy and Human Rights', pp. 111–16.   [23] Smith, *America's Mission*.

[24] B. Russett, *Grasping the Democratic Peace: Principles for a Post-Cold War World* (Princeton: Princeton University Press, 1993).

[25] Fukuyama, *The End of History and the Last Man*.

[26] S. Huntington, *The Third Wave: Democratization in the Late Twentieth Century* (Norman: University of Oklahoma Press, 1991).

illustrates the point most clearly when he writes 'For modern states, democracy (or polyarchy, following Dahl[27]) is usually identified with a voting franchise for a substantial fraction of citizens, a government brought to power in contested elections, and an executive either popularly elected or responsible to an elected legislature, often also with requirements for civil liberties such as free speech'.[28] My point is not to dispute Russett's claim as to the features of democracy but to point out that he elides Dahl's polyarchy with democracy despite the fact that Dahl's version has been very widely attacked as an extremely restricted version of democracy and one only really applicable to the US itself.[29] The main features of the critique are that it presents the degree of empirical fit as the main way of judging rival accounts of democracy; the value consensus that lay at the heart of Dahl's model did not actually exist in the US; Dahl's model had a very restricted notion of power, as illustrated by the seminal works by Schattschneider,[30] Bachrach and Baratz,[31] and Lukes;[32] and pluralism does not ensure that governments will act as brokers between competing views, and instead they will ignore some voices, listen only to elites, do nothing about some issues, and remain immune to influence from anyone other than the powerful.[33]

Moreover, not only has there been a massive amount of criticism of Dahl's pluralism, but he has himself changed his view in a way that seems to me to undermine substantially the reliance on his earlier work in the US literature on democracy promotion. In 1985, Dahl wrote of the economic obstacles to democracy, for both the citizen and the government. For the citizen, political equality was undermined by economic inequality: 'Ownership and control contribute to the creation of great differences among citizens in wealth, income, status, skills, information, control over information and propaganda, access to political leaders . . . differences like these help in turn to generate significant inequalities among citizens in their capacities and opportunities for participating as political equals in governing the state.'[34] For governments, political choices are limited by the need to work within the capitalist model of private accumulation. As Held neatly puts it: 'A government's policies must follow a political agenda that is at least favourable to, i.e. biased towards, the development of the system of private enterprise and corporate power.'[35] This seems to me to be such an important change in Dahl's position that the eliding of polyarchy and democracy is particularly problematic. I would claim that

---

[27] R. Dahl, *Polyarchy: Participation and Opposition* (New Haven: Yale University Press, 1971).

[28] Russett, *Grasping the Democratic Peace*, p. 14

[29] See Held, *Models of Democracy*, for an excellent summary of the main criticisms.

[30] E. Schattschneider, *The Semi-Sovereign People: A Realist View of Democracy in America* (New York: Holt, Rinehart and Winston, 1960).

[31] P. Bachrach and M. Baratz, 'The Two Faces of Power', *American Political Science Review*, 56 (1962), pp. 947–52; 'Decisions and Nondecisions: An Analytical Framework', *American Political Science Review*, 57 (1963), pp. 641–51.

[32] S. Lukes, *Power: A Radical View* (London: Macmillan, 1974).

[33] J. Lively, *Democracy* (Oxford: Blackwell, 1975).

[34] R. Dahl, *A Preface to Economic Democracy* (Cambridge: Polity Press, 1985), p. 55.

[35] Held, *Models of Democracy*, p. 215.

this simple equating of democracy with polyarchy runs throughout the literature on US democracy promotion, with the result that the notion of democracy used is both a very specific and historically located version, and one that its main theorist no longer accepts in the form adopted by those who write about US democracy promotion.

In summary, when the US talks of promoting democracy it has a very clear view of what a democracy is. The problem is that democracy is a very contested concept, and even within liberal democratic theory the elite model favoured in the US has been subject to serious criticism *in terms of its weaknesses as a model of democracy*. The debate in the US shows scant awareness of this, and presents democracy as a self-evident and uncontentious concept. Crucially, whereas promoting US-style democracy is a political choice, with strengths and weaknesses, it has instead been presented in such a way as to imply that there is one version of democracy and that this is applicable across cultures and societies—hence the comments about countries not being ready for democracy quite yet. As such, democracy is but the latest version of the modernization thesis with all its attendant assumptions about progress and the essential similarity between societies. In this light it can indeed look like a form of US dominance, a problem exacerbated by its relationship to the neoliberal economic policies of the Clinton administration.

Low-Intensity Democracy

Not only is the version of democracy promoted by the US a very specific form, it is also a very limited form, which, following Barry Gills and Joel Rocamora,[36] can be characterized as low-intensity democracy.[37] This argument has also been a constant theme in the work of Noam Chomsky.[38] Gills and Rocamora's central argument, based on a series of case studies—Argentina, Guatemala, the Philippines and South Korea—is 'that the institutions of formal democracy that have recently re-emerged in many countries in the Third World have failed to broaden popular political participation in a very meaningful way . . . [the case-studies] found little evidence to support the widespread assumption that formal electoral democratization alone would bring a lasting progressive breakthrough in these societies or that it is capable of solving their fundamental social and especially economic problems'.[39]

Gills and Rocamora note three ideological biases of the mainstream US literature on democracy promotion. First, democracy *per se* is a goal worth pursuing. They believe that unless democracy is combined with social reform then democracy gets undermined in the medium term. Without social reform

---

[36] B. Gills and J. Rocamora, 'Low Intensity Democracy', *Third World Quarterly*, 13/3 (1992), pp. 501–23.

[37] See also W. Robinson, *Promoting Polyarchy: Globalization, US Intervention, and Hegemony* (Cambridge: Cambridge University Press, 1996).

[38] For example N. Chomsky, *Deterring Democracy* (New York: Hill and Wang, 1992).

[39] Gills and Rocamora, 'Low Intensity Democracy', p. 501.

'the term "democracy" is largely devoid of meaningful content. Indeed, it is in danger of becoming a term of political mystification or obfuscation, serving as a euphemism for sophisticated modern forms of neo-authoritarianism'.[40] Second, they note that democracy is usually equated with capitalism, and moreover 'the particular forms of democracy pushed by the West in the Third World are specifically tailored to serve the interests of global capital in these countries'. Finally, there is the assumption that external factors do not play a major causal role in the political and economic development of Third World countries.[41]

Reviewing the role of the US in the four countries, Gills and Rocamora argue that the US did not support democracy until it was clear that the existing authoritarian regimes were in crisis, and then promoted a specific form of democracy that was able to serve as a means of justifying continuing intervention by the US in the affairs of these countries, yet was also able to pre-empt more radical change. In their words, 'low intensity democracy was conceived as a half-way house between previous "unstable" representative democratic systems in the Third World and the moribund and counter-productive military dictatorships of the 1960s and 1970s which had often been established and maintained with US support'. As such, low-intensity democracy had two purposes: to preempt more radical reforms and to legitimize the status quo. Indeed, as they note, the new 'democratic' regime can in fact impose even harsher adjustment policies on populations than could preceding authoritarian regimes: 'The paradox of low intensity democracy is that a civilianized conservative regime can pursue painful and even repressive social and economic policies with more impunity and with less popular resistance than can an openly authoritarian regime'.[42] They also make the telling point that the promotion of democracy dates back to the Reagan administration, when it was combined with a policy of opposing democratic movements wherever they threatened US interests. The most obvious examples of such activity were to be found in Latin and Central America where, 'at best, the USA tolerated, and at worst directly promoted, the most grotesque abuses of human rights in recent history'. Crucially, Gills and Rocamora argue that the driving force for these policies was the protection and promotion of US economic interests, insisting that the main threat to US interests in Latin and Central America since World War II was not communism 'but rather any nationalistic regime responsive to popular demands for immediate improvement in standards of living and which therefore interfered with US efforts to encourage private investment and repatriation of profits'.[43]

Low-intensity democracy is a form of democracy whereby the focus is on formal electoral rights, with little consideration paid to the wider socioeconomic power structure, and with the military often remaining in the wings

[40] Gills and Rocamora, 'Low Intensity Democracy', p. 502.
[41] Gills and Rocamora, 'Low Intensity Democracy', pp. 502–3.
[42] Gills and Rocamora, 'Low Intensity Democracy', pp. 504–5.
[43] Gills and Rocamora, 'Low Intensity Democracy', p. 511.

should reform go too far. This results in splits within progressive social movements over the issue of whether to participate in the democratic system. Gills and Rocamora see an important transition taking place between two phases of 'democratisation'. The first phase sees reform promised, a decrease in the level of repression, and the transformation of popular movements into political parties. The second phase sees a retreat from the promises of reform, the imposition of a conservative economic policy protecting the interests of both domestic and external elites, a widening of economic inequalities and an increase in repression. The result is that 'Despite what may seem to be major changes, precious little real change occurs under a regime of low intensity democracy'.[44]

In contrast, Gills and Rocamora propose 'progressive democracy', which involves three features: first, the democratization of formal democratic institutions by social reform, without which formal democracy will simply reinforce existing power divisions so that power effectively remains with the economic elite; second, a significant reduction in the size of the military; third, the achievement of genuine independence, which means economic as well as political independence, since the global market is inherently undemocratic.[45]

This view of US democracy promotion is shared by Noam Chomsky, for whom there is a fundamental link between the domestic and international aspects of the policy. He sees US foreign policy as promoting a democracy of a specific form in order to maintain the economic status quo, and manipulating democracy within the US to limit its effectiveness.[46] His is a very bleak portrayal of how the US deters democracy both at home and abroad, and, like Gills and Rocamora, he stresses the linkage between the policies of the US on democracy enlargement, which he sees as entirely tactical, and its policies on the development of a neoliberal international economic order. Democracy then becomes less of a goal of foreign policy and more a tool of economic policy.

Globalization, the Nation-State and Democracy

My concern here is that the US is promoting a form of democracy that seems to be ill-suited to the developing international political and economic order. The effects of globalization are such that states are increasingly unable to control their societies, polities and economies. There are two main aspects to this problem.

First, globalization reduces the effective sovereignty of nation states because it places increasingly large parts of formerly 'domestic' policy under external control. The most obvious such areas involve economic policy. The inter-

---

[44] Gills and Rocamora, 'Low Intensity Democracy', p. 522.
[45] Gills and Rocamora, 'Low Intensity Democracy', pp. 520–1.
[46] Chomsky, *Deterring Democracy*.

national market therefore regulates domestic economic activity, and this is not amenable to democratic control within state structures; indeed, all of this raises the question of to what extent economic actors are subject to democratic control at all. The central problem is that the formal model of democracy advanced by the US cannot deal with the dominance of the economic realm by forces outside the territorial state. The second, and related, problem is that the emphasis on formal electoral democracy results in a very narrow civil society being created, and this restricts the political realm considerably. Low-intensity democracy creates a civil society that cannot undertake major economic and social reforms, with the result that the arena of politics within the state is a very narrow one.

Together these two factors create a crisis for democracy in a wider sense than that used in US democracy promotion programmes. This problem has been well addressed by Benjamin Barber[47] and Jean-Marie Guehenno.[48] In his portrayal of the emerging world order as one of 'Jihad versus McWorld', Barber points to the twin forces of globalization and tribalism as together undermining the state. As he puts it, 'they both make war on the sovereign nation-state and thus undermine the nation-state's democratic institutions. Each eschews civil society and belittles democratic citizenship, neither seeks alternative democratic institutions'.[49] The nation-state becomes caught between two sets of forces which together create a world in which the individual citizen becomes either merely a consumer or the product of ethnic identity. Government becomes less and less effective in providing public goods, civil society declines, and politics becomes reduced to either the market or the barrel of a gun. Critically, both forces undermine civil society to such an extent that the very nature of politics narrows considerably. Barber is clear that in such a world it is no easy task to promote democracy: 'A people corrupted by tribalism and numbed by McWorld is no more ready to receive a prefabricated democratic constitution than a people emerging from a long history of despotism and tyranny. Nor can democracy be someone's gift to the powerless. . . To prepare the ground for democracy today . . . means laying a foundation in civil society and civic culture.'[50] For Barber, this civil society 'occupies the middle ground between government and the private sector. It is not where we vote and it is not where we buy and sell'.[51] For new democratic states, it is the creation of this civil society that he sees as the main priority, not the establishment of formal electoral procedures. For all states he sees the expansion of civil society as necessary for healthy democracy; he also proposes a global civil society in order to be able to subject McWorld to democratic control.[52] Barber's central concern is that 'Unless we can offer an alternative to the struggle between Jihad and McWorld, the epoch on whose threshold we stand—

[47] B. Barber, *Jihad vs. McWorld* (New York: Ballantine Books, 1996).
[48] J.-M. Guehenno, *The End of the Nation-State* (Minneapolis: University of Minnesota Press, 1995).
[49] Barber, *Jihad vs. McWorld*, p. 6.   [50] Barber, *Jihad vs. McWorld*, p. 279.
[51] Barber, *Jihad vs. McWorld*, p. 281.
[52] For a discussion of the problems of global democratic control, see David Held, *Democracy and the Global Order: From the Modern State to Cosmopolitan Governance* (Cambridge: Polity Press, 1995).

postcommunist, postindustrial, postnational, yet sectarian, fearful and bigoted—is likely also to be terminally postdemocratic'.[53]

Guehenno's argument is even starker. Indeed, the title of his book in French summarizes his main claim neatly: whereas the US edition was titled *The End of the Nation-State*, the (original) French edition was given the title *La Fin de la Démocratie*. Like Barber, Guehenno argues that democracy is in trouble because the nation-state is in decline. Like Barber, he asks whether democracy can exist without the nation-state. The world he sees developing is one in which states are losing control over their territories as a result of forces such as the information revolution, globalization and the domination of the market. This leads to the entire Enlightenment project being in crisis because the political community necessary for its realisation is being eroded. Individuals no longer have the ability to act politically because the spatial and geographical demarcations that accompanied the domination of the nation-state have become obsolete: 'From the beginning, since the Greek city (polis), politics has been the art of governing a collectivity of people defined by their rootedness in a location, city or nation. If solidarity can no longer be locked into geography, if there is no longer a city, if there is no longer a nation, can there still be politics?'[54] In short, for Guehenno the central idea of the nation-state—that there was a political sphere dealing with the search for consensus and the general interest—has been undermined by the forces of globalization with the result that citizens are reduced to atomised individuals lacking political reason: 'nations—even the most powerful of them all, the United States—no longer have the capacity, in a global world, of protecting the peoples whose destiny they claim to embody from the uncertainties of the outside world that have irreversibly irrupted into what used to be called their domestic affairs'.[55] Above all, politics becomes reduced in its scope so that the political realm becomes nothing more than the outcome of private interests. In such a situation, where politics is reduced to the function of a market,

the political space is immediately threatened with extinction, for there is no market that can establish the 'value' of the national interest and circumscribe the scope of solidarity. If the national collectivity is no longer a given but a choice, individuals no longer effectively have the means to base this choice on the same rational criteria that guide their actions in the functional management of the national interests. No economic law can replace the territorial and historical basis of the nation.[56]

Barber's and Guehenno's analyses suggest that while the problem of ensuring the survival of democracy in a globalized world is difficult enough because of the erosion of civil society, the possibilities of enlarging the democratic community of nations is going to be even more difficult. This is especially so because the kind of democracy being promoted by US policies is weakest precisely in the area that Barber and Guehenno say is under attack, namely, civil

---

[53] Barber, *Jihad vs. McWorld*, p. 20.   [54] Guehenno, *The End of the Nation-State*, p. 17.
[55] Guehenno, *The End of the Nation-State*, p. 138.
[56] Guehenno, *The End of the Nation-State*, p. 23.

society. By promoting low-intensity democracy the US supports a form of democracy that is least able to manage the forces of globalization. And, because of this, the long-term future of these democracies must be called into question. The dominant economic forces behind globalization cannot be resisted by low-intensity democracies, whereas, as Hirst and Thompson have convincingly argued, economic relations can be made subject to governance at both national and international levels. But at the national level they note that this will require precisely the kind of institutions, laws, and rules that are found in states with a strong civil society, and yet which are absent from low-intensity democracies.[57]

The Relationship between Democracy Promotion and NeoLiberal Economics

There are two aspects of this relationship that concern me: first, the emerging global pattern, and second, the linkage between the two in US foreign policy. As to the former, and as implied by the preceding analysis, the problem is that neoliberalism is so dominant in the world economy that the political is being increasingly reduced to the economic. The most obvious example of this is the way that the market is presented as an autonomous force that governments cannot manage, a force that slowly but surely removes more and more of what was previously politics into the market. These forces also reconstruct the subject with the effect of reducing the realm of what appears both politics and politically possible. In this light, the form of democracy being promoted by the US fits exactly into this reduced political role for government and the state. As such, US democracy promotion seems designed to put in place the type of state apparatus required by neoliberal economics. In short, low-intensity democracy is the type of democracy that best suits US economic interests. Yet Terry Lynn Karl has shown just how neoliberal economic policies restrict the development of democracy. Discussing the situation in Central America, Karl argues that 'the current implementation of stabilization and austerity measures with insufficient regard to social safety nets threatens to shrink the already narrow political space'.[58] For Karl, democracy and socioeconomic transformation cannot be pursued sequentially, but must be addressed simultaneously; given that the neoliberal economic model has considerably worsened existing economic inequalities, the medium-term stability of democracy will be undermined unless socioeconomic inequalities are addressed.

As for the linkage within US foreign policy, Douglas Brinkley has most convincingly shown just how intertwined democracy promotion is with US foreign economic policy.[59] That there is a massive linkage between the two is not

---

[57] P. Hirst and G. Thompson, *Globalization in Question: The International Economy and the Possibilities of Governance* (Cambridge: Polity Press, 1996).

[58] T. Karl, 'The Hybrid Regimes of Central America', *Journal of Democracy*, 6/3 (1995), p. 84.

[59] Brinkley, 'Democratic Enlargement'.

the main point at issue; what is really interesting is which aspect is in the driving seat. In my view, it is clearly the case that US democracy promotion policies serve US economic policy rather than the other way round. Brinkley shows that, from the outset, President Clinton saw the promotion of US economic interests as central for US foreign policy, citing Clinton's 1994 budget message to Congress: 'We have put our economic competitiveness at the heart of our foreign policy.'[60] US economic interests would be best served by global free trade, which would bolster US economic performance. Now, although Brinkley surveys the relationship between democratic enlargement and US foreign economic policy, he concludes that 'Put another way, enlargement was about spreading democracy through promoting the gospel of geoeconomics'.[61] This implies that geoeconomics was the path to democracy promotion. In my view it is the other way round, in that democracy has been promoted to support US economic interests. As Michael Cox has noted, for the Clinton administration geoeconomics replaced geopolitics at the central foreign policy goal, to which end 'it pursued an extraordinarily coherent strategy which gave lie to the argument that Clinton had, or has, no vision'.[62]

The administration tended to be rather vague over the relationship between the two aspects of foreign policy, often speaking of the need to enlarge the number of 'market democracies'—itself a fascinating term! This conflation is particularly revealing, since it shows that the kind of democracy to be promoted was to be one that fitted with the market, and that of course is exactly the low-intensity democracy discussed above. In other words, US democracy promotion was aimed not so much at expanding deep conceptions of democracy but instead at putting in place a form of democracy that would suit US economic interests. In this sense there has been a considerable continuity in US policy, since the previous policies of shoring up authoritarian regimes was also done to protect and promote US economic interests.

William Robinson has provided an extensive account of how this change in US policy has come about. Robinson's main claim is that:

The impulse to 'promote democracy' is the rearrangement of political systems in the peripheral and semi-peripheral zones of the 'world system' so as to secure the underlying objective of maintaining essentially undemocratic societies inserted into an unjust international system . . . Just as 'client regimes' and right-wing dictatorships installed into power or supported by the United States were characteristic of a whole era of US foreign policy and intervention abroad in the post-World War II period, promoting 'low-intensity democracies' in the Third World is emerging as a cornerstone of a new era in US foreign policy.[63]

Robinson presents a Gramscian account of these forms of democracy, focusing on Gramsci's concept of 'hegemony'. Accordingly, he sees these low-intensity democracies—polyarchies—as structures to ensure consensual domination, in the sense of being a way for the economic elite to obtain the

[60] Cited in Brinkley, 'Democratic Enlargement', p. 117.
[61] Brinkley, 'Democratic Enlargement', p. 125.
[62] Cox, *US Foreign Policy after the Cold War*, p. 36.   [63] Robinson, *Promoting Polyarchy*, p. 6.

active consent of other classes. For Gramsci, a dominant class exercises hege-mony over other classes by getting them to internalize their logic and world-view. Hegemony is exercised within civil society, as distinct from the formal political structure, and results in 'The "spontaneous" consent given by the great masses of the population to the general direction imposed on social life by the dominant fundamental group'.[64]

Robinson examines four case studies, the Philippines, Chile, Nicaragua and Haiti, in detail and much more briefly looks at the Soviet bloc and South Africa. In each case, he looks at US democracy promotion policies as they were implemented as distinct from the public presentation of the policies. His cen-tral conclusion is that, despite the shift in US foreign policy from supporting authoritarian regimes to promoting democracy, the policy goal remains essen-tially the same, and that is to 'gain influence over and try to shape . . . out-comes in such a way as to preempt more radical political change, to preserve the social order and international relations of asymmetry'.[65] The US turned to promote democracy only when the existing authoritarian regimes were in trouble. Crucially,

In all cases, the forces of global capitalism acted to strengthen projects of polyarchy and neo-liberalism and to weaken the projects of popular social change. The Unites States intervened when these national democratization movements were reaching crescendos, threatening not just the existing regime but the social order itself. The beneficiaries of this intervention were neither the popular sectors nor the old autocrats, dictators and 'crony' elites, but new technocratic sectors tied to the global economy that articulated the transnational agenda.[66]

Robinson argues that the linkage between democracy promotion and neolib-eral economics is that the former is used to construct a state structure con-ducive to the latter; he calls this the neoliberal state.

His case studies also illustrate the contradictions between low-intensity democracy—polyarchy—and popular democracy, with polyarchy concerned above all with social stability. Although in their influential study of the rela-tionship between democracy and capitalism, Rueschemeyer, Stephens and Stephens[67] argued that capitalism, by altering the class structure, enables democracy to be established, Robinson notes that their definition of demo-cracy essentially equates it with polyarchy. Capitalism is less able to coexist with wider notions of democracy, and, therefore, in a world that is witnessing a massive growth in inequalities—both within the richer states and between the 'haves' and the 'have-nots'—polyarchy cannot in the long run ensure social stability. Robinson notes that 'The tendency is for wealth to become concentrated in a privileged stratum encompassing some 20 percent of humanity, in which the gap between rich and poor is widening *within* each country, North and South alike, simultaneously with a sharp increase in the

[64] A. Gramsci, *Selections from the Prison Notebooks* (London: Lawrence and Wishart, 1971), p. 12.
[65] Robinson, *Promoting Polyarchy*, pp. 318–19.   [66] Robinson, *Promoting Polyarchy* , p. 334.
[67] D. Rueschemeyer, E. Stephens, and J. Stephens, *Capitalist Development and Democracy* (Cambridge: Polity Press, 1992).

inequalities *between* the North and the South'.[68] In terms of the future, the most significant point is that increasing inequalities have been highly correlated with the breakdown of polyarchies, and yet these forms of political system cannot deal with these inequalities without undermining capitalism. Robinson summarizes the problem perfectly:

the neo-liberal model is designed to prevent any interference with the workings of the free market, including state redistributive policies . . . The neo-liberal model therefore generates the seeds of social instability and conditions propitious to the breakdown of polyarchy. 'Democracy promotion' is an attempt at political engineering, at tinkering with the political mechanisms of social control, while simultaneously leaving the socioeconomic basis of political instability intact . . .This is a contradiction internal to the transnational elite's project.[69]

Robinson's detailed analysis of the practice of democracy promotion leads to a very stark view of the relationship between neoliberal economics and low-intensity democracy. It is a view that would most certainly not be accepted by most of those who work in the policy area, for whom promoting democracy is self-evidently morally correct. This of course takes us back to my earlier comments about the truth rules that allow claims to be made about policy areas. I will now turn to discuss this relationship in more detail.

Conclusion: The Relationship between Politics and Economics

My main conclusion is that US democracy promotion policies have been based on one form of democracy, presented as if it is the only form. This is not presented as a moral choice, nor is it treated as if it is a claim about what democracy consists of. Instead, it is presented as a given, beyond debate. Of course, it is admitted that there can be flexibility in exactly how this model is adapted to given circumstances, but essentially the same polyarchic and formal electoral model is applied in each circumstance. Not only this, but the model is one of low-intensity democracy, a model that happens to suit US economic interests far more than would any rival democratic model that involved more extensive notions of what democracy means. Such models would focus more on the values underlying democracy, and would therefore see political democracy as incompatible with massive socioeconomic inequalities. This form of low-intensity democracy seems ill-equipped to cope with the demands placed on it by globalization on the one hand and by rising socioeconomic claims on the other. Yet it is a form of democracy that fits perfectly with the goal of promoting US economic interests. In this sense, the Clinton administration did indeed have a 'big idea' and that was not democracy promotion but a geoeconomic strategy.

---

[68] Robinson, *Promoting Polyarchy*, p. 339.   [69] Robinson, *Promoting Polyarchy*, p. 344.

Yet this picture seems far removed from the rhetoric of the Clinton administration's public statements on the policy of democracy promotion. The reason for this gap lies not in deceit or bad faith, but in the truth rules that construct the discourse in this area. The policy debate about democracy promotion is constructed by a set of prior 'commonsensical' rules about the relationship between politics and economics. They are seen as separate, and therefore the linkage between neoliberal economics and democracy promotion is a linkage between two policy areas, ultimately between two separate areas of social life: the political and the economic. What is not accepted is that the two are inextricably intertwined, such that the economic realm determines the fate of the political. Indeed, the economic sphere constructs the space for politics. Now, precisely because the separation between economics and politics is presented as natural—in my view the ultimate political act—the contradiction between the majority of forms of democracy and the requirements of neoliberal economics is never brought out. In its place is the claim that democracy equals polyarchy, and this then becomes the benchmark for the policy of democracy promotion. The link between that form of democracy and neoliberal economics, and ultimately US economic interests, is never discussed, because according to the truth rules these are separate domains.

Karl Polanyi[70] provides the classic account of this move to treat politics and economics as separate domains under capitalism. In other words, it is only under capitalism that it is possible to see politics and economics as separate; before then, economics was embedded in a social structure, but in capitalism the market is separated from this social structure, and begins to determine social and political structures.[71] In time this division is seen as natural, and the sphere of politics becomes limited to the public domain, leaving economics as a private sphere. As Robinson points out, before capitalism any economic demand was by definition also a political demand, whereas under capitalism economic demands are not seen as also being political.[72] Formal democracy therefore deals with the public (non-economic) arena, and is firmly limited to that by the hegemony of the dominant economic class. Thus, when groups in low-intensity democracies make socioeconomic demands, the political system cannot satisfy them within the boundaries of the political realm as defined by polyarchy.

In conclusion, then, my claim is that US democracy promotion policies are based on the illusion of the separation of politics from economics. This illusion creates a discourse about democracy promotion that limits discussion to the 'political' realm, regardless of the complex embedding of political—and social—life within an economic context. Accordingly, the US promotes a culturally particular form of democracy, reflecting its own domestic form of the relationship between economics and politics. It takes these rules to be the rules of democracy *per se*. US-style democracy becomes the model, regardless of the

---

[70] K. Polanyi, *The Great Transformation: The Political and Economic Origins of Our Time* (Boston: Beacon Press, 1957), especially Ch. 6.

[71] Polanyi, *The Great Transformation*, pp. 70–1.   [72] Robinson, *Promoting Polyarchy*, p. 354.

particular historical and cultural conditions that gave rise to it, and this model is then transported to other countries. Not surprisingly, this model cannot deal with those countries' underlying socioeconomic inequalities, since these are seen as 'naturally' outside the political sphere. Moreover, given that the world economy is increasing these inequalities, both within and between the 'haves' and the 'have-nots' of the world economy, the form of democracy being promoted by US policy cannot resist this trend; indeed, it can be argued that there is a necessary fit between the type of democracy being promoted and the widening gaps between poor and rich created by neoliberalism.

What is particularly interesting is the extent to which the policy of democracy promotion, both historically and in the Clinton administration, is debated in such limited terms, as if no alternative views of democracy were tenable and as if the relationship between economics and politics was indeed 'natural'. Conservative or realist critics of the policy may argue that it does not support US military and political interests, and may harm them by diverting attention and resources, but there is little in the way of public debate arguing the case made in this chapter. This is because the policy is not treated as propounding a moral case; it is a question of pragmatics whether or not it aids or assists US interests. In fact, though, the policy is deeply normative in a much more important way. It is deeply normative because of the way in which the truth rules for discussing democracy are so narrowly drawn as to restrict debate considerably. Moreover, the dominance of geoeconomics in US foreign policy creates a very narrow political space, and it is this narrow political space that low-intensity democracies occupy. This totalism of economics results in a situation whereby the market does not just determine the state form, but also defines the political. US democracy promotion policy is based on the illusion of the separation of politics from its socioeconomic setting, and it is the internalization of this illusion that represents the strength of US hegemony over the emerging global system. It is the naturalization of this illusion that results in the regime of truth within which the debate over democracy promotion takes place.

II

Democracy Promotion as US 'Grand Strategy'?

4

National Security Liberalism and American Foreign Policy

TONY SMITH

It is not only the right thing to do, it is the smart thing to do.

(Secretary of State Madeleine Albright, on President Clinton's trip to Africa promoting trade, human rights, and democracy, 23 March 1998)

The chief proposition made by national security liberals is that self-interest—the enhancement of American influence in the world—and the morally correct thing to do—a foreign policy supporting human rights and the establishment of democratic governments abroad—may actually serve one another far more often and importantly than most commentators on the US role in world affairs generally suppose. Realists may recall the famous assertion of French diplomat Charles Talleyrand two centuries ago, 'it is worse than a crime, it is a mistake', but liberals may now recall the equally pithy assertion of Secretary of State Madeleine Albright in 1998 on the eve of President Bill Clinton's trip to Africa, 'it is not only the right thing to do, it is the smart thing to do'.

In fact, Albright's liberalism is only the latest expression of a long-standing, but widely misunderstood, tradition in American foreign policy. What were the principal reasons, according to the historical record, that the United States came early in the twentieth century, beginning most notably with the presidency of Woodrow Wilson (1913–21), to champion the promotion of democratic governments abroad? Twenty, perhaps even ten, years ago, asking such a question would have been virtually inconceivable, unless the intention had been to mock any such effort by deconstructing its pretensions into self-righteous and/or self-defeating categories allegedly typical of the American proclivity for moralistic and ideological thinking about power. The dominant academic theories of comparative politics and international relations had no concepts that endorsed any such undertaking in terms of recognizing the liberal project as being part of the serious pursuit of American interests in the world. Nor would it have been a simple thing to formulate such an argument: the dominant political thinkers deplored unabashed liberalism either as a

potentially dangerous obfuscation of national priorities—the realist critique—
or as a deliberate mystification of what this country was in fact doing—the
radical critique. Prior to the dramatic turn of events that accompanied the fall
of Soviet communism between 1989 and 1991, I myself would never have
thought to have written a book such as *America's Mission: The United States and
the World-wide Struggle for Democracy in the Twentieth Century.*[1]

Yet since 'Minerva's owl flies out at dusk', then today is a proper historical
moment at which to take stock of the past in order to try to make sense of the
future. Suddenly, much that was obscure becomes plain—the dynamism of
international capitalism, for example, and the role therein of Japan and
Germany, whose significance did not seem so great for a while. In a related
manner, the end of the cold war, with the clear-cut victory of one side over the
other, raises new questions about alliance structures, including the character
of the states within them, that at an earlier period might have seemed quite
hypothetical. In a word, in an epic contest in which one side scored a clear
win—terrible and unjustifiable as the cost of that victory may have been in
places like Vietnam, Iran, and Central America—the question of why the victory raises to new prominence the ingredients of America's success. Only now
does it become virtually obligatory to see the organization and exercise of
American power as distinctive and to recognize that its 'liberalism' was an
essential ingredient of its success.

Here is an opportunity to plough new ground. Not only our understanding
of historical trends but also our intellectual apparatus for studying them need
to be revised in order to come to terms with the question of what was distinctively American about the way the cold war was won. In order to aid in
rethinking the history of the twentieth century in light of the closing of the
enormous struggle between democracy and communism (which some might
prefer to call a struggle between market capitalism and state planning), and in
line with my assignment to present the historical forces giving rise to the
American commitment to foster democracy abroad, this essay seeks to establish four propositions.

Proposition I. The predilection in the literature on international relations
prior to a decade ago to call American efforts to promote democratic government abroad 'moralism', 'idealism', 'utopianism' and the like has inhibited
scholars from understanding the practical utility of democracy promotion by
the US government. At the same time, the predilection of comparative political analysis to look predominantly at internal events to explain country-
specific behaviour has been an additional intellectual force obscuring the
strength of international influences on domestic politics. The result has been
that the argument for what might be called 'national security liberalism'—
asserting that the US has both the ability and the interest to promote democracy abroad—has been extremely difficult to make given the intellectual
blinkers of a wide range of academic specialists. Only with the triumph of

[1] Tony Smith, *America's Mission: The United States and the World-wide Struggle For Democracy in the
Twentieth Century* (Princeton: Princeton University Press, 1994).

democracy over communism after 1989 are we ready to reconceptualize the past in terms of new frameworks of understanding and finally come to recognize that the values and institutions of democratic life functioned both domestically and internationally in ways of enormous historical importance.

Proposition 2. For a variety of reasons related to the peculiarities of American history, the US has long favoured the development of world order based on a framework of action that today is called 'liberal'. That is, the United States has tended to favour a plural world political order as opposed to one based on great power divisions of the globe through imperialism. This world has presupposed an open international economic system and a battery of international institutions to manage relations in a peaceful and stable manner. Whatever the deviations from this framework in terms of the demands of neutralism, isolationism, or containment, and whatever the allowances that need to be made for the evolution of the basic premises of American liberalism for world order since the birth of the Republic, there is nevertheless a striking continuity and purpose to American foreign policy since the Republic's founding.[2]

Proposition 3. It is not enough to study America domestically to see the origins of democracy promotion. World events viewed from the perspective of international history alone can show us the kind of challenges Washington faced, and thus offer part of the explanation for why the United States acted as it did and why its policy was relatively successful. In a nutshell, the rise of nationalism beginning more than two centuries ago in northern Europe, coming thence to North America, before progressively reaching every part of the globe over ensuing generations, introduced a 'crisis of modernity' in state-society relations. Liberal democratic government, championed for global purposes by the United States beginning with the Wilson presidency, corresponded to an international need in certain social milieus for blueprints for the reform of state-society relations. What Washington then found in practice is today what is called the 'democratic peace': that where liberal democratic forces consolidated themselves, there American interests were best served. American liberalism in world affairs thus needs to be understood not only ethnocentrically, as the expression of a domestic preference for a certain kind of political order, but also from the perspective of international history; that is, as part of a global change in state-society relations that made this American paradigm relevant to many forces abroad.

Proposition 4. Despite the affinity of American liberalism with the hopes of many global forces, there should be no easy presumption on the basis of the foregoing observations that the spread of democratic government world-wide will be either easy or likely. Studies of 'defensive modernization'—whether of Turkey and Japan in the nineteenth century, or China and Iran today—demonstrate that local forces may well oppose 'Americanization' or 'Westernization' in terms of local values, interests, and institutions backed by powerful

[2] Smith, *America's Mission;* John Gerard Ruggie, *Winning the Peace: America and World Order in the New Era* (New York: Columbia University Press, 1996).

sentiments of nationalist faith. While by any historical measure the prospects for the consolidation of democratic government are excellent in the northern parts of Eastern Europe, and good in many parts of Latin America, elsewhere—especially in China and most of the Muslim world and Africa—local conditions are less propitious. Therefore, while it may well be clearly in the interest of the United States that democratic government spreads globally, Washington must recognize that there are obstacles to its ambitions, that its power is limited, and that a liberal agenda is not the only, or at times even the principal, framework that should guide policy deliberations.

Let us now turn to each of these interrelated propositions in more detail.

Rethinking History

Historical watersheds such as the one we have been experiencing globally since the end of the 1980s not only permit but indeed require a rethinking of past conceptualizations of world affairs. Since the failure of Woodrow Wilson at Versailles in 1919, liberals have been made the scapegoats of American failures in world affairs, variously blamed for all manner of mistakes: from overselling the peace-making capacity of international institutions to underestimating the need to be ready to use force in defence of the national interest, and from breeding a self-righteous blindness to America's limitations that led to Vietnam to calling for intervention for the sake of human rights today, which if undertaken would overextend the country's involvement in world affairs at little or no return to its national interest.

Accordingly, to consult a range of textbooks on international relations is to see that prior to the 1990s—and often still today—liberalism was used as an exact synonym for 'moralism' and 'idealism'—and this not only in the usual academic trade publications but also by notables such as Walter Lippmann, Hans Morgenthau, Reinhold Niebhur, and George Kennan. Given that mainstream comparative political thinking in the academy was coincidentally dominated at much the same time by a mentality that looked only at the domestic evolution of countries, the door remained closed to any suggestion that international forces could have significant impacts on internal developments—other than provoking imitative-defensive efforts. As a consequence, mainstream American academic life was simply deaf to the notion that one might take seriously the proposition that the US actually could, or should, promote democracy abroad. Ironically, Marxism, the one field of comparative politics that allowed for international and domestic forces to intermix, saw authoritarian, not democratic, government as the likely outcome of the exercise of US power. Marxists may have come to the wrong conclusion, but clearly their theoretical apparatus was superior to that of most of their mainstream rivals.

To be sure, it was obvious to all these schools that a peculiarity of American foreign policy was its notion that could it change the way the peoples of the

world were governed, a more lasting peace might result. Give
unreality of this ambition—not only because of the lack of Amer.
assure any such transformation (the comparative argument) but a.
of the realist conviction that even should a world order such as thes
called for materialize then it would not actually be different in any m.
ful way from the kinds of international system it succeeded—what, then,
its origins? Two explanations readily presented themselves so far as this c .-
guard thinking was concerned. First, Americans were a singularly religious
people, at least for an advanced industrial power—a characteristic that was
reinforced by founding the nation's unity on an ideology that has been called
the American creed. The 'universalism' inherent in the Declaration of
Independence and the Constitution thus related synergistically to American
religiosity in a way that made the US in its foreign policy as well as in its
domestic policy a quintessentially moralistic and ideological country.

The second traditional explanation for American moralism in world affairs
complements the first: thanks to the country's geographic isolation and great
power, it never experienced the kinds of threats at the hands of foreign enemies that would correct this penchant and make the US more realistic in its
conduct in world affairs. Mighty oceans and weak neighbours thus combined
to protect the United States from a sobering encounter with history that would
have dampened its universalistic pretensions while making it aware of the
high price that moralism may exact from any people that assumes it is exempt
from learning how to sup with the Devil.

Critics of American liberalism thus fall into two camps: those realists or
radicals who find all talk of an American interest in promoting democratic
government abroad to be disingenuous nonsense, a mystification of power—
Charles de Gaulle thinking about F. D. Roosevelt, for example, or virtually any
of the writings of Noam Chomsky; and those who—like Hans Morgenthau or
Henry Kissinger in his study on *Diplomacy*—take liberalism as a serious expression of American identity in foreign affairs, but who try to 'educate' the dysfunctional aspects of this ethnocentrism as to the damage such thinking can
do either to American interests—the realists—or to foreign peoples—the radicals—or to both.

In short, until the end of the cold war there was an intellectual consensus
that thinking about the distinctiveness of America as a liberal world power,
with a correspondingly distinctive ideology, set of interests, and framework
for action, had no cachet. It is for this reason that Michael Doyle's arguments
that were first formulated in 1983 are so interesting: virtually alone at the
time, he was able to advance a set of propositions that, modest as they may
seem today, were harbingers of an argument that came into its own only a
decade later. For it is only today, with two world wars and the cold war behind
us, that we can look at the US as the dominant power of the world system and
ask what particular aspects of its values and interests and their political organization gave it the success it has had in world affairs. Of course, power is a
composite of many factors, from geographical location to population size and

resource base. But its primary ingredient is surely the organization of its people and the direction given them by its political leadership—all of which must be formulated in ideas. To investigate this primary aspect of American power is, then, to ask for an analysis of American international liberalism. The most remarkable point, perhaps, is that it has taken so long for America to come to this understanding of itself.

National Security Liberalism

I see no particular reason to doubt the traditional explanation that American liberalism has roots in the ideological and religious sources of this country's founding. But to leave the matter at that is not simply to understate by a large measure the much wider range of interests that have made the United States the champion of liberalism in world affairs, in both the nineteenth and the twentieth centuries, but also to leave as cultural explanations reasons that were far more practical in nature for the liberal framework for world order that America came to champion.

Let us first define liberalism, as it came to be understood by the time of Woodrow Wilson, as having three aspects: liberal democracy promotion abroad at the nation-state level—the central focus of our investigation, but not the sole meaning of liberalism; open markets for the world economic system; and international institutions to regulate conflict—especially the use of military force. This three-legged structure for world order rested on four characteristics of America in the world—two general to the country, two specific to domestic forces—features of American political life that underlay the country's ability not simply to tolerate but actually to encourage the emergence of a politically plural world based on what Wilson was the first to call 'national self-determination'.

The general factors were political and geostrategic; the particularistic factors were economic and—especially after 1945—ethnic. What they added up to was a definition of the American national interest based on a notion of world order that was anti-imperialist and pro-nationalist—so long as these nationalist movements were not themselves imperialist. Such a preference for a world order was already recognizably liberal in the nineteenth century with an American predilection for a plural political world and economic openness; but in the twentieth, with Woodrow Wilson's presidency, the US became quintessentially liberal as it embraced democracy promotion and the creation of international institutions to regulate the peace.

Consider, first, the history of US international economic policy. As with the British after the 1820s, American economic interests were well served in world affairs by a non-discriminatory international system. American economic leaders did not oblige their country to engage in direct imperialist undertakings and so permitted the US to avoid head-on clashes with foreign nationalists to control them politically. At its origins, the country was anti-mercantilist, revolting against British-imposed trade discrimination that stifled its livelihood. By the late nineteenth century, when the country's industrialization made it second to none, it likewise opposed mercantilism out of the conviction that American goods could out-compete those of other countries provided there was a level playing field. The anti-imperialism of both the Monroe Doctrine and the Open Door Notes thus reflected the economic calculations of American anti-mercantilism.

Nineteenth-century economic liberalism was obviously a far cry from what we see around us today. Yet in the Monroe Doctrine and the Open Door Notes were the basic building blocks that would turn into an appeal for an open international economic system by Wilson during World War I, that would be reiterated by Cordell Hull and F. D. Roosevelt after 1933, and that ultimately underlay the Bretton Woods Accords reached in 1944. Today, with the North American Free Trade Association, the World Trade Organization, Asia Pacific Economic Cooperation, and the agencies of the International Monetary Fund and the World Bank, we have moved an enormous distance from the thinking of a century ago. Still, the continuity of American international economic liberalism and its effect on stable democratic governments—most apparent in the political consequences of the economic reforms currently experienced in much of Latin America and Eastern Europe—is quite evident.

Complementing the economic arguments favouring an anti-imperialist posture in world affairs, a second reason that the US opposed imperialism—and so can be called liberal—grew from its domestic political structure; as a democracy, America could ill imagine annexing to its own domestic institutions peoples of cultures quite foreign to its own. Thus, the strongest arguments against taking more of Mexico than was claimed in 1848, or of assuming control over the Philippines 50 years later, concerned the unsuitability of these peoples for incorporation into American democratic life. Moreover, the need to rule them as subjects not only implied the militarization of the American state but denied as well these peoples' right to self-government, a value the American people could ill afford to deny.

Accordingly, from the Monroe Doctrine to the Open Door Notes, the United States made itself friendly to the assertions of nationalist government in Latin America and north-east Asia. Following in these traces, Wilson at Versailles was recognized to be the friend of many rising peoples including not only the East Europeans but also the Zionists and the Armenians. To be sure, African and Irish Americans might well criticize Wilson for his failure to extend his principles of national self-determination to their kinfolk abroad, but their protests illustrate more than they diminish the point that American liberalism and the rise of nationalism abroad could be forces that worked together harmoniously. Certainly both the Latin Americans and the Chinese had reason to feel this during the nineteenth century—and the Chinese through World War II.

Of course, on occasion the United States came into direct conflict with foreign nationalists. In 1848, America seized nearly half of Mexico in an unprovoked aggression. In 1898, the Hawaiian islands were similarly seized, and shortly thereafter the Philippines and Puerto Rico were taken as dependencies. Again, the Americans enjoyed with other Westerners the benefits from restraints on the exercise of Chinese sovereignty at about the same time. Clearly, foreign nationalism and American power were often at loggerheads. Yet none of these acts of imperialism seriously implicated the United States in anti-nationalist struggles. In the case of Mexico and Hawaii, native populations were extremely small—roughly 80,000 Mexicans in the territories including Texas, and some 70,000 natives in Hawaii. Although there is no disguising the arrogant use of American power, the fact remains that the United States resisted the temptation to bring under its control large numbers of ethnically different peoples whom it was unlikely easily to be able to assimilate politically. The single exception was the Philippines, which was taken against strong nationalist opposition organized by Emilio Aquinaldo. Yet here Washington categorically rejected any thought of permanent control and began almost immediately to speak of eventual self-government, leading to a proposal in the 1930s for independence that the Filipinos themselves asked to be postponed.

In a word, while France was adding more than four million square miles to its empire in the 40 years prior to World War I, while Britain added three million, and Germany and Russia one million each, the US exercised relative restraint, its policies preferring a plural world political order with an affinity to nationalist demands to one controlled from imperial centres.

In due course, certain forms of great power nationalism came into direct conflict with the United States in the twentieth century. Fascism was a variant of nationalism, as was communism. For reasons to be discussed below, both ideologies derived a good part of their vigour from their appeal to political forces seeking power both locally and internationally. But the point to underscore is that part of the American opposition to each of these ideologies was based on their perceived hostility to the US for its liberalism and on the imperialist intentions of the great powers that embraced them—especially the Soviet Union in the case of communism, and Japan and Germany in the case of fascism. To fail to see these epic struggles as related to earlier wars of religion—to reduce them to being largely materialist or power-centred contests, the fallacies of radical and realist accounts respectively—is to fail to see a critical element of their dynamic.

This combination of economic and political arguments for American liberalism in world affairs was complemented by yet a third: a bias against a strong military for political and geostrategic reasons. In geostrategic terms as well, the United States favoured liberalism, for the anti-militarist bias of its political culture made girding for war as an imperialist nation a difficult undertaking. Since the time of the Founding Fathers, the US had favoured a weak military establishment as a guarantee that its democratic institutions would not be overthrown by the government itself—a reasoning that also made for trial by juries rather than leaving too much power to judges. In consequence, as late as the Spanish-American war the country had fewer than 40,000 men in uniform in the navy and army combined. Better, then, regional balances of power rather than great-power spheres of influence, arrangements which would mean that the US itself might not have to arm and compete for foreign control.

While these general characteristics of liberalism were in place in American foreign policy by the late nineteenth century, they were not without their shortcomings and their contradictions. Unable to be assured that the Philippines would remain independent from German or Japanese designs, the United States pre-emptively took over the islands. Unable to assure that Latin American countries would meet their debts to European creditors and so forestall the kind of annexations that had occurred with Egypt and were threatened for China, the United States—through the Roosevelt Corollary to the Monroe Doctrine, passed by Congress in 1904—preemptively took over the custom houses of a series of Latin American republics. More ominously, as the war clouds gathered over Europe, it became evident that a more detailed plan for what the United States hoped to see in the world was necessary if the storms unleashed by ethnic and nationalist hatreds were not to destroy American interests in the process.

From Wilson to the Late Twentieth Century

The greatness of President Woodrow Wilson was to see that his call for 'national self-determination' in the wake of the collapse of the Austro-Hungarian, Russian, and Ottoman empires in 1918 meant that the United States had to do more than had been done before when Washington simply expressed its antipathy for imperialist schemes of world order. Under Wilson, the US for the first time proposed its own version of a stable world order, a framework that was in line with earlier elements of American liberalism but that in significant features was boldly new.

Three elements of Wilson's update of American liberalism in world affairs are worth special notice. First, it was no longer enough that the international order be composed of sovereign states; Wilson's assumption was that democratically constituted states were inherently more stable and peace-loving and hence were the most appropriate building blocks of the global system. Second, given that order was to be based on political pluralism and that aggression was a recurrent feature of world history, Wilson declared the need to create international institutions capable of defining and regulating state interactions. Third, in a world undergoing such basic changes, American foreign policy needed for the first time to be a consciously constructed design with the United States playing a leading role in international affairs. In short, under Wilson's guidance American national security liberalism came of age.

This coming to maturity was promptly followed by a series of terrible reversals. The American public refused to follow Wilson's leadership—in good measure because the ailing President himself was so inflexible and obstreper-ous in his politicking—and the US in due course turned to isolationism. Nor did the slogan 'democratic national self-determination' readily translate into a blueprint for action for Eastern Europe or the Middle East. Of the many new states and mandates created by the Versailles Peace Conference and the League of Nations, only Czechoslovakia emerged in a form that did credit to the President's hopes. The Depression ruined whatever chances there were for international economic cooperation. Bolshevism and fascism, not liberal democracy, seemed the more likely blueprint for the world's nationalists to follow.

Yet if Wilsonianism was in bad odour by the 1930s—a state of affairs from which it is only now beginning to recover—a blueprint was on the table that could serve as a starting point for the next generation of American leaders as they contemplated the world in 1945 and debated how they might best move from winning the war to winning the peace that followed. Thus, the first Roosevelt administration had promoted an open international economic sys-tem, while the last saw to the creation of the United Nations and sponsored the Bretton Woods system. The Truman administration oversaw the demo-cratization of Japan and Germany during their occupations and urged the Western Europeans on to a form of economic and political integration that fulfilled Wilson's hopes for Franco-German rapprochement based on a 'peace without victory'.

Yet, as was immediately apparent to F. D. Roosevelt, neither constructing the postwar peace nor, as was apparent to Truman, waging the cold war could be fought under a strictly liberal banner. The requirements of the struggle forced the United States to sup with the Devil in ways that made a policy of liberal ends and means impossible to pursue—although, that said, a more lib-eral policy was possible in many areas than was actually pursued. Still, the rehabilitation of Japan and Germany under the terms of a liberal agenda that actually proceeded apace served the purpose of winning the cold war as well, for their democratization and economic liberalization strengthened the power of the US *vis-à-vis* both countries, obstructed the hopes of their right wing movements to regain power, and brought them in as full partners—more the Germans than the Japanese—to the liberal international American order. Indeed, to the extent that the expansion of an American hegemony over Western Europe and parts of East Asia contributed to the cold war, liberalism gained as a consequence.

Given this history, it should be no surprise that, for the Bush and Clinton administrations, a neo-Wilsonian framework for world order in the post-cold war world seemed appropriate. Now more than ever, sovereign nation states, democratically based and economically open, might cooperate in a variety of already established international agreements and institutions that American power had provided for order in those parts of the world where such arrange-ments could be maintained. As the Soviet empire, and then the Soviet Union itself, disintegrated into its ethnic and nationalist constituencies, the

American-directed order had a tried and proven way to pick up at least some of the pieces.[3]

In the case of Eastern Europe, for example, the Bush administration called in no uncertain terms for the inauguration of democratic governments throughout the region. Such arrangements were to include the regular panoply of freedoms and institutions, including civilian control of the military and respect for minority rights. Failure to adhere to the liberal model domestically meant exclusion from liberal economic organizations internationally controlled by the West and from any thought of incorporation into other liberal regimes, either the European Union or the North Atlantic Treaty Organization.

Seen from this liberal perspective, as Czech president Vaclav Havel has repeatedly, and I think correctly, maintained, the expansion of NATO to include Poland, the Czech Republic, and Hungary represents not so much a defensive pact against Russia as a reassuring agreement on collective security entered into by the members of an enlarged liberal union. Should these ambitions succeed, they will crown more than 80 years of effort, stretching from the activism of Eastern European Americans, Eastern European political leaders, and Woodrow Wilson during World War I until today. Indeed, nothing could have been more Wilsonian than Secretary of State Madeleine Albright's rousing speech at Harvard University in June 1997, on the fiftieth anniversary of the announcement of the Marshall Plan, where this woman of Czech descent declared that 'American security and prosperity are linked to economic and political health abroad':

. . . we must take advantage of the historic opportunity that now exists to bring the world together in an international system based on democracy, open markets, law and a commitment to peace. Today the greatest danger to America is not some foreign enemy; it is the possibility that we will fail to heed the example of [the postwar] generation; that we will allow the momentum toward democracy to stall, take for granted the institutions and principles upon which our own freedom is based, and forget what the history of this century reminds us: that problems, if left unattended, will all to often come home to America. A decade or two from now, we will be known as the neo-isolationists, who allowed tyranny and lawlessness to rise again, or as the generation that solidified the global triumph of democratic principles.[4]

A final feature of American domestic life that deserves note in explaining the country's liberalism in world affairs is its ethnic make-up. In the three decades prior to World War II, ethnic groups could be deeply at odds with one another. In the 1910s, German, Scandinavian, and Irish Americans were in the forefront of neutralism and opposition to US membership in the League of Nations. With home rule for Ireland in 1922, and independence 15 years later, Irish Americans came to be less involved in trying to influence foreign policy,

---

[3] Smith, *America's Mission*; G. John. Ikenberry, 'The Myth of Post-Cold War Chaos', *Foreign Affairs*, 75/3 (1996), pp. 79–91; Strobe Talbott, 'Democracy and the National Interest', *Foreign Affairs*, 75/6 (1996), pp. 47–63.

[4] *New York Times* (6 June 1997).

but their place was taken by Italian Americans, who tended to support Mussolini and so to favour isolationism. After World War II, however, European—including Jewish—Americans could close ranks both with each other and with respect to any tensions they felt between their ethnic and their national loyalties. Whether it was Washington's support for Western European integration, its defence of eventual national self-determination in Eastern Europe, or its support for Israel, fighting the cold war in terms of democratic values for other peoples gained serious grassroots political support. Once again, then, American liberalism in world affairs corresponded to defined political values and forces at home.

While American liberalism in world affairs has grown from a rich brew of domestic values and interests—of which the much-touted religiosity, ideological founding, and innocence of the country are only minor ingredients—a good part of its success has come from the fact that it was in league with its times, able to secure the well-being of this country not simply because the United States has been so powerful but also because many world forces have found an affinity between their ambitions and American policy.

The principal political force in world politics over the last two centuries and more has been nationalism, a political spirit that insists on direct governmental contacts with the people, legitimized by some set of ideas as to who 'the people' is and what makes the structure of their relations with the state legitimate. As an ideology of ethnic unity, nationalism has recast the basis of state-society relations, forcing a new articulation of ties between the government and the people best seen in the emergence of party systems of popular political participation. New concepts of the rights and obligations of citizenship have emerged in league with new ideas of governmental legitimacy. The result may rightly be called 'the crisis of political modernity', an upheaval in political relations that spelled the death of authoritarian and imperial governments everywhere. While the process began first in northern Europe and North America—most vividly in the American and French Revolutions—it soon swept Latin America—leading to the uprisings against Spain in the early nineteenth century—thence to Eastern Europe in the revolutions of 1848, and shortly thereafter to Turkey, Japan, and Russia. By the turn of the twentieth century, the appeal of nationalism had given rise to Zionism and played a role in the fervour of World War I and in the reorganization of the state system that followed the collapse of the Ottoman, Russian, and Austro-Hungarian empires in 1918 as well as in the fall of the Manchu dynasty in China.

Nationalism was evident in the interwar years in the Arab Awakening, the progress of the Congress Party in India, and the origins of the forces that would lead the decolonization movement against European empires after 1945. Nationalism was also a primary force in the collapse of the Soviet empire and the Soviet Union itself between 1989 and 1991. Despite the intensified globalization of the world economy and the rise of a variety of transnational actors and issues in recent years, there is every reason to expect nationalism to remain a vigorous force in world affairs well into the future.

Now the important point to make with respect to nationalism and American liberalism is simply this: Wilsonianism provided something of a blueprint to nationalist forces abroad for the construction of a modern state authority when authoritarian and imperial government appeared deficient. But liberalism was not alone in its proposals. Communism and fascism too had responded to the crisis of modernity; each of them also had a blueprint of global relevance to promote. And given that each of these models for nationalist government was backed by a major international power, a host of minor states, and a wide range of domestic forces throughout the world—very roughly, the established traditional order coming to favour fascism, the exploited order communism, and the middle class liberal democracy—nationalist struggles were invariably internally divided, regionally fragmented, and globally mingled. Civil, regional, and global wars intersected with one another frequently and in a mutually aggravating manner.

In the three-sided struggle among communism, fascism, and liberal—supported by socialist—democracy for the allegiance of nationalist forces, the latter was ultimately successful for a variety of reasons, which limitations of space preclude reviewing even summarily here. Suffice it to say, however, that liberalism's strength came not only from the power of the American government and those like the British who fought with it, but from aspects of American policy that fell on fertile ground with peoples much farther afield. Still, the ultimate victory of liberal democracy was no foregone conclusion. From the 1910s through the 1980s, observers have understandably worried that the divisions, proceduralism, anti-militarism, and self-absorption of the democracies would prove their undoing.

American Liberalism in the Perspective of International History

In the preceding section, I suggested some of the principal reasons I think that the US was relatively uninterested in imperialism of its own and actively opposed it for others, and hence could be called liberal in world affairs. The basis of American commercial interests never prompted it to seek foreign dominion, for example, but the point for this section is that this relative restraint put American policy on the right side of history so far as many foreign nationalisms were often concerned. American policy was relatively successful because it corresponded to interests and forces abroad.

Thus, nineteenth century nationalist governments in Latin America or north-east Asia were relatively well disposed to Anglo-American liberal anti-mercantilism because they recognized that the tariff preferences usually called for by other great powers were mechanisms to gain informal—and perhaps later formal—political control. From the viewpoint of China or Argentina, better the international order that allowed them to treat with all comers equally than that which would assign economic privileges that could be converted into political liabilities; better, that is, the British and the Americans than the Russians, the Japanese, the French, or the Germans.

And so it remains today. A reason the American-sponsored liberal international economic order is one of the wonders of world political history is that it has managed simultaneously to respect the sovereignty of local states and to disarm many of the proponents of imperialist expansion, while assuring unprecedented levels of global prosperity. After the defeat of German and Japanese militaristic nationalism, Washington helped to reshape these countries politically, culturally, and economically. The incorporation of these two giants into today's world trade regimes was one of the ways the US pacified their nationalism. A major question of international relations currently is whether in the post-cold war order Russia and China will similarly be incorporated or whether instead they will come to define their national interests in opposition to this system.

In geostrategic terms, as well, the world's weaker peoples may favour the anti-militarism that has long dominated American thinking, for a disarmed world may serve their interests as well as those of the United States. As Eastern Europeans were well aware in the interwar years, for example, competitive imperialist neighbours made the sovereignty of the weak a tenuous affair. As the example of NATO illustrates, a democratic military alliance has virtues that often are not immediately apparent.[5] Hence, while weaker peoples opposed predatory grabs by mighty states in the name of their own independence, the US opposed such developments because of the wars in which they might embroil this country. By the same token, the spread of democratic government might appeal to foreign peoples and in turn serve American interests in world affairs. As Wilson was the first to argue, democratic government not only is a stable formula for the state but provides the kind of political system abroad most likely to be in harmony with American interests and values. Of course, as US experience with Nehru's India or de Gaulle's France illustrates, one should not exaggerate the point. Nor should one underestimate the enormous obstacles that may lie in the way of the consolidation of democratic government abroad.

Still, the fact that democratic countries are so unlikely to go to war with one another has bred in recent years a large and interesting 'democratic peace' literature, which usually invokes the spirit of Immanuel Kant but might with more reason reconsider the intentions of Woodrow Wilson. And in terms of American foreign policy, what better illustrates the liberal argument than Wilson's belief that the stability of Europe rested on Franco-German reconciliation, which itself could not be expected unless Germany, like France, were a democracy? The combined contribution of the Marshall Plan and the occupation of Germany to the realization of this idea is the single best demonstration in the history of US foreign policy of the strength of American national secur-

[5] Thomas Risse-Kappen, *Cooperation Among Democracies: The European Influence on U.S. Foreign Policy* (Princeton: Princeton University Press, 1995).

ity liberalism both to move history and to serve the American national interest in the process.

What I have tried to argue in this section is that American liberalism became confirmed national foreign policy not only because it corresponded to domestic interests and values but also because it corresponded to certain of the realities of world affairs in the twentieth century. Pacifists, peoples concerned by the tensions of ethnic diversity, the middle class and international business, secularists, nationalist leaders of weak states—all of these and more might find in liberal economic systems, international peacekeeping regimes, or democratic government proposals for world order that suited their needs and hence that elicited their support. As a consequence, the arguments in favour of American liberalism have been successful not only because they have a domestic constituency but because they have developed an international following as well.

Liberals Must Respect the Limits of Their Influence

Lest our enthusiasm for liberalism as the doctrine of American foreign policy become unbounded, it should be recalled that seldom have liberal precepts been the sole framework for conceptualizing America's role in world affairs, and seldom should they be. As the preceding section indicated, many forces in world affairs are deeply hostile to liberalism in all its manifestations. To assume that American power can overcome these obstacles is to inflate by a long measure what the US can do and to portend an 'end to history' as all peoples converge toward liberal government that no serious student of international history should take seriously.

Put differently, the strictures of comparative political theory that have us analyse local conditions in terms of their appropriateness for democratic government still need to be respected. It should come as no surprise, then, that the recent advent of democratic government has come in environments prepared for it by close contact with the West, or striving mightily to imitate it— Poland, the Czech Republic, Hungary, South Africa, South Korea, and most of Latin America. By contrast, in China, the Muslim world, and much of Africa, there is much less reason for confidence. A prudent policy might be bullish in the first cases, bearish in the second.[6]

To be sure, there are many initiatives the democratic world can take that can make a difference.[7] And in cases where nations of real importance to world affairs are poised at a fork in the road where democratic government is a viable option—today Russia, Mexico, and Turkey, for example—then even a marginal intervention may have a major outcome. But to assume that everywhere

---

[6] Fareed Zakaria, 'The Rise of Illiberal Democracy', *Foreign Affairs*, 76/6 (1997), pp. 22–43; Thomas Carothers, 'Democracy Without Illusions', *Foreign Affairs*, 76/1 (1997), pp. 85–99.

[7] Larry Diamond, *Promoting Democracy in the 1990s* (Carnegie Endowment for International Peace, 1995); Graham T. Allison and Robert P. Beschel, Jr. 'Can the United States Promote Democracy?', *Political Science Quarterly*, 107/1 (1992), pp. 81–98.

the West can make a difference is to exaggerate by a long measure what out-siders can achieve. As the occupation of Haiti or events in the former Yugoslavia or efforts to bring about stable, democratic government in Cambodia all indicate, vast sums of money and talent may be expended with little positive to show as a result. Imagine, then, the obstacles in China, the Muslim world, and much of Africa to any effort to promote liberal democracy from without when peoples far more open to Western influence have proved so recalcitrant to change. The United States must thus be prepared to work with the world in terms other than democracy promotion as a result. At times this may prove unpalatable—supping with the Devil for the sake of mutual advantage—or at other times enlightening—as other cultures reveal their dis-tinctive ways of promoting justice, beauty, and freedom. In either case, what America must understand is the limits on its power.

In its early days, the Clinton administration seemed to lack a clear sense of limits and announced that it would replace a foreign policy premised on con-tainment with one focused on the enlargement of the democratic community. In short order, however, the shortcomings of this new policy became evident. Sounding the trumpet of Wilsonianism was not to strike a note that all would follow—as was eventually recognized in May 1994, when the Clinton admin-istration issued a statement on military engagement that made it evident that the US would hazard little militarily for the sake of its heady rhetoric on the promotion of human rights and democracy abroad.[8]

Yet surely the conclusion to draw is not that Wilsonianism needs to be aban-doned as a pillar of America's role in the world, a framework for international order that still is the best indication of a grand design we have to work for. Still, just as in the interwar period, when much of eastern Europe was unpre-pared or unable to join a liberal world system, just as in the cold war when the United States found itself repeatedly obliged to work in balance of power terms with little regard for liberal principles, so today too the character of world events means that leaders must be prepared not only to act without guidance from liberal principles but on occasion actually to violate them as well.

For example, it is not obvious to me how a vigorous campaign in favour of human rights in China will interact with domestic forces there to bring about a favourable outcome. Indeed, I can easily imagine the opposite result. Similarly, the serious promotion of democracy in parts of the Muslim world critical to Western and Japanese energy supplies might well destabilize friendly governments there. Or again in Africa, the social openings dictated by democratization may result in terrible civil wars, as the Rwandan genocide of 1994 so starkly illustrates. Nor do I know what the United States and its allies might do more than very marginally to affect domestic threats to the estab-lished democratic order of India should they unfortunately materialize.

Coming from a liberal who thinks many of the most positive aspects of American foreign policy stem from the liberal tradition, the conclusion that

---

[8] For more information on the Clinton administration and democracy promotion, see Michael Cox in this volume.

American liberalism should be temperate in its undertakings is somewhat unpleasant to arrive at. Yet without it, should quixotic crusades based on unrealistic assessments of the country's power be entered into, honouring the kinds of demands that are often made by, for example, Human Rights Watch, Freedom House, or Amnesty International—organizations whose efforts I do not want to disparage but whose demands on democratic governments I often find breathtaking in their self-righteousness and lack of realism—the gains of the liberal order itself might be jeopardized. Moreover, there are surely abundant contradictions within the liberal democratic order itself so that Americans would be well-advised to attend to their own house before trying to put those of their distant neighbours in order. The temptations of self-righteousness lead directly enough to overextension and may damage not only our own interests but the well-being of other peoples.

'Who would be an angel becomes a beast', Pascal cautions us. And as Machiavelli reminds us, 'Men always commit the error of not knowing where to limit their hopes, and by trusting to these rather than to a just measure of their resources, they are generally ruined'. Liberals should be realistic enough to be able to cite repeated examples of where these admonitions have proved true and to remember them as we suggest how American foreign policy be conducted today.

Conclusion

To take liberalism seriously is to take seriously the notion that ideas make history. Of course ideas do not act by themselves; they are the expression of values and interests based on emotion and experience. But the fact that ideas have material origins does not mean that they do not have an independent logic of their own, whose repercussions on political life can be tremendous.[9] Marxism and realism—two enemies of what they can both agree is liberal 'idealism'—are themselves ideological constructs, ironically enough, and, as such, subject to the same strictures as liberalism—as the ultimate collapse of the Soviet Union so richly demonstrates and as realism's own difficulties dealing with its account of the cold war period also illustrate.

It is beyond the purview of this essay to speculate on why ideas are historically powerful, or why the recognition of this power is at moments obscured by other sets of ideas. Suffice it to say in conclusion that national security liberalism is a historical construct of a set of ideas reflecting the values and interests of individuals and groups predominant over a series of generations in the United States who, on the basis of a set of constantly evolving but none the less integrated ideas, built international economic, military, and political institutions and persuaded other peoples that it was in their interest to organize themselves in a similar manner.

[9] Tony Smith, *Thinking Like A Communist: State and Legitimacy in the Soviet Union, China, and Cuba* (New York: W. W. Norton, 1987), Ch. 1.

Like any complex set of ideas, liberalism has its contradictions, its short-comings, its lacunae. Nor has it been static; seen historically, it is a doctrine in constant evolution. Nor has it ever functioned alone: as a set of values and institutions, liberalism has had far from a monopoly on determining how the United States has acted in world affairs. Thucydides and Machiavelli should remain required reading in any introductory course on international relations. But that this set of ideas could serve to organize an international economic system of the kind we behold today, that it could have created a military alliance of the character of NATO, that it could have understood the importance of democratic values and institutions as a way of providing unity and direction to a wide variety of international actors, that liberalism could have done all of this in a way that served American national security recommends it to our continued study and reflection.

5

America's Liberal Grand Strategy: Democracy and National Security in the Post-war Era

G. JOHN IKENBERRY

Introduction

It is thought by many that America's preoccupation with the promotion of democracy around the world is essentially an 'idealist' impulse rooted in the moralism and exceptionalism of the American political tradition. To the extent that this American preoccupation with democracy spills over into actual foreign policy, it is seen as the triumph of American ideas and ideology—often at the expense of the more sober pursuit of American national interests. At best, the American democratic impulse is a minor distraction, rhetorical window dressing fashioned to make foreign policy commitments more acceptable to the American public. At worst, it is a dangerous and overweening moralistic zeal, built around profound misconceptions about how international politics really operates, and fuelling periodic 'crusades' to remake the world—and, as Woodrow Wilson discovered after 1919, this democratic impulse can get the country in serious trouble.

This common view is wrong. The American promotion of democracy abroad in the broadest sense, particularly as it has been pursued after World War II, reflects a pragmatic, evolving, and sophisticated understanding of how to create a stable international political order and a congenial security environment: what might be called an American 'liberal' grand strategy.[1] This orientation sees the character of the domestic regimes of other states as hugely important for the attainment of American security and material interests. Put simply, the United States is better able to pursue its interests, reduce security threats in its environment, and foster a stable political order when other states—particularly the major great powers—are democracies rather than non-democracies. This view is not an idealist preoccupation but a distinctively American

---

[1] The most sophisticated and systematic survey of American democracy promotion in this century is Tony Smith, *America's Mission: The United States and the Worldwide Struggle for Democracy in the Twentieth Century* (Princeton: Princeton University Press, 1994).

national security orientation that helps explain the American encouragement of democracy abroad as well as the wider imprint that the United States has left on the post-war world.

The argument of this chapter is three-fold. First, the American preoccupation with democracy promotion is part of a larger liberal view about the sources of a stable, legitimate, secure, and remunerative international order. This liberal orientation may be intellectually right or wrong, historically successful or unsuccessful, and in a given American foreign policy episode it may be a dominant or recessive characteristic. But it is a relatively coherent orientation rooted in the American political experience and an understanding of history, economics, and the sources of political stability. This American liberal grand strategy can be contrasted with more traditional grand strategies that grow out of the realist tradition and the foreign policy practices of balance of power, *Realpolitik*, and containment.

Second, this distinctively American liberal grand strategy is built around a wide-ranging set of claims and assumptions about how democratic politics, economic interdependence, international institutions, and political identity contribute independently and together to encourage stable and mutually acceptable political order. The richness and persistence of this American orientation is due in part to its manifold character; it is not just a single theoretical claim—for example, power transitions cause wars, democracies do not fight each other, stable order is built on a balance of power—but is a composite view built on a wide range of related claims about democracy, interests, learning, institutions, and economic change. Its richness and persistence is also due to the fact that various aspects of the liberal grand strategy are argued by different groups in the foreign policy community—this is what makes it a composite but also so stable. Some stressed democracy promotion, some stressed free trade and economic liberalization, and others stressed the construction of ambitious new international and regional economic and security institutions. But these separate emphases and agendas complemented each other—and together they came to constitute a liberal grand strategy.

Third, the dominance and appeal of this liberal grand strategy have survived the end of the cold war, even as most observers of American foreign policy do not fully recognize its character or accomplishments. It is an orientation that unites factions of the left and the right in American politics. Conservatives point to Ronald Reagan as the great cold war champion of the free world, democracy, and self-determination—ironically, Reagan is the great Wilsonian of our age. Liberals emphasize the role of human rights, multilateral institutions, and the progressive political effects of economic interdependence. For all the talk about drift and confusion in contemporary American foreign policy, the United States is seized by a robust and distinctive grand strategy.

I begin by sketching the basic debate about democracy promotion and American foreign policy, which took shape in the inter-war and post-war decades. Following this, I argue that the United States pursued two basic types of order-building strategies after World War II. One strategic orientation

emerged really as a response to the rise of Soviet power a
which culminated in the containment order. The other stra
which is more difficult to capture in a single set of policies, was
ing stable and open relations among the major democracies. It
order that bears the marks of America's liberal order-building de
next section, I sketch the major claims that are brought togethe
grand strategy and trace these claims to positions and groups withi
eign policy community. Finally, I reflect on the significance of thi .ioeral
democratic orientation for the current debate about American foreign policy.

Liberalism, Realism, and the Great Debate

The idealist image of American liberal internationalists was fixed in the intellectual and popular imagination during the great world upheavals of the 1930s
and 1940s. The seeming inability of the Wilsonian agenda to create order after
1919—the debacle of the League of Nations and the rise of German and
Japanese revisionist power in the 1930s—discredited liberal internationalism
and set the stage for the introduction of 'realist' thinking into American foreign policy. It was easy to argue that liberals had fundamentally misread the
character of twentieth century world politics, putting the country at danger by
substituting utopian thought and moral appeals for the more sober appreciation of material capabilities and power balancing. By the time the United
States emerged as a hegemonic power after World War II, the great debate in
American foreign policy was between an ascendant 'realism' and a beleaguered
'idealism'.

In one sense, the realist charge that liberals were sentimental idealists was
justified. Woodrow Wilson embraced the liberal internationalist agenda as he
sought to shape the post-war order, and in doing so he gave it a moralist cast.
As Wilson himself put it, foreign policy must not be defined in 'terms of material interest', and should be 'more concerned about human rights than about
property rights'. He brought to his political thinking and principles of political action deeply held religious and ethical beliefs that unified and defined his
orientation toward the outside world. 'In the conduct of foreign affairs', Link
notes, 'this idealism meant for him the subordination of immediate goals and
material interests to superior ethical standards and the exaltation of moral and
spiritual purposes'.[2]

Wilson's idealism had direct implications for his view about the goals of
American foreign policy, including the centrality of democracy to the emerging international order. 'His belief in the inherent goodness of man, in
progress as the law of organic life and the working out of the divine plan in
history, and in democracy as the highest form of government led him straight
to the conclusion that democracy must some day be the universal rule of

---

[2] Arthur S. Link, *Wilson the Diplomatist* (New York: New Viewpoints, 1974), p. 13.

political life.'[3] When the United States was finally drawn into the European war, Wilson appropriated the ideas and proposals of the British and American peace movements, and, in competing with Lenin to define a new path away from the old and bloody power politics of Europe, gave liberal internationalism a moral, universal, and idealist face.[4]

It was against this backdrop—the seeming impotence of Wilsonian ideas in the face of the brutal aggression of the 1930s and 40s—that realism took root in America. The first stroke was E. H. Carr's *Twenty Years' Crisis*, which was, as Stanley Hoffmann notes, 'the work of a historian intent on deflating the pretences of Liberalism, and driven thereby to laying the foundations both of a discipline and of a normative approach, "realism," that was to have quite a future'.[5] The liberals, Carr claimed, were seized by utopian illusions that were dangerously revealed when military aggression of Germany and Japan made a mockery of the Versailles order. Liberal democracy did succeed during the nineteenth century within a few countries, Carr observes. 'But the view that nineteenth-century liberal democracy was based, not on a balance of forces peculiar to the economic development of the period and the countries concerned, but on certain *a priori* rational principles which had only to be applied in other contexts to produce similar results, was essentially utopian; and it was this view which, under Wilson's inspiration, dominated the world after the first world war.'[6] It was the triumph of this rationalist idealism in the 1919 settlement, so Carr argued, that set the stage for the violence and failures of the next two decades.

The second stroke was Hans Morgenthau, whose *Politics Among Nations* crystallized and brought to dominance the realist 'paradigm' for the study and conduct of foreign relations. This was a work that advanced a series of law-like precepts about international relations distilled from the nineteenth century and early twentieth century European diplomacy and balance of power politics. Like Carr, he too was intent on exposing the illusions of liberal idealism. Trained in international law and a refugee from Hitler's Germany, Morgenthau sought to disabuse Americans of their faith in law, morality, and mutual interest as foundations of world order. The remarkable and long-lived influence of Morgenthau's book, first published in 1948, was facilitated by emerging cold war hostilities, which only underscored the stark realities of *Realpolitik* and the balance of power.

But the ascent of realism was accomplished in part by the misrepresentation of liberal thinking about international relations. Pre-1914 writings by British and American liberals were actually quite materialist in their arguments about economics and politics. Apart from Wilson, the most famous early twentieth century liberal thinker who seemed to evince an idealist disregard for the real-

[3] Link, *Wilson the Diplomatist*, p. 14.
[4] See Thomas J. Knock, *To End All Wars: Woodrow Wilson and the Quest for a New World Order* (New York: Oxford University Press, 1992).
[5] Stanley Hoffmann, 'An American Social Science: International Relations', *Daedalus*, 106/3 (1977), p. 43.
[6] E. H. Carr, *The Twenty Years' Crisis, 1919-1939*, 2nd edn (New York: Harper & Row, 1946), p. 27.

ities of power politics was Norman Angell. His 1909 book *The Great Illusion*, which was first published at the author's expense as an obscure essay but eventually became a world-wide best-seller with over a million copies in print, has long been cited as arguing that the rise of economic interdependence between nations made war impossible.[7] But the book actually presented a more sophisticated argument about how interdependence altered the costs and benefits of territorial gains through war, and how in Europe the costs of disruption to trade and investment were greater than the fruits of territorial conquest. Angell sought to establish that: 'a nation's political and economic frontiers do not now necessarily coincide; that military power is socially and economically futile, and can have no relation to the prosperity of the people exercising it; that it is impossible for one nation to seize by force the wealth or trade of another; . . . that, in short, even when victorious, war can no longer achieve those aims for which peoples strive.'[8]

When critics of Angell argued that the 1912 Balkan War seemed to disprove his theories, Angell replied: 'War is not impossible . . . it is not the likelihood of war which is the illusion, but its benefits.'[9] As Miles Kahler notes, Angell's 'underlying argument was not idealist, it was materialist: The contemporary state system and its competitive nationalism was a poor fit with underlying economic reality'.[10] Angell and other liberals of that era were making arguments about the changing relationship between an increasingly interdependent world economy, a rising transnational society, and the military and political capacities of governments.

The liberal internationalists before and after World War I did not represent a coherent 'school' of thinking. The professionalization of the study of international relations had not yet taken off and liberal thinkers mingled with the League of Nations societies and peace movements. But rather than being unalloyed idealists, they were making arguments that were decidedly materialist and bear the marks of liberal thinking more generally: that modern industrialism and the expanding world economy were creating demands and incentives for new types of cooperative relations between states; that international institutions can and need to provide mechanisms for the governance of interstate relations; that free trade and open markets created opportunities for joint economic gains between countries; that new types of cosmopolitan identities and affiliations between societies were subversive of nationalism and facilitated international cooperation; and that democracy was a commanding force in history that had—or would—transform states and interstate relations.

Liberal thinking was cast in the shadows by the upheavals of world war and the cold war crisis. Not only was realist thinking seemingly more relevant in making sense of the realities twentieth-century world politics, it was more

---

[7] Norman Angell, *The Great Illusion: A Study of the Relation of Military Power to National Advantage* (New York and London: G. Putnam and Sons, 1910).

[8] Angell, *The Great Illusion*, p. x.   [9] Angell, *The Great Illusion*, pp. 386–7.

[10] Miles Kahler, 'Inventing International Relations: International Relations Theory After 1945', in Michael Doyle and G. John Ikenberry (eds), *New Thinking in International Relations Theory* (Boulder, CO: Westview Press, 1997), p. 23.

coherent and straightforward as a doctrine that could inform American foreign policy. It was easy to conclude that the liberal doctrine—in the guise of Wilson's statecraft at Versailles—had been tried and failed. It was also easy to confuse Wilson's own idealism with the core of the tradition, and this confusion was quite useful to realists as they began the process of articulating realism within the academic and foreign policy community. A great and single statement of 'liberal theory' and its implications for American foreign policy was never produced in the inter-war or post-war decades. Liberal internationalism remained a collection of arguments, assumptions, and constructs that were never fully pulled together as a coherent theory or doctrine.

The failure of liberal internationalism was most evident in the mid-twentieth century professionalizing world of international relations and in the American foreign policy establishment. But in the shadows it retained a presence in the practical work of American officials as they sought to rebuild order after World War II—particularly in the work to reconstruct Europe and open the post-war world economy. Ideas were brought forward from the Wilsonian and League of Nations era, but the agenda of liberal internationalism became more complex and multifaceted. It became less centred on the creation of global institutions and universal principles. Lessons were learned from the earlier period, and the inter-war problems of capitalism and the modern management of industrial societies infused the new post-war thinking. But liberal ideas and accomplishments remained obscured by the cold war.

The Liberal Post-War Settlement

Even as liberal internationalism experienced a practical breakthrough after World War II, its agenda remained scattered and successes unheralded. In explaining this, it is useful to observe that American foreign policy after 1945 produced two post-war settlements. One was a reaction to deteriorating relations with the Soviet Union, and it culminated in the 'containment order'. It was a settlement based on the balance of power, nuclear deterrence, and political and ideological competition. The other settlement was a reaction to the economic rivalry and political turmoil of the 1930s and the resulting world war, and it culminated in a wide range of new institutions and relations among the Western industrial democracies—call it the 'liberal democratic order'. This settlement was built around economic openness, political reciprocity, and institutionalized management of an American-led liberal political order.[11]

The two settlements had distinct political visions and intellectual rationales, and at key moments the American president gave voice to each. On 12 March 1947, President Truman gave his celebrated speech before Congress announcing aid to Greece and Turkey, wrapping it in a new American commitment to

---

[11] This section draws on G. John Ikenberry, 'The Myth of Post-Cold War Chaos', *Foreign Affairs*, 75/3 (1996), pp. 7991.

support the cause of freedom around the world. The Truman Doctrine speech was a founding moment of the 'containment order'—rallying the American people to a new great struggle, this one against the perils of world domination by Soviet communism. A 'fateful hour' had arrived, Truman told the American people. The people of the world 'must choose between two alternative ways of life'. If the United States failed in its leadership, Truman declared, 'we may endanger the peace of the world'.[12]

It is forgotten, however, that six days before this historic declaration, Truman gave an equally sweeping speech at Baylor University. On this occasion, Truman spoke of the lessons the world must learn from the disasters of the 1930s. 'As each battle of the economic war of the thirties was fought, the inevitable tragic result became more and more apparent. From the tariff policy of Hawley and Smoot, the world went on to Ottawa and the system of imperial preferences, from Ottawa to the kind of elaborate and detailed restrictions adopted by Nazi Germany.' Truman reaffirmed American commitment to 'economic peace', which would involve tariff reductions and rules and institutions of trade and investment. In the settlement of economic differences, 'the interests of all will be considered, and a fair and just solution will be found'. Conflicts would be captured and domesticated in an iron cage of multilateral rules, standards, safeguards, and dispute resolution procedures. According to Truman, 'this is the way of a civilized community'.[13]

The 'containment order' is well known in the popular imagination. It is celebrated in our historical accounts of the early years after World War II, when intrepid American officials struggled to make sense of Soviet military power and geopolitical intentions. In these early years, a few 'wise men' fashioned a coherent and reasoned response to the global challenge of Soviet communism.[14] The doctrine of containment that emerged was the core concept that gave clarity and purpose to several decades of American foreign policy.[15] In the decades that followed, sprawling bureaucratic and military organizations were built on the containment orientation. The bipolar division of the world, nuclear weapons of growing size and sophistication, the ongoing clash of two

---

[12] H. Truman, 'Address to Joint Session of Congress on Aid to Greece and Turkey', 12 March 1947. For historical accounts of this foreign policy turning point, see Dean G. Acheson, *Present at the Creation: My Years at the State Department* (New York: Norton, 1969); Howard Jones, *'A New Kind of War': America's Global Strategy and the Truman Doctrine in Greece* (New York: Oxford University Press, 1989). On whether the Truman Doctrine was a cold war watershed, see John Lewis Gaddis, 'Was the Truman Doctrine a Real Turning Point?', *Foreign Affairs*, 52 (1974), pp. 386–92.

[13] H. Truman, 'Address on Foreign Economic Policy' (Baylor University: 6 March 1947).

[14] For a popular account of the 'founding fathers' of the containment order, see Walter Isaacson and Evan Thomas, *The Wise Men: Six Friends and the World They Made* (New York: Simon and Schuster, 1986).

[15] The seminal role of George Kennan as architect of containment policy is stressed in John Lewis Gaddis, *Strategies of Containment* (New York: Oxford University Press, 1984). More recently, Melvyn Leffler has argued that many American officials and experts from across the foreign and defence establishment independently began to embrace containment thinking. See *A Preponderance of Power* (Stanford: Stanford University Press, 1992). On Kennan's changing views of containment, see Kennan, *American Diplomacy, 1925–50* (Chicago: University of Chicago Press, 1951); *Memoirs, 1925–50* (Boston: Little, Brown and Co, 1967); and the interview with Kennan in 'X-Plus 25', *Foreign Policy*, 7 (1972), pp. 353.

expansive ideologies—all these circumstances gave life to and reinforced the centrality of the 'containment order'.

By comparison, the ideas and policies of the liberal democratic order were more diffuse and wide-ranging. It was less obvious that the liberal democratic agenda was a 'grand strategy' designed to advance American security interests. As a result, during the cold war it was inevitable that this agenda would be seen as secondary—a preoccupation of economists and American business. The policies and institutions that supported free trade and economic openness among the advanced industrial societies were quintessentially the stuff of 'low politics'. But this is an historical misconception. The liberal democratic agenda was built on a robust and sophisticated set of ideas about American security interests, the causes of war and depression, and the proper and desirable foundations of post-war political order. Indeed, although the 'containment order' overshadowed it, the ideas behind post-war liberal democratic order were more deeply rooted in the American experience and a thoroughgoing understanding of history, economics, and the sources of political order.

The most basic conviction behind the post-war liberal agenda was that the closed autarkic regions that had contributed to world depression and split the world into competing blocs before the war must be broken up and replaced by an open and non-discriminatory world economic system. Peace and security were impossible in a world of closed and exclusive economic regions. The challengers to liberal multilateralism occupied almost every corner of the advanced industrial world. Germany and Japan, of course, were the most overt and hostile challengers. Each had pursued a dangerous pathway into the modern industrial age that combined authoritarian capitalism with military dictatorship and coercive regional autarky. But the British Commonwealth and its imperial preference system was also a challenge to liberal multilateral order.[16] The hastily drafted Atlantic Charter was an American effort to insure that Britain signed on to its liberal democratic war aims.[17] The joint statement of principles affirmed free trade, equal access for countries to the raw materials of the world, and international collaboration in the economic field so as to advance labour standards, employment security, and social welfare. Roosevelt and Churchill were intent on telling the world that they had learned the lessons of the inter-war years—and those lessons were fundamentally about

---

[16] For arguments that the great mid-century struggle was between a open capitalist order and various regional autarkic challengers, see Bruce Cumings, 'Trilateralism and the New World Order', *World Policy Journal*, 8/2 (1991), pp. 195–226; and Charles Maier, 'The Two Postwar Eras and the Conditions for Stability in Twentieth-Century Western Europe', in Charles Maier, *In Search of Stability: Explorations in Historical Political Economy*, part 1 (New York: Cambridge University Press, 1987), pp. 153–84. A similar sweeping historical argument, described as a struggle between 'liberal' and 'collectivist' alternatives, is made in Robert Skidelsky, *The World After Communism* (London: Macmillan, 1995).

[17] Churchill insisted that the charter did not mandate the dismantlement of the British empire and its system of trade preferences, and only the last-minute sidestepping of this controversial issue ensured agreement. See Lloyd C. Gardner, 'The Atlantic Charter: Idea and Reality, 1942–1945', in Douglas Brinkley and David R. Facey-Crowther (eds), *The Atlantic Charter* (London: Macmillan, 1994), pp. 45–81.

the proper organization of the Western world economy. It was not just America's enemies, but also its friends, that had to be reformed and integrated.

It was in this context that the post-1945 settlement within the advanced industrial world can be seen. It was a scattering of institutions and arrangements, reflecting the lessons of the 1930s and the new imperatives that emerged from a collapsed war-ravaged world and a newly powerful America. The cold war did overpower the thinking of American officials sooner or later, but the principles and practices of Western order came earlier and survived longer. They were principles and practices that emerged as officials grappled with real post-war problems—the liberal post-war agenda emerged as officials sought to stabilize, manage, integrate, organize, regulate, reciprocate, control, and achieve agreement. The specific ideas and operational visions can be identified more precisely and linked to the post-war transformation.

American Liberal Visions and Strategies

America's liberal grand strategy is an amalgam of related but distinct claims about the sources of political order—and each has been pushed into the post-war foreign policy process by different groups and parts of the foreign policy establishment. Post-war presidents have stressed different aspects of this agenda, even though the various strategies complement and reinforce each other. Five strategies can be identified, each with its own theory and claims about international relations and each with its own distinctive impact on American foreign policy. In each instance these are liberal ideas that emerge from the American experience and its conceptions of the sources of desirable political order.

Democracy and Peace

Ideas about democratic peace, traced to Kant and developed recently by many analysts, hold that liberal constitutional democracies—or what Kant called 'republics'—tend to have peaceful relations with one another, because of both their internal structures and shared norms.[18] Some argue that the structures of democratic government limit and constrain the types of conflicts over which democratic leaders can mobilize society. Others stress the norms of peaceful resolution of conflict and the ways in which reciprocal democratic legitimacy places limits on the use of violence, while others emphasize the effect of democratic institutions on information and signalling in strategic interaction.

---

[18] See Michael Doyle, 'Kant, Liberal Legacies, and Foreign Affairs', *Philosophy and Public Affairs*, 12 (1983), pp. 205–35, 323–53; Michael Doyle, 'Liberalism and World Politics', *American Political Science Review*, 80/4 (1986), pp. 1151–69; Bruce Russett, *Grasping the Democratic Peace: Principles for a Post-Cold War World* (Princeton: Princeton University Press, 1993); James Lee Ray, *Democracy and International Conflict: An Evaluation of the Democratic Peace Proposition* (Columbia: University of South Carolina Press, 1995); William J. Dixon, 'Democracy and the Peaceful Settlement of International Conflict', *American Political Science Review*, 88/1 (1994), pp. 14–32.

Behind these institutional dynamics, others focus on the way in which democracies are built on shared social purposes and an underlying congruence of
interests that limit the rise of conflicts worthy of war.[19]

American officials at various junctures have acted on this basic liberal view.
Wilson, of course, placed the role of democracy at the centre of his optimism
about the durability of a post-war peace. It was also his conception of the
sources of war that led to his distinction between the German people and the
German government: the former the legitimate source of authority and interest and the latter a dangerous militarist autocracy. The United States did not
have a quarrel with the German people, but with their military dictators who
had brought war to Europe. 'A steadfast concert of peace can never be maintained except by a partnership of democratic nations. No autocratic government could be trusted to keep faith within it or observe its covenants.'[20]

Wilson's claim was just the most emphatic version of a long tradition in
American diplomacy arguing that the United States would be able to trust and
get along better with democracies than non-democracies. The American decision to use its post-war occupation of Japan and Germany to attempt ambitious and unprecedented reforms of their states and societies was driven in
large part by this belief in the security implications that would flow if
Germany and Japan developed more democratic polities.[21] This impulse, of
course, was not absolute, and cold war imperatives moderated the extent of
actual democratic reform, particularly in Japan. But the argument that the
world wars were caused fundamentally by the rise of illiberal, autocratic states
and that American post-war security was dependent on the successful transition of these states to democracy was widespread and at the heart of American
foreign policy. It was echoed recently by an American official who summarized the view:

Our answer to the sceptics, the critics, and the self-styled realists is straightforward: look
at history, and look at the world around us. Democracy contributes to safety and prosperity, both in national life and in international life—it's that simple. The ability of a
people to hold their leaders accountable at the ballot box is good not just for a citizenry
so enfranchised—it is also good for that country's neighbours, and therefore for the
community of states.[22]

Beyond the democratic peace thesis, other arguments abound that link democracy and the rule of law to international agreement and the stable functioning of international institutions. One argument is that democracies are able to
develop relations based on the rule of law rather than political expediency,

---

[19] Many of these arguments are brought together in Michael E. Brown, Sean Lynn-Jones, and
Steven Miller (eds), *Debating the Democratic Peace* (Cambridge, MA: MIT Press, 1996).

[20] Address to a Joint Session of Congress, 2 April 1917; in Arthus S. Link (ed.), *The Public Papers of
Woodrow Wilson*, 41 (Princeton: Princeton University Press, 1983), pp. 519–27.

[21] See Smith, *America's Mission*, Ch. 6.

[22] 'Democracy and the International Interest', remarks by Deputy Secretary of State Strobe Talbott
to the Denver Summit of the Eight Initiative on Democracy and Human Rights, 11 October 1997,
p. 2. See also Strobe Talbott, 'Democracy and the National Interest', *Foreign Affairs*, 75/6 (1996), pp.
47–63.

and this facilitates stable and mutually beneficial dealings.[23] Another argument is that democracies are better able to cooperate in alliance organizations and establish binding institutional relations. The open and permeable character of democracies allows potential institutional partners to overcome uncertainties about domination or abandonment. This is true for three reasons. Democracies are more transparent than non-democracies, and this allows states to observe the domestic system of the other states, and therefore to have more confidence in promises and commitments. Democracies are also more open and accessible to the direct representations of other states, allowing potential partners to not just make agreements, but also to create a political process that allows them to actually influence policy in the other democracies. Finally, the multiple power centres of democracies make abrupt and untoward state actions more difficult—sharp change in policy requires more actors and institutions to sign up to it than in non-democracies.[24]

Overall, the liberal claim is that democracies are more capable of developing peaceful, continuous, rule-based, institutionalized, and legitimate relations among each other than is possible with or between non-democracies. This thesis was put forward by former National Security Council Director Anthony Lake in 1995 in explaining American foreign policy after World War II:

We led the struggle for democracy because the larger the pool of democracies, the greater our own security and prosperity. Democracies, we know, are less likely to make war on us or on other nations. They tend not to abuse the rights of their people. They make for more reliable trading partners. And each new democracy is a potential ally in the struggle against the challenges of our time—containing ethnic and religious conflict; reducing the nuclear threat; combating terrorism and organized crime; overcoming environmental degradation.[25]

Free Trade, Economic Openness, and Democracy

Another liberal argument that found its way into American post-war policy stresses the importance of trade and economic openness in creating and reinforcing democracy. The claim is that open markets have a salutary impact on the political character of the regimes of other countries, dissolving autocratic and authoritarian structures and encouraging more pluralistic and accountable regimes. Because trade and economic openness have liberalizing political impacts, international order that is organized around free markets promotes

---

[23] See Anne-Marie Burley, 'Toward the Age of Liberal Nations', *Harvard International Law Journal*, 33/2 (1992), pp. 393–405; and 'Law Among Liberal States: Liberal Internationalism and the Act of State Doctrine', *Columbia Law Review*, 92/8 (1992), pp. 1907–96.

[24] These arguments are developed in G. John Ikenberry, 'Liberal Hegemony: The Logic and Future of America's Postwar Order' (unpublished paper, 1997). See also Daniel Deudney and G. John Ikenberry, 'Liberal Competence: The Performance of Democracies in Great Power Balancing' (unpublished paper, 1994). For a good summary of this literature, see Kurt Taylor Gaubatz, 'Democratic States and Commitment in International Relations', *International Organization*, 50/1 (1997), pp. 109–39.

[25] Anthony Lake, 'Remarks on the Occasion of the 10th Anniversary of the Center for Democracy' (Washington, DC: 26 September 1995).

and reinforces the types of states that are most inclined to pursue free markets. It is a self-reinforcing order.

Several different lines of argument are advanced. The most general argument is that trade has a positive impact on economic growth and this in turn encourages democratic institutions, and this in turn creates more stable and peaceful international relations. The logic is straightforward: FREE TRADE ⟹ PROSPERITY ⟹ DEMOCRACY ⟹ PEACE. The two claims that are introduced in this area are that trade promotes economic growth and that economic growth encourages democracy. The first of these arguments is an almost undisputed truth, at least among economists and theorists of economic growth. Economists understand why trade stimulates growth faster than within closed economies—factors of production are employed more efficiently, allowing the development and spread of technology and stimulating productivity gains. Opponents of free trade rarely dispute the growth effects of trade, but rather focus on its potentially adverse distributive, social, or national security implications.[26]

The argument that economic growth encourages democracies is more complicated and debated. But as two scholars recently summarize one version of the argument, 'it is only under conditions of prosperity and capitalism that elites can accept defeat peacefully at the polls, secure in the knowledge that they will have fair opportunities to regain political power, and opportunities for economic benefit when they are out of power'.[27] Moreover, there is strong empirical evidence to support the claim. Not all democracies are high-income and prosperous, but there is a strong correlation.[28]

The classic statement of the theory was advanced by Lipset in the 1950s, who attempted to explain why economic development had a positive effect on the likelihood of a country establishing and maintaining democracy. Two intervening factors were most important. First, economic development tends to produce increases in education, which in turn promotes a political culture and political attitudes that are conducive to democracy; and second, economic development tends to produce a social structure dominated by a rising middle class, which moderates class struggle and the appeal of anti-democratic parties and ideologies and increases the size of the population that supports democratic parties.[29] In this view, a rising middle class is the key to the rise and maintenance of democratic institutions, and this class increases in size and importance with economic growth and capitalist development.[30]

---

[26] See Douglas A. Irwin, *Against the Tide: An Intellectual History of Free Trade* (Princeton: Princeton University Press, 1996).

[27] Thomas J. Volgy and John E. Schwarz, 'Free Trade, Economic Inequality and the Stability of Democracies in the Democratic Core of Peace', *European Journal of International Relations*, 3/2 (1997), p. 240.

[28] See John B. Longregan and Keith Poole, 'Does High Income Promote Democracy?', *World Politics*, 49 (1996), pp. 1–30.

[29] Seymour Martin Lipset, 'Some Social Requisites of Democracy: Economic Development and Political Legitimacy', *American Political Science Review*, 53 (1959), pp. 69–105.

[30] The literature is summarized in Dietrich Rueschemeyer, Evelyne Huber Stephens, and John D. Stephens, *Capitalist Development and Democracy* (Chicago: University of Chicago Press, 1992). These authors modify the Lipset model, stressing the specific role of the urban working class.

Subsequent debate on this argument has stressed complicating factors, particularly the role of income inequality, which some argue tends to counteract the positive influence of economic development on democracy. There also seem to be non-linear and threshold effects on the relationship: economic growth is most important at the lower and medium levels of development, and after some threshold the level of democracy tends to hold regardless of further economic development.[31]

This claim about the positive impact of trade on economic development and economic development on politics has had a long and well-established hold on official American foreign policy thinking. The American embrace of free trade and open markets gained its most secure foothold at the turn of the twentieth century with the articulation of the Open Door policy, driven most forcefully by American efforts to gain market access in Asia. Later, during the progressive era, arguments in favour of free trade moved beyond the simple struggle for markets or the restatement of Ricardo's classic claims. It was Wilson who claimed that free trade would have the added benefit of checking or undercutting domestic monopoly. Protectionism encouraged collusion and reinforced the dominance of big business, and this in turn distorted democratic politics.[32] This progressive era view was seen to hold outside the United States as well—free trade was a necessary condition for the spread of democracy abroad.

This liberal view makes an intensely materialist assumption: that economics shapes politics. Free trade and open markets strengthen society and create zones of autonomy that limit the reach of the state, empowering individuals and altering what they want and expect out of politics. This view lies at the core of American foreign policy efforts at 'engagement'—whether it is directed at South Africa, the Soviet Union, or China. Often unappreciated by the anti-democratic elites whose countries are engaged, trade and market openings are the sharp end of a liberalizing wedge that ultimately promotes economic development and democracy.

Free Trade, Economic Interdependence, and Peace

A related argument is that free trade and open markets promote not just economic advancement and democracy, but also encourage more intense and interdependent relations between states, which in turn foster mutual dependence and new vested interests that favour greater restraint and stability in international relations. This claim takes several forms. Some argue that trade makes states more prosperous, and therefore they are less likely to have grievances that lead to war. 'Prosperous neighbours are the best neighbours',

---

[31] See Edward N. Muller, 'Economic Determinants of Democracy', *American Sociological Review*, 60 (1995), pp. 966–82.

[32] See Arthur S. Link, *Woodrow Wilson and the Progressive Era, 1910–1917* (New York: Harper and Row, 1954).

remarked Roosevelt era Treasury official Harry Dexter White.[33] Others argue that trade creates more mutual dependencies, societies expand their mutual interests, and more stable relations result. Still others stress the transnational linkages that are fostered which help reshape political processes and identities. But the basic argument is clear: free and open trade breaks down the sources of antagonism and war.

These claims were advanced by American officials involved in the creation of an open trading system after World War II. The most forceful advocates of this position came from the Department of State and its Secretary, Cordell Hull. Throughout the Roosevelt presidency, Hull and other State Department officials consistently held the conviction that an open international trading system was central to American economic and security interests and was also fundamental to the maintenance of peace. Hull believed that bilateralism and the economic blocs of the 1930s, practised by Germany and Japan but also Britain, were the root cause of the instability of the period and the onset of war.[34] Charged with responsibility for commercial policy, the State Department championed tariff reduction agreements, most prominently in the 1934 Reciprocal Trade Agreement Act and the 1938 US-British trade agreement. Trade officials at the State Department saw liberal trade as a core American interest that reached back to the Open Door policy of the 1890s.[35] In the early years of World War II, this liberal economic vision dominated initial American thinking about the future world order and became the initial opening position as the United States engaged Britain over the post-war settlement. Emerging from the war with the largest and most competitive economy, an open economic order would serve American interests. An open system was also seen as an essential element of a stable world political order; it would discourage ruinous economic competition and protectionism that was a source of depression and war. But just as importantly, this vision of openness—a sort of 'economic one worldism'—would lead to an international order in which American 'hands on' management would be modest. The system would, in effect, govern itself.[36]

The connection between trade and the sources of order is made at several levels. There is an expectation that trade will create new forms of mutual

[33] Alfred E. Eckes, Jr., *A Search for Solvency: Bretton Woods and the International Monetary System, 1944–71* (Austin: University of Texas Press, 1971), p. 52. This was a reflection of the Cobdenite philosophy that trade protection and tariffs were linked to political conflict and, ultimately, war.

[34] As Secretary Hull argued, 'unhampered trade dovetailed with peace; high tariffs, trade barriers, and unfair economic competition, with war'. Cordell Hull, *The Memoirs of Cordell Hull*, vol. 1 (New York: Macmillan, 1948), p. 81.

[35] Herbert Feis, the State Department's economic adviser, noted the continuity of the department's position when he argued during the war that 'the extension of the Open Door remains a sound American aim'. See Herbert Feis, 'Economics and Peace', *Foreign Policy Reports*, 30 (April 1944), pp. 14–19. On the State Department's commitment to a post-war open trading system, see Lloyd Gardner, *Economic Aspects of New Deal Diplomacy* (Madison: University of Wisconsin Press, 1964); Richard Gardner, *Sterling-Dollar Diplomacy: The Origins and the Prospects of Our International Economic Order* (New York: McGraw Hill, 1969); and Alfred E. Eckes, Jr., *Opening America's Market: U.S. Foreign Policy Since 1776* (Chapel Hill: The University of North Carolina Press, 1995), Ch. 5.

[36] This argument is made in G. John Ikenberry, 'Rethinking the Origins of American Hegemony', *Political Science Quarterly*, 104 (1989), pp. 375–400.

dependence through the progressive evolution of specialization and functional differentiation of national economies. This process in turn creates a blurring of national economic borders and interests, which in turn debilitates the capacity of the state to determine and act upon narrow nationalist economic interests. The state's interests are broadened to include a stake in the stability and functioning of the larger international order. At the level of the state, the expansion of trade and investment creates new vested interests in economic openness and the political organization of international politics that is congenial with openness. For example, there is evidence that when firms invest overseas they not only develop an interest in international conditions that foster and protect those operations, but they also become a new voice back home in advocating the opening of the domestic market.[37]

More generally, when American foreign policy has sought to bring countries into the open trade order, they have had expectations that these involvements would have 'socializing' effects on these countries that would be conducive to the maintenance of order. Nowhere was this more explicit than in the Clinton administration's approach toward China. The administration argued that a 'China as a power that is stable, open, and non-aggressive, that embraces free markets, political pluralism, and the rule of law, that works with us to build a secure international order—that kind of China, rather than a China turned inward and confrontational, is deeply in the interests of the American people'. To move China in this direction, the administration embraced the dynamic vision of liberalism: that integration into the international economic order would promote reform at home, encourage the development of the rule of law, and socialize China into the prevailing order. This liberal vision was put directly by Clinton:

China's economic growth has made it more and more dependent on the outside world for investment, markets, and energy. Last year it was the second recipient of foreign direct investment in the world. These linkages bring with them powerful forces for change. Computers and the Internet, fax machines and photo-copiers, modems and satellites all increase the exposure to people, ideas, and the world beyond China's borders. The effect is only just beginning to be felt.[38]

This is essentially the same argument made by Wilson, Roosevelt, Truman, and other American presidents. It now takes a more sweeping and vivid form because of recent developments: the dramatic collapse of the Soviet Union, the rapid rise of new technologies, and the continuing work of the relentless integrating forces of trade and investment. Free markets tend to force open societies, liberalize politics, and integrate and socialize countries.

---

[37] Helen Milner and David B. Yoffie, 'Between Free Trade and Protectionism: Strategic Trade Policy and a Theory of Corporate Trade Demands', *International Organization*, 42/2 (1989), pp. 239–72; Hidetaka Yoshimatsu, 'Economic Interdependence and the Making of Trade Policy: Industrial Demand for an Open Market in Japan', *The Pacific Review*, 11/1 (1998), pp. 28–50.

[38] White House Press Release, 'Remarks by the President in Address on China and the National Interest' (24 October 1997).

Institutions and the Containment of Conflict

Another enduring and strongly held liberal view that is deeply entrenched in American foreign policy thinking is that institutions matter. The claim is that when states create and operate within international institutions, the scope and severity of their conflicts are reduced. The reasons involve a series of arguments about the relationship between states, interests, and the logic of dispute resolution. But fundamentally, when states agree to operate within international institutions (within a particular realm), they are in effect creating a political process that shapes, constrains, and channels state actions in desirable ways. Interstate institutions establish a political process that helps to contain conflict by creating mechanisms that can move the dispute toward some sort of mutually acceptable resolution.

At the heart of the American political tradition is the view that institutions can serve to overcome and integrate diverse and competing interests—state, section, ethnicity, class, and religion. American constitutionalism is infused with the belief that state power can be restrained and rights and protections of individuals insured though the many institutional devices and procedures that they specify. Separation of power, checks and balances, and other devices of the balanced constitution were advanced as ways to ensure limits on power. Theories of institutional balance, separation, oversight, and judicial review have an intellectual lineage that traces from Aristotle to Locke and Montesquieu. By specializing functional roles and dispersing political authority, the concentration of power and the possibility of tyranny is prevented.[39] In this way, institutional design can help define and ensure the durability of desirable political order.

It is this deeply held view that has made American officials so inclined to build and operate international institutions. Indeed, the historical record is striking. When the United States has had an opportunity to organize international relations—such as after the two world wars—it has been unusually eager to establish regimes and multilateral institutions.[40] After 1919 it was the League of Nations, and after 1945 it was a flood of institutions with different purposes, functions and scope. The American architects of post-war order are justly famous for their efforts to institutionalize just about everything: security, monetary relations, trade, development assistance, peacekeeping and dispute resolution.[41] When one compares and contrasts *Pax Britannica* and *Pax Americana*, one of the first things to note is that the American era was much more institutionalized.[42]

[39] See M. Richter, *The Political Theory of Montesquieu* (Cambridge: Cambridge University Press, 1977).

[40] Of course, the United States has also been assiduous is ensuring that there are limits and escape clauses in the binding effects of institutions.

[41] On the post-war surge in institution building, see Craig Murphy, *International Organization and Industrial Change* (New York: Oxford University Press, 1994).

[42] For comparisons of American and British hegemony, see Robert Gilpin, *U.S. Power and the Multinational Corporation: The Political Economy of Foreign Direct Investment* (New York: Basic Books, 1975); and David Lake, 'British and American Hegemony Compared: Lessons for the Current Era of

Of course, American interest in institutionalizing international relations is driven by a variety of factors. It mattered that the United States was in an unprecedented power position after the war. The sheer asymmetry of power relations between the United States and its potential post-war partners made institutions an attractive way to reassure Europe and Japan that it would neither dominate nor abandon them, and a functioning political process made possible by the wide array of institutions was useful in legitimizing America's post-war hegemony.[43] Likewise, the industrial great powers at mid-twentieth century passage were much more complex and interdependent than in the early nineteenth century—so there was just a lot more stuff to organize than before. The political calculus and social purpose of states had evolved, and this was reflected in the functional imperatives of the 1940s.[44]

But there are specific expectations that Americans had about how states operating within international institutions would dampen conflict and mitigate anarchy. Two types of general institutional 'effects' are most important: institutions constrain and socialize. Institutions constrain in that the rules and roles that institutions set out for states serve to create incentives and costs that channel states in particular directions. Violating the rules may create costs by provoking responses by others—such as sanctions and retaliation—or constraints may be manifest by creating 'sunk costs' that make it relatively more expensive to start from scratch and create a new institution. International institutions are not unlike domestic institutions; they create a 'political landscape' that provides advantages, constraints, obstacles, and opportunities for actors who inhabit them.[45] Properly engineered, they can bias state actions toward the desired rules and roles.

International institutions can also socialize states, which happens when they influence the way in which states think about their interests. In becoming socialized to accept certain ways of thinking, as Martha Finnemore argues, states 'internalize the roles and rules as scripts to which they conform, not out of conscious choice, but because they understand these behaviours to be appropriate'.[46] The underlying view is that the interests and preferences of states are not completely fixed, and that institutions could play a role on cultivating certain types of foreign and domestic policy orientations. States might initially agree to operate in an international institution because of the manipulation of incentives by the hegemon, but after a while through a complex

Decline', in Michael Fry (ed.), *History, the White House, and the Kremlin: Statesmen as Historians* (New York: Columbia University Press, 1991), pp. 106–22.

[43] These arguments are made in G. John Ikenberry, *After Victory: Institutions, Strategic Restraint, and the Rebuilding of Order After Major Wars* (Princeton: Princeton University Press, 2000).

[44] See John G. Ruggie, *Winning the Peace: America and World Order in the New Era* (New York: Columbia University Press, 1996).

[45] For an overview of this perspective on institutions, see James G. March and Johan Olsen, 'The New Institutionalism: Organizational Factors in Political Life', *American Political Science Review*, 78 (1984), pp. 734–49.

[46] Martha Finnemore, *National Interests in International Society* (Ithaca: Cornell University Press, 1996), p. 29.

process of socialization the rules and values of the institution would be embraced by the state as right and proper.[47]

American officials hoped that the post-war institutions would 'rub off' on the other states that agreed to join. In creating the United Nations, officials worked under the assumption that the establishment of mechanisms for dispute resolution would channel conflicts in non-violent directions.[48] In creating the GATT, officials also anticipated the economic conflicts could be trapped and diffused in framework of rules, standards, and dispute resolution procedures. In establishing the Marshall Plan for aiding post-war Europe, American officials insisted that the Europeans create an joint institution that would force them to work together in allocating funds, and the hope was that a habit of cooperation would emerge.[49]

Both these ways in which institutions matter echo the American political tradition. The notion of institutional constraints is implicit in republican political theory, where the constitution, separation of powers, and the institutional layers and limits on authority create power distribution and checking mechanisms that inhibit the aggrandizement of power. The view that institutions can socialize is also an extension of the classical liberal view that the political system is not simply a mechanical process where preferences are aggregated, but it is a system where persuasion and justification matter as well.

Community and Identity

A final liberal claim is that a common identity among states facilitates the establishment of a peaceful and durable order. Values and a sense of community matter as sources of order—not just power and interests. Again, there are several layers of argument. One is that states with similar political values and social purposes will be more likely to understand each other, which facilitates cooperation. Another is that if the common values are liberal and democratic, substantive norms exist that specify expectations about how conflicts are to be resolved.

American foreign policy thinkers have been attracted to this liberal view, but the specific way they have sought to identify and develop common identity and community has varied. Wilson talked about a 'community of power' and associated common identity with democracy. This followed directly from his view that the world stood on the brink of a great democratic revolution, and so to build order around a universal democratic community was obvious. The problem was that the world did not culminate in democratic revolution after 1919; Russia, of course, moved in a different direction, but continental Europe also failed to develop democratic societies in the way Wilson expected.

[47] See G. John Ikenberry and Charles Kupchan, 'Socialization and Hegemonic Power', *International Organization*, 43/3 (1990), pp. 283315.

[48] See Ruth B. Russell, *A History of The United Nations Charter: The Role of the United States, 1940–1945* (Washington, DC: The Brookings Institution, 1958).

[49] See Ernst H. Van Der Beugel, *From Marshall Plan to Atlantic Partnership* (Amsterdam: Elsevier Publishing Co., 1966).

As a result, the universalism of the League of Nations was built on unfulfilled expectations.

This failure was a central lesson of the generation of American leaders who followed Wilson. The lesson was not that democracy was unrelated to American security and a durable post-war order, but that universalism was a bridge too far. Democracy was not as easily spread or deeply rooted as Wilson had assumed. Building order around like-mind democracies was still a desired goal of Roosevelt and Truman, but the realm of world politics that would fit within this order and the way the order would be institutionalized differed after World War II.[50] The democratic community would exist primarily within the Atlantic world, and its institutional foundations would be more complex and layered.

This view was articulated by a variety of officials and activists in the 1940s who were primarily concerned with creating political order among the democracies of the North Atlantic region. The vision was of a community or union between the United States, Britain, and the wider Atlantic world. Ideas of an Atlantic union can be traced to the turn of the twentieth century and a few British and American statesmen and thinkers, such as John Hay, British Ambassador to Washington Lord Bryce, American Ambassador to London Walter Hines Page, Admiral Alfred T. Mahan, and Henry Adams. These writers and political figures all grasped the unusual character and significance of Anglo-American comity, and they embraced a vision of closer transatlantic ties.[51] These ideas were articulated and rearticulated over the following decades. During World War II, Walter Lippmann gave voice to this view, that the 'Atlantic Ocean is not the frontier between Europe and the Americas. It is the inland sea of a community of nations allied with one another by geography, history, and vital necessity'.[52]

Various experiences and interests fed into the Atlantic idea. One was strategic and articulated during and after the two world wars. Suspicious of Woodrow Wilson's League of Nations proposal, French Premier Georges Clemenceau proposed in 1919 an alliance between France, Britain, and the United States—an alliance only among what he called 'constitutional' countries.[53] The failure of the League of Nations reaffirmed in the minds of many Americans and Europeans the virtues of a less universal security community that encompassed the North Atlantic area.

Others focused on the protection of the shared democratic values that united the Atlantic world. These ideas were most famously expressed in

[50] On the lessons drawn by order builders in 1945 from the failures of 1919, see David Fromkin, *In the Time of the Americans: The Generation that Changed America's Role in the World* (New York: Alfred Knopf, 1995).

[51] See James Robert Huntley, *Uniting the Democracies: Institutions of the Emerging Atlantic-Pacific System* (New York: New York University Press, 1980), p. 4.

[52] Walter Lippmann, *U.S. Foreign Policy: Shield of the Republic* (Boston: Little, Brown, 1943), p. 83.

[53] The French proposal was to transform the League of Nations into a North Atlantic treaty organization—a union complete with an international army and a general staff. See Thomas J. Knock, *To End All Wars: Woodrow Wilson and the Quest for a New World Order* (New York: Oxford University Press, 1992), pp. 221–2.

Clarence Streit's 1939 book, *Union Now: The Proposal for Inter-democracy Federal Union*.[54] Concerned with the rise of fascism and militarism and the fragility of the Western democracies in the wake of a failed League of Nations, Streit proposed a federal union of the North Atlantic democracies.[55] In the years that followed, a fledgling Atlantic Union movement came to life. An Atlantic Union Committee was organized after the war and prominent Americans called for the creation of various sorts of Atlantic organizations and structures. American and European officials were willing to endorse principles of Atlantic community and unity—most explicitly in the 1941 Atlantic Charter—but they were less interested in supranational organization.

In more recent years, American officials have returned to this theme. In the aftermath of the cold war, the Bush administration was quick to remind its allies that they were more than a defensive alliance against communism—that the alliance was equally a positive embodiment of the values and community that they shared. In major speeches both President Bush and Secretary of State Baker talked about Euro-Atlantic Community and the 'zone of democratic peace'. It had been relatively easy during the cold war to talk about the unity of the 'free world'. After 1991, this became more difficult and the older notions of democratic community were rediscovered. The Clinton administration also came to evoke similar sentiments about democratic community in making the case for NATO expansion.

There is an inherent ambiguity is specifying the precise character of democratic community, and this is reflected in foreign policy thinking. Some draw the borders of shared community rather narrowly. Samuel Huntington's famous argument about civilization, for example, has a rather limited notion of the West and shared community. It exists primarily in the Atlantic world. Others have more expansive notions. James Huntley has developed an elaborate set of criteria for determining the 'like-mindedness' of states, which in turn explains why 'some countries and their governments are more ready than others to engage in sophisticated forms of international cooperation'. These include a stable, experienced, and advanced democratic regime, advanced and knowledge-based modern economies and societies, and a substantial body of diplomats, civil servants, political leaders, and other elites who are oriented toward international cooperation.[56] In this view, democratic community is not absolute, but runs along a gradient, concentrated in a core of states and moving outward to less similar states.

---

[54] Clarence Streit, *Union Now: The Proposal for Inter-democracy Federal Union* (New York: Harper and Brothers, 1939).

[55] It would be a 'union of these few peoples in a great federal republic built on and for the thing they share most, their common democratic principle of government for the sake of individual freedom'. Streit, *Union Now*, p. 4.

[56] James Robert Huntley, *Pax Democratica: A Strategy for the Twenty-first Century* (London: Macmillan, 1998), Appendix A.

The Coalitional Basis of Liberal Grand Strategy

These liberal claims and strategies are compatible, even synchronous, in some deep sense, and they have come together at various historical junctures, most fully after World War II. They have rarely been thought of or championed as a single package. But in the 1940s they came together. Today, with the end of the cold war, they are ideas and strategies that can be seen more clearly as a distinctive American grand strategy.

In the 1940s the various pieces came together. The free traders at the State Department had a clear line on the post-war order: it would be a free trade system. Others at the Treasury and New Dealers were eager to see international institutions established that would provide fixed mechanisms for the governance of the post-war economy. Other activists were focused on the United Nations and the creation of political governance institutions. Still others, such as George Kennan, were interested in rebuilding Europe, as a stable counterweight to the Soviet Union.

In the background, other officials were focused on American geopolitical interests and the Eurasian rimlands. This is where American strategic thinkers began their debates in the 1930s, as they witnessed the collapse of the world economy and the emergence of German and Japanese regional blocs. The question these thinkers pondered was whether the United States could remain as a great industrial power within the confines of the western hemisphere. What were the minimum geographical requirements for the country's economic and military viability? For all practical purposes this question was answered by the time the United States entered the war. An American hemispheric bloc would not be sufficient; the United States must have security of markets and raw materials in Asia and Europe.[57] It must seek openness, access, and balance in Europe and Asia.

This view that America must have access to Asian and European markets and resources, and must therefore not let a prospective adversary control the Eurasian land mass, was also embraced by post-war defence planners. Defence officials also saw access to Asian and European raw materials, and the prevention of their control by a prospective enemy, as an American security interest. Leffler notes that 'Stimson, Patterson, McCloy, and Assistant Secretary Howard C. Peterson agreed with Forrestal that long-term American prosperity required open markets, unhindered access to raw materials, and the rehabilitation of much—if not all—of Eurasia along liberal capitalist lines'.[58] Some defence studies went further, and argued that post-war threats to Eurasian access and openness were more social and economic than military. It was economic

---

[57] The culmination of this debate and the most forceful statement of the new consensus was presented in Nicholas John Spykman's *America's Strategy in World Politics: The United States and the Balance of Power* (New York: Harcourt, Brace, 1942).

[58] Melvin Leffler, 'The American Conception of National Security and the Beginnings of the Cold War, 1945–48', *American Historical Review*, 89/2 (1984), p. 358.

turmoil and political upheaval that were the real threats to American security, as they invited the subversion of liberal democratic societies and Western-oriented governments. Access to resources and markets, socioeconomic stability, political pluralism, and American security interests were all tied together.

The desirability of open markets, democratic states, and international institutions was something that liberal visionaries and hard-nosed geopolitical strategists could agree upon. Indeed, the durability of America's liberal grand strategy is partly due to the multiple agendas that are served in the process. This was true in 1945 as well as today. State Department officials advancing notions of an open world economy were reinforced by defence planners who linked American security interests to market and resource access to Asian and European regions. State Department planners, such as George Kennan, who were primarily concerned with rebuilding the economic and political infrastructure and wherewithal of western Europe made common cause with other officials who were concerned with encouraging the emergence of continental European governments committed to an open and integrated Western order. This convergence on liberal democratic order was facilitated by the reluctance of the Truman administration to pursue more far-reaching options, such as simple free trade or world government. An institutionalized and managed Western order that centred on openness and democracy was an appealing objective to some and an indispensable means to an end to others.

Conclusion

For those who thought cooperation among the advanced industrial democracies was primarily driven by cold war threats, the last few years must appear puzzling. Relations among the major Western countries have not deteriorated or broken down. What the cold war focus misses is an appreciation of the other and less heralded post-war American project: building a liberal democratic order within the West. The ideas, practices, lessons, and designs that American officials brought to bear on the problem of rebuilding order among the Western states was, taken together, a distinctively American grand strategy.

The robustness of the ideas behind Western liberal democratic order was partly a result of the manifold lessons and experiences that stimulated these ideas. It is sometimes argued that what differentiated the 'successful' settlement after 1945 from the 'unsuccessful' settlement after 1919 is that it was based on more 'realist' understandings of power and order. Roosevelt, for example, was sensitive to considerations of power, and his notion of the 'Four Policemen' was a self-conscious effort to build a post-war settlement around a great-power collective security organization. But the actual post-war settlement reflected a more mixed set of lessons and calculations. 'Realist' lessons from the League of Nations debacle of the 1920s were combined with 'liberal' lessons from the regional imperialism and mercantilist conflict of the 1930s.

The United States did show more willingness to use its military victory and occupation policy after 1945 to implement its post-war aims in Germany and Japan, but those aims were manifestly liberal in character.

It is commonly argued today that post-cold war American foreign policy has lost its way. The loss of containment as an organizing concept and grand strategy has left some bewildered. But if the other elements of American post-war grand strategy sketched in this paper are recognized, this perspective is less compelling. The United States has a deeper and more sophisticated set of policies and practices than a narrow focus on American cold war diplomacy would reveal. So to analysts who equate grand strategy with 'containment' and 'managing the balance of power', the liberal strategies of the United States will not be recognized, and these analysts will acknowledge the arrival of a new American grand strategy only when a new threat emerges that helps stimulate and organize balancing policies. But this is an intellectually and historically impoverished view, and it misses huge foreign policy opportunities in the meanwhile.

What is striking, in fact, and perhaps ironic, about American foreign policy after the cold war is how deeply bipartisan liberal internationalism is in foreign policy circles. Reagan and Bush pursued policies that reflected a strong commitment to the expansion of democracy, markets, and the rule of law. The Reagan administration's involvements in El Salvador, the Philippines, Chile, and elsewhere all reflected this orientation. Its shift from the Nixon-Kissinger 'permanent coexistence' approach to the Soviet Union toward a more active pursuit of a human rights and democracy promotion agenda also revealed this orientation. Following in line with a view articulated by Wilson, Roosevelt, Truman and others, the Reagan administration articulated the democratic peace argument—that the regime type of other states matters, and if they are democracies they will be less threatening to the United States. Jeane Kirkpatrick and other Kissinger-type realists were brought into the administration, but their view that democracy promotion was a counterproductive luxury did not dominate.

Today, a foreign policy agenda organized around business internationalism, multilateral economic and security organizations, and democratic community building is embraced by elites in both parties. It is a coalition not unlike the one that formed in the 1940s. Some elites embrace democracy, the rule of law, and human rights as an end in itself; others see its promotion as a way to expand and safeguard business and markets; and others see indirect payoffs for national security and alliance management. The Clinton administration's doctrine of 'enlargement' and its policy of engagement toward China were mere reflections of this long-standing liberal American orientation.[59] Many of the speeches that Clinton administration officials made on enlargement and engagement could just as easily have been generated by Reagan and Bush

---

[59] See Douglas Brinkley, 'Democratic Enlargement: The Clinton Doctrine', *Foreign Policy*, 106 (1997), pp. 111–27.

speech writers. There were differences of details, but the two major parties did not articulate two radically—or even moderately—different world-views.

Part of the reason for the stability of this general liberal strategic orientation is that the overall organizational character of the American system encourages it. International business is a coalition partner. Engagement of China, for example, was really the only option, given the huge stakes that American multinationals have in the Chinese and Asian markets. The United States also has a huge domestic constituency for democracy promotion and numerous non-government organizations keep the issue on the agenda. The groups and associations that have sought to build a more formal Atlantic community are also at work articulating notions of wider democratic community. Transnational groups that support the United Nations, the IMF and World Bank, and other major multilateral organizations also feed into the American foreign policy process. In other words, American foreign policy is only part of what generates and sustains the American liberal orientation. Democracies— particularly big and rich ones like the United States—seem to have an inherent sociability. Democracies are biased, structurally speaking, in favour of engagement, enlargement, interdependence, and institutionalization, and they are biased against containment, separation, balance, and exclusion. The United States is doomed to pursue a liberal grand strategy.

6

America's Identity, Democracy Promotion and National Interests: Beyond Realism, Beyond Idealism

HENRY R. NAU

Introduction

What role does or should democracy play in foreign policy? Two answers come from traditional perspectives on American foreign policy. The idealist tradition concludes that democracy should play a big role, such that the purpose of American foreign policy becomes either to perfect democracy at home and stay out of foreign affairs—isolationism—or to promote democracy abroad and transform world affairs—internationalism. The realist tradition, conversely, argues that democracy should play only a minor role, if any. The true purpose of foreign policy, realists say, is to defend the national interest, and that is best done by balancing power among states and preventing the domestic political values of any one state, apparently including democracies, from dominating the values of other states.

The idealist and realist traditions confound the effort to assess the real influence of democracy on American foreign policy. Democracy matters either a lot or not at all, when in fact it probably matters some or most of the time depending on the circumstances. Even in extreme circumstances, such as direct attack, democracy is not irrelevant. The United States seeks to survive as a liberal democratic society, not as a piece of geography that hosts a despotic or democratic society—that is, whatever it takes to survive.

To assess the real influence of democracy on US foreign policy, analysis has to surmount the dualism of the idealist and realist traditions. Both traditions pose a sharp dichotomy between a democratic society at home, which eschews force, and a balance of power system abroad, which uses force. This New World-Old World dichotomy, while it may have captured America's situation at its founding, is no longer applicable as America enters the twenty-first century. Today, the entire industrial world is democratic, and much of the rest of the world is democratizing. At the same time, the United States and other democracies face growing conflicts and potential violence at home—from racial divisions, cultural clashes, immigrant issues and terrorist threats. In short, much of the Old World has become New, while the New World encounters more of the ethnic and cultural tensions of the Old.

A new approach is needed that combines idealism and realism. Such an approach must take into account a nation's internal agenda and self-image as well as its external national interests. It examines under what kind of external circumstances a country's internal characteristics are likely to play a role in that country's foreign policy. Internal factors shape the foreign policy of any country, democratic or non-democratic. In the case of the United States, this approach helps us to judge better where the promotion of democracy fits in America's foreign policy relations with other countries.

An Identity Approach

The new approach centres on national identity as the starting point of foreign policy. Every country behaves abroad, at least in part, on the basis of its domestic ideals and politics. America's domestic ideals are those of a diverse democratic society. These ideals constitute a self-image that evolves over time and influences how the United States organizes its own power to pursue foreign affairs as well as how it perceives the power of other nations in the international system. This self-image is not more important than power or national interests, as idealists would claim. But it does affect how the United States mobilizes and legitimizes its power and whether the power of other countries, great or small, threatens US foreign policy objectives—all of which realism ignores. Foreign policy becomes a consequence of both how much wealth and power a country has, relative to other nations, *and* whether that country perceives the wealth and power of other nations to be potentially helpful or harmful to its foreign policy purposes.

The traditional way of approaching US—or any country's—foreign policy is to define the national interest. The guru of such thinking was Hans J. Morgenthau.[1] In a seminal textbook on political realism, Morgenthau penned the doctrine of national interest: 'The main signpost that helps political realism to find its way through the landscape of international politics is the concept of interest defined in terms of power.' By this concept, Morgenthau meant that states act mainly to acquire wealth and defend national survival. This does not mean, as Morgenthau hastened to add, that nations always or only pursue national interest and power, any more than economists, who make a similar assumption about self-interest, claim that individuals always pursue materialist goals. States also act on moral or ideological grounds. 'Political realism', Morgenthau insisted, 'is aware of the moral significance of political action' but, Morgenthau added, 'political realism refuses to identify the moral aspirations of a particular nation with the moral laws that govern

---

[1] See Hans J. Morgenthau, 6th edn, *Politics Among Nations: The Struggle for Power and Peace* (New York: Alfred A. Knopf, 1985). The quotations in this paragraph are from pp. 5, 12 and 13.

the universe'. States pursue different moral aspirations. Yet they all pursue power to achieve those aspirations. Thus, the pursuit of power is more universal and fundamental to international affairs than the pursuit of moral purpose. For Morgenthau, this fact created the possibility of a 'science' of international politics. A statesman who did not believe in the pursuit of power was like a scientist who did not believe in the law of gravity.[2] He could make no sense out of the world of international politics and, more importantly, could not act effectively to influence international politics.

The assumption in this traditional approach is that states have different and often conflicting moral or political aspirations. In short, they have different internal self-images: different governments, economic systems, cultures, and historical experiences. They pursue wealth and power externally because they need to defend and promote these self-images internally. What if, however, states begin to share similar political self-images or, in Morgenthan's terms, to pursue common moral aspirations? That is the case today among the United States and a growing number of other democratic countries. All these countries share liberal political systems that constrain the pursuit of power domestically. In each, military and police power is subjected to the rule of law, and economic power is tempered by social justice. Although liberal democracies differ in other areas—cultural and historical characteristics—their common political systems appear to override other differences and reduce the significance of military conflict in their relations with one another. Democracies do not or almost never fight other democracies. This democracy-peace phenomenon is not well understood.[3] Nevertheless, it is a striking feature of contemporary international reality. The great industrialized powers, all of which are democratic, do not threaten or seek to defend themselves against one another by the deployment or use of military force. Lest we forget, these are the same nations that have been fighting each other continuously for over 500 years, creating the very system of national interests and balance of power that Morgenthau investigated. Contrary to Morgenthau's logic, however, these countries now pursue common internal political aspirations that visibly circumscribe the competitive external pursuit of military power.

There is powerful evidence that domestic self-images matter in foreign policy as much as national interests. When these self-images converge, they mitigate conflict; when they diverge, they exacerbate it. This is true among non-democracies as well as democracies. The Holy Alliance was a nineteenth century alignment among conservative monarchies in Russia, Prussia and Austria. These countries joined together to protect their common monarchic political systems and to prevent revolution against the monarchy in other countries. While Great Britain joined this group initially to balance power against external threats, it broke away from the group as its domestic

---

[2] See Hans J. Morgenthau, *In Defense of the National Interest* (New York: Alfred A. Knopf, 1952), pp. 323.

[3] For a sceptical summary of this research and evidence, see Steve Chan, 'In Search of Democratic Peace: Problems and Promise', *Mershon International Studies Review*, 41/1 (1997), pp. 59–93.

institutions evolved toward more liberal representative standards. For Great Britain, a diverging liberal self-image made foreign policy cooperation with conservative monarchies more difficult.[4]

Diverging self-images may also exacerbate conflict. The cold war was particularly dangerous not just because the United States and the Soviet Union were nuclear superpowers. They also disagreed about the political purposes that power served. One sought a liberal democratic future for Europe; the other a totalitarian communist future. In central Europe, they disagreed to the point that they created two Germanies and two halves of Europe—one liberal, one communist.[5] If their domestic systems had been more similar, their conflict would have been less severe. John Lewis Gaddis, perhaps the most respected historian of the cold war, makes the point: 'If the Soviet Union had been the superpower that it actually was, but with a system of checks and balances that could have constrained Stalin's authoritarian tendencies, a Cold War might have happened, but it could hardly have been as dangerous or as protracted a conflict.'[6]

Thus, foreign policy begins with how a nation thinks about and organizes itself internally to project its economic and military power abroad. Mutual self-images are as much a part of the relationships among nations as military balances and trade. Indeed, in a reversal of conventional national interest logic, states do not start in isolation and pursue wealth and power toward one another. Rather, military balances and trade exist (or do not exist) between states because of the particular way in which they view themselves and one another. Between countries that value fundamentally different principles for organizing their riches, military balances may predominate. Between countries that value similar principles, military balances may be irrelevant. The United States has a First Amendment prohibiting the establishment of religion by the state; Iran has a state established by religion. Neither society considers the principle of the other society to be legitimate. The two societies may tolerate one another, but if they live in close proximity to one another they are likely to keep a keen eye on the relative balance between their military and economic power. Conversely, Canada and the United States have similar protection for religious diversity. For this and other reasons of similar political identity, they relate to one another mostly by trade and interactions between civil societies, despite a dramatic imbalance in military power.

---

[4] For a helpful discussion of the Holy Alliance, see Henry Kissinger, *Diplomacy* (New York: Simon and Schuster, 1994), Ch. 4.

[5] This ideological or, less pejoratively, political aspect of the cold war was always present, but it was played down during the cold war for fear that it might exacerbate the conflict and trigger a nuclear war. See my essay 'Rethinking Economics, Politics and Security in Europe', in Richard Perle (ed.), *Reshaping Western Security: The US Faces a United Europe* (Washington, DC: The American Enterprise Institute Press, 1991), pp. 11–39; and Thomas Risse-Kappen, 'Collective Identity in a Democratic Community: The case of NATO', in Peter Katzenstein (ed.), *The Culture of National Security: Norms and Identity in World Politics* (New York: Columbia University Press, 1996), pp. 357–400.

[6] John Lewis Gaddis, 'The Tragedy of Cold War History: Reflections on Revisionism', *Foreign Affairs*, 73/1 (1994), p. 145.

Combining Identity and Interests

The self-image of any nation affects its foreign policy. This is true for non-democracies as well as democracies. It would be quite astonishing if the United States behaved consistently abroad like a non-democratic totalitarian power, or if China behaved consistently abroad like a liberal democratic power. To be sure, both countries practice imperialism. But they do so in very different ways because their domestic personalities differ. The United States expands its power through commercial or ideological imperialism, China through cultural and military imperialism. Paying attention to domestic identity, therefore, is a starting point for understanding the foreign policy behaviour of all countries.

In this sense, the United States is not unique because its domestic democratic ideals influence its foreign policy. It may be unique because its foreign policy promotes domestic ideals more self-consciously than the foreign policy of other countries. But why is this so? One easy answer is that its superpowers status allows it to do so. The United States has no significant military rivals and, with the triumph of democracy, it has no ideological rivals as well. Not surprisingly, in this situation, the promotion of democracy has become a bigger feature of American foreign policy today than it has been in the past. To ascertain the role of domestic politics in foreign affairs, therefore, one needs to look first at the situation defined by the relationships among the identities and power capabilities of relevant states. The particular configuration of identity and power within the system as a whole helps us to sort out when domestic identities play a role in international affairs and what kind of role these identities play.

Figure 6.1 takes up this exercise for American foreign policy—but it bears repeating that the same exercise can be done for any country's foreign policy. It juxtaposes America's domestic identity and its national interests or power, allowing America's identity *vis-à-vis* other countries to vary across the x-axis from similar to dissimilar and America's power to vary up the y-axis from relatively equal to relatively unequal. The two axes describe a continuous spectrum of situations involving different structural configurations of identity and power.[7] Within each configuration, we can assess the relative influence of power and identity and specifically the role of democracy in American foreign policy. For convenience, we can divide Fig. 6.1 into four general areas or boxes—remembering that these are continuous possibilities, not categories.

The top-left area—box (1)—of Fig. 6.1 depicts a situation in which power is centralized and identity is homogeneous. This situation does not exist at the global level, except in the extreme case of world government. But such a situation may be emerging in selective cases at the regional level. The North

---

[7] Figure 1 portrays *structural* features of the international system. Both power and identity are measured in terms of the relative positions actors occupy in the system. The identity or power of an individual actor is not important, but the relationships of identities and power among actors are.

Configuration of self-Images

		Similar (converge)	Dissimilar (diverge)
Distribution of power	Unequal (centralized)	(1) Hierarchical institutions (NATO?)	(2) Western hegemony (WTO, IMF, WB)
	Equal (decentralized)	(3) Democratic peace (G-7, EU)	(4) Balance of power (NATO–Russia in Europe, U.S.–China in Asia, Arab–Israeli conflict in Middle East)

Figure 6.1. U.S. Domestic Identity and National Interests

Atlantic Treaty Organization (NATO) is not, strictly speaking, an hierarchical institution. Yet it does exhibit centralized decision-making processes to command and control the military power of separate NATO member states in defence against selective threats. This centralized structure was initially a response to a common threat from the former Soviet Union, but it survives after that threat has disappeared because the national identities of NATO members are now tightly integrated around similar internal democratic values and institutions. As some critics have suggested, NATO today is more a collective democratic identity in search of interests, than a traditional multinational alliance to protect existing national interests—as it was at the beginning when it included non-democratic as well as democratic countries. While these critics imply that such a collective democratic identity cannot survive without traditional threats, NATO does survive, at least for the moment, and indeed is expanding to include new members—the Czech Republic, Hungary and Poland—and new missions—so-called out-of-area threats. In box (1), the collective identity of nation states is more important than their relative power, and thus the role of democracy is paramount if the member states are democratic—or the role of some other identity factor, such as conservative monarchism, if the member states are non-democratic.

Box (1) in Fig. 6.1 also depicts the domestic situation of a given country—that is, centralized power and unified identity—and directs our attention to the domestic agenda or debate within that country about what kind of country it is and how its self-image may be changing. This domestic debate is normally neglected in national interest approaches to the study of foreign policy. The national interest is assumed to be objective, discernible by experts but less accessible to the broader public. But the domestic debate is a crucial place to begin the analysis of the role of identity in foreign affairs. If a country is badly divided about what kind of country it is—as the former Soviet Union was in the late 1980s—it is not likely to project a very strong image in its foreign policy or indeed to conduct an active foreign policy at all. On the other hand, no country is ever static or fully complacent about what kind of country it is. Debate goes on all the time, and politicians and citizen groups vie for influence and power, not just to gain economic and social (status) rewards but also to decide what purposes or self-images economic and social power in that country will serve.

One conclusion that can be drawn from box (1) about the role of democracy in American foreign policy is that it will depend in good part on the health of democracy within America itself. If the country is confused or divided about its domestic situation, democracy promotion is not likely to be a big part of its foreign policy. The preoccupation with democracy promotion today may reflect the relatively satisfied state of affairs within the American economy and society—a democracy fresh from success in the cold war against communism and a competitive, 'goldilocks' economy once again leading the industrialized world in productivity and growth.[8]

The top-right box in Fig. 6.1 illustrates a situation in which one country is dominant in terms of power but its self-image is contested by many smaller powers. Since the end of the cold war, this situation may have characterized US relations with the world in general, but it is particularly true today in US relations with developing countries. The United States is the lone nuclear superpower and leads the world economy through Western institutions such as the World Trade Organization (WTO), International Monetary Fund (IMF) and World Bank (IBRD). Yet other countries, especially developing nations in Asia, Africa and the Middle East, resist the projection of American identity, even as they are able do little about America's dominant power. They criticize democracy promotion and reject the globalization of capitalism. In the situation described by box (2), the United States faces the greatest dilemma with respect to democracy promotion. If it does too much by way of projecting democracy and free markets because its power is unchallenged, it reaps creeping resentment and eventual backlash. If it does too little because its national interests are not at stake—in the sense that no other country seriously contests American power—it risks offending other countries by neglecting them or appearing to be condescending toward them.

---

[8] Recognizing the favourable state of affairs in the American economy is not to glorify it or expect it to last for ever. Moreover, there are serious social and cultural issues that persist and divide the country. Nevertheless, there is a reluctance within the academic world and media to acknowledge, let alone explain, success. American leaders have made some good policy choices over the past 15 years, beginning with Ronald Reagan's determination to free up American markets to shift resources into the information age—not unlike the shift from agriculture to industry a century before—and ending with Bush's and Clinton's determination to restore sound fiscal policies. In between, two Federal Reserve chairmen, Paul Volker and Alan Greenspan, conducted the most successful monetary policy perhaps in Fed history. For one account that anticipated America's success, see my book *The Myth of America's Decline: Leading the World Economy in the 1990s* (New York: Oxford University Press, 1990).

The bottom-left box in Fig. 6.1 captures situations in which countries have converging self-images and are more equal in relative power and wealth. Military threat in this situation is sharply reduced. A security community—as opposed to a security dilemma—emerges in which countries do not perceive each other as military threats, even though the distribution of power is decentralized and a condition of anarchy prevails, in the sense that no single centre of legitimate power exists. Countries remain independent and compete. But they compete now largely for economic power and do not militarize this competition because they do not believe that other countries in the community will use a relative gain in economic power to threaten or harm them politically or militarily.[9]

All countries agree on the basic political purposes for which they pursue power, whether those purposes are democratic—for example, today's Group of Seven—or non-democratic—for example, the Holy Alliance—and this convergence of self-images mutes the threat or use of military force among them. Countries in the security community may, of course, continue to disagree on how to deal with third countries, those that fall outside the security community. The United States and European democracies disagreed, for example, on how to deal with the ethnic crisis in the former Yugoslavia. If such disagreements escalate and rebound into relations within the security community, security communities may weaken. If, in addition, domestic self-images diverge, security communities may dissolve. Great Britain eventually left the Holy Alliance not only because it could not agree to preserve monarchies in Greece and other European areas but also because over time it had less in common with the domestic political systems of the continental monarchies in Russia, Prussia and Austria.

In box (3) in Fig. 6.1, domestic self-image plays a crucial role in a nation's foreign policy. In the case of US foreign policy, democracy mutes, if not suppresses altogether, military conflict with Europe and Japan and prevents economic competition with these democracies from escalating rapidly to political and military conflicts. If this common democratic bond weakened, trade wars might become real wars. Thus, democracy promotion or, better put, democracy preservation is absolutely vital to America's national interests in relations with other democracies. Otherwise, the United States would have to arm and compete for military power with these countries, all of whom are rich and could afford substantial, even nuclear, arms. Yet, paradoxically, most of the concern with democracy promotion in contemporary American foreign policy has little to say about these relations with other existing democracies.

The bottom-right box in Fig. 6.1 portrays international relationships in which nations have differing self-images and relatively equal wealth and power. This is the traditional setting of European international politics, at least

---

[9] On the critical role that the use of force plays in orienting relationships among states toward cooperation or conflict, see Robert Powell, 'Absolute and Relative Gains in International Relations Theory', in Robert A. Baldwin (ed.), *Neorealism and Neoliberalism* (New York: Columbia University Press, 1993), p. 211.

until the modern democratic era. Because nations aspire to preserve and promote different domestic political systems, they are more easily threatened by one another's power. They resist any one country achieving dominant power and therefore act to preserve a relative balance of power. On the other hand, one or more countries, depending on how they view themselves and their purposes, may always be tempted to disrupt the balance and seek disproportionate power. For balance of power theorists, this is the familiar problem of the revisionist state. The revisionist state aspires to change the prevailing equilibrium or conquer other states.[10] Bismarck jettisoned the conservative consensus of the Holy Alliance to preserve independent monarchies when he attacked and coerced separate monarchies to form the new nation of Germany.

Box (4) in Fig. 6.1 characterizes contemporary US relations with former communist countries in Europe, especially Russia, and remaining communist powers in Asia, such as China. Russia is not a democracy by any of the significant tests that characterize peaceful relations among democraciesas discussed further below. It has initiated a process of democratization that could at some point lead to closer convergence with Western democracies. But it starts with a long legacy of authoritarian and militant nationalist traditions and an ongoing internal debate as to whether democracy is an appropriate form of government for the Russian people.[11]

Other former communist states in Europe are further along the road to democracy. Hungary, Poland and the Czech Republic have met the political requirements to join NATO—which in a sense symbolizes the democratic peace—and have begun negotiations, along with Cyprus and Slovenia, to join the European Union (EU). The Baltic and other former communist states are potentially next in line. In Asia, China remains firmly outside the community of democratic nations. It has reaffirmed its authoritarian political system but moved smartly to reduce its totalitarian grip on economic and other aspects of civil life in China. While its power is growing, its relations with the United States straddle boxes (2) and (4) in Fig. 6.1. At the moment, the United States is clearly an imperial power *vis-à-vis* China—more so than it is *vis-à-vis* Russia, which has a more substantial nuclear arsenal—but China seeks actively to alter the status quo and is therefore more competitive with the United States.

In box (4), democracy promotion is moderately relevant to US foreign policy. Where countries are struggling to democratize, democracy assistance may be useful. Because democracy is by nature an indigenous, bottom-up form of government, however, such assistance can be overdone or insensitive. American assistance may be provided best in concert with other European democracies. Where countries resist democracy, as in China's case, democracy promotion—or the promotion of domestic values more generally—may be not

---

[10] On the role of revisionist states in the balance of power, see Randall L. Schweller, 'Bandwagoning for Profit: Bringing the Revisionist State Back In', *International Security*, 19/1 (1994), pp. 72–108.

[11] On this debate, see Peter Rutland's essay in this volume.

only irrelevant but also dangerous, adding ideological conflict on top of power competition.

Implications for American Foreign Policy

On the basis of this discussion combining the factors of national identity and power, where does democracy promotion fit in US foreign relations with other countries? First, democracy promotion will reflect the evolution of American democracy itself and in particular the debate about contemporary domestic issues in the United States. Second, the role of democracy in American foreign policy is most crucial in relations with other democracies. Although democracy promotion is not appropriate or necessary in this context, democracy enhancement and preservation are. Third, democracy promotion is most troublesome in relations with weaker, non-Western developing countries that have little capability to resist American power and resent projection of American democracy and capitalism. Fourth, democracy promotion is more, perhaps most, useful in relations with democratizing states, states that seek democracy assistance but because of historical and cultural traditions remain sensitive, even allergic, to Western and especially US democracy. Fifth, in relations with both developing and democratizing counties, the United States and other democracies will often disagree about what kind of democracy assistance to provide. They advocate different prescriptions because they practise different varieties of democratic liberalism at home. In the rest of this chapter, I comment briefly on each of these points, drawing on the discussion in other contributions to this volume.

America's Self-Image

Self-images are not snapshots; they evolve. America's democratic self-image has evolved through four stages.[12] From its origins to the civil war, America was *a dual and conflicted country*. On the one hand, it was a new nation based on the belief that all 'men' were created equal and possessed inalienable rights to participate in self-government. On the other, it was an old nation of racial homogeneity and class identity. Free citizens were predominantly Anglo-Saxon and Protestant, and only white propertied males had the right to vote—though this franchise was larger than that of any other nation at the time, including Great Britain.[13] Black Americans were slaves.

[12] For more details of the following discussion, see my forthcoming publication *At Home Abroad: America's Identity and National Interests in the 21st Century*, a book prepared for The Twentieth Century Foundation, New York, Ch. 3.

[13] See Henry Steele Commager, *Commager on Tocqueville* (Columbia, Missouri: Missouri University Press, 1993), p. 22. In the United States, both houses of Congress and the executive were elected—albeit indirectly by State legislatures in the case of the Senate—while in Britain neither the executive—who was still appointed by the crown—nor the upper house was elected. Great Britain did lead in freeing slaves, doing so in 1833.

From the civil war through the 1920s, America became a 'thin' *electoral or institutional democracy*. The franchise extended eventually, at least in a legal sense, to all citizens—all men, blacks and women. Progressive Era reforms focused on good government, effective institutions and market competition (trust-busting). Two great waves of immigration—the first in the 1850s and the second around 1900—made America much less homogeneous, although still predominantly European. Participatory—especially local—government and robust capitalism effectively assimilated new Americans. What social class there was in America diminished, but economic inequalities increased.

In the third stage, from the 1930s to the mid-1960s, America became a limited—compared with Europe—*social democracy*. The New Deal and wartime—World War II and then the cold war—government expanded significantly the role of federal institutions. Social security and other federal programmes addressed basic poverty and income inequalities, the GI bill expanded equal opportunity in education, and cold war defence programmes shaped a new partnership between government and corporations, both supporting and regulating the new 'military-industrial complex'.

The fourth stage began in the mid-1960s and is still ongoing. In this stage, America is confronting the challenges of a mature *liberal democracy*. A third great wave of immigration, this time from non-European countries, principally Latin America and Asia, and the full emancipation of America's black citizens have brought a level of racial and ethnic diversity that America has never experienced before. Today, almost one-third of America's citizens are non-white, a proportion of ethnic minorities higher than that in any other democratic country with the exception of Switzerland and Belgium.[14] By the end of the twenty-first century, white Europeans in America may be in a minority. Is the new nation created in the belief that all human beings are equal regardless of race, creed or national origin up to the task of actually being a new nation of multiethnic and multicultural citizens? This issue penetrates to the core of the country's identity. It has triggered a spirited constitutional debate between the traditional liberal belief that the individual is the bedrock of democracy regardless of race, creed or national origin and the more radical view that the individual's ethnic, cultural or racial group—by which black Americans have been judged for more than three centuries—is the basis of social justice before the law, necessitating preferential discrimination or affirmative action in areas such as education, employment and contracting.

At least in part, American foreign policy reflects this evolution of America's self-image.[15] When America's self-image was conflicted before the civil war, its foreign policy was minimalist and ambivalent. Toward Europe, America withdrew. Across the continent, it expanded but this expansion reflected the torn

---

[14] In both Switzerland and Belgium, the diversity is among European nationalities. In the United States, it is increasingly between European and non-European ethnic groups.

[15] For an interpretation of American foreign policy from this perspective, see Tony Smith, *America's Mission: The United States and the Worldwide Struggle for Democracy in the Twentieth Century* (Princeton: Princeton University Press, 1994).

self-image of free versus slave America.[16] During the stage of electoral democracy, American foreign policy—especially under Woodrow Wilson—emphasized elections and good government. Not surprisingly, it became more cohesive and interventionist on behalf of democracy and national self-determination in the Caribbean, Central America and Europe after World War I. In the New Deal era, American diplomacy went beyond good institutions and for the first time pursued significant economic and social reforms in the democratic reconstruction of postwar Germany and Japan and in the Alliance for Progress programmes toward Latin America. Finally, today, American foreign policy champions human rights and promotes not only electoral and social but also entrepreneurial and constitutional democracy—the protection of inalienable civil liberties, including freedom from unjustified imprisonment, exile, torture and religious oppression and the right to own and exchange property, a partial but important economic means of defending individual liberties.

American foreign policy in the future hinges critically on the outcome of the ongoing domestic debate between traditional liberalism, nativism and multiculturalism.[17] A unified country that assimilates non-European cultures and blends diversity with unity is likely to be not only a more attractive example for multiethnic societies abroad but also a more cohesive and activist participant in foreign affairs. On the other hand, a nativist America, fearful of immigrants and foreign economic influences, is likely to retreat and project a harsher and more astringent image abroad. And a divided, multicultural America may be too distracted and weak to have much influence abroad and may succumb to greater foreign influences at home. Various ethnic groups—Black Americans, Jewish American, Irish Americans, Hispanic Americans—may dominate American foreign policy toward specific countries or regions and project an episodic and incoherent American presence on the world stage. This domestic debate motivates and channels American power and is at least as important to the future of American foreign policy as the relative weight of American economic and military resources.

America's Relations with Other Democracies

Democratic government is no longer unique to America or the New World. Old World countries have also evolved democratically. The western European countries and Canada have similar democratic features that are most important in reducing the role of military competition among states: (1) free, fair and

---

[16] While America's relatively modest power is also an explanation of American foreign policy in this period, it is not the only explanation.

[17] For discussions of these different images of America in the past and future, see Jack Citrin, Ernst B. Haas, Christopher Muste, and Beth Rheinigold, 'Is American Nationalism Changing?: Implications for Foreign Policy', *International Studies Quarterly*, 38/1 (1994), pp. 1–33; Ernst B. Haas, *Nationalism, Liberalism and Progress* (Ithaca: Cornell University Press, 1997); and Michael Lind, *The Next American Nation: The New Nationalism and the Fourth American Revolution* (New York: The Free Press, 1995).

broadly participatory elections in which competing political parties rotate in government; (2) governmental institutions, including particularly the military, that are responsive and accountable to elected officials; and (3) fundamental protection of civil liberties, including impartial judiciaries. By these standards, Japan is also a democracy, especially in comparison with other Asian societies. In comparison with Europe and North America, however, Japan may be less developed democratically. It has less experience with opposing issue-oriented parties that rotate in government; it has a bureaucracy that is more powerful and less accountable to elected officials; and it has a consensual, group-oriented political culture that offers fewer bulwarks against violation of basic civil rights.

As noted earlier and now widely acknowledged, countries with the above features appear not, or almost never, to fight against one another. The reasons for this dramatically different interstate behaviour among democracies are not fully understood. Important roles may be attributed to democratic norms and institutions within democratic countries, to trade and economic interdependence among them, and to shared membership in international institutions—all of which may be related to the democratic phenomenon broadly defined.[18] On the other hand, democracies until recently have been too few in number to confirm these conclusions statistically.[19] Moreover, since World War II, when more democracies have existed, they have been allied most of the time against the former Soviet Union.[20] Hence sceptics question whether peaceful behaviour among these countries will persist now that the need for democracies to ally against the Soviet Union is gone. Some, such as Randall Schweller in this volume, doubt that it will persist even if the entire world were to become democratic.

As Schweller suspects, because democracies evolve, they also change. There are many types of liberal democracy. If democracies differ sufficiently in their degree or strength of democracy, they may fall out with one another and even fight.[21] Some analysts find that this process of political estrangement may

[18] See, *inter alia*, Bruce Russett, John Oneal, and David R. Davis, 'The Third Leg of the Kantian Tripod for Peace: International Organization and Militarized Disputes, 1950–1985', *International Organization*, 52/3 (1998), pp. 441–69; and John R. O'Neal and Bruce Russett, 'The Classical Liberals Were Right: Democracy, Interdependence, and Conflict, 1950–1985', *International Studies Quarterly*, 41/2 (1997), pp. 267–94. Immanuel Kant first speculated that the three ingredients—republic constitutions (domestic norms and institutions), commerce (economic interdependence), and pacific union (international law and organization—were all essential components of the liberal peace.

[19] See David Spiro, 'The Insignificance of the Liberal Peace', *International Security*, 19/2 (1994), pp. 50–87, and other articles in that and following issues of the same journal.

[20] See Joanne Gowa, 'Democratic States and International Disputes', *International Organization*, 49/3 (1995), pp. 511–23. The argument that alliances cause peace among their members follows from dyadic and systemic perspectives. On the basis of expected utility theory, alliances may actually increase the incidence of war among allies. For this conclusion, see Bruce Bueno de Mesquita, *The War Trap* (New Haven: Yale University Press, 1981).

[21] Spencer R. Weart has done some interesting work on this proposition. He argues that it is not the specific features of democracy in any one country—for example, norms or institutions—that cause peaceful behaviour but the degree of difference among these features between two democracies. This thesis implies a layered view of democratic development—as suggested by the three criteria used in this essay—and is consistent with research that shows that democratizing or single-layer—i.e. thin—democracies may sometimes fight more mature or multi-layered democracies. See

have already started between Japan and the United States.[22] Hence the democratic peace may not eliminate a certain rivalry among liberal democracies. Whether this rivalry takes on a military character, as opposed to pure economic competition, depends on perceptions of threat. If one democracy comes to believe that another democracy may use relative gains from economic competition to harm it politically or militarily, the democratic peace ends. A crucial aspect of the democratic peace, therefore, is the mutual perception between two countries that they do not differ so much politically that one country begins to wonder if the other country will use its economic wealth or military power to impose its differing political views.

From this perspective, democracy promotion is not irrelevant in US foreign policy toward other democracies, although it is seldom mentioned in this context. America has a huge stake in preventing, for example, a political drifting apart between the United States and Japan. Democracy programmes to deepen relationships between the civil societies of these two countries would seem to be just as important as tough trade negotiations. Indeed, without the former, the latter will only accelerate the political estrangement. Rival capitalisms slowly engender and inflame rival liberalisms, which may eventually explode into traditional rival nationalisms. The US Information Agency (USIA) used to be concerned about this kind of democratic backsliding among Western allies. It was responsible for much of the deepening of political ties that took place between the United States and western Europe during the cold war. As Tom Carothers points out in this volume, however, since the end of the cold war USIA has taken a back seat to the National Endowment for Democracy, with its focus on democracy promotion in developing or newly democratizing states. Democracy promotion *per se* is not needed among states that are already democratic. But democracy enhancement to facilitate contacts between political parties, parliamentarians, government institutions—at the local well as the national level—and non-governmental organizations in the civil society is useful and might prevent existing democracies from drifting apart on the essential features that ensure peaceful relations among democracies.

America's Relations with Developing Countries

America's relations with developing countries in Asia, Latin America, the Middle East and Africa reflect two overriding facts. With the exception of Latin America, the political cultures of developing nations differ significantly from those of the United States and the West. This reality leads some analysts to ask if the next great defining conflict in international politics will be a 'clash of

Weart's *Never At War: Why Democracies Will Not Fight One Another* (New Haven: Yale University Press, 1997). On the tendency of democratizing states to fight other democracies, see Edward D. Mansfield and Jack Snyder, 'Democratization and the Danger of War', *International Security*, 20/1 (1995), pp. 5–39.

[22] See, for example, Michael Mastanduno, 'Do Relative Gains Matter?: America's Response to Japanese Industrial Policy', *International Security*, 16/1 (1991), pp. 73–113.

civilizations'.[23] The second reality is that of hegemony. For the most part, America's military power predominates in the developing world. American soft power penetrates this world as well. While many developing countries are struggling to become democratic, their democracies are nascent and thin. Domestic politics includes the panoply of elections and multiple parties but often lacks the traditions of bureaucratic transparency and accountability and, most important, the civic culture of individual rights and religious tolerance.[24] Some important developing countries remain solidly authoritarian—China— and a few continue to be totalitarian—North Korea, Iran, and Cuba. In general, therefore, America's relations with developing countries fall into the imperial or hegemonic configuration of power and identity in box (2) in Fig. 6.1.

In this situation, democracy promotion looms large in US foreign policy if only because American power and identity are so overwhelming. For the same reason, however, democracy promotion is frequently resented. As Sørensen, Steve Smith, Robinson and Gills point out in their essays in this volume, weaker nations often see democracy promotion as a thin disguise for US economic and military interests. When the latter are not at stake, the United States pushes democracy and human rights—as is the case, for example, in much of Africa and parts of Latin America. But when economic or security interests prevail, the United States quickly soft-pedals democracy—the more likely case in relations with China or oil-producing monarchies in the Middle East. In the 1970s, for example, the United States aligned with a totalitarian and violent China to counterbalance the Soviet Union, and, after the Tiananmen Square killings in 1989, quickly patched up relations with China to take advantage of trade opportunities. In some cases during the cold war, as Steve Smith notes, the United States undermined rather than promoted democracy—Guatemala, Chile, Zaire, the Philippines, and so on. Today, according to such critics, global capitalism may be undermining democracy in developing economies, weakening national communities and state institutions in smaller states, and reinforcing local elites who resist real social and democratic reforms.

The problems for democracy promotion that these criticisms highlight are not problems unique to American foreign policy, however. They are problems that derive, at least in part, from the structure of power and identity in which the United States has had to act. During the cold war, the United States confronted the Soviet Union in a situation of anarchy. It was acting in circumstances described by box (4) in Fig. 6.1. In that situation, the United States did

---

[23] See Samuel Huntington's widely read article, 'The Clash of Civilizations?', *Foreign Affairs*, 72/3 (1993), pp. 22–50; and his *The Clash of Civilizations and the Remaking of World Order* (New York: Simon and Schuster, 1996).

[24] Larry Diamond finds, for example, that ten of the 22 principal countries in Latin America, all of which are nominally democratic, have levels of human rights abuses that would disqualify them as liberal democracies. See 'Democracy in Latin America: Degrees, Illusions and Directions for Consolidation', in Tom Farer (ed.), *Beyond Sovereignty: Collectively Defending Democracy in a World of Sovereign States* (Baltimore: Johns Hopkins University Press, 1996), pp. 52–104. See also Fareed Zakaria, 'The Rise of Illiberal Democracy', *Foreign Affairs*, 75/6 (1996), pp. 47–63.

not undermine democracy. It played the key role in defending and strengthening democracy. As the essays in this volume by Ikenberry and Tony Smith show, the United States not only fostered the democratic reconstruction of Germany and Japan; it also forged the liberal community of democratic nations that persists to this day even though the threat of force from the former Soviet Union has disappeared. In the Third World, however, the United States often had to make choices. It needed allies to support democracy; but it needed even more to prevent the Soviet Union from acquiring allies to support communism. Where it was a choice between a non-democracy and communism, the United States chose the non-democracy: the Philippines, South Korea, Dominican Republic, Chile, and so forth.[25] European democracies made similar choices—France in Africa and Great Britain in the Middle East.

The end of the cold war shifted the structure of power and identity closer to that of hegemony—box (2) in Fig. 6.1. No longer entangled in an anarchic structure, US democracy promotion became more consistent. American policy shifted to put the same pressure on right-wing governments in the Philippines and elsewhere that it traditionally placed on left-wing governments. At the same time, Third World countries lost leverage. There was no Soviet Union to play off against the United States. American power became overweening. The door was open for unconstrained democracy promotion, because the United States no longer feared that it might provoke a communist reaction.

What can be done to temper America's 'democracy' power and avoid a severe backlash of Asian or Muslim countries deeply offended by American values and arrogance? From a structural perspective, only two things can help. Developing countries can escalate the confrontation with American values. Some Asian countries, at least before the recent financial crisis, took this tack with their emphasis on 'the Asian way'. Second, developing countries can adopt long-term strategies to expand their power. This is probably done most effectively, as Europe and Japan demonstrated after World War II and the Asian 'tigers' more recently, by working with the United States and other industrial nations to expand trade and growth, eventually shifting the balance of power in more equitable directions.

The United States promotes a private market model to enhance trade and growth with developing countries. Although some essays in this volume criticize this approach as subversive of local institutions and reforms, this model may actually be less intrusive than more radical, government-promoted reforms. Based on limited government—expanded now by a sense of social justice and racial equality following from the New Deal and civil rights experiences—America's style of capitalism creates space for domestic as well as foreign initiatives. If local elites are stripped of government protection and

---

[25] John Kennedy captured this dilemma best. When the dictator, Rafael Trujillo, died in the Dominican Republic in 1961, he outlined the choices as follows: 'There are three possibilities in descending in order of preference: a decent democratic regime, a continuation of the Trujillo regime, or a Castro regime. We ought to aim at he first, but we really can't renounce the second until we are sure we can avoid the third.' Quoted in Smith, *America's Mission*, p. 226.

subsidies, the market approach may actually facilitate more equal income distribution. A more radical approach that bans foreign and domestic competition in favour of government-directed industries and reforms is not only more coercive, it usually impedes growth and makes smaller countries even more vulnerable to foreign meddling—for example, Cuba under Castro or Nicaragua under the Sandinistas. Historically, America has exhibited a relatively cautious or soft imperial self-image, and, as Michael Cox points out, continues to do so today.[26] Moreover, as Ole Holsti shows, there is no groundswell of enthusiasm among the American public or its leaders for 'helping to bring a democratic form of government to other nations'.[27] Countering America's political weight, therefore, may be more easily done than said. Some Asian nations, such as Singapore, Malaysia and China, are following alternative 'democratic' models of authoritarian government, guided economic liberalization, and social consensus. African nations, which, as Georg Sørensen argues, suffer particularly from a lack of national identity, are also searching for various alternatives such as Museveni's one-party democracy in Uganda. For its part, the United States does not have to accept these alternatives to welcome the debate. As South Korea may be demonstrating, Malaysia's authoritarian version of Asian democracy may be neither authentic nor necessary, and Museveni's one-party democracy in Uganda may avoid multiethnic parties and violence only at the price of enfranchising one party and one set of ethnic elites. The United States and other democracies can engage in this debate and recognize that it may be necessary to strengthen the self-images of weaker or poorer states.

Debate between governments may be nice, critics respond, but what about the power of private actors? Does not the cautious, low-intensity—that is, private sector—democracy that America peddles simply open up a developing country to the more vicious, less accountable private interests of multinational corporations that undermine local sovereignty and prevent genuine social change? Is not low-intensity democracy nothing more than a Trojan horse for high-intensity private capitalism? Would it not be better if the hegemon simply withdrew altogether and allowed developing nations to get on with their own social reforms and self-image building?

Withdrawal of the hegemon defies structural logic and is probably naïve to expect. It seems to happen only when a hegemon collapses—as the Soviet Union did—or, by some stroke of good luck, has a self-image of caution and self-restraint so strong that this image overrides opportunities to exercise preponderant power—a rare occurrence in history. Moreover, would it actually be in the interest of weaker states if the hegemon withdrew to that extent? How would weaker states acquire new technology, gain economic experience, and eventually compete in global markets? It may be legitimate for weaker states to worry about how they can manoeuvre against highly advanced partners to

---

[26] See Michael Cox, *US Foreign Policy after the Cold War: Superpower Without a Mission?* (London: Pinter for the Royal Institute of International Affairs, 1995).

[27] See Ole Holsti's essay in this volume.

promote their own industries and development in brutally competitive global markets, but it is probably foolish for them to believe that autarky is a viable model. Too many developing countries that adopted the closed socialist model during the cold war found out the hard way that this model is a dead end.

Asian countries, especially China, suggest another approach. They developed and are developing through integration with, not separation from, global markets. Yes, there are risks, as the current financial crisis in Asia reveals. But even with these risks, Asian countries and China are far ahead of the game compared with African, Middle East and Latin American counterparts. They have not only grown more rapidly; they have also strengthened their cultural autonomy and been the most vocal states attacking the American hegemon when it crosses the line of political insensitivity and invades sovereign space.

The United States also comes out ahead in this game. Low-intensity democracy and global capitalism do not always erode space for civil society in weaker countries. These forces also create such space. Who would argue that the average citizen in China today does not have more freedom and opportunity than he or she did in the days when China cut itself off from world markets? Foreign capitalists may cut deals with elites; but neither they nor those elites control all the forces they unleash. Integrating with world markets may not only help over time to reduce hegemony, it may also help perhaps to reduce authoritarianism. That is certainly the experience of many countries. No fully industrialized country today is non-democratic. At the same time, some, at least thinly, democratic countries are poor, suggesting that democracy need not wait for full industrialization, as advocates of a more authoritarian style of democracy sometimes argue.

In a situation of hegemony, democracy promotion may be too self-serving and offensive to succeed. Democracy presentation and preparation may be a better approach: (1) welcoming a vigorous debate between a US or Western democracy model and its alternatives; (2) insisting at a minimum on respect for human rights and participatory political processes, but not being too quick to endorse or praise elections that rest on weak political institutions and governmental accountability; and (3) encouraging more economic openness to create space in civil society for greater freedom of movement, more legal contracting and enforcement, wider educational opportunities, and enhanced local authority. This combination of political debate and economic support offers the best formula under hegemony—box (2) in Fig. 6.1—to respect foreign cultures, promote greater equality of power, and nurture convergence of political self-images such that states move progressively toward security communities—box (3) rather than anarchy—box (4).

America's Relations with Former Communist Countries in Europe

Democracy promotion under condition of anarchy confronts different dilemmas. In this situation, US democracy promotion is less likely to be overweening than inconsistent. As we noted in the case of the cold war, the United States defended some democracies—for example, in western Europe—at the expense of democratic groups in other countries—for example, in the Philippines, Zaire, and so forth. Power and identity are both contested under anarchy. No country is powerful enough to impose order or its values. Hence, because both democracy and stability are at stake, the United States will blow hot and cold on democracy promotion, even more so if there is no overriding power conflict in the anarchic system as there was in the cold war—that is, under multipolar as opposed to bipolar anarchy.

This situation seems to characterize US democracy promotion in the former communist countries in Europe, particularly in Russia. Although the power balance in Europe is no longer bipolar or even multipolar in the sense of fully equal competitors, Russia remains the most significant military power in the world besides the United States. It is also not yet a democracy. On all three internal features that characterize democracies that live in peace with one another, Russia comes up short.[28] On the other hand, it is democratizing. It no longer stands in a hostile confrontation with Western democracies or categorically rejects democracy as a possible form of government for Russia—although, as Peter Rutland points out in this volume, it is far from united on whether democracy is the appropriate form. Hence, although the structural aspects of anarchy are still at play in US-Russian relations, they are for the moment muted, and the chance that Russia may converge with Western states in the future is no longer the chimera it seemed to be only a few years ago.

Democracy promotion in the anarchic context is not only appropriate; it is also less offensive and may actually be welcomed. More advanced and democratizing states in Europe are not as vulnerable as poorer developing countries, and democratic support groups in these states are large enough to give the democratizing process an indigenous character. Accordingly, US democracy promotion in Europe has been substantial not only in Russia but also in eastern Europe and the newly independent states. In eastern Europe, democracy programmes have been largely successful. These countries not only had previous democratic experience; they were also reacting against the communist model and political oppression of the former Soviet Union. They embraced democracy and immediately applied for membership in the Western institutions of NATO and the EU.

---

[28] Russia has not yet experienced one, let alone several, peaceful transitions in which opposing parties rotate in the most powerful institution of governmentin Russia's case, the presidency. The Russian military as well as powerful civilian bureaucracies may not be fully accountable to elected officials, and civil rights in Russia are still in an infant stage of development.

Democracy promotion in Russia and the former Soviet republics that make up the Commonwealth of Independent States (CIS) has been more troubled. Self-images in this context still diverge—between Russia and the Westernized Baltic states, and between Russia and Muslim central Asia and Caucasus; and anarchy, though muted, nevertheless introduces complications and even contradictions. Again, as Rutland argues, US democracy promotion in Russia has been extensive, but, as predicted by anarchic structures, it has blown hot and cold depending on the internal struggle in Russia between nationalists and communists on the one hand, and liberal reformers on the other. American support was apparently crucial at key points—for example, Yeltsin's election in 1996; and early privatization programmes, while sharply criticized both inside and outside Russia, did enlarge the democratic support groups, including now an economic oligarchy with a stake in Russian democracy—or at least in not backsliding to Russian communism or nationalism. On the other hand, NATO expansion induced by muted anarchy complicated—some would argue contradicted—the democracy support effort. It strengthened Russian nationalists by making the United States and other Western states appear aggressive. At the same time, others argued that NATO expansion weakened nationalists by ensuring that a nationalist attempt to recreate the former Soviet Union would now involve a direct confrontation with NATO.

Similar contradictions afflict US democracy promotion in other CIS countries. Here US efforts are compromised by a concern for stability along Russia's southern frontier with Islam—from Iran through the Caucasus and central Asia to Afghanistan. Pushing democracy too hard in Uzbekistan and Turkmenistan inflames Muslim opposition and reinforces existing domestic military conflicts in Tajikstan and Afghanistan. Supporting rapid change in Azerbaijan and Georgia jeopardizes oil supplies in the Caspian Sea and opens up opportunities for Iranian meddling. In Kazakhstan, Kyrgyzstan, and the Baltic states, US democracy confronts large Russian ethnic minorities. Pushing their democratic rights risks separatism and possible reabsorption of these minorities—and their territories—into Russia.

None of these factors excuses the ambivalence of US democracy programmes in these countries. But it does suggest the complications induced by anarchic structures. As in the cold war, the United States needs to set clear priorities. Democracy promotion is probably most vital in Russia because the progress or failure of democracy there weakens or strengthens the anarchic pressures at work in the rest of the system. As the nationalists in Russia are weakened, separatist problems in the Baltic states, Kyrgyzstan and Kazakstan abate. Democracy programmes can pay more attention to the rights of Russian minorities in these states without encouraging their independence. Problems with Muslim populations in other central Asian and Caucasus republics may be more intractable, even if Russia progresses. Here the problems have to do with diverging religious and cultural self-images. Power balancing concerns intensify not only because the frontier with Islam is unstable but because Iran and Afghanistan are key states that connect the Middle East—the Persian

Gulf—and South Asia—Pakistan, India. Democracy promotion in the cumstances is likely to remain conflicted by crosscutting concerns for sta and liberal reforms.

Different Varieties of Democracy Promotion

Democracy promotion is not new. In the limited sense of setting an example, democracy promotion has been around since the first democracy. George Washington exhorted the new American republic 'to give to mankind the magnanimous and too novel example of a people guided by an exalted justice and benevolence'.[29] John Quincy Adams urged it to 'recommend the general cause by the countenance of her voice, and the benignant sympathy of her example'.[30] All nations express their political self-image in foreign policy, not just democracies. It is the means by which states activate their power in foreign affairs and decide whether the power of other nations obstructs or supports their objectives.

Democracy promotion is also not unique to the United States. Other democracies express their self-images as well. Inoguchi reminds us in his essay in this volume that while the United States tends to moralize in foreign policy, Europe has a penchant to ideologize, and Japan to commercialize foreign issues. In Europe, the state and nation developed before democracy. In many cases, social revolutions and great ideological struggles were necessary to democratize the state. In the United States, democracy developed before the state and became a critical factor in forging the nation through the crucible of the civil war. No social revolution was necessary of the sort familiar in Europe.

It is not surprising, therefore, that European critics of US democracy programmes advocate deep-seated, high-intensity reforms to transform class structures and state institutions in developing countries—see Steve Smith and Georg Sørensen in this volume, in particular—while US democracy programmes emphasize private sector and local self-help initiatives that assume market activity can dissolve—or at least not be obstructed by—class differences. Democracy programmes reflect different state characteristics in Europe and the United States. During the cold war, for example, European states with large domestic welfare programmes were the biggest donors of foreign aid to developing counties, often to countries that pursued similar statist domestic programmes—for example, Tanzania.[31] By contrast, US aid programmes encouraged private sector trade and foreign investment, principally in Latin

---

[29] Quoted in Richard B. Morris (ed.), 'George Washington: Farewell Address 1796', in Daniel Boorstin, *An American Primer* (New York: New American Library, 1966), p. 222.

[30] See John Quincy Adams, *An Address Delivered at the Request of the Citizens of Washington; on the Occasion of Reading the Declaration of Independence, on the Fourth of July, 1821* (Washington, DC: Davis and Force, 1821).

[31] See David Halloran Lumsdaine, *Moral Vision in International Politics: The Foreign Aid Regime 1949–1989* (Princeton: Princeton University Press, 1993).

American countries, often supporting commercial elites and relatively neglecting income inequalities.

These differences are natural expressions of different varieties of liberal democracy.[32] They are not peculiar eccentricities of any one particular democracy. What has changed since the end of the cold war is that American power is now preeminent in most parts of the world. That does give the United States a unique opportunity to promote its particular version of liberal democracy. Add to that a stronger religious tradition in the evolution of American democracy, unlike religion in Europe, which was closely identified with the earlier non-democratic state and you have the exaggerated magnitude and moral fervour of democracy promotion programmes in US foreign policy today.

Power shifts, however, and democracy promotion encounters resentment as well as support. Hence, the current situation will not last for ever. The United States would do well to think more carefully about the varying circumstances of power and identity within which it seeks to promote democracy. If it does, it can potentially guide shifts in identity and power such that more states wind up in security communities in which relationships do not threaten militarily either their interests or US interests. In the end, much also depends on how US and other liberal democracies evolve and whether they learn from one another to promote an attractive and inclusive example of democracy that other nations will find congenial and acceptable to emulate.

[32] Michael Doyle elucidates the variety of liberalisms in his contribution to this volume.

III

US Democracy Promotion: The Domestic Context

7

Promotion of Democracy as Popular Demand?

OLE R. HOLSTI

Introduction

One of the continuities linking the foreign policies of the Bush and Clinton administrations was support for expanding the 'zone of democracy'. Both of the post-cold war presidents used State of the Union addresses and many other vehicles to promote the proposition that this goal could provide one of the foundations of American foreign policy, much as containment of Soviet expansionism did during four and a half decades after World War II.[1]

The idea of an American mission to expand democracy has a venerable history, dating back to the early days of the republic.[2] It has not, however, been free of controversy.[3] Is it either a desirable or a feasible goal of foreign policy?

I am indebted to the National Science Foundation for five grants that supported the Foreign Policy Leadership Project surveys of American opinion leaders; to the Duke University Research Council and the Trent Foundation for additional grant support; to Eugene R. Wittkopf for sharing some of his data from the Chicago Council on Foreign Relations and *Times-Mirror* surveys; to Robert Jackson for obtaining relevant data from the Roper Center; to David Priess for research assistance; to Daniel F. Harkins for many years of programming assistance; to Rita Dowling for secretarial assistance; and to participants in the January 1988 SSRC-sponsored conference on US promotion of democracy for useful comments and suggestions.

[1] These themes may be found in President Bush's State of the Union addresses in 1990, 1991, and 1992, and in those by President Clinton in 1994, 1995, and 1996. For example, in 1994 the latter stated: 'Ultimately, the best strategy to ensure our security and to build a durable peace is to support the advance of democracy elsewhere. Democracies don't attack each other. They make better trading partners and partners in diplomacy.'

[2] For an excellent overview, see Tony Smith, *America's Mission: The United States and the Worldwide Struggle for Democracy in the Twentieth Century* (Princeton, NJ: Princeton University Press, 1994). The recent policies are effectively analysed in Rick Travis, 'The Promotion of Democracy at the End of the Twentieth Century: A New Polestar for American Foreign Policy?', in James M. Scott (ed.), *After the End: Making U.S. Foreign Policy in the Post-Cold War Environment* (Durham, NC: Duke University Press, 1999), pp. 251–76; Thomas Carothers, 'Democracy and Human Rights', *Washington Quarterly*, 3 (1994), pp. 109–20; Carothers, 'Democracy Without Illusions', *Foreign Affairs*, 76/1 (1997), pp. 85–99; and Carothers, 'US Democracy Assistance', in this volume.

[3] Those who support promoting democracy abroad include Terry L. Deibel, 'Strategies Before Containment: Patterns for the Future', *International Security*, 16 (1992), pp. 79–108; Larry Diamond, *Promoting Democracy in the 1990s* (New York: Carnegie Corp., 1991); G. John Ikenberry, 'The Myth of Post-Cold War Chaos', *Foreign Affairs*, 75/3 (1996), pp. 79–91; G. John Ikenberry, 'America's Liberal Grand Strategy: Democracy and National Security in the Postwar Era', in this volume; Charles A.

Is it best implemented actively by policy or passively by example? Woodrow Wilson placed the expansion of democracy squarely among American war aims in his Fourteen Points and his speech on 2 April 1917, requesting that Congress declare war against Germany. The Atlantic Charter and other allied proclamations during World War II also asserted that the war against the Axis powers was guided in part by such Wilsonian goals. Both world wars found major democracies such as the United States, Great Britain, and France among the victors but, except in the defeated countries—Japan, Germany and Italy— there were only limited successes in promoting democracy in formerly author- itarian countries after World War II.

Expressions of American support for expanding democracy were not hard to find during the cold war. For many years Congress went through the annual ritual of voting for the 'Captive Nations Resolution', for example, but some important barriers stood in the way of moving beyond symbolic and rhetor- ical exercises for promoting democracy in areas where it did not exist. The first was a lack of agreement about the appropriate targets of such efforts. Conservatives typically limited their support to promoting democracy in Soviet bloc countries. In contrast, liberals were more inclined to argue that the US should use its leverage to promote political reform in countries such as South Africa or among allies that were also recipients of American military and economic assistance. The second barrier was international. Where was it desir- able or feasible to promote democracy at other than the rhetorical level with- out the risks of provoking a world war or uprisings against faithful allies in the confrontation with the Soviet Union?

The end of the cold war largely dismantled these barriers. Not only were the potential costs associated with expanding democracy significantly reduced, but this goal also seemed to offer a unifying focus for American foreign policy, thereby helping to rebuild the foreign policy consensus that had been one of the notable casualties of the Vietnam War. In short, this has appeared to be a foreign policy goal that not only promised a very favourable risk-reward ratio abroad, but that also offered the promise of rich domestic political dividends.

This chapter examines the role of American public opinion in promoting and sustaining the expansion of democracy: To what extent has the public been the driving force behind Washington's efforts to promote political

Kupchan, 'Reviving the West', *Foreign Affairs*, 75 (1996), pp. 92–104; James Kurth, 'America's Grand Strategy', *The National Interest*, 43 (1996), pp. 3–19; Joshua Muravchik, *Exporting Democracy: Fulfilling America's Destiny* (Washington: American Enterprise Institute, 1991); Bruce Russett, *Grasping the Democratic Peace: Principles for a Post-Cold War World* (Princeton, NJ: Princeton University Press, 1993); Tony Smith, 'National Security Liberalism and American Foreign Policy', in this volume; and Strobe Talbott, 'Democracy and the National Interest', *Foreign Affairs*, 75 (1996), pp. 47–63. Critics include Eugene Gholz, Daryl G. Press, and Harvey Sapolsky, 'Come Home America: The Strategy of Restraint in the Face of Temptation', *International Security*, 21 (1997), pp. 79–108; Randall Schweller, 'US Democracy Promotion: Realist Reflections', in this volume; Steve Smith, 'US Democracy Promotion: Critical Reflections', in this volume; Fareed Zakaria, 'The Rise of Illiberal Democracy', *Foreign Affairs*, 75/6 (1996), pp. 47–63; and Thomas J. McCormick, 'Troubled Triumphalism: Cold War Veterans Confront a Post-Cold War World', *Diplomatic History*, 21 (1997), pp. 481–92. The lat- ter dismisses Tony Smith's neo-Wilsonian prescription of expanding democracy as 'both wrong- headed and dangerous' (p. 491).

reform abroad? The next section briefly describes how both aspects of the question—the role of public opinion in the foreign policy process and the goal of promoting democracy in other countries—are among the issues that most clearly divide proponents of the realist and liberal perspectives on international affairs.[4] The third section presents some evidence on how both the general public and opinion leaders have assessed the goal of expanding democracy during the past two decades. The analysis is based on a broad rather than a restrictive view of expanding democracy. Competitive elections are a crucial element of democracy, but governments may in fact gain electoral victories by pledges to repress some minority or other. For example, generations of politicians in the American South won elections by promising to maintain second-class citizenship for blacks.[5] Thus, this section will also include evidence about some related issues, including the promotion and defence of human rights abroad. The data are intended to shed some light on several questions:

1. How strong is public support for promoting democracy in other countries?
2. To what extent do the views of the general public diverge from those of opinion leaders?
3. How, if at all, has the end of the cold war affected support for expanding democracy abroad?
4. To what extent has the goal of expanding democracy abroad served to bridge the partisan and ideological gaps that have characterized most foreign policy issues since the Vietnam War?

The conclusion presents several possible explanations for the dominant patterns in the public opinion data and touches briefly on the policy implications of the findings.

Liberals vs. Realists on Public Opinion and Promotion of Democracy Abroad

At first glance it might appear that this discussion addresses two quite distinct issues: the role of public opinion in the formulation of foreign policy, and the promotion of political reform in other countries as a foreign policy goal. Both issues are at the core of the venerable debates between advocates of realism and liberalism, the two dominant perspectives on the conduct of foreign affairs. Proponents of these two schools of thought generally hold sharply divergent views on the role of public opinion in the foreign policy process as well as on the appropriate weight that should be accorded to reforming domestic institutions abroad.

---

[4] See Michael Doyle and Randall Schweller in this volume for a theoretical discussion of liberalism and realism.

[5] The tensions between promotion of democracy and human rights are more fully discussed in Thomas Carothers, 'Democracy and Human Rights: Policy Allies or Rivals', *Washington Quarterly*, 3 (1994), pp. 109–20.

The first issue centres on the role of public opinion and its ability to make a useful contribution to the quality of foreign policy and diplomacy. A long liberal tradition, dating back to Immanuel Kant and Jeremy Bentham and continuing through Woodrow Wilson, asserts that democracies are more peaceful at least in part because the public can play a constructive role in constraining policy makers. Elihu Root, a distinguished Republican foreign policy leader, eloquently summarized the case for democratizing foreign policy in the initial issue of *Foreign Affairs*:

When foreign affairs were ruled by autocracies or oligarchies the danger of war was in sinister purpose. When foreign affairs are ruled by democracies the danger of war will be in mistaken beliefs. The world will be the gainer by the change, for, while there is no human way to prevent a king from having a bad heart, there is a human way to prevent a people from having an erroneous opinion.[6]

In contrast, Alexis de Tocqueville, Walter Lippmann, E. H. Carr, Hans J. Morgenthau, George F. Kennan and most other realists have been intensely sceptical of the public because the effective conduct of diplomacy requires long-term strategic visions of the national interest, combined with the ability to pursue those interests with speed, secrecy, and flexibility. These requirements would often be jeopardized were the public, whose preferences are allegedly driven by emotions and short-term considerations, to have a significant role in foreign affairs. Lippmann's indictment of the public would gain the support of many realists:

The unhappy truth is that the prevailing public opinion has been destructively wrong at the critical junctures. The people have impressed a critical veto upon the judgements of informed and responsible officials. They have compelled the government, which usually knew what would have been wiser, or was necessary, or what was more expedient, to be too late with too little, or too long with too much, too pacifist in peace and too bellicose in war, too neutralist or appeasing in negotiations or too intransigent. Mass opinion has acquired mounting power in this country. It has shown itself to be a dangerous master of decision when the stakes are life and death.[7]

By the late 1960s or early 1970s a near-consensus had developed among public opinion analysts on three points: public opinion is *volatile, lacks any coherent structure*, and is largely *irrelevant* in the conduct of foreign affairs. Were these three propositions generally valid, it would scarcely be of more than modest academic interest to devote much effort to analysing public attitudes on expanding democracy. However, during the past quarter-century some powerful challenges have been mounted against all three of them. Although the debate about the nature and impact of public opinion is far from over, we now have a growing body of evidence that public attitudes are in fact quite stable, have at least a moderate degree of structure, and often play a significant role in foreign policy decisions.[8]

---

[6] Elihu Root, 'A Requisite for the Success of Popular Diplomacy', *Foreign Affairs*, 1 (1922), p. 5.

[7] Walter Lippmann, *Essays in the Public Philosophy* (Boston: Little, Brown, 1995), p. 20.

[8] See for example, Eugene R. Wittkopf, *Faces of Internationalism: Public Opinion and American Foreign Policy* (Durham, NC: Duke University Press, 1990); Ronald H. Hinckley, *People, Polls, and*

Realists and liberals also disagree about the extent to which the nature of domestic institutions and practices in other countries are proper concerns of foreign policy. The realist thesis in opposition to such policies is grounded in three propositions. First, an effective foreign policy requires that national interests be pursued with sober understanding of the balance between risks and rewards on the one hand, and relevant resources on the other. It is necessary and sufficient that such policies be focused on the demanding task of influencing the international behaviour of other states, without taking on the added and extraneous burden of judging and seeking to reform their domestic institutions and practices as well. Realists often cite with approval the 1821 Independence Day address by Secretary of State John Quincy Adams, in which he answered demands that the United States should assist other nations in gaining their freedom: 'Wherever the standard of freedom and independence has been or shall be unfurled, there will her [US] heart, her benedictions and her prayers be. But she does not go abroad in search of monsters to destroy. She is the well-wisher to the freedom and independence of all. She is the champion and vindicator only of her own.'[9]

The doctrines of state sovereignty and non-interference in the internal affairs of other countries constitute the second pillar in the realist argument against efforts to reform political institutions and practices abroad. In an imperfect world, these norms are essential to avoid constant conflict. Without them, the international system would more closely approximate a state of perpetual war because no political grievance—real or perceived—would lie beyond the reach of external powers that might be tempted to launch crusades to redress them. Although realists generally are not counted among the staunchest defenders of international institutions, they frequently remind their liberal critics that Article 2, paragraph 7 of the UN Charter explicitly endorses the doctrine of non-interference: 'Nothing contained in the present Charter shall authorize the United Nations to intervene in matters which are essentially within the domestic jurisdiction of any state or shall require Members to submit such matters to settlement under the present Charter.'

The third point usually emphasized by realists is that, even if it were desirable to give a high priority to political reform abroad, this is not a feasible goal. Political institutions, including democratic ones, must originate in indigenous cultural values and practices. They can be imposed from abroad only in the most unusual circumstances; for example, it required the total defeat of Germany and Japan in World War II, followed by long periods of post-war occupation, to impose effective democratic institutions on those two countries. It is simply not feasible, according to most realists, for the United States

Policy-Makers: American Public Opinion and National Security (New York: Lexington Books, 1992); Benjamin I. Page and Robert Y. Shapiro, *The Rational Public: Fifty Years of Trends in Americans' Policy Preferences* (Chicago: University of Chicago Press, 1992); Ole R. Holsti, *Public Opinion and American Foreign Policy* (Ann Arbor, MI: University of Michigan Press, 1996); and Douglas Foyle, *Counting the Public In: Presidents, Public Opinion, and Foreign Policy* (New York: Columbia University Press, 1999).

[9] For example, this passage is quoted by Henry F. Kissinger, *Diplomacy* (New York: Simon and Schuster, 1994), p. 35.

to take on such an agenda, even in an era in which it is the world's only super-power. As three critics of an active American effort to promote democracy put it, 'there is no surer way to turn millions of America's admirers into America's opponents than to force an unfamiliar social system on them'.[10]

Liberals bring forth a number of responses to the realist brief against according a priority to the promotion of democracy abroad. They can muster evidence about the emergence of at least some international consensus on acceptable internal institutions and practices. The 1926 international agreement to abolish slavery is a pre-World War II example. The United Nations Declaration on Human Rights and additional international and regional treaties and institutions created in the wake of the Nazi Holocaust constitute further indications of widening agreement that the doctrines of sovereignty and non-interference in internal affairs are not absolute barriers against international concern with what goes on within a country's borders. Although events in Cambodia, Somalia, Burundi, Rwanda, Bosnia, Chechnya, Haiti and elsewhere provide ample evidence that progress on reforming internal institutions is at best slow and uneven, there is a discernible international trend in the direction of more rather than less concern for such issues. Thus, according to liberals, it is in its national interest for the United States to be a leader rather than a laggard in the undertaking.

The role of public opinion in the policy process and the priority to be assigned the expansion of democracy are intimately linked in the realist-liberal debate. Not the least reason for realist scepticism about public opinion is the fear that the public will give undue weight to reformist and humanitarian impulses—what Michael Mandelbaum has derisively called 'foreign policy as social work'.[11] Indeed, one of the worst realist nightmares is that the public, aroused by vivid television presentations of egregious denials of basic political and human rights in some country of no vital American national interest, will press Washington to undertake a costly and ill-fated intervention at the risk of major losses while achieving little more than salving the American national conscience. Moreover, should the undertaking result in even modest casualties, the public may then clamour for immediate withdrawal, further damaging America's credibility and reputation for mature international leadership.[12]

The liberal rebuttal to the realist case begins with the propositions that promoting democracy abroad constitutes the 'right thing' and that doing so is consistent with the most basic American values, including those articulated in the Declaration of Independence and the Bill of Rights. Liberals further assert

---

[10] Gholz et al., 'Come Home America', p. 43. Because the term 'democracy' is hardly self-evident, an important part of the debate on this issue concerns the conception of democracy being promoted. In addition to previously cited chapters in this volume by Thomas Carothers and Steve Smith, see also the chapter by Georg Sørensen.

[11] Michael Mandelbaum, 'Foreign Policy as Social Work', *Foreign Affairs*, 75/1 (1996), pp. 16–32.

[12] For example, George F. Kennan, 'Somalia, Through a Glass Darkly', *New York Times* (30 September 1993), A25.

that their concerns are not merely a reflection of dedication to fundamental democratic values, but are also grounded in a sober appreciation of three important political realities. First, long-term domestic support, a prerequisite for success in any significant international undertaking, can be sustained only when the public is persuaded that the ends and means of foreign policy are consistent with basic American values. As Jimmy Carter put it in his May 1977 speech at Notre Dame: 'I believe that we can have a foreign policy that is democratic, that is based on fundamental values, and that uses power and influence for humane purposes. We can also have a foreign policy that the American people both support and understand.'[13] Moreover, although the public may not be sufficiently informed or sophisticated to understand all the nuances of international affairs, they correctly believe that regimes which consistently deny fundamental political and human rights to their own citizens cannot be trusted to behave responsibly toward other countries, much less to carry out their international agreements. Finally, liberals point out that because democratic regimes don't go to war with each other, expanding the 'zone of democracy' is a significant contribution to peace.[14]

Data

Through much of the cold war, promotion of democracy was largely limited to rhetoric about America's adversaries. Washington's response to the East German uprising in 1953 and the Hungarian revolution in 1956 revealed that campaign slogans about 'liberation' and 'rolling back the iron curtain' were just that—campaign slogans. Nor was there much interest in promoting democracy among America's authoritarian allies for fear that successor regimes might prove to be less faithful cold war partners or, worse, to be dominated by radical leftists. It took the conjunction of the domestic civil rights movement, intense controversy over the costly but failed military effort in support of South Vietnam, and a backlash against the *Realpolitik* foreign policy strategies of the Nixon-Kissinger period to stimulate serious debates about the role of democratization and human rights in American foreign policy.

It is thus not surprising that there are relatively few public opinion survey questions about the promotion of democracy or human rights abroad prior to the 1970s. Even for the period since the mid-1970s we have nothing that comes close to approximating the almost monthly surveys assessing presidential approval or performance ratings. There are, however, two continuing survey projects, both initiated in the wake of the war in Vietnam and continuing

---

[13] Jimmy Carter, Text of President's Address at Notre Dame on Foreign Policy', *New York Times* (23 May 1977), 12:1.

[14] The seminal essay on this issue is Michael Doyle, 'Liberalism and World Politics', *American Political Science Review*, 80 (1986), pp. 1151–70. See also Doyle's chapter in the present volume. Doyle's original essay has stimulated a huge literature that generally finds liberals arrayed against realists. Many of the contributions to this spirited debate may be found in the pages of *International Security, International Organization, American Political Science Review*, and *International Studies Quarterly*.

into the post-cold war era, that provide at least some evidence about American attitudes toward promoting democracy and human rights abroad. In 1974, the Chicago Council on Foreign Relations (CCFR) undertook a major survey of attitudes toward foreign affairs. Subsequent replications of that study have been conducted at four-year intervals.[15] The CCFR studies included both the general public and much smaller samples of leaders. The Foreign Policy Leadership Project (FPLP) surveys of American opinion leaders, first conducted in 1976, have also included follow-up studies at four-year intervals—1980, 1984, 1988, 1992, and 1996.[16] Much of the evidence for this paper is drawn from the CCFR and FPLP surveys. Some additional data about the desirability and feasibility of promoting political change abroad has been drawn from surveys conducted by such major polling firms as Gallup as well as some that have been sponsored by major newspapers and networks.

Findings

Since its inception, the CCFR surveys have asked both the general public and leaders to rate the importance of various foreign policy goals for the United States, including 'helping to bring a democratic form of government to other nations'. Table 7.1, a summary of the results for each of the six surveys, includes responses to all of the goals in the questionnaire, not merely the promotion of democracy, in order to convey a better sense of how assessments of that goal have compared with others. It is clear that promoting the spread of a democratic form of government to other nations has not been a high foreign policy priority for the general public. Indeed, more often than not it has been the foreign policy goal that was assigned the fewest 'very important' ratings, and in none of the surveys did as many as one-third of the respondents accord the top rating to this goal. Although some observers have criticized American diplomacy for misguided zeal in attempting to propagate the country's values and institutions abroad, there is little in these data to suggest a groundswell of public enthusiasm for such undertakings.

Nor does the evidence in Table 7.1 indicate that the end of the cold war and the disintegration of the Soviet Union kindled any burning desires to promote the spread of democracy, even though the risks of igniting a superpower confrontation with Moscow by doing so have virtually vanished. Notwithstanding the fact that the Bush and Clinton administrations placed expanding democracy near the top of their foreign policy agendas, since 1986

---

[15] John E. Rielly (ed.), *American Public Opinion and U.S. Foreign Policy, 1975* (Chicago: Chicago Council on Foreign Relations, 1975). Rielly is also the editor of similarly titled monographs in 1979, 1983, 1987, 1991, and 1995.

[16] The FPLP surveys are described in Ole R. Holsti and James N. Rosenau, *American Leadership in World Affairs: Vietnam and the Breakdown of Consensus* (London: Allen and Unwin, 1984); Holsti, *Public Opinion and American Foreign Policy*, and Ole R. Holsti, 'Continuity and Change in the Domestic and Foreign Policy Beliefs of American Opinion Leaders' (presented at the 1997 Annual Meeting of the American Political Science Association).

Table 7.1. The Importance of American Foreign Policy Goals: Assessments by the General Public in the Chicago Council on Foreign Relations Surveys, 1974–1994 (% 'very important' ratings)

'For each [foreign policy goal], please say whether you think that it should be a very important foreign policy goal of the United States, a somewhat important foreign policy goal, or not an important goal at all.'

	1974	1978	1982	1986	1990	1994
World order security issues						
A. Preventing the spread of nuclear weapons	—	—	—	—	59	82
B. Worldwide arms control	64	64	64	69	53	—
C. Strengthening the United Nations	46	47	48	46	44	51
D. Protecting weaker nations against aggression	28	34	34	32	57	24
World order economic and environmental issues						
E. Improving the global environment	—	—	—	—	58	58
F. Combatting world hunger	61	59	58	63	—	41
G. Helping to improve the standard of living in less developed countries	39	35	35	37	41	22
US economic interest issues						
H. Stopping the flow of illegal drugs into the US	—	—	—	—	—	85
I. Controlling and reducing illegal immigration	—	—	—	—	—	72
J. Securing adequate supplies of energy	75	78	70	69	61	62
K. Reducing the US trade deficit with foreign countries	—	—	—	62	56	59
L. Protecting the jobs of American workers	74	78	77	78	65	83
M. Protecting the interests of American business abroad	39	45	44	43	63	52
US values and institutions issues						
N. Promoting and defending human rights in other countries	—	39	43	42	58	34
O. Helping to bring a democratic form of government to other nations	28	26	29	30	28	25
Cold war/security issues						
P. Maintaining superior military power worldwide	—	—	—	—	—	50
Q. Defending our allies' security	33	50	50	56	61	41
R. Matching Soviet military power	—	—	49	53	56	—
S. Containing communism	54	60	59	57	56	—

Source: John E. Rielly (ed.), *American Public Opinion and US Foreign Policy 1975* (Chicago: Chicago Council on Foreign Relations, 1975). Also, similar monographs edited by Rielly in 1979, 1983, 1987, 1991, and 1995.

there has in fact been a slight decline in support for promoting democracy abroad.

The five most recent CCFR surveys have also asked respondents to rate the importance of 'promoting and defending human rights in other countries'. Improving the state of human rights abroad has rarely been a top priority for the American public. The high point occurred in 1990, just a year after the Berlin Wall had come down, when 58 per cent of the general public rated it as 'very important', but even then it ranked only sixth, well behind such economic and security goals as protecting the interests of American workers and businesses abroad, securing adequate supplies of energy, defending allies, and preventing nuclear proliferation.

Just as the end of the cold war failed to stimulate heightened enthusiasm for promoting democracy abroad, the post-cold war period has also witnessed a precipitous decline in the priority to be accorded to human rights in American foreign policy. By 1994 only about one-third of the public rated it as a 'very important' goal, the lowest figure since the question was introduced to the CCFR surveys in 1978.

The CCFR surveys have also included much smaller samples of political and other leaders. Their assessments of possible American foreign policy goals are summarized in Table 7.2. As was true of the general public, the leaders taking part in the CCFR surveys have expressed very muted support for efforts to bring democratic institutions to other nations. This ranked as the least important goal in four of the six studies, and it never gained a 'very important' rating from as many as one-third of the leaders.

The related goal of promoting and defending human rights abroad has fared somewhat better than expanding democracy in the judgement of opinion leaders surveyed by the CCFR, but not substantially so. At no time did it rank among the most important goals of American foreign policy, nor did it ever gain a top rating from a majority of the respondents. Moreover, although improving the state of human rights abroad was never among the top priorities during the 1970s and 1980s, the period since the end of the cold war has witnessed reduced rather than heightened enthusiasm for this foreign policy goal among leaders, paralleling the trend among the general public. The decline in support was especially notable during the period between the 1990 and 1994 surveys.

The six Foreign Policy Leadership Project (FPLP) surveys of American opinion leaders have borrowed the CCFR cluster of questions asking respondents to rate the importance of various foreign policy goals. The questions have been worded identically with those in the CCFR surveys, making it possible to undertake cross-survey comparisons. It should be noted, however, that the FPLP samples are substantially larger, employ different sampling designs, and include an additional leadership group: senior military officers. Assessments of foreign policy goals during the 1976–96 period are summarized in Table 7.3. Once again, responses to the entire cluster of items are included in order to permit a comparison of views about promoting democracy and human rights abroad with other foreign policy goals.

The results reveal a very tepid response to expanding democracy abroad, as this goal ranked at or near the bottom in each of the six FPLP surveys. Even at the peak of support in 1988 only one-quarter of the opinion leaders judged it to be a 'very important' foreign policy goal. By 1996 fewer than one leader in

Table 7.2. The Importance of American Foreign Policy Goals: Assessments by Leaders in the Chicago Council on Foreign Relations Surveys, 1974–1994 (% 'very important' ratings)

'For each [foreign policy goal], please say whether you think that it should be a very import-ant foreign policy goal of the United States, a somewhat important foreign policy goal, or not an important goal at all.'

	1974	1978	1982	1986	1990	1994
World order security issues						
A. Preventing the spread of nuclear weapons	—	—	—	—	94	90
B. Worldwide arms control	86	81	86	83	80	—
C. Strengthening the United Nations	31	25	25	22	39	33
D. Protecting weaker nations against aggression	26	30	43	29	28	21
World order economic and environmental issues						
E. Improving the global environment	—	—	—	—	72	49
F. Combatting world hunger	76	64	64	60	—	41
G. Helping to improve the standard of living in less developed countries	62	64	55	46	42	28
US economic interest issues						
H. Stopping the flow of illegal drugs into the US	—	—	—	—	—	57
I. Controlling and reducing illegal immigration	—	—	—	—	—	28
J. Securing adequate supplies of energy	77	88	72	72	60	67
K. Reducing the US trade deficit with foreign countries	—	—	—	—	62	49
L. Protecting the jobs of American workers	34	34	43	43	39	50
M. Protecting the interests of American business abroad	17	27	25	32	27	38
US values and institutions issues						
N. Promoting and defending human rights in other countries	—	36	41	44	45	26
O. Helping to bring a democratic form of govern-ment to other nations	13	15	23	29	26	21
Cold war/security issues						
P. Maintaining superior military power worldwide	—	—	—	—	—	54
Q. Defending our allies' security	47	77	82	78	56	60
R. Matching Soviet military power	—	—	52	59	20	—
S. Containing communism	34	45	44	43	10	—

Source: John E. Rielly (ed.), *American Public Opinion and US Foreign Policy 1975* (Chicago: Chicago Council on Foreign Relations, 1975). Also, similar monographs edited by Rielly in 1979, 1983, 1987, 1991, and 1995.

six gave it that rating. As was the case with responses to the CCFR surveys, although promoting human rights in other countries garnered somewhat stronger support than the goal of expanding democracy among opinion lead-ers taking part in the FPLP studies, it never ranked very high when compared with other foreign policy goals. And once again the data indicate that the end

Table 7.3. The Importance of Foreign Policy Goals: Assessments by American Opinion Leaders in the Foreign Policy Leadership Surveys, 1976–1996 (% 'very important' ratings)

Please indicate how much importance should be attached to each goal

	1976 [N=2282]	1980 [N=2502]	1984 [N=2515]	1988 [N=2226]	1992 [N=2312]	1996 [N=2141]
World order security issues						
A. Preventing the spread of nuclear weapons	—	—	—	—	87	83
B. Worldwide arms control	66	55	70	68	73	60
C. Strengthening the United Nations	25	32	27	27	44	26
D. Protecting weaker nations against aggression	18	23	—	—	28	18
World order economic issues						
E. Fostering international cooperation to solve common problems, such as food, inflation, and energy	70	73	66	70	71	56
F. Protecting the global environment	—	47	53	69	66	47
G. Combatting world hunger	51	51	56	57	55	36
H. Helping to improve the standard of living in less developed countries	38	44	59	51	43	28
US economic interests						
I. Securing adequate supplies of energy	72	78	84	75	68	52
J. Protecting the jobs of American workers	31	30	—	36	32	29
K. Protecting the interests of American business abroad	14	19	22	—	24	19
US values and institution issues						
L. Stopping the flow of illegal drugs into the US	—	—	—	—	—	58
M. Controlling and reducing illegal immigration	—	—	—	—	—	33

	1976	1980	1984	1988	1992	1996
N. Promoting and defending human rights in other countries	—	27	33	39	38	24
O. Helping to bring a democratic form of government to other nations	7	10	18	25	23	15
Cold war/security issues						
P. Maintaining superior military power worldwide	—	—	—	—	—	40
Q. Defending our allies' security	37	44	47	51	34	36
R. Containing communism	39	41	38	37	13	15
S. Matching Soviet military power*	—	—	40	33	18	—

* 'Russian' instead of 'Soviet' in 1992.

of the cold war has not heightened support for efforts to improve and protect the state of human rights abroad. To the contrary, by 1996 'very important' ratings for this goal had declined to 24 per cent, the lowest figure recorded in any of the FPLP surveys.

At least some tentative answers to several of the questions posed earlier appear to have emerged at this point. First, there has been a remarkably consistent absence of strong support for either of the closely related goals of promoting democracy and human rights abroad. Second, the end of the cold war does not appear to have provided an impetus for moving these goals higher on the foreign policy agenda; indeed, to the extent that there have been changes since the Berlin Wall came down, they are in the direction of reduced rather than increased support for both of them. It is noteworthy that such consistent results have emerged from the twelve surveys undertaken by two organizations over a period of more than two decades. Finally, the evidence in Tables 7.1–7.3 indicates that differences between the general public and opinion leaders are rather limited. These results certainly do not provide a great deal of support for realist fears that a poorly informed and emotional public might drive leaders, who know better, into feckless crusades to make the world over in the American image.

The foregoing analyses have focused on questions asking respondents to assess the importance of foreign policy goals. Although these questions have the virtue of having been asked over a span of more than two decades with precisely the same wording, they have the disadvantage of being rather abstract and removed from the specific context of actual decisions and policies.[17] Stated differently, the 'goals' questions may provide evidence about what respondents believe to be *desirable*, but they tell us much less about what they regard as *feasible* in given circumstances, or about how they may assess *trade offs* between goals. Two of the more difficult and controversial issues touching on such trade offs have involved American policies toward the Soviet Union and China. To what extent should the United States have pressed for democratization within the Soviet Union or for better treatment of Jews and other minorities within the USSR if doing so might have endangered negotiations on arms control and other strategic issues, or even given rise to serious deterioration in relations between Washington and Moscow?[18] Should the United States insist upon political reform and improvement of China's human rights record as a condition for better relations, including normalization of trade, with Beijing?[19]

Table 7.4 summarizes the results of a dozen questions concerning Soviet-American relations posed by several survey organizations over the span of the Carter and Reagan administrations. Although the wording of the questions varied quite substantially, making it hazardous to make any direct comparison of responses, the data suggest that the American public usually ascribed a higher priority to concerns other than expanding democracy and human rights in the Soviet Union. One exception occurred in 1977, just two months after Carter's inauguration but before the Brezhnev regime demonstrated that it, too, could play the 'linkage game' in response to such actions as Carter's open letter to Soviet dissident Andrei Sakharov. In a *Time* magazine survey, a majority—55 per cent—agreed that the President should continue to complain to the Soviets about the suppression of human rights 'even if it slows down détente and the chances for an arms agreement'. Two other 1977 surveys revealed considerable ambivalence about whether Carter's criticisms would in fact damage the chances of achieving an arms control agreement.

By 1978, however, a strong majority felt that a US human rights emphasis had in fact hurt efforts to achieve an arms control treaty, and an even larger majority rejected the proposition that Washington should break off such negotiations because of Soviet human rights violations. Further, in five surveys undertaken during the Reagan era the public repeatedly accorded a higher priority to arms control than to regional conflicts, Third World tensions, and other points of contention between the two superpowers, including the state of human rights in the Soviet Union. By 1988, two-thirds of the public rejected the proposition that the US should press the Gorbachev regime

---

[17] Several surveys, including those conducted by the Chicago Council on Foreign Relations, have asked whether respondents would favour or oppose the use of US troops in various hypothetical scenarios. Support for doing so is consistently higher, among both elites and the general public, if the victims of aggression are democracies (for example, western Europe or Israel) rather than autocracies (for example, Saudi Arabia). But the extent to which these responses reflect support for democracies, formal alliance commitments, or traditional friendships is not clear. In short, differences in public support for using US troops in these scenarios may be overdetermined.

[18] See the comments on Russia by Jason Ralph and Peter Rutland in this volume.

[19] See Minxin Pei, 'Is China Democratizing?', *Foreign Affairs*, 77/1 (1998), pp. 68–82.

Table 7.4. Public Opinion on the Role of Democracy and Human Rights in US Policy Toward the Soviet Union, 1977–1988

Date/Survey	Question	Responses	%
March 1977 Time	President Carter says that he is trying to bring more morality to our country's foreign policy. Some people feel that he is doing the right thing, others that he is making unwise decisions. Do you personally feel that [he] should or should not continue to complain to the Russians about the suppression of human rights even if it slows down détente and the chances for an arms agreement?	Should Should not Not sure	55 26 19
March 1977 Harris	Tell me if you tend to agree or disagree [that] President Carter hurt his chances of getting an agreement on SALT because he kept talking about how the Russians were violating human rights.	Agree Disagree Not sure	46 25 29
May 1977 Roper	We are currently engaged in talks to reach an arms agreement with Russia, and Russia is one of the countries President Carter has criticized for denying its citizens human rights. Do you think Carter's criticism will decrease. . . , increase. . . , or won't affect the chances of reaching an [arms] agreement?	Decrease Increase Won't affect outcome Don't know	31 9 46 15
July 1978 Harris	Do you feel that President Carter's continuing emphasis on the Russian violations of human rights of dissidents in that country has . . . made it more difficult to reach agreement with the Russians on SALT arms control and other important issues?	Has Has not Not sure	62 26 12
August 1978 NBC/AP	Do you think that the US should break off negotiations with Russia aimed at limiting nuclear weapons because of Russian violations of human rights, or do you think negotiations should continue?	Continue Break off Not sure	76 15 9
November 1985 Gallup	Some people think that the US should make agreement on the arms control treaty dependent on progress in other areas of difference between this country and the Soviet Union—including human rights and regional conflicts. Others believe that arms control is so important we should negotiate in that area regardless of progress in other areas of difference between our nations. Which comes closer to your views?	Yes, dependent Negotiate regardless Don't know	29 62 10

Table 7.4. cont.

Date/Survey	Question	Responses	%
November 1985 LA Times	What do you think is the most important topic that should be discussed at the Geneva summit meeting: nuclear weapons disarmament, a nuclear test ban, outlawing nuclear weapons in space, reducing missiles stationed in Europe, peace talks for regional trouble-spots, human rights, cultural exchanges, or what? [Adds up to more than 100% due to multiple responses.]	Nuclear disarmament	50
		Regional trouble-spots	31
		Human rights	22
		Space weapons	18
		Test-ban	12
		Missiles in Europe	9
		Cultural exchanges	6
		Other	1
November 1987 ABC News/ Washington Post	Which of these is the most important in America's policy toward the Soviet Union: human rights, reducing nuclear weapons, situations like Afghanistan, or making Western Europe safe?	Nuclear weapons	45
		Human rights	31
		Western Europe	18
		Afghanistan	5
		Don't know	1
July 1988 Americans Talk Security	I'd like to read you three things the Soviets could do that many Americans would think of as positive steps for the Soviets to take. If the Soviets were to do only one of them, which one would be the most important?	Nuclear arms agreement	46
		Ease Third World tensions	25
		Improve human rights	21
		All (vol.)	5
		Don't know	3
July 1988 Americans Talk Security	Which viewpoint is closest to your own—that we should hold up arms agreements until the Soviets improve human rights, or that we should go ahead with arms agreements regardless of whether or not the Soviets have improved human rights in their country?	Go ahead with agreements	60
		Hold up agreements	28
		Neither (vol.)	4
		Don't know	8

September 1988
Peter D. Hart*

I'd like to focus on some specific goals the next president might give priority to. Which one or two would you say are the most important for the next president to address?

Slow down arms race	47
Stop terrorism	35
Stop world hunger	22
Ensure strong defence	16
Stop communism in Central America	15
Ensure respect for US	13
Promote human rights and democracy	11
Middle East peace	11
Avoid US military involvement abroad	10
End apartheid	8
None (vol.)	1
Not sure	2

December 1988
Gallup

Some people feel that now is a good time for the US to put pressure on Gorbachev to make concessions on human rights, regional conflicts, and other areas of difference between our countries. Others feel that we should not put pressure on Gorbachev so that his attempts to reform the Soviet system have a better chance to succeed. Which view comes closer to your own?

Do not pressure	66
Pressure now	27
Don't know	7

*Sample limited to ages 18–44.

for concessions on the grounds that such pressures might damage the Soviet leader's own efforts at reform.

The public has been somewhat more ambivalent about its preferences when faced with a trade off between, on the one hand, improving relations and expanding trade with China, and, on the other, pressing the leaders in Beijing for political reform, including improvement of its human rights record. Few recent issues have more clearly divided American leaders along realist-liberal lines. Henry Kissinger, George Bush, and other realists have been vocal advocates of the view that relations with China were too important to be held hostage to American preferences about Beijing's domestic institutions and practices; in any case, they argued, expanding trade relations was the best vehicle for promoting political reform. After rejecting this position during the 1992 presidential campaign, Bill Clinton joined the realist camp. Representatives Richard Gephardt and Nancy Pelosi, *New York Times* columnists A. M. Rosenthal and Anthony Lewis, and the Christian right were among the more vocal proponents of the opposing view that China's record on democratization and human rights should play an important role in Sino-American relations.

Since the mid-1980s questions relating to American policy toward China have been posed in various forms at least 14 times, with results that fail to yield a clear pattern of public preferences. Prior to the Tiananmen Square massacre of pro-democracy dissidents in June 1989, a majority of the public was disinclined to let US relations with China depend on human rights considerations. Six months after the massacre an overwhelming majority of those taking part in a *Los Angeles Times* survey asserted that the US should 'stand up for human rights as a condition of our friendship' with China, but soon thereafter the public mood began to shift toward a more ambivalent stance. For example, between January 1990 and October 1991 four CBS/*New York Times* surveys asked, 'when the United States deals with China, which do you think is more important: to criticize the way China suppressed human rights, or to avoid criticism in order to maintain good relations with China?'[20] In none of these surveys did either option garner support from a majority of the respondents; the 'good relations' policy prevailed in the first two surveys by 4 per cent and 2 per cent, whereas the 'human rights' position was favoured by margins of 11 per cent and 4 per cent in the two later polls. However, more recent surveys indicate that public attitudes are shifting in the direction of a more accommodating stance toward China despite the absence of visible steps toward democratizing that country's political system or improving its human rights record. For example, a 1995 *Times-Mirror* survey revealed that 62 per cent of the respondents believed that 'the US should not get involved in China's

---

[20] Respondents in opinion surveys often are offered only two starkly different options, thus excluding the possibility of uncovering the strength of public support for other options. It would be impossible to list all possible approaches to complex foreign policy issues, but in the case of the questions on China, it would have been useful to have offered at least one additional response option: 'To press Chinese leaders on human rights issues, but only in private discussions.'

domestic affairs, even if it means overlooking human rights abuses', whereas fewer than half that number stated that 'the US should try to promote democracy in China, even if it risks worsening relations with China'.

In summary, there is little evidence in Table 7.5 to support the charge that a moralistic and unrealistic public is pushing the United States toward an unwise confrontation with China. If anything, the data suggest that those who are reluctant to undertake actions that might spoil relations with Beijing slightly outnumber those who would press for a China that is more democratic and sensitive to the human rights of its citizens.

Party, Ideology and Support for the Promotion of Democracy

There is ample evidence that during the decades since the Vietnam War most foreign policy issues have divided leaders and the general public along partisan and ideological lines.[21] The end of the cold war has not given rise to a dramatic change in the direction of bridging these partisan and ideological cleavages, although there are some important issues, notably trade and protectionism and relations with Israel, on which the fault lines run along somewhat different dimensions. The question to be addressed here is whether the promotion of democracy abroad has been another of the many issues that pits Republicans against Democrats and liberals against conservatives.

Whereas Table 7.1 provided aggregate summaries of responses to the promotion of democracy goal question, Table 7.6 reports assessments of that goal according to party affiliation and ideological self-description by members of the general public who took part in the Chicago Council surveys. The results indicate that, contrary to many other foreign policy issues, partisan and ideological differences on this foreign policy goal have been rather narrow. Neither Republicans nor Democrats have expressed much support for the promotion of democracy abroad and the gaps between them have ranged between 1 per cent and 8 per cent. A very similar pattern is evident when respondents are classified according to ideology. Moreover, support for expanding democracy reached a peak—if that is the appropriate term to describe 'very important' ratings that never rose above 30 per cent—during the 1980s, and it has declined among all partisan and ideological groups since the end of the cold war.

Table 7.7 summarizes assessments of the human rights foreign policy goal by both leaders and the general public in five Chicago Council and one *Times-Mirror* surveys. As in Table 7.6, respondents are classified according to party and ideology. The results yield several conclusions. First, Democrats generally have accorded higher importance to the goal of defending and promotion of

---

[21] On this point, see I. M. Destler, Leslie H. Gelb, and Anthony Lake, *Our Own Worst Enemy* (New York: Simon and Schuster, 1984); Wittkopf, *Faces of Internationalism*; and Holsti, *Public Opinion and Foreign Policy*.

Table 7.5. Public Opinion on the Role of Democracy and Human Rights in US Policy Toward China, 1985–1995

Date/survey	Question	Responses	%
March 1985 Gallup	Do you think that the human rights situation in China is such that the United States should make our relations with them depend on the human rights situation there?	Yes No Don't know	34 51 15
December 1989 LA Times	Which course of action do you think better serves America's long-term interests: should we be conciliatory to the Chinese, or should we stand up for human rights as a condition of our friendship?	Stand up Conciliatory Not sure Refused	83 8 8 1
January 1990 CBS/NYT	When the United States deals with China, which do you think is more important: to criticize the way China suppresses human rights, or to avoid criticism in order to maintain good relations with China?	Criticize Good relations Both (vol.)	42 46 3
May 1990 CBS/NYT	Same question as above	Criticize Good relations Both (Vol.)	42 44 2
June 1991 CBS/NYT	Same question as above	Criticize Good relations Both (Vol.) DK/NA	48 37 2 13
October 1991 CBS/NYT	Same question as above	Criticize Good relations Both (Vol.) DK/NA	44 40 4 12
December 1993 NBC/WSJ	Which one of the following comes closer to your point of view: We should maintain good trade relations with China, despite disagreements we might have with its human rights policies? We should demand that China improve its human rights policies if China wants to continue to enjoy its current trade status with the United States?	Good trade Human rights Neither (Vol.) Not sure	29 65 2 4

March 1994 NBC/WSJ	Same question as above	Good trade	31
		Human rights	61
		Neither (Vol.)	2
		Not sure	6
May 1994 NBC/WSJ	Same question as above	Good trade	40
		Human rights	51
		Neither (Vol.)	3
		Not sure	6
June 1994 NBC/WSJ	Same question as above	Good trade	42
		Human rights	50
		Neither (vol.)	3
		Not sure	6
April 1994 LA Times	Do you think Congress should make Chinese progress in human rights a requirement for extending that country's most favoured nation trade status, or would it be better to keep human rights discussions separate from our trade agreements with China?	Requirement	36
		Separate	56
		Neither/other	1
		Don't know	7
May 1994 Time/CNN	Which of these two policy goals do you think is more important in dealing with China? Encouraging China to exercise human rights in the treatment of its citizens. Establishing a strong trading relationship with China.	Human rights	62
		Trade	29
		Not sure	9
July 1995 NBC/WSJ	Should First Lady Hillary Clinton attend the UN World Conference on Women, to be held in China, or should she not attend because Harry Wu, an American citizen and human rights activist, is being held by Chinese authorities on espionage charges?	Should attend	55
		Not attend	33
		Not sure	12
August 1995 Times-Mirror	Do you think the US should try to promote democracy in China, even if it risks worsening relations with China? Or, do you think the US should not get involved in China's domestic affairs, even if it means overlooking human rights abuses?	Promote democracy	29
		Not get involved	66
		DK/Refused	5

Table 7.6. Assessments of 'Helping to Bring a Democratic Form of Government to Other Nations' by the General Public in the Chicago Council on Foreign Relations Surveys, 1974–1994
(% 'very important' ratings)

	1974	1978	1982	1986	1990	1994
All respondents	28	26	29	30	28	25
By party *						
• Republicans	27	27	28	37	30	23
• Democrats	30	30	33	29	29	24
• Independents	25	23	25	27	23	20
By ideology *						
• Conservatives	28	33	33	32	31	24
• Middle of the road	31	23	29	30	26	25
• Liberals	22	22	28	29	25	28

* Not all respondents were asked about party and ideology in the 1978–1994 surveys

human rights abroad, although partisan differences among the general public were quite small during 1986 and 1990, the years of strongest support for human rights. The partisan gap was only 4 per cent in the latter survey as a majority of Republicans, Democrats, and independents assigned the highest rating to that goal. Second, compared with the general public, partisan gaps have consistently been much wider among leaders. Differences between Republicans and Democrats reached a peak of 37 per cent in 1994, when only 9 per cent of the Republican leaders rated human rights abroad as a 'very important' foreign policy goal.

When members of the general public are classified according to ideology, the range of judgements about the pursuit of human rights abroad has typically exceeded the partisan differences—the 1982 survey represents the one exception—and there is little evidence that the gaps have been narrowing since the end of the cold war. The five CCFR surveys reveal that liberals consistently have given higher priority to human rights goals. As was true of partisan gaps on this question, the ideological differences were more pronounced among leaders than among general public, with the gaps ranging between 27 per cent and 39 per cent.

Levels of partisan differences among opinion leaders taking part in the FPLP surveys are presented in Table 7.8. The goal of promoting democracy abroad has given rise to relatively narrow gaps linked to party identification. Although responses to the most recent survey in 1996 yielded statistically significant differences, the more important points that emerged from the data are, first, that 'helping to bring a democratic form of government to other nations' was a rather low priority goal among all opinion leaders, whether Republicans, Democrats, or independents, and second, that its importance fell rather sharply between 1992 and 1996 for members of all three groups.

A somewhat different pattern may be seen in the bottom half of Table 7.8. Sharp and consistently significant partisan differences are evident in each of the five surveys that asked opinion leaders to appraise the importance of 'promoting and defending human rights in other countries'. In each case Democrats were significantly more inclined than their Republican counterparts to rate the human rights goal as 'very important,' and they did so by margins exceeding 20 per cent. In each survey, responses by the independents placed them between members of the two major parties.

Table 7.9 reports responses to the goals of promoting democracy and human rights abroad when those taking part in the FPLP surveys are classified according to self-placement on a standard five-point ideology scale. Although most analyses have shown that ideology is a very strong source of differences on a wide array of foreign policy issues, the goal of promoting democracy has yielded rather muted differences across the ideology scale. Moreover, the

Table 7.7. Assessment of 'Promoting and Defending Human Rights in Other Countries', Leaders and the General Public 1978–1994
(% 'very important' ratings)

	1978 [CCFR]	1982 [CCFR]	1986 [CCFR]	1990 [CCFR]	1993 [T-M]*	1994 [CCFR]
GENERAL PUBLIC						
All respondents	39	43	42	58	22	34
*By party:***						
• Republicans	34	35	43	57	20	23
• Democrats	44	48	42	61	26	37
• Independents	39	42	41	56	21	34
*By ideology:***						
• Conservatives	38	41	37	57	NA	29
• Middle of the road	36	46	41	56	NA	34
• Liberals	47	44	52	64	NA	43
LEADERS						
All respondents	36	41	44	45	28	26
By party						
• Republicans	20	18	24	23	14	9
• Democrats	37	46	54	48	36	46
• Independents	46	32	42	47	26	24
By ideology						
• Conservatives	16	15	26	27	12	NA
• Middle of the road	24	25	35	40	23	NA
• Liberals	55	53	59	54	42	NA

NA   Question not asked.
T-M   Times-Mirror Center for the People and Press survey.
CCFR   Chicago Council on Foreign Relations.
*   Reported percentages are for 'top priority' responses.
**   Not all respondents were asked about party and ideology in the 1978-1994 CCFR surveys.

Table 7.8. The Importance of Promoting Democracy and Human Rights Abroad in the Foreign Policy Leadership Surveys of American Opinion Leaders Classified by Party, 1976–1996
(% 'very important' ratings)

'For each [foreign policy goal], please say whether you think it should be a very important, a somewhat important, or not an important goal at all.'

	1976	1980	1984	1988	1992	1996
Helping to bring a democratic form of government to other nations						
Republicans	6	7	19	28	21	12
Democrats	9	12	18	25	26	20
Independents	6	8	18	20	21	12
Differences significant at .001 level in 1980 and 1996						
Promoting and defending human rights in other countries						
Republicans	NA	15	16	25	25	12
Democrats	NA	36	47	53	52	34
Independents	NA	26	35	36	35	23
Differences significant at .001 level in all years						

NA Question not asked

pattern of ideological differences has varied across surveys. In four of them, including the 1996 study, liberal leaders expressed the strongest support for this goal, but in the other two studies, both of them during the Reagan era, the conservatives were slightly more enthusiastic about exporting democracy. No doubt the conservative support arose largely from a hope such efforts would be targeted at the Soviet Union and its cold war allies rather than, for example, South Africa.[22]

In contrast, promoting human rights abroad as a foreign policy goal has consistently given rise to exceptionally large chasms between liberals and conservatives. The gaps ranged from a low of 34 per cent in 1980 to a high of 53 per cent twelve years later. In each instance the 'very liberal' opinion leaders ascribed the greatest importance to human rights abroad, and there was a steady erosion of support as one moved toward the 'very conservative' end of the ideological spectrum. Although the importance of human rights has declined among all five groups since the end of the cold war, the range of opinions has remained very wide.

Some additional questions in the FPLP surveys gave opinion leaders further opportunities to express their views on issues related to the promotion of

[22] For evidence on this point, see Ole Holsti, 'Public Opinion and Human Rights in American Foreign Policy', in David P. Forsythe (ed.), *The United States and Human Rights: Looking Inward and Outward* (Lincoln, NE: University of Nebraska Press, 2000, forthcoming).

democracy abroad. The 1980 study was undertaken after the fall of the Shah of Iran, the authoritarian ruler who had become the designated pillar of American interests in the Persian Gulf region. It included a question that asked respondents to assess the proposition that, 'The US should not become aligned too closely with authoritarian regimes'. A very slight majority—53 per cent— including two-thirds of the Democrats, agreed, whereas a majority of the Republicans dissented. The 1992 and 1996 surveys asked opinion leaders whether 'The US may have to support some dictators because they are friendly toward us'. Wide partisan gaps emerged from their responses, with strong support from members of the GOP and equally strong disagreement from Democrats. In 1996, however, all three groups expressed a somewhat greater willingness to support friendly tyrants than they had four years earlier.

The two most recent FPLP surveys also included the dictum that the US should be prepared 'to intrude upon the domestic affairs of other countries' with a view to establishing and preserving 'a more democratic world order'. That proposition gained the support of fewer than one leader in five in 1992, with somewhat greater approval from Republicans. Four years later, when experiences in Somalia, Haiti, and Bosnia had revealed some of the risks of

Table 7.9. The Importance of Promoting Democracy and Human Rights Abroad in the Foreign Policy Leadership Surveys of American Opinion Leaders Classified by Ideology, 1976–1996
(% 'very important' ratings)

'For each [foreign policy goal], please say whether you think it should be a very important, a somewhat important, or not an important goal at all.'

	1976	1980	1984	1988	1992	1996
Helping to being a democratic form of government to other nations						
Very liberal	13	16	20	29	26	25
Somewhat liberal	9	12	18	23	26	18
Moderate	8	9	16	23	28	14
Somewhat conservative	6	7	17	24	19	13
Very conservative	7	11	24	32	17	12
Differences significant at .001 level in 1980 and 1996						
Promoting and defending human rights in other countries						
Very liberal	NA	48	61	67	70	48
Somewhat liberal	NA	41	53	55	52	36
Moderate	NA	26	30	36	38	22
Somewhat conservative	NA	17	17	24	22	11
Very conservative	NA	14	10	21	17	11
Differences significant at .001 level in all years						

NA Question not asked.

Table 7.10. Assessments of Foreign Policy Guidelines Relevant to Democratization in US Foreign Policy in the Foreign Policy Leadership Surveys of American Opinion Leaders Classified according to Party (% agree strongly + agree somewhat)

Please indicate how strongly you agree or disagree with each statement	Year	All Respondents	Republicans	Democrats	Independents
The US should not become too closely aligned with authoritarian regimes	1980*	53	44	68	54
The US may have to support some dictators because they are friendly toward us	1992*	44	62	29	44
	1996*	52	66	39	52
The US should not hesitate to intrude upon the domestic affairs of other countries in order to establish and preserve	1992*	19	23	17	17
a more democratic world order	1996	10	8	12	8

*Differences significant at the .001 level

interventions, even this limited level of support had been cut in half, as only one opinion leader in ten agreed with it. Republicans, Democrats, and independents expressed almost equally strong disapproval toward such interventionist policies (Table 7.10).

Finally, Table 7.11 reports results for the same three propositions when respondents are classified according to ideological rather than partisan self-identifications. The first two items, concerning alignment with authoritarian regimes and support for friendly tyrants, revealed a consistent pattern in which the more conservative opinion leaders were by far the most supportive of the *Realpolitik* position that the domestic institutions and practices of other countries—especially of friendly ones—should not govern American relations with them. The gaps between the most conservative and liberal groups on these questions are huge, exceeding 40 per cent in each case. The final proposition in Table 7.11 yielded mixed results. Conservatives were somewhat more prepared than liberals to undertake interventions on behalf of a more democratic world order in 1992, but on balance even they were strongly against undertakings of this kind. By 1996 respondents in all five ideological groups expressed an overwhelming distaste for such interventions, with only minor differences among them.

Conclusion

With a few scattered exceptions, the data presented in the foregoing tables point quite clearly to the conclusions that there is very limited support among either the general public or opinion leaders for the expansion of democracy abroad, and that the end of the cold war has not given rise to heightened approval for that goal. At the very least, it is hard to find any evidence to sustain realist fears that the public is the driving force behind ill-conceived efforts to export American values and institutions to other countries. Moreover, support for such goals is often a source of sharp partisan differences, and even sharper ideological ones. Indeed, such gaps seem to narrow only when Republican and Democrats, and liberal and conservatives, are united in overwhelming *opposition* to policies directed at expanding democracy and human rights abroad.

What can explain these findings, including an apparent paradox: as the opportunities for promoting democracy have increased with the end of the cold war, and as the costs and risks of doing so have fallen, why has public enthusiasm for pursuing this goal declined? One possible argument is that perhaps the survey data are simply inadequate to capture public sentiments on expanding democracy abroad; because of such deficiencies as poor wording of the questions, respondents have not been offered an opportunity to express their real views on these issues. While this explanation cannot be ruled out with certainty, it seems rather implausible when a wide range of surveys undertaken across a period of more than two decades by several organizations

Table 7.11. Assessments of Foreign Policy Guidelines Relevant to Democratization in US Foreign Policy in the Foreign Policy Leadership Surveys of American Opinion Leaders Classified according to Ideology (% agree strongly + agree somewhat)

Please indicate how strongly you agree or disagree with each statement

	Year	Respondents	Very liberal	Somewhat liberal	Moderate	Somewhat conservative	Very conservative
The US should not become too closely aligned with authoritarian regimes	1980*	53	88	76	54	33	31
The US may have to support some dictators because they are friendly toward us	1992*	44	14	29	44	62	66
	1996*	52	20	40	54	64	67
The US should not hesitate to intrude upon the domestic affairs of other countries in order to establish and preserve a more democratic world order	1992*	19	14	15	21	21	26
	1996	10	11	10	12	8	8

* Differences significant at the .001 level

have yielded such consistent results. Moreover, surveys of both the general public and opinion leaders, which have often revealed large gaps between the two groups on many issues, have pointed to similar conclusions about the low priority assigned to democratization as well as the declining support for that goal during the post-cold war era. If we can at least tentatively assume that the survey data are valid on these issues, then we must look elsewhere for explanations. Three possible lines of reasoning depict the public in quite different ways: as irrational and ostrich-like, rational and prudent, and cynical.

The first of these explanations may be found in the 'return to the womb' thesis articulated by Arthur Schlesinger and other critics who believe that, in the absence of cold war imperatives and effective leadership in Washington, an isolationist and unilateralist public has endangered the 'magnificent dream' of American global leadership directed at a more stable and humane world order.[23] It is not hard to find evidence of post-cold war 'compassion fatigue' in survey data such as those presented in Tables 7.1–7.3. But a number of other analysts have challenged Schlesinger's gloomy assessment of contemporary public opinion about foreign affairs and America's proper role in the world, and they have presented evidence to buttress their doubts that the public has abandoned support for important aspects of global leadership.[24]

Hints about a second possible source of the findings emerge from Jentleson's studies showing that a 'pretty prudent public' is prepared to use American armed forces abroad to prevent aggression but not to alter the nature of governments or institutions in other countries.[25] The evidence presented here suggests a somewhat broader and more general version of the Jentleson thesis: the public is reluctant to have the United States involved in promoting internal changes abroad, and this lack of support is not limited to situations that require the use of American armed forces. This reluctance might arise from several sources. For example, perhaps there is agreement with the proposition that democratic institutions and practices cannot be exported successfully, least of all by the United States, because they can only emerge indigenously. It is thus neither feasible nor desirable to assign a high priority to the expansion of democracy. This view, if valid, is largely consistent with realist warnings against allowing reformist ideals, however laudable in themselves, to govern the conduct of foreign affairs.

A third and somewhat different explanation for indifference to the expansion of democracy would emphasize public cynicism about such undertakings,

---

[23] Arthur Schlesinger, Jr, 'Back to the Womb?' *Foreign Affairs* 74 (1995), pp. 2–8. For a fuller analysis of the dangers of a 'recrudescence of realist unilateralism', see John Gerard Ruggie, *Winning the Peace* (New York: Columbia University Press, 1996).

[24] Steven Kull, 'What the Public Knows that Washington Doesn't', *Foreign Policy*, 101 (1995–6), pp. 10215; Eugene R. Wittkopf, 'What Americans Really Think About Foreign Policy', *Washington Quarterly*, 19 (1996), pp. 91–106; Holsti, 'Continuity and Change'; and Steven Kull and I. M. Destler, *Misreading the Public: The Myth of a New Isolationism* (Washington: Brookings Institution, 1999).

[25] Bruce Jentleson, 'The Pretty Prudent Public: Post-Vietnam American Opinion on the Use of Force', *International Studies Quarterly*, 36/1 (1992), pp. 49–73; and Bruce Jentleson and Rebecca L. Britton, 'Still Pretty Prudent: Post-Cold War American Public Opinion on the Use of Military Force', *Journal of Conflict Resolution*, 42/4 (1998), pp. 395–417.

arising in part from a revulsion about the rag-tag band of dictators and human rights abusers that have received American approbation as 'democrats', 'friends of democracy', or 'the moral equivalent of the Founding Fathers', especially during the cold war. These friendly tyrants included but were not limited to the various regimes in Saigon during the Vietnam War, the Shah of Iran, Ferdinand Marcos and the contras in Nicaragua. Even President Carter, who was far more sensitive to human rights issues than his predecessors or successors, was not immune to this tendency to mislabel some of America's cold war friends; recall, for example, his extravagant toast to the Shah during a visit to Iran. The cynicism explanation would also take into account the mountains of survey data revealing public disenchantment with virtually all American institutions, especially political ones at the federal level, including the White House, Congress, and much of the bureaucracy.[26] If the public has lost faith in the efficiency, effectiveness, and fairness of American public institutions, is it surprising that they have consistently expressed only lukewarm support for efforts to export them to other countries?

We thus have three quite different explanations for the data. According to proponents of the first, an ostrich-like American public is quite prepared to turn its back on more than half a century of effective world leadership with consequences that are likely to be tragic. The second emphasizes a public that, because it is rational, prudent, and discriminating, is unwilling to endorse goals that seem beyond reasonable reach. The third posits a public that is not irrational, but which has grown cynical in the face of perceptions that the rhetoric of American leaders about the virtues of democracy has not been matched by reasonable standards of probity and performance, either at home or abroad.

Perhaps there is some element of truth in all three of these theses and there may also be other sources of public disinterest in expanding democracy. But wherever one finds an explanation for the evidence presented above, it seems clear that leaders who propose to place expansion of democracy at or near the top of the country's post-cold war foreign policy agenda surely cannot count on a powerful groundswell support from either the general public or opinion leaders. To the contrary, it appears that policymakers who propose to pursue such goals will have to make frequent and effective use of the 'bully pulpit' to persuade a sceptical public that promotion of democracy and human rights abroad is indeed a vital national interest.

---

[26] Evidence on public assessments of major American institutions may be found in the annual General Social Survey conducted by the National Opinion Research Center at the University of Chicago. For a recent summary, see 'Americans Rate Their Society: The NORC Series on Confidence in Leaders of National Institutions', *The Public Perspective*, 8/2 (1997), pp. 2–5.

8

Taking Stock of Democracy Assistance

THOMAS CAROTHERS

Introduction

Since the early 1980s, democracy assistance—aid explicitly designed to promote democracy abroad—has become an increasingly important component of US foreign aid and of US foreign policy generally. The US government currently spends more than $500 million annually, in over 50 countries, on democracy assistance. A number of US government agencies, ranging from the United States Agency for International Development (USAID) to the Department of Defense, sponsor these activities, as do several government-funded semi-autonomous organizations such as the National Endowment for Democracy (NED), the Asia Foundation and the Eurasia Foundation. In countries as diverse as Guatemala, Mongolia, Malawi, Bulgaria, Haiti, and Egypt, the United States government has a wide-ranging portfolio of assistance programmes designed to stimulate or further democratic transitions.

Despite the significant growth of democracy assistance, it has been only sporadically examined by US policy analysts and scholars, and remains poorly understood by most persons outside the immediate circle of practitioners. The origins and evolution of the assistance are murky to many. Only superficial attention is given to the variety of forms of such aid, with a few categories—most notably, international election observing and the sending abroad of US law professors to write foreign constitutions—dominating the public image. Basic facts about the magnitude of the aid are not widely known, leading to disproportionate responses, such as the tendency of journalists to pay much more attention to the activities of the NED than USAID, even though the latter spends more than ten times the former on democracy aid. In general, what debate does exist over democracy assistance lurches unhelpfully and unrealistically between extremes; occasional cynical observers who dismiss the democracy programmes as either far-flung foolishness or sinister scheming and fervent practitioners who argue that such assistance is critical to democracy's future.

This chapter aims to redress this informational and analytical gap. It traces the rise of democracy assistance since the 1960s and positions such aid in the overall toolbox of US democracy promotion policies. After outlining the basic types, sources, and forms of US democracy aid, it analyses key questions of strategy and impact. The chapter does not attempt to assess the degree to which democracy promotion is in fact a part of US foreign policy or the reasons why the United States does or does not make democracy one of its goals toward specific countries. These topics are the subject of other essays in the volume. The chapter is part of a series of writings on democracy assistance by this author and is intended to serve as an up-to-date overview of the subject that will complement existing analyses of specific facets of the subject, including the relationship between democracy promotion and human rights promotion, the role of the NED, the value of election observers, the role of democracy promotion in Clinton's foreign policy, and the question of strategy, as well more in-depth regionally-focused studies of democracy promotion in Latin America and eastern Europe.[1]

The Rise of Democracy Assistance

Prior to the 1980s, little US foreign aid was specifically aimed at fostering democracy. In the 1950s, US aid was heavily security-oriented and consisted primarily of economic and military assistance to bolster governments friendly to the United States. In the 1960s, economic development rose as a priority of US aid, both as a goal in and of itself and as an objective tied to US security interests—the idea being that promoting economic development in the Third World would deter countries from 'going' communist. Encouraging the establishment or maintenance of *democratic* governments in developing countries as opposed simply to *non-communist* governments was not a wide concern of most US policymakers of the period, at least after the disillusionment in the Kennedy administration with its initial efforts to promote democracy in Latin America. To the extent that democracy promotion was a goal of US foreign aid, it was pursued largely through economic aid, under the general 'modernization theory' rationale that economic development would produce political development, or democracy.

The passage in 1966 of Title IX of the Foreign Assistance Act—directing USAID to assure 'maximum participation in the task of economic development on the part of the people of the developing countries, through the encouragement of democratic private and local government institutions'—produced a brief bout of attention in the US government toward using aid to foster democracy. However, USAID interpreted Title IX much more in terms of

---

[1] See, for example, Thomas Carothers, *Aiding Democracy Abroad: The Learning Curve* (Washington, DC: Carnegie Endowment, 1999); 'Democracy Assistance: The Question of Strategy', *Democratization*, 4/3 (1997), pp. 109, 132; 'The Rise of Election Monitoring: The Observers Observed', *Journal of Democracy*, 8/3 (1997), pp. 17–31; *Assessing Democracy Assistance: The Case of Romania* (Washington, DC: Carnegie Endowment, 1996); 'Democracy Promotion Under Clinton', *The Washington Quarterly*, 8/4 (1995), pp. 13–25; 'Democracy and Human Rights: Policy Allies or Rivals?', *The Washington Quarterly*, 17/3 (1994), pp. 10920; 'The NED at 10', *Foreign Policy*, 73 (1994), pp. 123–38; and *In the Name of Democracy: US Policy Toward Latin America in the Reagan Years* (Berkeley: University of California Press, 1991).

increasing participation in economic development than of promoting demo-cratic institutions *per se*, and created few programmes explicitly aimed at pro-moting democracy. A number of programmes established by USAID in the 1960s reached similar sectors—legislatures, legal systems, labour unions, civic organizations, and so forth—as the democracy programmes of the 1990s. These programmes were often carried out in dictatorships, however, and were more about increasing participation in economic development than about democratization.[2]

With the 1970s came the 'basic human needs' doctrine in foreign aid, a back-to-basics trend prompted by disillusionment over the overall course of Third World development and foreign aid itself. This approach eschewed the idea of a natural connection between economic development and political development and pointed aid sharply away from any explicit concern with democracy. The emergence of human rights as a goal of US foreign policy in the second half of the 1970s led to some diplomatic initiatives that could be interpreted as pro-democratic—although they were not generally put in those terms—but little change on the assistance front. In 1978, Congress enacted Section 116(e) of the Foreign Assistance Act authorizing the use of assistance funds for projects to promote human rights. Some small efforts were under-taken in this direction, such as funding legal aid centres in Latin America, but they were at most a minor footnote to the overall portfolio of US aid.

The emergence of US democracy assistance in the 1980s had its roots in the renewed anti-communist emphasis of the first Reagan administration. President Reagan and his early foreign policy team were concerned about what they believed to be an inadequate US engagement in the 'war of ideas' with the Soviet Union. They developed plans for an ambitious public diplomacy campaign to promote the idea of democracy around the world; and in 1982, before the British Parliament, President Reagan announced that the United States would undertake a new assistance effort to promote democracy abroad. Congress did not approve the plans for the public diplomacy campaign, but in 1983 it did approve a related plan for the establishment of a governmentally funded but privately operated organization devoted to democracy promotion: the National Endowment for Democracy. The Endowment represented the major first step toward the establishment of the broad programme of US democracy assistance.[3]

The growth of democracy assistance within official US assistance started soon after the founding of the NED. In Central America, the State Department and USAID initiated a new set of assistance efforts in the mid-1980s, some aimed at supporting transitional elections and some at improving the

[2] On Title IX, see Robert Packenham, *Liberal America and the Third World* (Princeton: Princeton University Press, 1973) and Elizabeth Fletcher Cook, 'Political Development as a Programme Objective of US Foreign Assistance: Title IX of the 1966 Foreign Assistance Act', unpublished doctoral dissertation, 1971.

[3] See Carothers, *In the Name of Democracy*, Ch. 6; Christopher Madison, 'Selling Democracy', *National Journal* (28 June 1986), pp. 1603–08; Howard Wiarda, *The Democratic Revolution in Latin America: History, Politics, and US Policy* (New York: Holmes and Meier, 1990), Ch. 6.

administration of justice. These initiatives were one part of the Reagan administration's effort in that region of supporting transitions to democracy—or, more accurately, elected civilian rule—which in turn was a part of the larger policy of resisting the spread of what the Reagan administration believed to be Soviet-sponsored leftist subversion of the region. They quickly gained momentum of their own, however, and USAID began to sponsor elections assistance, rule-of-law aid, and other types of aid directly aimed at fostering democracy in various parts of Latin America and the Caribbean. Although initially rooted in the strident anti-communist policy toward Central America, this new wave of democracy aid spread in response to the democratic trend in the region. As country after country in Latin America underwent encouraging transitions away from military rule toward democracy, the US government, and US aid, attempted to support that trend. By the end of the second Reagan administration, the United States was involved in extensive democracy assistance efforts in countries such as Chile, Haiti, and Paraguay where anti-communist strategic concerns were not the primary motivating factor.[4]

Latin America was the main locus of the early wave of US democracy assistance, but as countries in other parts of the world began to democratize in the second half of the 1980s, US democracy assistance followed. This was most noticeable in Asia, where US democracy assistance efforts supported transition processes in the Philippines, South Korea, Taiwan, Pakistan, and elsewhere. To an extent that is often now forgotten, President Reagan and his top aides constantly made what they called 'the worldwide democratic revolution' a major stated theme of US foreign policy. Although Reagan's policies were in fact a mix of pro- and anti-democratic actions—as for example the support for a number of anti-communist 'friendly tyrants' such as President Mobutu of Zaire and President Suharto of Indonesia, democracy promotion was a genuine goal in some countries and democracy assistance was becoming an accepted policy tool.

In the 1990s, democracy assistance mushroomed, driven by a confluence of trends including the fall of communism in eastern Europe, the demise of the Soviet Union, the surprisingly widespread trend of political openings in sub-Saharan Africa, further democratic transitions in Asia, and a mild but recognizable liberalization trend in parts of the Middle East. For the most part, where democracy seemed to be emerging, the United States attempted to be supportive, both diplomatically, economically, and with democracy aid. A second key factor was the end of the cold war. The falling away of the US-Soviet global rivalry reduced ideological tensions around the world and made it much easier for the United States and other countries to engage in assistance programmes with an explicit political purpose. It also reduced divisions within the US policy community and allowed conservatives and liberals to agree on the value of democracy assistance and democracy promotion rather than to

---

[4] Carothers, *In the Name of Democracy*, Ch. 6; Tamar Jacoby, 'The Reagan Turnaround on Human Rights', *Foreign Affairs*, 64 (1986), pp. 1066–86.

treat those subjects as further points in a long-standing argument over the relationship of ideals and interests in US foreign policy.[5]

American democracy aid expanded most rapidly in eastern Europe and the former Soviet Union as an integral part of the Bush and then the Clinton administration's policy of supporting the transition away from communism. Under the Support for Eastern European Democracy Act of 1989, the US government has provided significant amounts of democracy aid to eastern Europe since 1989.[6] Similarly, under the Freedom Support Act of 1991, large amounts of democracy aid have gone to the former Soviet Union since 1991.[7] Russia and Ukraine have been by far the largest recipients of such aid in the former Soviet Union, with major programmes on elections, parties, rule of law, and civil society.

Although US aid officials were initially sceptical at the beginning of the 1990s about the idea of democracy-related aid to sub-Saharan Africa, they were brought around to it by both policymakers and Africans themselves who sought help from Western donors for their attempted democratic transitions. A major elections programme established by USAID aided almost every transitional election in Africa in the first half of the 1990s. A host of other programmes, ranging from civic education to legislative strengthening, were initiated and by the mid-1990s a majority of countries in the region were receiving some type of US democracy aid.

Democracy assistance increased to Asia, at least to those countries attempting democratic transitions, such as Cambodia, Mongolia, and Nepal. In Asia more than in any other region, however, some US aid officials held to the idea that it might be better just to focus on economic development and let political development take care of itself. In the Middle East, a few modest programmes were initiated, primarily aimed at supporting either legislative elections or newly established legislatures, such as in Kuwait and Jordan. In Latin America, the United States continued to be heavily involved with democracy assistance. The initial focus on elections assistance in Latin America faded as elections became more regularized. The additional strong emphasis on programmes of judicial and legal reform largely continued. New programmes were added on civil society development and decentralization and the largest recipient of such aid passed from being El Salvador to Haiti, reflective of the changes in overall US policy toward the region.

In the 1990s, US democracy aid increased not only as part of US foreign assistance but as a part of the aid programmes of many other countries and of a number of international organizations. Almost every major aid donor has developed democracy-related programmes, with some becoming very actively involved, such as Sweden, the Netherlands, Germany, the European Union,

---

[5] See Catharin E. DalpiNo, *Anchoring Third Wave Democracies* (Washington, DC: Institute for the Study of Diplomacy, Georgetown University, 1998), Ch. 1.

[6] See 'SEED Act Implementation Report Fiscal Year 1996', Department of State Publication 10443 (February 1997).

[7] 'US Government Assistance to and Cooperative Activities with the New Independent States of the Former Soviet Union: FY 1996 Annual Report', Department of State (January 1997).

Denmark, Norway, and Spain.[8] The United Nations, the Organization of American States, the Organization for Security and Cooperation for Europe, the Council of Europe, the Commonwealth Association, and other multilateral institutions also now undertake democracy assistance.[9] In addition, multilateral banks, including the World Bank, the Inter-American Development Bank, the European Bank for Reconstruction and Development, and the Asian Development Bank, have moved into governance-related activities that often have much in common with democracy assistance.[10] The growth of US democracy assistance is thus just one part of a much larger trend in the international community.

The Democracy Policy Toolbox

When the US government does decide to try to promote democracy in a country, democracy assistance is just one of a number of tools available for the task. Very generally speaking, most policy measures aimed at promoting democracy in other countries fall into the categories of either 'stick' or 'carrot'. The types of sticks are several. The US government can exert *diplomatic pressure* on countries for their democratic failings. This may consist of critical remarks by high-level US officials, not inviting the leaders of the country to Washington, and generally maintaining 'cool' diplomatic relations, with such measures taken in reaction either to a specific visible event, such as a stolen election, or to a more diffuse trend of democratic stagnation. At least in Latin America, where there is some regional consensus on the norm of democracy, pro-democratic diplomacy can also entail mobilizing multinational coalitions to exert pressure on a backsliding country, such as occurred in relation to Paraguay in late 1996.[11] Another stick is *economic pressure*, measures such as denying trade benefits or most favoured nation status, working to reduce or cut off loans to the country from the international financial institutions, and reducing US economic aid. In more extreme circumstances, the United States sometimes imposes economic sanctions to try to overturn a disliked authoritarian ruler, such as those imposed against General Manuel Antonio Noriega in Panama in 1988. The ultimate stick is *military intervention*—military action to restore democracy in

[8] See Michael Pinto-Duschinsky, 'The Rise of Political Aid', in Larry Diamond, Marc Plattner, Yun-han Chu, and Hung-mao Tien (eds), *Consolidating the Third Wave Democracies* (Baltimore: Johns Hopkins University Press, 1997), pp. 295–324.

[9] See Larry Diamond, *Promoting Democracy in the 1990s* (Washington, DC: Carnegie Commission on Preventing Deadly Conflict, 1995), pp. 31–8.

[10] On the World Bank's governance work see 'Governance: The World Bank Experience' (Washington, DC: The World Bank, 30 November 1993), and 'Governance and Development' (Washington, DC: The World Bank, 1992). On the Inter-American Development Bank's governance work see 'Modernization of the State' (Washington, DC: Inter-American Development Bank, July 1994). For a critical analysis of the concept of governance employed by the multilateral development banks see David Williams and Tom Young, 'Governance, the World Bank and Liberal Theory', *Political Studies*, 42/1 (1994), pp. 84–100.

[11] Arturo Valenzuela, 'The Coup That Didn't Happen', *Journal of Democracy*, 8/1 (1997), pp. 43–55.

a country that has experienced a military coup or other type of democratic reversal. Such actions are rare. Military interventions by the US are often given the label of pro-democratic ventures—such as the 1994 Haiti intervention and the 1990 Panama intervention—but tend to be rooted in other motives, whether relating to security concerns or to domestic political pressures.

The carrots are the mirror image of the sticks. The United States can encourage democratic progress with diplomatic favour: official praise, state visits for newly elected leaders, a regular stream of higher-level official contacts, and the like. Economic rewards may also be granted. American economic aid is sometimes tied to democracy. In Africa in the 1990s, for example, the United States set economic aid levels to specific countries in some part on the basis of their democratic performance. Trade and other commercial benefits are also used. After the relatively successful local elections in Romania in 1992, for example, the Bush administration reversed its opposition to most favoured nation status for Romania, opposition that had been based primarily on the administration's dissatisfaction with the weak democratic path of the Iliescu government.

Alongside these various sticks and carrots is democracy assistance. Democracy aid is best thought of as neither carrot nor stick. When the United States gives such aid to countries that are not democratic or are moving backward away from a political opening, the aid is not considered a type of punishment—at least by the providers—but rather as a sort of pro-democratic medicine. Similarly, when democracy aid is provided to countries that are moving forward with democratization, it is not given as a reward but rather as a supplementary boost.

Publicly funded democracy programmes are one tool of US foreign policy. Yet just as there is talk at times of a separation between US foreign aid and US foreign policy, and the need to make foreign aid more strictly serve US policy goals, the relationship between democracy aid in a specific country and US policy toward that country is not always simple. Democracy aid is the work of a subset of the aid bureaucracy, and there exists the tendency of some enthusiasts of such assistance to push to do it in every possible setting whether or not democracy promotion is really an element of the broader policy line. For example, in Indonesia USAID sponsored some small democracy programmes—mostly consisting of aid to independent human rights groups—for much of the 1990s despite the fact that the main thrust of US policy was stability and a positive relationship with President Suharto. Similarly, in Kazakhstan some low-key democracy programmes coexisted in the 1990s with a broader embrace of the not very democratic President Nazabayev. State Department officials typically tolerate such discrepancies, in large part because they do not take the democracy programmes very seriously. If by chance the political situation is upended, such as with the sudden fall of Indonesian President Suharto in 1998, the State Department does not hesitate to take credit for what suddenly appear to have been far-sighted, effective democracy promotion efforts.

The Types, Sources and Forms of Democracy Aid

Types

The term 'democracy assistance' is sometimes used broadly to mean all aid to a government that is attempting to lead a democratization process. For example, in some budget documents submitted to Congress, the Clinton administration listed all aid to the former Soviet Union, whether focused on health, privatization, or banking regulation, as 'democracy building' on the ground that all of the aid contributed to the overall post-Soviet project of transition toward democracy and market economics. A more specific meaning of the term is intended here. Democracy aid is all aid for which the primary purpose, not the secondary or indirect purpose, is to foster democracy in the recipient country. It does not therefore include economic and social aid programmes.

Democracy aid falls into three general categories.

1. *Political process*. This includes aid to promote free and fair elections: technical aid to election commissions for better administration of elections, support for both international and domestic election observation, and aid to promote voter registration and voter education. It also consists of aid to strengthen political parties, both their overall institutional base and their more specific election-related capabilities.
2. *Governing institutions*. This aid takes numerous forms: programmes to strengthen national legislatures, judicial reform efforts, police training and restructuring, and local government strengthening programmes. It may consist of efforts to help a country rewrite its constitution. The military may also be a target: programmes to develop pro-democratic attitudes within a military, to increase civilian control over a military, or otherwise improve civil-military relations.
3. *Civil society*. American aid to foster civil society development has taken four major forms in the 1990s: support for non-governmental organizations (NGOs) engaged in public interest-oriented advocacy work, such as human rights, women's issues, or election monitoring; assistance to build independent media; support for independent labour unions; and programmes that seek to promote better citizen understanding of democracy, such as civic education projects, conferences and seminars on democracy, and educational exchange programmes.

Actors

Many different agencies and organizations have a role in US democracy assistance. By far the largest actor is USAID, the main foreign aid agency of the government. It formally made democracy promotion one of its four core priorities in 1990, a status that was fortified when the Clinton administration came to power and Brian Atwood, formerly head of the National Democratic Institute for International Affairs, a democracy promotion organization, took over the leadership of USAID. During the 1990s, USAID devoted approximately $400 million a year to democracy programmes, the funds going to programmes of all the types outlined above. By the mid-1990s, democracy work was a part of the portfolios of most, although not all, USAID missions around the world.[12]

The second most important governmental agency for democracy assistance is the United States Information Agency (USIA), now reincorporated into the State Department. For many years, but especially since the early 1980s when the Reagan administration increased attention within USIA to democracy advocacy as part of the intensified 'war of ideas' with the Soviet Union, USIA has emphasized democracy promotion in its work. Through conferences in other countries, speakers sent on foreign tours, educational exchanges, short-term visitor programmes and other methods, USIA has promoted democracy as a political ideology and helped disseminate abroad specific knowledge about the functioning of democratic systems.

The State Department is also responsible for a certain amount of democracy-related assistance. The State Department oversees some of the 'Section 116(e) funds', the special pool of funds established in 1978 for assistance programmes to promote human rights abroad. During the 1980s the mandate for these funds began to be interpreted by the State Department and USAID as including democracy promotion, and they are now used for human rights and democracy programmes interchangeably. The State Department's Bureau for Democracy, Human Rights, and Labor also has responsibility for some democracy assistance funds, although most of the actual programming is implemented by USAID.

The Department of Defense has in recent years increasingly emphasized democracy promotion as one of the goals of its foreign military training programmes. In 1991, Congress mandated that the International Military Education and Training (IMET) programme of the Pentagon be expanded to address the needs of new democracies. Under 'expanded IMET' (E-IMET), the Defense Department's assistance to foreign militaries gives greater emphasis than before to civilian control of militaries, human rights, and other democracy-related topics.

The Department of Justice is also involved in democracy programmes, primarily relating to judicial and police reform. The Overseas Prosecutorial Development Assistance and Training (OPDAT) programme trains foreign prosecutors. A number of major foreign police assistance efforts at the Department of Justice, including the International Criminal Investigative Training Assistance Programme (ICITAP), and the police training programmes

---

[12] It is difficult to arrive at a single figure for all of USAID's democracy programmes because there are many different ways of defining a democracy programme. The $400 million figure represents programmes which directly aim to promote democratic institutions and processes and was obtained through interviews with USAID officials in the Center for Democracy and Governance in the USAID Bureau for Global Affairs. The annual USAID Congressional Presentations give considerable information about USAID's democracy programming.

of the Drug Enforcement Agency and the FBI, work to strengthen foreign police forces. Of these programmes, only ICITAP specifically has pro-democratic intentions; the others are more focused on law enforcement goals.[13]

Alongside these US government agencies, several organizations primarily funded by the US government but operating as private, non-profit organiza-tions with independent boards of directors and non-US government employee staffs are heavily involved in democracy assistance. The most visible of these is the NED, which, as noted previously, was established in 1983. The essential idea was to create an organization whose sole purpose was democracy promo-tion and which would use government funds but not be a part of the govern-ment, and would therefore have greater latitude than the government in acting politically abroad. The NED, which in the 1990s had an annual budget in the range of $25 million to $35 million, gives at least half of its grant funds to four core institutions—the International Republican Institute, the National Democratic Institute for International Affairs, the American Center for Labor Solidarity, and the Center for International Private Enterprise—representing respectively the Republican and Democratic parties, the AFL-CIO, and the US Chamber of Commerce. Each of these institutions carries out assistance pro-grammes abroad relating to its areas of specialty: the political party institutes work primarily on elections and political party assistance, with some attention to legislatures, local government, and civic education; the labour institute supports labour unions; and the business institute seeks to further free enter-prise abroad. The rest of the NED's grant funds, known as NED's 'discretionary' funds, go in relatively small grants to organizations in the United States and abroad that are working to promote civic education, democratic awareness, independent media, human rights, and other similar goals, often in non-democratic countries, ranging from Nigeria to Vietnam.[14]

The Asia Foundation, established in 1954, receives the bulk of its funds from the US government, in several forms: a yearly line item grant from Congress, some USAID grants, and some funds from the State Department. The Asia Foundation has for many years sought to foster pluralistic governing institu-tions in Asia. Since the early 1980s, it has stepped up its emphasis on demo-cracy promotion and broadened its focus beyond governing institutions to encompass civil society and democratic education. The 1996 budget of the foundation was just under $40 million, with between one-half and two-thirds of its work bearing some relation to democracy promotion.

Finally, the Eurasia Foundation, established in 1993 to assist the post-Soviet states, also gives democratic aid. Through its offices in the field and its main office in Washington, the foundation sponsors programmes on issues such as

---

[13] On ICITAP, see '1996 Annual Report of Organizational Development and Training Activities', International Criminal Investigative Training Assistance Programme (Washington, DC: US Department of Justice), and Charles Call, 'Police Aid and the New World Disorder: Institutional Learning Within the US International Criminal Investigative Training Assistance Programme (ICI-TAP)', unpublished paper (Stanford University, 3 July 1997).

[14] For basic information on the NED see its annual reports. See also, Carothers, 'The NED at Ten'.

local government reform, public administration strengthening, NGO development, the rule of law, and media development. The Eurasia Foundation operates almost exclusively with US government funds, with a 1997 budget of $25 million.

Forms

The term 'aid' conjures up the idea of money flowing from a donor to a recipient. Most US democracy aid, however, does not consist of such transfers. The most common form of such aid is training and technical assistance: advice, counsel, knowledge, know-how, and information given by the aid provider to the aid recipient. Thus, election assistance generally consists not of funds to hold an election but of advice about how to administer it and training on election administration. Legislative assistance usually consists of training for parliamentarians and staff, advice on how to run committees, efforts to encourage the setting up of constituent offices, and so forth. Media assistance is typically less about money to cover operating costs of newspapers, radio stations, or television networks and more about training for journalists or reporters, advice on how to run media operations as a business, and efforts to establish better legal protections for independent media.

US democracy assistance does sometimes entail direct grants or other transfers to organizations in recipient countries. This is most common with aid to civil society development, with USAID setting up some small direct grant programmes for local NGOs. These grants are relatively small, usually in the range of $10,000 to $50,000 and are often accompanied by technical assistance on management and accounting.

Most USAID-funded democracy assistance projects involve a US intermediary organization that receives the actual funds and delivers the training and technical assistance to the recipient country. These intermediary organizations are many. Some are groups that specialize in democracy assistance: the political party institutes and the labour institute that are core grantees of the NED, the International Foundation for Election Systems, and the Central and Eastern European Law Initiative of the American Bar Association. The other type of intermediary organizations are for-profit development consulting firms that do many types of development work for USAID but have added capacity to take on democracy-related projects as such funds have increased. The major such development firms involved in democracy assistance include Management Systems International, Chemonics International, Development Associates Inc., Creative Associates, Checchi & Co., PACT, and World Learning.

The Question of Strategy

A fundamental question about democracy assistance is the question of strategy, which can be sub-divided into two parts. First, on what model of *democracy* are democracy assistance programmes based? And second, on what model of *democratization* is such assistance built? Stated differently, toward what specific end do democracy programmes point and how do they presume to move countries there?

The conception of democracy underlying most US democracy assistance is hardly arcane. It has the following basic features: regular, free, and fair elections; a constitution that enshrines democracy and a full set of civil and political rights; a governmental system based on the separation of powers and consisting of an accountable, lawful executive branch, a representative legislature, and an independent judiciary; viable local government structures; national political parties that aggregate and articulate citizens' interests; and some independent trade unions, independent media, and independent advocacy NGOs. It is, in short, the liberal democratic model, although defined in somewhat more detailed institutional terms than conventional political science definitions, which tend to emphasize elections and respect for political and civil rights.

Whereas the model of democracy underlying democracy assistance programmes is clear, the model of democratization is less so. It is not stated explicitly in aid strategy documents and project papers. It is rarely articulated in speeches or statements. Rather, it is implicit in the programmes themselves and has to be deduced from their content. Basically this model assumes a two-part sequence of democratic transition and consolidation. In the transition phase, a non-democratic government experiences a loss of legitimacy and power due either to the accumulation of its own shortcomings, rising public desire for democracy, external pressures or a combination of the three. The government either permits a political opening or is driven completely out of power. Open national elections are held and a democratic government arrives to power. In the consolidation phase, the new government progressively reforms the major governing institutions to make them more representative, accountable, and effective. At the same time, civil society grows stronger and more diverse and increasingly serves to articulate citizens' interests and to check the power of the state.

A central process in this model is *institutional modeling*: the notion that democratizing countries progressively shape their major socio-political institutions in the form of such institutions in established democracies. It is this process that democracy assistance seeks to advance. Each area of democracy assistance aims to help reshape a particular institution: trade union assistance seeks to make the recipient unions take on the key characteristics of Western unions; legislative programmes aim to mould legislatures in the form of Western models; elections assistance seeks to produce elections that resemble Western democratic elections; and so forth. The idea is that if each major socio-political institution in a transitional country can manage to attain the basic features of such institutions in democratic societies, the political system as a whole will become democratic.[15]

---

[15] A fuller account of the 'institutional modeling' approach is given in Carothers, 'Democracy Assistance: The Question of Strategy'.

Although the model of democracy underlying US democracy assistance is clearly drawn from the US experience, the model of democratization is not. Providers of US aid do not refer in their studies and project designs to the specific patterns of democratization in America: how press freedom was established and maintained, what led to judicial reform in the late nineteenth century, how labour unions formed, and so forth. Nor is the model drawn from the academic literature on democratization. There is remarkably little borrowing by aid officials engaged in democracy promotion of ideas and concepts from the burgeoning scholarly literature on democratic transitions. A crucial concept in the extensive 'transitology' literature of the 1980s on Latin American democratic transitions, for example, was that of pacts and pact formation.[16] Yet that concept is entirely missing from project documents on US democracy assistance to Latin America of that period and from the projects themselves. The reasons for the lack of close connection between democracy assistance and scholarly inquiries into democratization are various and can only be mentioned here. They include the differing purposes of the two endeavours—finding ways to produce change as distinct from finding concepts to explain change—the tendency of practitioners not to follow academic debates and writings, and the tendency of scholars not to seek to engage directly the assistance community.

The source of the democratization model is thus neither US history nor academic theory. It appears instead to derive from a certain common-sense style of assistance design. When assistance officials attempt to assess the state of democracy in a transitional country they tend to go through an institutional checklist, examining the state of the parliament, the judiciary, the unions, the media, and other institutions that they hold to be crucial to democracy, assessing how those institutions compare with counterparts in established democracies. They then design programmes to address the perceived shortcomings in the various institutions. In other words, aid providers assess transitional countries in terms of what they themselves know best—which are the endpoints rather than the processes of democratization. They then create programmes to reproduce those endpoints with the assumption that the achievement of the correct endpoints will solve the problem of process.

These models of democracy and democratization underlying US democracy assistance do have some strengths. They are relatively simple and clear, which are useful features to aid officials struggling to explain democracy aid to policymakers, congressmen, journalists, and others within the US policy community. Telling a sceptical US congressman that promoting democracy in some far-off country, say Malawi or Mongolia, consists of familiar activities like training parliamentary staff, building up a legislative library, and helping legislators in those countries learn to hold public hearings is likely to be reassuring for the congressman. These models also provide aid officials with a sense of direction. Democracy assistance has spread very rapidly and widely in

---

[16] The role of pacts was highlighted, for example, in Guillermo O'Donnell and Philippe C. Schmitter, *Transitions from Authoritarian Rule* (Baltimore: Johns Hopkins University Press, 1986).

the past ten years and aid providers have needed an approach that will allow them to land in very unclear, fluid situations and rapidly produce a clear set of next steps. The US model of democracy and the institutional modeling approach fit that bill.

The shortcomings of these models are varied and serious. One problem relating to the model of democracy is that US democracy promoters push to create political attributes that are quite specific to American democracy yet hold them out as features of liberal democracy generally. Thus, for example, US legislative strengthening programmes often focus on elements that are not common features of legislatures in established democracies but instead are *distinguishing* features of the US Congress, such as a large, powerful staff, an outstanding library, powerful committees, a confrontational posture toward the executive branch, and a high degree of openness to advocacy or lobbying from outside interest groups. Similarly, US media assistance programmes often emphasize training for investigative reporting, the importance of non-partisanship, and private rather than public ownership—cardinal features of US media but not of the media of all other democracies. Many of the persons involved in US democracy aid programmes are surprisingly unaware of the numerous different institutional forms in other established democracies, and in particular of the fact that American democracy is quite different from, and in some ways rather isolated from, democracy in many western European countries. They confuse American democracy with liberal democracy itself and promote a form of democracy that is over-specific and strongly rooted in particular political traditions that may not apply in other countries, even countries that may fully intend to be democratic.

A major problem with the institutional modeling idea in the model of democratization is that it encourages aid providers to ignore the underlying relationships and structures of power at work in any particular sector they are trying to change. They assume that it will be possible to help change the basic key political institutions without actually grappling with the entrenched interests dominating them, that some modest amounts of technocratic training and technical assistance will fix fundamental problems. For example, assessments of judicial systems in transitional countries regularly find that cases move too slowly, judges lack training, and the judicial infrastructure is weak. The aid response is to design new case management systems, increase judicial training, and rebuild infrastructure rather than to delve into why the judiciary is in a terrible state, whose interests its deficiencies serve, and what configuration of political actors might be willing to fight for reform. This tendency to treat the symptoms rather than the causes of democratic shortcomings is a pervasive feature of democracy assistance and often a fatal flaw. Programmes end up foundering on the lack of any real will to reform, on obstacles put forward by countervailing, entrenched interests, and on a lack of understanding of the essential political dynamics at play.

Another major problem with the institutional modeling strategy is that it assumes that democratization is essentially a natural process in which countries move from dysfunctional dictatorship to peaceful pluralism without great upheaval, violence or doubt. With the passage of time, however, it is increasingly evident that many of the putative 'democratic transitions' of the late 1980s and early 1990s, especially in Africa, Central Asia, the Caucasus, and south-eastern Europe, are not following the path of initial opening, elections, and progressive consolidation. Openings are sometimes leading to failed elections. And even when legitimate elections are held, subsequent efforts at consolidation are sometimes lapsing into semi-authoritarianism, outright authoritarianism, or even civil conflict. When this occurs, the basic strategy of democracy assistance proves of little use. Assisting elections is futile if the elections are held merely to legitimize the rule of an aspiring strongman leader. Providing support to reform government institutions does little good when there is little internal will to reform. Strengthening civil society runs rapidly into sharp limits when the space in which civil society operates is harshly restricted. An assistance strategy rooted in the notion of gradual, positive change works poorly when the underlying political dynamic is very different.

American aid providers are taking note of these shortcomings of the basic strategy and beginning to formulate corrective responses. The tendency to promote highly US-specific democratic forms is being increasingly leavened with a recognition of the need to provide comparative models and to use experts and trainers from other countries. Aid providers are also attempting to take much greater account of the underlying interests and power structures at play in any given political situation. They are paying much more attention, for example, to whether there exists significant will to reform within an institution before attempting to help reform it or how to help engender such impetus if it is not present. The tools for assessing and dealing with issues of power and vested interests are still not highly developed, but the necessity of facing these issues is increasingly accepted.

Similarly, as aid providers confront the reality of democratic stagnation or backsliding in many countries they are beginning to develop alternative strategies. For example, in countries with semi-authoritarian leaders, such as Kenya and Ethiopia, US democracy aid often emphasizes civil society development, in the hope that it will serve as a means of preserving the existing political space and possibly widening it. In countries attempting political transitions as part of a process of ending a civil war, US democracy efforts sometimes grapple with reconciliation, as in El Salvador and Guatemala. Where the central institutions are nominally democratic but seem unable to respond effectively to the needs of the population, such as in Nepal and Bangladesh, democracy assistance sometimes emphasizes decentralization and partnerships between local civil society organizations and local government. The trend, in short, is away from a uniform, unilinear strategy toward a typology of strategies that conform to the numerous varieties of political transitions clustered under the very general heading of 'democratization'.

Effects and Experiences

Despite the fact that the United States has spent at least several billion dollars on democracy assistance during the past two decades, surprisingly little is known about the actual effects of these efforts. Only a few outside studies of such assistance have been carried out.[17] Some of the agencies or organizations that provide the assistance do carry out evaluations of their own programmes. These evaluations provide some insight into the effects of the programmes, as well as some lessons learned about what works and what does not. The value of such 'in-house' evaluations is limited, however, in several ways. Although outside consultants are sometimes employed as evaluators, the studies have an officialist character, are rarely very critical, and tend to gloss over mistakes and failures. Until recently, the evaluations focused on the specific 'outputs' of the programmes, such as the number of persons trained or the number of fax machines delivered, rather than the actual political impact. Impact is now a major concern, at least at USAID, but the process of evaluation has become caught up in a frantic search for highly specific, quantitative indicators of democratic progress. The evaluations now produce reductionistic fragments of information about the effects of assistance efforts, fragments that are generally not placed in any larger, more meaningful context. Thus, for example, an evaluation might show that a parliamentary programme increased the number of public hearings held by a parliament but give no explanation of whether the public hearings actually constituted significant events, increased public information about the parliament's actions—as opposed to getting publicity for a particular parliamentarian—or resulted in more informed action by the parliament.

Although few in-depth studies of the effects of democracy assistance exist, some basic points about the experience of US democracy assistance in the three basic areas of assistance can be put forward. Elections assistance is the most developed area of democracy assistance. After having worked on elections in countless countries since the mid-1980s, US aid providers have refined sophisticated methods for helping election administrators and for carrying out election observing.[18] Election aid has helped many elections go more smoothly and has generally increased understanding of and respect for the principle of free and fair elections in many parts of the world. Elections assistance cannot, unfortunately, guarantee a good election. In Central Asia, the Caucasus, sub-Saharan Africa, and elsewhere entrenched rulers determined to stay in power have been able to manipulate elections to their advantage

[17] American programmes to promote labour unions in Russia are examined in Linda J. Cook, *Labor and Liberalization: Trade Unions in the New Russia* (New York: Twentieth Century Fund, 1997). American democracy assistance to Eastern Europe is analysed through a single in-depth country case study in Carothers, *Assessing Democracy Assistance: The Case of Romania.*

[18] See Larry Garber and Glenn Cowan, 'The Virtues of Parallel Vote Tabulations', *Journal of Democracy*, 4 (1993), pp. 95–107; Neil Nevitte and Santiago A. Canton, 'The Role of Domestic Observers', *Journal of Democracy*, 8 (1997), pp. 47–61; Thomas Carothers, 'The Observers Observed', *Journal of Democracy*, 8 (1997), pp. 17–31.

despite the existence of externally-sponsored assistance on election administration and the presence of international observers. Furthermore, the record of
the many transitional elections of recent years has also demonstrated that
even when well-designed election assistance efforts are implemented and elections go very well, the political process may nonetheless go off the tracks
sooner or later as elected leaders turn out to be anti-democratic—such as in
Zambia and Belarus, or political consensus on the outcome breaks down—as
in Cambodia, Burundi, and Angola.

A sobering number of democracy aid projects targeted at state institutions
have ended in disappointment or even outright failure. It turns out to be very
difficult to help political institutions such as parliaments, judiciaries, and local
governments undertake fundamental reforms. The power structures in which
such institutions are embedded often lie outside the reach of the assistance
efforts and undercut what is done. A genuine will to reform matched with
leadership skills and real technical capacities is exceedingly rare in such institutions, rendering them poorly positioned to take advantage of assistance.
Even when such leadership exists, the rank and file personnel of the institutions often resist reforms out of fear of a loss of security, perquisites, or power.
Despite over ten years and hundreds of millions of dollars of support for judicial, legal and police reform in Latin America, for example, the administration
of justice in most countries of the region remains seriously troubled. Aid
providers are learning to work more within the interstices of institutions
rather than on the surface and to accept very modest incremental gains as a
reasonable return for major investments. They have also been developing
ways to help promote institutional change by empowering non-state actors
that seek to exert constructive pressure for change. None the less, democracy
aid to governing institutions remains a difficult area of endeavour.

Concerning civil society development, US aid providers, usually in conjunction with similar programmes by various European and multilateral
donors, are able to help create burgeoning NGO sectors in countries coming
out of authoritarianism. These NGOs exert some pressure on transitional governments for free and fair elections, better laws on governmental transparency, greater respect of political and civil rights, and other elements of
democratic governance. Although these new NGO sectors generally have
many positive features and constitute the possible start of a broader pattern of
civic participation, they usually also have serious limitations. They often are
dominated by a limited circle of small, elite-run organizations that have little
popular support, few means of local sustainability, and vague agendas that
change with each new donor fashion. The gap between creating NGOs and
creating civil society is generally wide. In transitional countries where leaders
are slipping into semi-authoritarian rule, these NGO sectors are able to keep
alive a certain amount of political space but rarely have the power on their
own to challenge the regime seriously.

American civic education efforts in a number of countries to promote voter
education in preparation for first-time transitional elections have helped make

citizens more aware of the purpose of elections and probably increased the value of the elections. The many more general civic education programmes that have been sponsored around the world have had uncertain effect. Presenting persons with basic information about democracy, political participation, human rights, and the like may contribute in some amorphous ways to democratic development. But there is no good evidence to show that it is possible to change the basic political attitudes and political behavioural patterns of large numbers of people through short-term educational programmes in contexts where the overall political context is itself not much changing.[19]

Very generally speaking, it is certainly possible to find many examples of democracy assistance programmes that appear to have been helpful to the particular people participating in the programme and that have helped achieve some modest improvements in particular institutions or organizations involved in a country's democratic development. Yet democracy assistance rarely has very decisive effects. It is most effective in countries which are themselves on a clearly forward-moving path. If the leaders of a country's major political institutions are trying to democratize, assistance can help provide the know-how and sometimes the financial resources to help speed the process. Yet if a country that started to democratize has since begun to stagnate or move backward, democracy assistance cannot usually reverse that pattern or even slow it much. The relatively modest overall weight of democracy assistance programmes is cast in sharp relief by democratic breakdowns such as in Cambodia in 1997. The United States and numerous other Western countries invested tens of millions of dollars in democracy aid to Cambodia after the 1993 elections, after spending almost $2 billion on the elections themselves. Despite all this activity, the level of pluralism and respect for human rights declined sharply in 1996 and the first half of 1997. And in July 1997, a coup steamrollered the fragile democratic practices that the United States and other countries had worked hard to nurture.

Only in very limited circumstances can democracy assistance have catalytic effects. Occasionally a particular election may be critical to putting a country on a democratic path, such as the snap elections in the Philippines in 1986 or the Chilean plebiscite of 1988. In such cases, external assistance aimed at supporting that election may help hold the process together or make it widely known if the process has failed. In countries coming out of civil war and facing devastated political institutions along with a ruined economy, large-scale, emergency-style democracy aid to rebuild police, legislatures, local governments, and other basic institutions may at least help hold the situation together. As the case of Haiti after 1994 demonstrates, however, even major assistance efforts of this type may do little more than keep a semblance of multi-party political life together.

---

[19] The most systematic study of democratic civic education found a general pattern of modest to negligible effects of such assistance. See Christopher Sabatini, Gwendolyn G. Bevis and Steven Finkel, *The Impact of Civic Education Programmes on Political Participation and Democratic Attitudes, Final Report* (Washington, DC: Management Systems International, 27 January 1998).

Conclusions

Discussions of the proper role of democracy promotion in US foreign policy are too often carried on with little reference to the actual policy tools available for the task. To the extent the tools are mentioned, their actual effectiveness is rarely very well understood. Democracy assistance is one of the most widely used such policy tools; yet it remains a confused subject in the public debate, with much oscillation between unrealistically optimistic and negative accounts of its significance. A more accurate understanding proceeds from a set of five neither black nor white propositions advanced in this essay:

1. Democracy assistance is not a passing fad, nor the exclusive pet province of hubris-ridden Americans. It is an element of the foreign assistance programmes of most major donors and reflects both the expansion of democracy in the world and the growing view that development ultimately depends as much on certain forms of political organization and behaviour as on economic pre-conditions and policies.
2. Aid for democracy has travelled on a steep, often punishing, learning curve in the past two decades, but in fact is progressing. American aid providers are moving away from the simplistic application of made-in-America templates, resorting less often to the sending abroad of inexperienced, heavy-handed American consultants, and coming to the recognition that technical fixes will not solve deeply entrenched political problems. Aid providers still often fail to write down and share their learning but real learning is nonetheless occurring.
3. The recurrent debate over 'top-down'—focusing on state institutions—versus 'bottom-up'—targeting civil society—approaches is giving way to a productive consensus around the idea that assisting democracy requires working from both directions and that the two approaches can be mutually reinforcing, such as programmes that help government officials and civil society representatives work together more effectively.
4. At least in the field, aid providers are gaining a more realistic picture of what can and cannot be achieved through such assistance. Democracy aid can help a country that is genuinely democratizing move faster along that path. It generally cannot, however, reverse the direction of a country retreating from an attempted transition, although it may help preserve a limited amount of political space.
5. Aiding democracy is likely to become more challenging in the coming decades. The global democratic trend has lost much of its momentum and many countries are experiencing democratic stagnation or backsliding. Large parts of the former Soviet Union, the Middle East, and sub-Saharan Africa remain undemocratic and are not fertile environments for existing democracy aid approaches. Much new thinking and learning remains to be done concerning how to promote democracy in contexts where conventional transitions have failed.

9

'High Stakes' and 'Low-Intensity Democracy': Understanding America's Policy of Promoting Democracy

JASON G. RALPH

THIS chapter discusses the gap between rhetoric and practice in the American policy of promoting democracy. It examines the validity of two explanations for the gap and offers a third that suggests future analysis should be rooted in a study of American democracy itself. The first suggests that America cannot always fulfil the ideological agenda set by its rhetoric because doing so may undermine an unsatisfactory but nevertheless tolerable order. When the stakes are high in relations between states, it may choose to concede on the policy of promoting democracy within states for the sake of maintaining stability. Because order is to be considered a normative goal in itself, it is argued that the unfulfilled promises some consider to be hypocritical may none the less be excusable.

The second explanation, informed by William Robinson's book *Promoting Polyarchy*,[1] argues that the low-intensity and market oriented democracy that America promotes advances an order based on transnational elite interests rather than the popular democracy that its rhetoric suggests is America's aim. It is argued here, however, that while US policy does contribute to the problems Robinson identifies, this should be seen not in terms of a capitalist elite conspiracy but as a consequence of America's image of its own success. In contrast to that image, it is further argued that America's success has less to do with the liberal insistence on small government than with the exceptional socioeconomic circumstances at America's founding. When those circumstances changed in the 1930s, capitalism was rescued by the state's intervention in the marketplace. This lesson should be used to inform a foreign policy that seeks to promote democracy in areas that are not suited to the imposition

The author would like to thank Maggie Smolen for her assistance with the empirical research for this chapter.

[1] William I. Robinson, *Promoting Polyarchy: Globalization, U.S. Intervention, and Hegemony* (Cambridge and New York: Cambridge University Press, 1996).

of a free market. Failure to heed this lesson means that the policy of extending the democratic community has little chance of success.

America's commitment to sustaining the community that already exists, moreover, depends on the link that is made between liberal internationalism and America's self-interest. Should the policy of promoting liberal democracy succeed only in encouraging those alienated by the free market to rebel against US hegemony, it is likely that America's international role will come under increasing domestic pressure. To pre-empt this isolationist attack, America's foreign policy has to demonstrate that its internationalist commitment is making the world safe for democracy. To do that it must rethink the nature of the democracy it seeks to promote. American foreign policy, in other words, should be more sensitive to exceptional socioeconomic circumstances and be prepared to promote liberal *and* social democracy.

High Stakes Mitigate the Democratic Ideal

While the United States is able to define itself, and to be seen by others, as an agent of a political philosophy, it also represents and pursues the interests of Americans, who, because of their citizenship, make additional claims on their government. Beyond the rights that the American Declaration of Independence recognizes as inalienable across humanity, Americans demand that their government promote their material interests as well. This first section discusses how the policy of promoting democracy interacts with US interests in terms of traditional state security and international order.

Throughout the cold war the policy of promoting democracy was simultaneously supported and undermined by realist considerations of power relations with the Soviet Union. Where it risked undermining geopolitical allies it was opposed by realists, and where the policy sought to undermine communist regimes it was, in the main, supported. In the latter case, however, the alliance between liberal internationalists and realist internationalists was undermined when the policy risked provoking a Soviet reaction that could upset the carefully constructed order between the superpowers. While some extreme realists may have welcomed an opportunity to revise the status quo in the pursuit of primacy, most realists prudently accepted the unsatisfactory but none the less tolerable order. Thus, the ideological agenda was mitigated in the name of order in Hungary in 1956, Cuba in 1962 and eventually in Vietnam when the material consequences of disorder proved too costly.

During the 1980s and early 1990s, as Soviet power began to retreat, the liberal constituency became stronger as the opportunity to promote democracy emerged out of a disorder that was in fact instigated by the Soviets. If they themselves sought a more satisfactory order based on principles that at first sight seemed to reflect those of the US, then promoting democracy would be geopolitically risk-free. Yet the uncertainty of the reform process provided realists with sufficient reason to be sceptical about the benefits of linking issues of state security to the liberal democratic agenda. The Bush administration was, therefore, torn between on the one hand those wishing to promote democracy by recognizing its agents in Yeltsin and the independence movements, and on the other hand those unwilling to undermine the less than democratic Gorbachev because he held the key to interstate order.[2]

The same dilemma persists in US policy towards post-Soviet Russia, as its democratic progress is filled with uncertainty. Again, administration policy appears to have been influenced by the high stakes involved in a breakdown of relations with Russia. Rather than condition interstate cooperation on democratic reform, and thereby cut relations with the Russian government or undermine its domestic position and provoke the rise to power of an anti-American government, the administration chose to overlook complaints against Russia's less than liberal behaviour. Thus a blind eye was effectively turned towards President Yeltsin's use of force to resolve crises with parliament and the regions. The US expression of 'concern' over events in Chechnya, for example, fell short of meeting the demands of those calling for outright condemnation and the imposition of sanctions.[3] Further questions have been raised over the manner in which Yeltsin won the 1996 presidential election[4] and Congress has sought to link aid to Russian law on religion.[5]

The administration, however, has expressed concern that Congress's 'sanctions-oriented approach fails to recognize the value of incentives and dialogue in promoting religious freedom and encouraging further improvements in some countries'. It also believes that the sanctions provisions will be counter-productive. 'In particular, while the imposition of sanctions is likely to have little direct impact on most governments engaged in abuses, it runs the risk of strengthening the hand of those governments and extremists who seek to incite religious intolerance.'[6] Critics of this 'engagement' policy argue that the administration is simply trying to have its cake and eat it. Indeed, if one is unconvinced by the logic of the engagement argument, one may cynically dismiss the administration's enthusiasm for promoting democracy as mere rhetoric. Yet this inconsistency can be understood, even justified, in the context of political realities statesmen must consider if not necessarily accept. '[P]olitics as an art', Tony Smith reminds us, 'requires the desirable in terms of the possible. The dilemma of leadership is to decide when it is weakness to fail to exploit the inevitable ambiguities, and therefore possibilities, of the histor-

---

[2] See Jason G. Ralph, 'From the Security Dilemma to the Emancipation Dilemma: A Critical Perspective on U.S. Policy Towards the Soviet Union, 1983-1991', PhD War Studies Thesis (King's College, London, 1998).

[3] Jim Nichol, *Russia: Chechnya at Peace? Recent Developments and Implications for U.S. Interests* (Congressional Research Service [CRS] Report for Congress, 2 December 1996).

[4] Jim Nichol, *Russia's Presidential Election: Outcome and Implications for U.S. Interests* (CRS Report for Congress, 12 July 1996).

[5] Jim Nichol, *Russia's Religion Law: Assessments and Implications* (CRS Report for Congress, 29 May 1998).

[6] John Shattuck, Assistant Secretary for Democracy, Human Rights and Labour, statement before the Senate Committee on Foreign Relations (Washington, DC, 12 May 1998).

ical moment, and when it is foolhardy to attempt to overcome immovable constraints set by a combination of forces past and present'.[7]

In this context, Harold Elleston's comment that 'the myth of Yeltsin the democrat should have been buried beneath the rubble of Grozny',[8] implying the West should have withdrawn support long ago, should only be taken conditionally. Given Yeltsin's influence on arms control and proliferation, NATO expansion and the Balkans, it would have been 'foolhardy' to isolate him in a manner that jeopardized not only American interests in these areas but also the evolving European and international order that protected the rights of perhaps many more individuals. Indeed, the administration opposes the extension of sanctions for it fears 'an adverse impact on our diplomacy in places like the Middle East and south Asia, undercutting Administration efforts to promote the very regional peace and reconciliation that can foster religious tolerance and respect for other human rights'.[9] The point is that order between states is, in many cases, considered a prerequisite for any policy that seeks to advance democracy.

An American foreign policy that prioritizes interstate order over support for democratic movements is, of course, vulnerable to accusations of double standards. These are inspired by the natural inclination to expose the hypocrisy of universal values applied selectively. Applying individual ethics to a state, however, is to misunderstand the foreign policy process. Individual statesmen rarely change their opinion of the importance of democracy; they are either consistent realists or consistent liberals. What those who execute policy must recognize, however, is the necessity of gaining enough support across the foreign-policymaking community to implement a course of action that can correctly be called 'American' foreign policy. When American material interests are at stake or interstate order threatened, realists will have a strong case which is reflected in their support amongst the public, Congress, the elite and the administration. Even if the president is absolutely determined to pursue a different policy, he will find it almost impossible, given the foreign policy powers of Congress, to implement that course of action.

The result of this duality in the American security discourse and political system is a policy that proclaims universal principles but inevitably, given the limitations on American influence, applies them selectively. The gap between rhetoric and practice is born of a political reality that idealistic statesmen face when seeking to mobilize an egoistic democracy to support the democratic aspirations of people elsewhere. Yet the issue should not simply be seen in terms of altruism versus state interest. Promoting democracy is in America's long term interests. Dogmatically pursuing such a policy, however, can run the risk of war, which not only defeats the original purpose but can also

---

[7] Tony Smith, *America's Mission: The United States and the Worldwide Struggle for Democracy in the Twentieth Century* (Princeton: Princeton University Press, 1994), p. 107.

[8] *The Times* (25 August 1998).

[9] John Shattuck, Assistant Secretary for Democracy, Human Rights and Labour, statement before the Senate Committee on Foreign Relations (Washington, DC, 12 May 1998).

violate more rights than the initial non-democratic order. Faced with such a situation, prudence is a moral virtue. It may be morally justifiable, in other words, that America sometimes renege on rhetorical promises to promote democracy.

Manipulating the Stakes in the Interests of Capital

The debate would, therefore, seem to rest on a consequentialist view of human rights and revolve around the definition of 'stakes'. Yet it is a criticism of such arguments that these stakes were manipulated by the government so that it could ignore opportunities to promote democracy and support authoritarian regimes that assisted the interests of American and transnational capital. 'Labour leaders, peasant organizations, priests and organizing self-help groups, any one with the priorities separate to the interests of transnational capital' were, according to this view, labelled communist. As such they were then easily linked to the Soviet threat to national security, which easily mobilized support for an intervention against such groups.[10]

Such interventions, it was claimed, were necessary to deter and defeat the Soviet Union. This view, however, misperceived the source of communism's strength in the Third World and generally exaggerated the Soviet threat. Indeed, the theoretical assumptions on which the rationale for neoconservative interventions rested were undermined by subsequent events. For example, the charge that revolutions were inevitably followed by communism was proven false as was the claim that authoritarianism was more open to reform than Soviet-type totalitarianism.[11] While that rationale did inform US policy, however, authoritarian dictators found it easy to manipulate the US security discourse. By raising the spectre of chaos and communism, they could almost guarantee US assistance. Steinmetz cites Marcos as a particularly good exponent of this practice.[12] According to some, post-cold war Russian leaders have been playing a similar game. Alan Philps, for example, writes 'Russia is no ordinary country. The spectre of chaos in a nuclear-armed Russia—*artfully orchestrated by the Kremlin*—has ensured that Mr. Yeltsin's begging bowl is kept topped up'.[13]

In other words, American commercial interests have been the real force behind the realist dominance of US policy. Threats to national security and international order were exaggerated, though not to the point that precluded prudent intervention, so that commercial interests could guarantee the ser-

---

[10] Noam Chomsky, *Deterring Democracy* (London: Vintage, 1992), p. 49; see also Barry Gills, Joel Rocamora and Richard Wilson, 'Low-Intensity Democracy', in Barry Gills, Joel Rocamora and Richard Wilson, *Low-Intensity Democracy: Political Power in the New World Order* (London: Pluto Press, 1993), p. 17.

[11] Sara Steinmetz, *Democratic Transition and Human Rights: Perspectives on US Foreign Policy* (New York: State University of New York Press, 1994), pp. 195–6.

[12] Steinmetz, *Democratic Transition and Human Rights*, pp. 164–5.

[13] *The Daily Telegraph* (25 August 1998; emphasis added).

vices of the state. While liberals protested that America was unnecessarily sub-verting its values in the name of national security and sought to treat regimes on genuine democratic records regardless of their geopolitical allegiances, the realist opinion was for the most part strong enough to maintain control of policy.

As the cold war disappeared, however, it became increasingly difficult, Robinson argues, for the realist cloak to hide the transnational elite interests that drove foreign policy. With Wilsonianism resurgent, the label 'national security' was dropped and 'promoting democracy' was adopted as a banner that would rally enough support for a US policy that continued to guarantee elite interests. This time a quasi-consensual rather than coercive approach would do what policy had always sought to do: maintain the interests of transnational capital.[14] Those interests, according to Robinson, not only clash with, but seek to repress, the interests of a majority that, despite the wave of 'democratic' revolutions, remains socially and economically repressed. By promoting 'polyarchy' or 'low-intensity democracy', American policy simply reinforces unequal socioeconomic circumstances. Yet this is of little concern, for it is the main aim of that policy, according to Robinson, to make sure transitional states contribute to the processes of globalization in a manner suited to transnational capital.

Low-Intensity Democracy

Tony Smith identifies a consensus on what is meant by 'democracy'. While he recognizes 'differences on the best institutional form of government', there is, he suggests, agreement that 'democracy is a political system' characterized by 'the rule of law', 'autonomous civil society', 'political parties' and 'freely contested elections'.[15] Most likely the result of focusing solely on 'America's mission', Smith is able to get away with calling this narrow definition a consensus. Its political rather than socioeconomic focus, however, stands apart from other definitions of democracy.

To William Robinson, for instance, the absence of socioeconomic considerations means such definitions fall short of true democracy. 'Popular democracy', on the other hand,

is seen as an emancipatory project of both form and content that *links the distinct spheres of the social totality, in which the construction of a democratic political order enjoys a theoretically internal relation to the construction of a democratic socioeconomic order. In sharp contrast to polyarchy, popular democracy is concerned with both process and outcome.* Popular democracy . . . posits democracy as both a process and a means to an end—a tool for change, for the resolution of such material problems as housing, health, education, access to land, cultural development and so forth.[16]

---

[14] Robinson, *Promoting Polyarchy*, p. 16.
[15] Smith, *America's Mission*, p. 13 (emphasis added).
[16] Robinson, *Promoting Polyarchy*, pp. 57–8 (emphasis added).

By limiting the focus to political contestation through procedurally free elections, as Smith appears to do, 'the question of who controls the material and cultural resources of society . . . becomes extraneous to the discussion of democracy'.[17] According to this view, US objectives may merge with the majority against a dictatorship or totalitarian regime. When it is clear a transition is inevitable, however, its interests and policies converge with a minority elite that seeks to protect the socioeconomic order by obstructing the populist programme of reform.[18] Thus the US, according to Robinson, made sure that Aristide, elected on a popular mandate, was returned to Haiti only when it became impossible for him to fulfil his reformist agenda.[19]

Robinson considers American interventions as part of a long-term strategy to consolidate the global neoliberal economic order by imposing a political superstructure made up of neoliberal states—that is, open to foreign capital—professing to be democratic. 'The new formal [low-intensity] democratization is', Gills, Rocamora and Wilson note in the same vein, 'the political corollary of economic liberalization and internationalization'.[20] The point is that the political superstructure merely secures the socioeconomic conditions of an undemocratic substructure.

Low-Intensity Liberalism

Fareed Zakaria also attacks the US policy of promoting democracy. In contrast to Robinson, however, he suggests US policy in fact encourages majority rule, but this often means sanctioning illiberal regimes. Where Robinson argues US policy encourages too much liberalism and not enough democracy, Zakaria suggests its focus is too much on democracy at the expense of liberalism. American policy towards Russia, Zakaria would argue, has overlooked illiberal acts by Yeltsin because it, like Yeltsin, has been blinded by the supposed mandate the President got from the Russian people. American policy, he suggests, should rediscover liberalism and promote that ahead of democracy.[21]

Given that Zakaria's article talks exclusively about constitutional liberalism—that is, the rule of law that respects human rights and civil liberties—Robinson may not disagree with his arguments. Indeed, Robinson insists that such rights are 'pre-conditions for the processes of democratization'. What Robinson would object to is the tendency to see constitutional liberalism as an end in itself rather than as a means toward popular democracy.[22] So long as American policy insists on a neoliberal economic order and promotes a liberal democratic political order to sustain it, then the material aspirations of a majority will be denied. So long as the ends of this policy combination remain

---

[17] Robinson, *Promoting Polyarchy*, p. 58.
[18] Robinson, *Promoting Polyarchy*, pp. 62–3; Gills *et al.*, 'Low-Intensity Democracy', pp. 23–4.
[19] Robinson, *Promoting Polyarchy*, pp. 256–316.
[20] Gills *et al.* 'Low-Intensity Democracy', p. 4.
[21] Fareed Zakaria, 'The Rise of Illiberal Democracy', *Foreign Affairs*, 76/6 (1997), pp. 22–43.
[22] Robinson, *Promoting Polyarchy*, p. 58.

unchallenged, socioeconomic inequalities will persist and popular democracy will be repressed.

That the free-market substructure has a non-negotiable presence in US policy goes to the heart of Robinson's criticism. In this sense, the 'democratic' choice of citizens in states engaged in the world economy is little more than Hobson's choice. Local economies may benefit from foreign investment, financial deregulation, and reductions in government expenditure and budgetary deficits. By abolishing protection and subsidies as viable policies, however, the global economy makes even the most democratic governments powerless to implement socioeconomic policies that challenge the state's contribution to the neoliberal international order.[23] In other words, the 'means by which domestic societies could be managed to reduce inequalities produced by inherited social structures and accentuated by the natural workings of the market, [have] declined significantly'.[24] Governments are now judged in terms of 'comparative "hospitality" to foreign capital: that is, they must offer the most attractive investment climates to relatively scarce supplies of money. This gives the foreign investment community enormous influence over the course of the nation's economic development, and constitutes a significant diminution in the country's economic sovereignty'.[25] Thus, according to *The Economist*, one of the most committed supporters of the neoliberal agenda, the Russian government '*has* to show that it will *not* succumb to populism [read democracy] but rather commit itself to the creation of a functioning market economy'.[26] Robinson would thus argue that unconditional US support for Yeltsin, despite his illiberal acts, has little to do with it being blinded by Yeltsin's democratic mandate, or with concerns about its geopolitical interests and interstate order. Rather, Yeltsin's governments have represented the best opportunity to promote a free market in which Western financial interests could prosper.

Identifying Yeltsin as a pro-free marketeer who defends the interests of a few 'oligarchs' against the rest of the Russian population is easy. Yet the flagrant disrespect for constitutional liberalism would suggest that the Russian oligarchs are less than perfect partners in any transnational agenda. Grigory Yavlinsky, who as leader of the reformist Yabloko party is one such partner, identifies the new Russian business elite as 'neither democratic nor communist, neither conservative nor liberal—merely rapaciously greedy'.[27] A more significant criticism of Robinson's thesis, however, can be levelled at the nature of what he identifies as an American foreign policy elite.

[23] Andre Gunder Frank, 'Marketing Democracy in an Undemocratic Market', in Gills *et al.*, *Low-Intensity Democracy*, pp. 40–4.
[24] Scott Burchill, 'Liberal Internationalism', in S. Burchill, R. Devetak, A. Linklater, M. Paterson and J. True (eds), *Theories of International Relations* (London: Macmillan, 1996), p. 55.
[25] Burchill, 'Liberal Internationalism', p. 59.
[26] *The Economist* (29 August 1998) (emphasis added).
[27] Grigory Yavlinsky, 'Russia's Phony Capitalism' *Foreign Affairs*, 77/3 (1998), p. 69.

Does a Transnational Elite Determine US Foreign Policy?

American policy undoubtedly advocates a path to democracy that is consistent with a neoliberal security and economic order that in turn reinforces, and is reinforced by, low-intensity rather than popular democracy. The source of that policy, however, should not go unquestioned. Were the American capitalist elite, leaders of an emerging transnational elite, really responsible for the hegemony realism exercised over cold war policy? Did American post-cold war policy seek to promote democracy that not only furthered the interests of that elite but was dictated by those interests?

It can reasonably be argued, as Tony Smith does, that US support for authoritarian regimes during the cold war was motivated by the genuine belief that no alternative existed that would guarantee US security interests as they were perceived at the time. Smith quotes President Kennedy's thoughts on the Dominican Republic:

There are three possibilities in descending order of preference: a decent democratic regime, a continuation of the Trujillo regime, or a Castro regime. We ought to aim at the first, but we really can't renounce the second until we are sure we can avoid the third.[28]

To continue the example of US policy towards Russia, one can easily ask what alternative American policy has in the absence of a popular and responsible opposition. In this sense, US policy has faced a similar dilemma in condemning Yeltsin to that which faced Kennedy when condemning Trujillo. As former Bush official Philip Zelikow remarked, in reference to Yeltsin's 1993 suppression of parliament, 'it was inconceivable that any American administration could have lined up behind Ruslan Khasbulatov and Aleksandr Rutskoi'.[29] Such a dilemma was even more apparent when the December 1993 parliamentary elections produced alarming results.

The electoral breakthrough of the extreme Russian nationalist Liberal Democratic Party, headed by the maverick Vladimir Zhirinovsky, provoked a fundamental rethink not only in the Kremlin but also in Washington, particularly as Zhirinovsky and the resurgent communists implicated the US in Russia's troubles and looked set on reviving the Soviet Union or at least greater Russia. With presidential elections approaching it became imperative that the US not further weaken Yeltsin, who was perceived as the only non-communist candidate capable of carrying the election. Warren Christopher, for example, sought to put the best gloss on the intervention in Chechnya by suggesting that public debate in Russia and the independent media coverage were 'reflections of Russia's emerging democracy and civil society'.[30] Yet it was Richard Holbrooke who perhaps more accurately reflected US policy when he stated that 'the Chechnya conflict, terrible though it is, has not changed the

---

[28] Smith, *America's Mission*, p. 226.
[29] Philip Zelikow, 'Beyond Boris Yeltsin', *Foreign Affairs*, 73/1 (1994), p. 44.
[30] Warren Christopher, 'America's Leadership, America's Opportunity', *Foreign Policy*, 98 (1995), p. 11.

nature of U.S. interests'.[31] So long as Yeltsin was the least worst option in terms of the liberal and realist agenda, he would receive American assistance.

One can further question the influence of Robinson's elite by attacking his notion of an extended policymaking community. It can be argued that America is more of a functioning democracy than these critics admit and, as such, its foreign policy is responsive to a broader constituency than the financial elite. While Robinson and Chomsky would argue that American foreign policy is controlled by commercial interests,[32] Robinson does add that this 'does not preclude circumstantial convergence of interests among different classes or groups, or foreign-policy development that is influenced, although not determined, by subordinate classes and groups'.[33] He goes on to adopt the Gramscian concept of an extended policymaking community that goes beyond the immediate policymaking community, which is the usual focus of analysis. The true focus of analysis is a community that 'extends backwards into civil society, goes well beyond the specific elected administration, spans the panoply of institutions in which power is exercised, and brings together the formal state apparatus with the network of universities, think-tanks, corporate groups, and so forth. It conducts ongoing regenerative processes of policy formation and implementation over extended periods'.[34] It is suggested here that an analysis of US policy needs to extend further than Robinson's focus on transnational capital.

The increasing role of Congress in the process of making foreign policy has been a common theme among recent texts.[35] If this is the case, then it has had the effect of opening that process up to wider influences. If one also considers the increased decentralization of Congress, then constituency interests and single-issue lobbyists all have a greater chance of influencing foreign policy. While the influence of those lobbying on behalf of transnational capital cannot be doubted, other interests advocating different approaches to security are too strong for policymakers to ignore. For example, there are those who seek to promote human rights irrespective of its implications for transnational capital. As a result it is misguided to say that an elite driven by commercial interests controls US policy. In introducing an amendment to the Foreign Aid Appropriation Act, for example, Senator Gordon Smith stated in July 1997 that Congress should send 'a strong signal to President Yeltsin that American tax dollars will not find their way to support any country that treats religious freedom in such a manner'.[36] As is noted above, 'tax dollars' *were* sent to assist Yeltsin despite what some saw as a violation of religious freedoms. The point here, however, is that the decision was not determined by the capitalist agenda, but was the result of a political debate between competing ideologies.

---

[31] Richard Holbrooke, 'America, A European Power', *Foreign Affairs*, 74/2 (1995), p. 49.
[32] Robinson, *Promoting Polyarchy*, pp. 25–7.
[33] Robinson, *Promoting Polyarchy*, p. 27.   [34] Robinson, *Promoting Polyarchy*, p. 28.
[35] See Randall B. Ripley and James M. Lindsay (eds), *Congress Resurgent: Foreign and Defense Policy on Capitol Hill* (Ann Arbor: University of Michigan Press, 1993).
[36] Nichol, *Russia's Religion Law*, p. 6.

Perhaps of greater importance is the strength of the isolationist constituency that sees globalization and democratization, not as opportunities for American interests to exploit, but as a process that takes advantage of America. One should ask why, if American policy is controlled by capitalist interests, an increasingly isolationist Congress is considering a cut in the funds it appropriates to the IMF, the institution at the heart of the neoliberal agenda.[37] This surely shows that not all US foreign policy is conducted in the interests of an elite that Robinson claims dominates policy, and not all the constituencies that contribute to that policy have the same motivation as the financial elite. American policy, in other words, is the result of a continuous political process.

Democracy versus Economic Interests: A Fundamental Dilemma?

Understanding the source of Congress's latent isolationism—or, as Ruggie prefers to call it, unilateralism[38]—is also a reminder that any internationalist policy seeking to assist the democratic aspirations of other peoples finds it necessary to promote US material interests simply to maintain domestic support. That support must come from a wider constituency than the transnational elite. President Bush's treatment by the electorate in 1992 is the most recent and, given the democratic advances taking place during his presidency, probably the best example of the role material interests of the electorate as a whole continue to play in formulating American foreign policy.[39] While Clinton's promise to promote US jobs within the neoliberal order appealed to many, it was the anti-liberal protectionism advocated by Pat Buchanan and Ross Perot that harmed Bush. While a majority did not want to withdraw from and thereby threaten the open international system, another majority sought a better deal for Americans. The result was, to use Robinson's words, a 'circumstantial convergence of interests among different classes or groups'[40] that suited but was not determined by agents of the transnational capitalist agenda.

Alongside the promotion of democracy and the protection of the neoliberal international order, therefore, President Clinton sought to address the growing dissatisfaction of the American electorate. His geoeconomic strategy of promoting American jobs through contracts in the international market involved an unprecedented level of government intervention on behalf of US exporters.[41] Given these aims, it was inevitable American policy would be

[37] *The Economist* (5 September 1998).

[38] John Gerrard Ruggie, *Winning the Peace: America and World Order in the New Era* (New York: Columbia, 1996).

[39] See Jason G. Ralph, 'Review Article: Realising Realism's Role in U.S. Policy Towards Europe', *European Security*, 7/4 (1998), pp. 172–86.

[40] Robinson, *Promoting Polyarchy*, p. 27.

[41] Michael Cox, *U.S. Foreign Policy After the Cold War: Superpower Without a Mission?* (London: Royal Institute of International Affairs, 1995), p. 17.

faced with difficult choices. This was clearly illustrated in the debate over renewing China's most favoured nation status in May 1994 after China had met only two of the seven human rights conditions Clinton had set a year earlier.[42]

It may be that the policy of 'comprehensive engagement' through trade is, as the administration insists, the best way to advance liberal democracy in China. Maintaining a cooperative relationship with the Chinese government is also prudent given its influence on regional security.[43] Yet 'comprehensive engagement' is also suspiciously consistent with Clinton's geoeconomic agenda. If one believes that liberal democracy is best advanced through linking human rights abuses to trade sanctions, then the Clinton administration has, by pursuing economic interests in the Chinese market, reneged on earlier promises to assist democratization. As Roger Burbach suggests, the US is caught in 'a fundamental dilemma between its declared support for democracy and *its perception* of its economic needs and interests abroad'.[44] Given the material circumstances of the American electorate relative to those in democratizing states, it is perhaps an inappropriate excuse for the gap between American rhetoric and practice. Sacrificing the fundamental rights of others for the indulgence of material desire is hardly the consequence of a dilemma. It is surely another example of self-interest betraying promises of altruism.

Yet it is argued here that concern for America's material 'needs' is a necessary part of maintaining America's commitment to the liberal internationalist agenda. American foreign policy is obliged, that is, to pursue the material interests of its electorate, alongside idealistic goals if those goals are to be pursued at all. In this sense the material interests of the American electorate is a political reality that idealistic policymakers cannot escape. Moreover, given the potential disorder created by an American retreat into isolationism, those interests unfortunately become a normative goal in themselves. That is, America's commitment to the neoliberal economic order is related to how the American electorate perceives its own material circumstances within that order. American policy, therefore, is again faced with the dilemma of having to choose between two potentially unsatisfactory courses of action: on the one hand, promoting democracy that could, by contradicting its material interests and thereby reducing support for internationalist policies, undermine an international order that protects more individual rights than it denies; and on the other hand, maintaining those material interests and with it the support to uphold an international order that is less than democratic.

Being aware of these realities, however, does not mean statesmen should accept them and hide behind consequentialist ethics. Nor indeed does the

---

[42] See Jason G. Ralph, 'Persistent Dilemmas in post-Cold War U.S. National Security Policy', in Clive Jones and Caroline Kennedy-Pipe (eds), *International Security: Issues of the Contemporary Age* (London: Frank Cass, 1999).

[43] Testimony by Kent Weidemann, Deputy Assistant Secretary of State for East Asian and Pacific Affairs Before House Ways and Means Subcommittee on Trade (Washington, DC: 23 May, 1995).

[44] Roger Burbach, 'The Tragedy of American Democracy', in Gills *et. al.*, *Low-Intensity Democracy*, p. 101 (emphasis added).

American identity let them. The pressures of an American mission are as real to any president as those of ensuring the material welfare of the electorate. It is a persistent dilemma encountered by any democratically elected statesman, but especially an American president. Given these pressures, it is to the Clinton administration's credit that 'comprehensive engagement' has achieved some sort of credible balance.

This dilemma, however, does not fully explain the gap between American rhetoric and practice. One may ask why, given a situation in which American security and economic interests are guaranteed, the democracy it seeks to promote meets the needs of the few rather than the many. The final section of this chapter examines the argument that this has less to do with the demands of a transnational financial elite, even though it is consistent with their interests, but is again reflective of a broader constituency. Indeed, it is reflective of America itself and its image of its own democratic evolution.

American Democracy: Open in Form, Confined in its Ends

Zakaria's article 'Illiberal Democracy' does the service of reminding us of the distinction between liberalism and democracy. Yet his conclusion that American policy has to rediscover constitutional liberalism and promote it ahead of democracy is misplaced.[45] In defence of the administration's policy that they helped to create, Shattuck and Atwood argue convincingly that US policy seeks to promote elements of a liberal civil society alongside electoral democracy.[46] Robinson also demonstrates how US policy has targeted civil society through the National Endowment for Democracy and the Agency for International Development.[47] Recipients of this aid recently hit the headlines in Indonesia, where groups opposing the Suharto regime, including the Indonesian Legal Aid Society, have received $16 million since 1995.[48] The absence of a liberal influence on a policy of promoting democracy would be strange given the fact that America itself could easily be described as more liberal than democratic. The Founding Fathers saw democracy not as an ongoing process but as a type of society. They considered it dangerous to allow democracy, like monarchy and aristocracy, to become dominant. Foley articulates their fears: 'A preponderance of monarchy would lead to despotism, a preponderance of aristocracy would produce oligarchy and a preponderance of democracy would run into violent anarchy.'[49]

Given the absence of a centralizing heritage and the consequent lack of any 'natural' balance to majoritarian rule, the Founding Fathers' aim was 'to con-

[45] Zakaria, 'The Rise of Illiberal Democracy', p. 41.
[46] John Shattuck and J. Brian Atwood, 'Defending Democracy: Why Democrats Trump Autocrats', *Foreign Affairs*, 77/2 (1998), pp. 16770; see also Marc Plattner, 'Liberalism and Democracy: Can't Have One Without the Other', *Foreign Affairs*, 77/2 (1998), pp. 171–80.
[47] Robinson, *Promoting Polyarchy*, pp. 13–72.   [48] *The Guardian* (21 May 1998).
[49] Michael Foley, *American Political Ideas: Traditions and Usages* (Manchester: Manchester University Press, 1991), p. 68.

trol the governed; and in the next place oblige it to control itself'.[50] While the system of checks and balances they created was outwardly chosen by the people, it in effect 'disaggregated democracy' by institutionalizing competing mandates. Thus, 'Instead of the government being constituted and informed by the single beam of a popular mandate in a unified election, it takes on the character of a kaleidoscope, full of colourful activity but possessing very little in the way of coherence and direction'.[51]

In this sense the evolution of American society had little to do with any socioeconomic ideology that was implemented politically. Rather, it has been a consequence of a political system that fractures such attempts and allows exceptional socioeconomic circumstances the freedom to shape civil society. Moreover, the fluidity of early social conditions in the United States and the Protestant tradition all contributed to an economic individualism that meant capitalism could prosper.[52] For example, the frontier acted both as a safety valve for the propertyless workers and as a continuous drain on the working population of the eastern cities, with the result that the labour supply remained limited and industrial wages were kept high. The affluence and mobility of the American workers compared with those of their European counterpart was thought to have made them far less receptive to radical politics and far more interested in moving up the ladder of social status. Even those workers who were not so taken with the individualist promises of success, and who favoured greater solidarity with one another, found that any collective consciousness stopped at racial, ethnic and religious barriers, which were consistently reinforced by the flow of immigrants.[53] Moreover, the disaggregative effects of local laws in the federal system meant that 'there was, in effect, no national pattern of law, legitimization or repression to confirm a socialist critique'.[54] Finally, the American 'celebration of its exceptionalism as a counterweight to socialism and as a rebuttal of Marxism undoubtedly contributed towards the civic integration of the United States'.[55]

Thus the systemic guarantees against mob rule were in effect redundant as a majority challenge to the socioeconomic order was diluted by the particular circumstances of that order. America's initial 'success', in other words, had less to do with liberal political management of democratic majorities than exceptional socioeconomic circumstances. Yet because capitalism thrived under those circumstances, and because America was democratic in the sense that it accommodated free—although not universal—elections, capitalism became equated with democracy in the American psyche. As Foley puts it, capitalism is seen as 'embodying such American ideals as liberty, individualism,

---

[50] James Madison, 'Federalist Paper No.51', in Alexander Hamilton, James Madison and John Jay, *The Federalist Papers* (New York: Mentor, 1961), p. 322. Cited in Foley, *American Political Ideas*, p. 72
[51] Foley, *American Political Ideas*, p. 77.
[52] Foley, *American Political Ideas*, pp. 28, 64–5.
[53] Foley, *American Political Ideas*, pp. 56–7.
[54] Theodore J. Lowi, 'Why Is There No Socialism In The United States?: A Federal Analysis', *International Political Science Review*, 5/4 (1984), p. 377. Cited in Foley, *American Political Ideas*, p. 58.
[55] Foley, *American Political Ideas*, p. 59.

emancipation, democracy and even equality'.[56] No other people, he suggests, 'are more dependent upon the meaning and value of capitalism for the conception of themselves, their history and their purpose in the world'.[57]

In theory, the political implications of the democratic electoral process were open to the whim of the voters. Yet with the cultural connection between democracy and capitalism, and the disaggregation of any mandate that sought to challenge that assumption, the socioeconomic ends of society were predetermined.[58] Furthermore, as the financial constraints of running for office grew, the support of 'big business' became a prerequisite. While the electorate may have been free to choose, the choice was and remains restricted. In these circumstances it is not surprising that less than half the electorate voted in the 1996 presidential election and only a third in the 1998 mid-term Congressional elections. American elections, the point is, have merely confirmed the capitalist order. To this extent, an uncritical American, unaware of other definitions of democracy, would deny the inconsistency of a foreign policy that sought to promote democracy alongside free market capitalism.

The Need for Liberal—and Social—Democracy

The system resting on this cultural acceptance of capitalism was secure so long as the exceptional socioeconomic circumstances that favoured the free market were sustained. Yet as those circumstances changed with depression in the 1930s, a repressed majority looked to the state. The question facing the system was whether it could translate this democratic need into political action, or whether the liberal safeguards against a dictatorship of the majority would protect the privileged few who had the power to survive, even to exploit, those circumstances.

The implementation of Roosevelt's New Deal and the rise of a socioeconomic liberalism that sought to construct and then defend a welfare state demonstrated that in this instance the system was responsive to the needs of the majority even when constitutional liberalism continued to protect the rights of the minority. While Roosevelt's legacy remains mixed—was the New Deal meant to set up a permanent welfare state, or was it simply to work temporarily with business to save capitalism from itself?—it is clear that when socioeconomic circumstances changed from the exceptional, and exceptionally fortunate, ones that founded the American state, questions confronted the liberal democratic political system that had allowed free market economics to continue uninterrupted. In this sense questions should be levelled at the present American foreign policy of promoting the kind of democracy it does when the global socioeconomic circumstances are not amenable to global free market economics. More important, because the circumstances that underpinned America's success were exceptional, it is unlikely that other societies

---

[56] Foley, *American Political Ideas*, p. 65.   [57] Foley, *American Political Ideas*, p. 64.
[58] Foley, *American Political Ideas*, p. 80.

will be able to accommodate a US-type system. A US foreign policy that insists on promoting the free market alongside liberal democracy is likely to find its task complicated by the resistance of local political culture.

In *America's Mission*, Tony Smith makes the distinction between American policies that have been sensitive to the particular socioeconomic circumstances of a state and those that simply seek to impose a liberal democratic regime. The former, usually implemented by domestic New Dealers, have been among America's greatest foreign policy achievements. The success of US policy in promoting German and Japanese democracy can be attributed, in part, to 'New Dealers, for whom the prerequisites of democracy included strong labour unions, land reform, welfare legislation, notions of racial equality, and government intervention in the economy'. Smith is also sympathetic to Kennedy's Alliance for Progress, which was 'for the most part cut of the same cloth as the New Dealers'.[59]

The point should be clear. The tradition that American foreign policy should rediscover is not, as Zakaria claims, constitutional liberalism—it has not forgotten it—but the socioeconomic liberalism of the New Deal. Democratizing states engaged in the world economy are failing to meet the needs of a majority of their citizens. In this respect they are merely low-intensity democracies. The arguments advanced here suggest America's support for these regimes has less to do with it being an agent of transnational capital than with its image of its own success. It must remember that when that success was challenged by the failings of the free market, it was responsive to a popular majority that voted for a New Deal. The socioeconomic circumstances of new democracies in the contemporary global system are not like the exceptional American circumstances. In this sense they are not ideal hosts for free market capitalism. An American foreign policy sensitive to this fact and ready to support intervention in the marketplace would be a more appropriate approach to promoting democracy.

Conclusion

The gap between America's claims to promote democracy and its actual foreign policy exists on two levels. When the policy of promoting democracy is at variance with the security and economic interests of the American state, policymakers find they have to apply universal values selectively. Yet this is not simply a political problem. Given the central role American multilateralism plays in contributing to order in the international system, the question confronting American foreign policy is not merely one of altruism versus self-interest. There is also a normative concern in guaranteeing American interests when one considers that a breakdown in international security not only harms those particular interests but may also violate more individual rights

---

[59] Smith, *America's Mission*, p.18.

than the undemocratic status quo. Furthermore, a breakdown in the international economic order caused by a disillusioned American electorate voting for protectionist policies may cause economic violence to a greater number than do the injustices of the present system.

As is argued above, this is unfortunate given the fact that the American electorate often confuses material desires with economic needs. It is, however, a political reality idealist statesmen must face. Reforming the structural circumstances of this dilemma is the real challenge for US foreign policy. If promoting democracy is in America's long-term interests, then a greater willingness to forgo the short-term gains offered by unilateralism is appropriate. Likewise, a greater willingness to bear the short-term costs of multilateralism is also required. The multilateral international order must not be threatened because the American electorate does not immediately see the gains of its commitment to liberal internationalism.

What if policy cannot meet this challenge? If America cannot keep its commitment to support democracy through a policy that acts on rhetoric, then what, if anything other than undermining America's credibility, is the role played by the liberal discourse? At one level it is apparent that the rhetoric itself can play a positive role. Benigno Aquino told an interviewer in May 1980, for example: 'When [President] Carter came onto the scene and spoke about human rights it gave us new hope. . . . It was the best thing that ever happened to the Third World.'[60] This sentiment was echoed by Polish human rights activist and former Prime Minister Tadeusz Masowiecki when asked by the author how he rated the influence of the human rights (Basket III) accords of the Helsinki process. In answering the question he focused on the important influence Carter's foreign policy had on encouraging activists like himself and suggested it far outweighed the influence of Reagan's cold war policy.[61]

Not to address the gap between rhetoric and practice may be inconsistent and even hypocritical, but, as these cases show, there are, to use Louis Henkin's phrase, 'benign consequences of certain kinds of hypocrisy'. By maintaining human rights as an ideal, 'repressive states are compelled to deny and conceal, but concealment can be uncovered and lies exposed'.[62] The very existence of ideals, in other words, delegitimizes repressive practices that would otherwise have gone unnoticed. Furthermore, repressive regimes that would otherwise be stable are undermined as the simple act of espousing an ideal denies them any legitimacy.

A foreign policy resting on such logic, however, is less than satisfactory. The gap between rhetoric and practice can be justified only by the mitigating circumstances considered above. When such circumstances do not exist, hypocrisy is unjustified and the consequences are unlikely to be benign. As

---

[60] Steinmetz, *Democratic Transition and Human Rights*, p. 185.

[61] Tadeusz Masowiecki (Exeter University: 5 February 1998).

[62] Louis Henkin, *International Law: Politics and Values* (Dordrecht: Nijhoff Publishers, 1995), p. 183. Cited in Rein Mullerson, *Human Rights Diplomacy* (London and New York: Routledge, 1997), p. 35.

this chapter has argued, in situations when US policy can guarantee its material interests and thereby guarantee its continued contribution to international order, its failure to live up to its rhetorical promises is inexcusable. Moreover, the promise of increased wealth that attends the advice to adopt free-market liberal democracy based on the American model does a disservice to the broader democratic project. This is a clear danger in US policy towards Russia. As is the tendency among Americans, so Russians too now equate democracy with capitalism. Unlike the American experience, however, capitalism in Russia has failed. The danger that Russia will also see that as a failure of democracy is very real. It is likely, moreover, that this will translate into support for an illiberal and undemocratic regime that seeks to undermine international order.

If this is the case, then the promotion of liberal democracy based on the American model does not provide the basis for enduring stability. Combined with a free market, it alienates individuals who do not enjoy the socioeconomic opportunities that Americans did at their founding and only the privileged do today. Recognizing this source of future instability, moreover, is to recognize that the liberal democratic peace theory is premature in its declaration of perpetual peace. More significantly, the implication of this insight is not simply theoretical. The promise of perpetual peace underpins America's policy of promoting democracy and is often used to convince a reluctant electorate that continued internationalism is in their interest. Given the centrality of that assumption, and given the inconsistencies exposed here, a fundamental rethink is required.

It is another conclusion of this paper that individual integrity can be guaranteed in today's global market only if socioeconomic rights are also considered important. The liberal discourse in American foreign policy has always been sensitive to violations of individual security and the threat they pose to international security. It should easily recognize, therefore, the threat posed by the socioeconomic alienation of an increasing number of the world's population. If America is to credibly justify its democratic mission to a sceptical electorate, it must realize that making the world safe depends first and foremost on refining the democracy that it seeks to promote in a manner that addresses these concerns. In this sense, it is not only appropriate to talk of the liberal *and* social democratic peace that existed in the past, but necessary to practice a policy informed by liberal *and* social democracy if that peace is to persist in the future.

10

Wilsonianism Resurgent? The Clinton Administration and the Promotion of Democracy

MICHAEL COX

E ACH time at the end of the two great wars that did so much to shape the course of the twentieth century, the United States attempted to define the outlines of a new world order—one that would not only make all the sacrifice seem worthwhile but over time lay the foundation for a more open and ulti- mately more democratic international system.[1] Just how seriously American policymakers took their own rhetoric in 1919 and 1945 has, of course, been the subject of a good deal of anguished comment; and while supporters feel that US efforts to make the world a better place should be taken at face value, others have dismissed such visions as so much rhetorical hot air either designed to mask its larger hegemonic ambitions or likely to lead to a danger- ous American over-commitment.

It was George Kennan who, perhaps more than anybody else, articulated the most persuasive critique of what he termed this 'diplomacy of dilettantism'; and in a powerful broadside written in 1951 lambasted the tendency of sub- stituting moral and legal formulae for careful calculations about 'national interest'.[2] Written when the US was engaged in a bitter ideological crusade against communism, his beautifully crafted polemic, delivered in the intellec- tual home of realism at the University of Chicago, was interpreted as much as an attack upon the excesses of the cold war as an attack upon the ambitious plans of Wilson and Roosevelt. His more general point, however—that America had always been inclined to substitute hard thinking about the bal- ance of power with dubious idealistic statements about how the world ought to be rather than how it was—was one that strongly influenced the way many Americans tended to think about their past. It was also repeated regularly thereafter: by other realists like the influential Hans J. Morgenthau, who orig-

---

[1] See Torbjørn L. Knutsen, *The Rise and Fall of World Orders* (Manchester: Manchester University Press, 1999). The issue is explored for the post-cold war era in John C. Hulsman, *A Paradigm for a New World Order* (Basingstoke: Macmillan Press, 1997).

[2] See George F. Kennan, *American Diplomacy: 1900–1950* (London: Secker and Warburg, 1953).

inally encouraged Kennan to set down his thoughts on paper; by more centrist opponents of the Vietnam War like George Ball; by those attempting to sell superpower détente to an increasingly sceptical American public in the 1970s; and finally by all those opposed to Ronald Reagan's tough stance against the evil empire better known as the USSR. It is remarkable, in fact, how frequently those opposed to what they saw as the less acceptable face of American foreign policy after 1950 often turned to Kennan and what they believed was his sound advice to the United States to behave more like a normal country and less like a political crusade. Reading later attacks on realists, one could easily be forgiven for thinking that they had been apologists for the excesses of the cold war rather than some of its more effective intellectual opponents.[3]

With the end of the cold war, one might have predicted that this persistent and somewhat overheated debate would have died out. But this was not to be. Indeed, the apparent urge in some quarters to build a new world order and in others to find a new post-cold war 'mission' for the United States led to renewed speculation that America was once again succumbing to the old temptation of wanting to refashion the international system in its own liberal democratic image. Even George Bush was not immune to the disease—or so it was suggested—but at least he had sufficient experience not to be seduced by the siren calls of political idealism.[4] The same, it seemed, could not be said of the less experienced Clinton. Guided by his own liberal instincts, buoyed up by electoral victory over the republicans in 1992, and keen to develop a 'doctrine' of his own in a world without a clear point of ideological opposition, Clinton, it was argued, soon gave in to those calling for a new foreign policy based on principle rather than considerations of power. For this he was severely assailed and soon came under fire from a battery of opponents who pointed out that, while the idea of promoting freedom was all very well in theory, in practice it provided policymakers with little or no guide as to how to deal with a host of pressing problems on an everyday basis. It also ignored the obvious lesson of history. This taught that a policy based on the virtues of democracy was bound to fail. One only had to look at what had happened after Word War I to see this. From this perspective, it was thus most unfortunate that the Clinton administration had fallen for the old Wilsonian fallacy of trying to make other countries assume a form of government for which they were probably not suited and almost certainly unwilling to adopt. As one of Clinton's many critics pointed out, while Wilsonianism embodied a legitimate, 'enduring and uniquely American approach to foreign policy', as a tradition it had proven to be less than useful when it came to dealing with the 'real' world of autocratic enemies and friends, powerful economic competitors, and limited American resources.[5]

---

[3] See Michael Cox, 'Requiem for a Cold War Critic: George F. Kennan, 19461950', *Irish Slavonic Studies*, 11 (1990–1), pp. 13–35.

[4] The best discussion on the Bush foreign policy is by the British scholar, Steven Hurst. See his *The Foreign Policy of the Bush Administration: In Search of a New World Order* (London: Pinter, 1999).

[5] Richard Haass, *The Reluctant Sheriff: The United States after the Cold War* (New York: A Council On Foreign Relations Book, 1997), especially pp. 60–3.

This chapter seeks neither to defend Clinton nor to endorse his critics. Instead, it tries to explore the many facets of democracy promotion as a grand strategy after 1992. It begins, however, not with a general statement of principle but by examining the fairly concrete reasons why the Clinton administration opted for the strategy of 'democratic enlargement' in the first place. Let me be clear. There is little doubt that there was far more continuity in this particular policy area than either Clinton or Bush cared to admit.[6] It is also clear that Clinton rather effectively used the issue of 'democracy' to put clear blue water between himself and Bush during the presidential campaign.[7] Furthermore, having raised the issue in 1992, Clinton then had to spend a good deal of his time sorting out the mess his earlier promises had created. To this extent, Clinton was hoisted on his own electoral petard, and this is one of the reasons—amongst others—why 'American foreign policy' appeared to be in such 'disarray and confusion' after he assumed office.[8] But none of this really helps us understand why Clinton played the democratic 'card' in the process of constructing his foreign policy. Nor would it explain why, in spite of the various attacks made upon the policy,[9] his administration continued to emphasize its attachment to democracy promotion—a point that was affirmed in a major statement outlining national security objectives in February 1996,[10] and restated in no uncertain terms a few

---

[6] This point is very well made by Thomas Carothers, 'Democracy Promotion Under Clinton', *The Washington Quarterly* 18/4 (1995), pp. 13–25.

[7] In his first major foreign policy speech at Georgetown on 12 December 1991, Clinton argued that Bush had not only 'coddled China' but more generally seemed to 'favor stability and his personal relations with foreign leaders over a coherent policy of promoting freedom and economic growth'. In his next address to the Foreign Policy Association on 1 April 1992 he continued his attack, adding that, aside from appeasing China, Bush had also 'poured cold water on Baltic and Ukrainian aspirations for independence' and had failed to recognize 'Croatia and Slovenia'. In the summer issue of the *Harvard International Review*, Clinton was in even more expansive form. 'President Bush', he opined, 'too often has hesitated when democratic forces needed our support in challenging the status quo. I believe that President Bush erred when he secretly rushed envoys to resume cordial relations with China barely a month after the massacre in Tiananmen Square; when he spurned Yeltsin before the Moscow coup; when he poured cold water on Baltic, Ukrainian, Croatian and Slovenian aspirations for independence; and when he initially refused to help the Kurds'. On 13 August in a speech given to the World Affairs Council in Los Angeles, he again assailed Bush, not just for being indifferent to democracy and the 'democratic revolution' but in daring to criticize Israel, 'America's only democratic ally in the Middle East'. Finally, in an address delivered at the University of Wisconsin in Milwaukee on 1 October 1992, Clinton more or less accused Bush of being 'un-American' and of not appearing to be 'at home in the mainstream pro-democracy tradition of American foreign policy'. Cited in *Clinton on Foreign Policy Issues* (London: United States Information Service, n.d.).

[8] See David C. Hendrickson, 'The Recovery of Internationalism', *Foreign Affairs*, 74/5 (1994), pp. 26–43.

[9] For a very small sample of the attacks made upon Clinton's Wilsonian or neo-Wilsonian views see, *inter alia*, Fareed Zakaria, 'Is Realism Finished', *National Interest*, 30 (1992–3), pp. 21–32; Robert W. Tucker, 'Realism and the New Consensus', *National Interest*, 30 (1992–3), pp. 33–6; Christopher Layne, 'Kant or Cant: the Myth of the Democratic Peace', *International Security*, 19/2 (1994), especially pp. 47–9; John Mearsheimer, 'The False Promise of International Institutions', *International Security*, 19/3 (1994–5), especially p. 5; Godfrey Hodgson, 'American Ideals: Global Realities', *World Policy Journal*, 10/ 4 (1993–4), p. 16; and Richard Haass, 'Paradigm Lost', *Foreign Affairs*, 74/1 (1995), pp. 43–58.

[10] See Bill Clinton, *A National Security Strategy of Engagement and Enlargement* (The White House, February 1996), pp. i, ii, 2, 32–3.

months later in an important article authored by the Deputy Secretary of State and published in *Foreign Affairs*.[11]

This in turn raises a second question: to what extent was the Clinton administration ever as idealistically committed to the promotion of democracy as its critics suggested and its own rhetoric sometimes seemed to imply? Certainly, to read some commentators, one could easily conclude that Clinton and his team were the most naive of foreign policy practitioners, carelessly intervening here and there to promote the cause of political freedom around the world. Abandoning the truths of realism and jumping on the liberal bandwagon, the new Democratic leadership, it has been argued, was leading America into very dangerous waters indeed. As I shall try to show, this attack against the purported idealism of the Clinton administration probably tells us much less about Clinton than it does about his various critics. Obviously, he and his administration saw definite advantages in supporting the cause of democracy. However, Clinton was hardly a liberal Rambo in search of new frontiers to conquer. Pragmatic in outlook and keen to assuage key domestic constituencies, ultimately he always viewed democracy promotion as a policy instrument to advance American power rather than as a moral duty. Thus, if he supported the cause of democracy, he did not do so for idealistic reasons, but because he felt this supported US national security and America's economic goals in the wider international system.

This logically brings us to a third issue: the complex relationship between democracy promotion and Clinton's stated goal of aggressively pursuing America's foreign economic objectives. This is an especially important area given that his administration not only saw the need to pursue both goals, but, unlike many of its more vocal opponents, saw no necessary contradiction between the two. In fact, what is so striking about the Clinton administration is the extent to which it seemed to see no real difference at all between politics and economics. Certainly, in its own mind it saw them as being intimately connected rather than mutually opposed. The market, it was believed, provided the only suitable material foundation for democracy—democracy being the most obvious superstructural accompaniment to the market.[12] The question this leads to, inevitably, is why the Clinton administration viewed the relationship between the two spheres in this way, and why it thought and acted as if democracy and markets were mutually compatible.

The issue of Clinton's apparent naivety and attachment to the ideals of Wilsonianism necessarily raises a fourth, more historical, question about how 'we', or more precisely the practitioners of foreign policy, 'construct' or 'read' the past. This is not just of academic importance. As Ernest May has pointed out in his classic study of the cold war, it was precisely the manner in which

[11] See Strobe Talbott, 'Democracy and the National Interest', *Foreign Affairs*, 74/6 (1996), pp. 47–63.
[12] For a critique from the left that disputes the connection between markets and democracy, see Ellen M. Wood, *Democracy Against Capitalism: Recovering Historical Materialism* (Cambridge: Cambridge University Press, 1995).

US foreign policymakers understood the past, and in particular the history of the 1930s and the nature of Hitler's Germany, that helped shape the international history of the 1950s and US views of the Soviet Union.[13] In the same way, I would want to suggest that a large part of the current debate about democracy promotion has been very much determined not just by an agreed set of 'facts' about the past, but by a particular and in many ways none too accurate reading of what happened after World War I under Woodrow Wilson, possibly the most misunderstood and difficult to understand foreign policy president of the twentieth century. Seen by the foreign policy community today as the quintessential symbol of American utopianism, his role in history was altogether more complicated. And significantly, whereas contemporary pundits have a very clear picture of what Wilson's purpose was, historians of the Wilson presidency are deeply divided about his role.[14] It might therefore be useful to explore this issue—partly to set the record straight, partly to see who it was exactly that Clinton purportedly was trying to emulate, and partly to deconstruct what seems to have become one of the most overused and misleading terms of the modern period: Wilsonianism.

Finally, and very briefly, I want to take up an issue raised in the critically important volume by Michael Hunt on the relationship between ideology and US foreign policy. In a major reinterpretation of American diplomatic history, Hunt suggests that the outlook of policymakers has been shaped less by a desire to advance democracy than by other, rather less idealistic, notions. Indeed, according to Hunt, it was not political freedom in general that has inspired the United States from the late nineteenth century onwards, but a fear of instability combined—until the late 1960s—with a belief in the natural hierarchy of races. Hunt may or may not be right, but his challenging argument forces us to confront the age-old issue of the extent to which America has ever had a singular mission to promote democracy.[15] It also raises the equally important problem of what America 'exports' to the rest of the world. Democracy may indeed be part of the overall package, but as all presidents, including Clinton, have discovered, the United States is bound to promote more than just its highest political ideals. Given its tempestuous past, the complexity of its social system, the diversity of its people, the dynamism of its economy and its sheer weight within the international system, it could not be otherwise.

However, before turning to this issue, let us go back to the beginning and the rather surprising election of Bill Clinton—a man with enormous political skills but without any real experience in foreign policy.

---

[13] See Ernest May, 'Lessons of the Past': The Use and Misuse of History in American Foreign Policy (New York: Oxford University Press, 1973).

[14] For a classic example of the way Wilson has been portrayed in the modern foreign policy debate, see Robert W. Tucker, 'The Triumph of Wilsonianism', World Policy Journal, 10/4 (1993–4), pp. 83–99.

[15] See Michael Hunt, Ideology and U.S. Foreign Policy (New Haven: Yale University Press, 1987).

Clinton and the Politics of Promoting Democracy

Bill Clinton was both the first elected post-cold war president and the first 'new' Democrat to occupy the White House. More concerned with domestic issues than with international affairs, his most pressing task, as he perceived it, was to build upon and extend his base of support at home. The most obvious means of achieving this, he felt, was by doing nothing rash abroad while focusing like the metaphorical laser beam on the one issue which almost certainly won him power in 1992: the belief that he could more effectively manage the American economy than George Bush.[16] The fact that Bush had not been helped in his bid for a second term by what the electors saw as his preoccupation with global issues only convinced the new Clinton team that it had to approach foreign policy with very great care. Above all, it had to avoid any unnecessary commitments and, in particular, ensure that there would be no military casualties in conflicts in faraway places whose names ordinary Americans would not recognize and whose importance to their lives appeared to be entirely marginal. Always sensitive to public opinion, and determined not to sacrifice his presidency on the altar of foreign wars, Clinton's foreign policy inclinations were from the outset extraordinarily cautious, even minimalist.[17]

This not illogical response by the administration to the world as it was did not, of course, mean it had no foreign policy at all. Nor is to imply that Clinton himself was uninterested in the world at large. He had after all made some effort to articulate a vision for the world in his campaign to become president, notably in his Georgetown speech of December 1991. None the less, his concentrated focus on the home front did leave him open to the charge of being indifferent to international affairs and unwilling to forge an overarching vision to guide the United States through the uncharted waters created by the end of the cold war and the collapse of the Soviet Union.

It was this, in part, that led to what Brinkley has rather tellingly referred to as the 'Kennan sweepstakes':[18] a bureaucratically driven exercise organized in late 1993 to come up with a notion or phrase that would most accurately encapsulate the foreign policy design of the Clinton presidency. Fearful of rhetorical overkill, but concerned to show a degree of serious thinking about America's role in the world, the term ultimately decided upon was 'democratic enlargement'. The phrase appeared to have many political advantages. It was conceptually simple; it pointed to the self-evident fact that with the end of the cold war the possibilities of expanding the zone of political freedom had grown enormously; and, unlike all the self-proclaimed competitors like 'clash

---

[16] See Bryan Jones (ed.), *The New American Politics: Reflections on Political Change and the Clinton Administration* (Boulder: Westview Press, 1995).

[17] I discuss this point at greater length in Michael Cox, *US Foreign Policy After the Cold War: Superpower without a Mission?* (London: The Royal Institute of International Affairs, 1995).

[18] Douglas Brinkley, 'Democratic Enlargement: the Clinton Doctrine', *Foreign Policy*, 106 (1997), pp. 111–27.

of civilizations', it had a positive rather than a negative sound to it. It also had an end goal in mind, though one so distant that it would be almost impossible to know whether the policy was really succeeding. For an administration keen to keep negative foreign policy news off the airwaves and the front pages of the major newspapers, this was not an unimportant consideration.[19]

The point at which the notion of 'enlargement' became official policy is not entirely clear. The consensus would seem to be, however, that after some period of discussion—though much less than one would have expected—it was finally adopted in the autumn of 1993. It was certainly alluded to by the apparently less than enthusiastic Secretary of State, Warren Christopher, in a speech he made at Columbia University on 20 September 1993. It was then made the centrepiece of a far more important address made at the School of Advanced International Studies by Anthony Lake, Clinton's National Security adviser. Two days later, Secretary of State Madeleine Albright referred to it in a speech at the Naval War College. And finally, in a keynote statement to the United Nations on 27 September, the president himself talked quite openly about America's 'overriding purpose' to 'expand and strengthen the world's community of market-based democracies'. Presumably having had three of his most important foreign policy advisers float the idea to largely academic gatherings, Clinton decided it was time to give the idea of enlargement the official seal of approval. The fact that he chose to do so before a mainly international audience, and not an American one, was perhaps a measure of the importance to which he now attached to the notion.[20]

The launch of any big foreign policy idea is of necessity a potentially problematic exercise. Other more pressing issues, like the cost of housing and interest rates, are likely to be of greater concern to the average American. Moreover, unless the idea in question can capture the public imagination or play upon popular fears, it is likely to be greeted with indifference rather than enthusiasm—particularly so in a country whose people are not known for their interest in the outside world. No doubt for all these reasons—and more— enlargement turned out to be what one observer has called a public relations dud, with few, it seems, taking more than 'a passing interest' in the possibility, as Lake put it, of strengthening and extending the 'community of core major market democracies'.[21] Even those who did take the trouble to decode its meaning could not detect anything especially original. Republicans in particular—though apparently not House Leader Newt Gingrich—viewed the whole idea as little more than window dressing designed to hide the fact that the emperor was conceptually naked when it came to foreign policy. Certainly, the general consensus seemed to be that a great opportunity had been lost, and that, instead of permitting the US to make the necessary transi-

---

[19] For a critique of Clinton's fear of foreign policy engagement, see Jim Hoagland, 'Signs of Global Decline in America's Ability to Command Respect', *The International Herald Tribune* (21 April 1995).

[20] Clinton's speech can be found in *Clinton Warns Of Perils Ahead Despite Cold War's End* (London: United States Information Service, 28 September 1993).

[21] See Anthony Lake, *Lake Says U.S. Interests Compel Engagement Abroad* (London: United States Information Service, 22 September 1993).

tion from containment to something more appropriate for the post-cold war world, the whole exercise had led only to confusion.[22] Clinton and his foreign policy team may have done a lot of hard thinking but there was very little, it seemed, to show for it all. Lake in particular came in for some especially tough comment, and the conclusion seemed to be that, although he was a decent human being, he was no Henry Kissinger or even a Zbigniew Brzezinski. Concepts, it seemed, did not become him. He was, to use the title of a slashing review of the man who had set out to win the 'Kennan stakes', Lake Inferior.[23]

Promoting Democracy Promotion

If the idea of democracy promotion did not fire the imagination of the American people, it did even less perhaps to quieten Clinton's political enemies. Even more moderate figures within the foreign policy establishment had their doubts. This was perhaps to be expected. For a generation hand-reared on the truths of realism and the doctrine of power politics, the idea that a change in the form of other countries' governments would enhance US security must have sounded a little odd, especially coming from someone so inexperienced in the ways of the world as Bill Clinton.[24] The response by the White House to these various criticisms, however, was not to sound the retreat but to mount a fairly muscular defence of the policy. Refusing to see the world in simple binary terms in which there were fine moral principles on one side and the real world on the other, and convinced in its own mind that democracy promotion was not just some idealistic add-on but something that would actually enhance world order, the administration thus decided to soldier on—partly because it would have been politically damaging to have abandoned the policy, but more obviously because it felt there were good reasons to do so. The question is: why?

One small part of the answer lies in the American experience and the widely shared belief that the United States was not just a successful democracy but a shining example for others to follow.[25] Clinton, in fact, was quite adamant that the character of a nation's foreign policy had to reflect its core values; and there was nothing more important in the American value system, he believed, than the principle of democracy. This, in the words of the title of a famous study by the historian Daniel Boorstin, was an essential part of the American genius.[26] But this was not all. While theorists of a more realist persuasion might try to build neat conceptual walls between the international system and

---

[22] See Fareed Zakaria, 'Internationalism as a Way of Life', *World Policy Journal*, 12/2 (1995), pp. 59–61.
[23] Jacob Heilbrunn, 'Lake Inferior', *The New Republic* (20 and 27 September 1993), pp. 29–35.
[24] For a useful summary of the arguments for and against democracy promotion, see Christopher Layne and Sean M. Lynn-Jones (eds), *Should America Promote Democracy?* (Boston: MIT Press, 1998).
[25] De Tocqueville, *Democracy in America* (1835; London: Oxford University Press, 1946), p. 370.
[26] Daniel J. Boorstin, *The Genius of American Politics* (Chicago: Chicago University Press, 1958).

domestic politics, Clinton refused to. In his view there was a close, almost intimate, connection between the two spheres. They were, as he pointed out, two sides of the same coin. As he made clear in an early speech defining US strategy in the post-cold war era, in the new world where so much had changed it was absolutely vital 'to tear down the wall in our thinking between domestic and foreign policy'. This was necessary if America wanted to compete economically, and it was essential too if it wished to promote a more stable international system.[27]

This outlook was allied with another, equally important idea: the notion that democracy had become the political gold standard of the late twentieth century. Talbott put the case particularly forcefully to a largely British audience in a speech delivered at Oxford University in October 1994. The world had altered beyond recognition over the past 25 years, he noted, with dictatorships from Latin America to the old Soviet bloc finally succumbing to the attractive pull of democracy. This had not only changed the lives of millions of people but had forced those who once believed otherwise to accept the self-evident truth that democracy was 'the best form of political organization'.[28] The facts—for once—spoke for themselves. As official US figures showed, in 1972 there had been 44 democracies in the world: 21 years later there were 107,[29] leaving very few outside the democratic fold.[30] Moreover, those that remained would never be regarded as wholly legitimate in a world where, according to Huntington, democracy had become the norm.[31] Hence, why oppose the inevitable?[32] Why stand against the tide of history? Indeed, why not ride the liberal wave and give it a nudge in the right direction? This not only made intellectual sense. From an American perspective it made foreign policy sense as well.

The assumption that democracy represented the wave of the future also became connected in the administration's mind with a theorem made popular by political theorists like Michael Doyle and Bruce Russett: namely, that for a variety of structural and cultural reasons, democracies in general tended not to go to war with each other.[33] Possibly no other idea emanating from the academic community exercised as much influence as this one on the White House. To be sure, the more general relationship between war and political forms was, as Warren Christopher conceded, a complex one; and he agreed

---

[27] Bill Clinton, *A New Covenant for American Security*, speech delivered at the Georgetown University School of Foreign Service (Washington, DC, 12 December 1991).

[28] See Strobe Talbott, *The New Geopolitics: Defending Democracy in the Post-Cold War Era*, speech delivered at Oxford University (20 October 1994).

[29] See Doh Chull Shin, 'On the Third Wave of Democratization', *World Politics*, 47/1 (1994), pp. 135–70.

[30] Doh Chull Shin, 'On the Third Wave of Democratization', p. 136.

[31] Samuel Huntington, *The Third Wave Democratization in the Late Twentieth Century* (Norman: University of Oklahoma Press, 1992), p. 58.

[32] See Francis Fukuyama, *The End of History and the Last Man* (New York, The Free Press, 1992), pp. 39–51.

[33] See Michael Doyle, 'Liberalism and World Politics', *American Political Science Review*, 80/4 (1986), pp. 1151–69, and Bruce Russett, *Grasping the Democratic Peace: Principles for a Post-Cold War World* (Princeton: Princeton University Press, 1993).

that it would be far too simple to conclude that democracies were 'incapable of aggression' or that war was 'always caused by dictatorship'.[34] Nevertheless, there was very strong evidence to support the more specific argument that democracies behaved peacefully toward each other. Clinton certainly seemed to believe so, and as early as December 1991 noted that it should matter to the United States 'how others govern themselves'; for, as he pointed out, using words once confined to the classroom, 'democracies don't go to war with each other'.[35] Talbott later went even further. In his view, the proposition was not just a self-evident truth or a 'bromide', but represented a fundamental law of politics. Indeed, in his opinion, it was 'as close as we're ever likely' to get 'in political science to an empirical truth'.[36]

Finally, the administration backed the idea of enlargement because it was convinced that democracy more generally contributed to global stability and security, especially in those countries that were in transition from communism to capitalism.[37] Here, it argued, democracy was absolutely essential if nations like Ukraine and Russia were to become normal members of the international community.[38] The same political rule also applied to the old 'Third World' where democracy, it was felt, might even help alleviate suffering and poverty. Talbott in fact believed there was a close relationship between democratic forms and food supply, and cited the famous economist Amartya Sen to the effect that famines did not occur where democracy flourished.[39] Clinton added a few more advantages to the ever-lengthening list, and noted, in a significant speech made before his election to the White House, that democracies did not sponsor terrorist acts; they were reliable trading partners; they protected the global environment; and they abided by international law. They were also likely to be more friendly towards the United States. Here he cited the examples of France and the United Kingdom. They had once been rivals of the US; and they possessed nuclear weapons. But precisely because they were members of the larger democratic club nobody seriously saw either as a threat. Hence, even though they had the capacity to destroy the United States, Americans did not fear 'annihilation at their hands', not because they did not possess the means, but because they shared the same political values. The existence of democracy in other countries, therefore, was not merely reassuring but of vital importance to American security. As Clinton noted, 'how others' governed 'themselves' was not a matter about which the United States could be indifferent. [40]

---

[34] Warren Christopher, 'U.S. Strategy To Defend Human Rights and Democracy', *U.S. Department of State Dispatch*, 6/15 (10 April 1995), p. 295.

[35] Clinton, *A New Covenant for American Security*.   [36] Quoted in Talbott, *The New Geopolitics*.

[37] For a more sceptical view of the relationship between academic theory and foreign policy practice, see Thomas Carrothers, 'Democracy', *Foreign Policy*, 107 (1997), pp. 11–18.

[38] See Michael Cox, 'The Necessary Partnership: The Clinton Presidency and Post-Communist Russia', *International Affairs*, 70/4 (1994), pp. 635–58.

[39] See Talbott, 'Democracy and the National Interest', pp. 51–2.

[40] Clinton, *A New Covenant for American Security*.

Clinton: The Pragmatic Crusader

The administration's strong defence of democracy promotion as a policy objective was certainly robust. Yet at the same time, Clinton and his various aides were extremely careful not to oversell the policy—a point often overlooked by critics. Clinton, however, was adamant. His administration would attempt to situate US grand strategy within the larger American democratic tradition, all the time implying that Bush had failed to do so. But it would not engage in what he more than once referred to as 'reckless crusades' to expand the realm of international freedom.[41] Clinton made it abundantly clear that he would not be doing so in an important, but rarely cited, speech he made on the campaign trail in 1992. Speaking to an enthusiastic student audience in the University of Wisconsin, Clinton was at his rhetorical best as he denounced Bush's poor record on democracy promotion. Bush, he claimed, was too much of a realist and as a result tended 'to coddle dictators' rather than support liberal values abroad. But he then went on to stress that, if he were elected to the White House, he would not be upsetting established US relations with important autocratic allies either. China in particular had nothing to fear from a Clinton administration. 'I will say again, I do not want isolate China', he emphasized. Nor, it seems, did he want to alienate other countries of equally dubious political probity. America, he accepted, had a special destiny. But this did not mean it could, or would, force its ideals on other people. 'Our actions' abroad, he agreed, had always to be 'tempered with prudence and common-sense'. After all, he continued, there were 'some countries and some cultures' that were 'many steps away from democratic institutions' and it would be foolish to think they could adopt democratic forms overnight. Moreover, though the United States under his leadership would do more than its predecessor to support the cause of democracy with tax dollars—for instance, by establishing a 'democracy corps' and reinforcing the work of 'the bipartisan National Endowment for Democracy'—it would not act rashly or without due consideration to America's other obligations. As he pointed out, there would be times 'when other security needs or economic interests' would compromise America's 'commitment to democracy and human rights'. Democracy promotion, he thus suggested, was not a moral duty that would override all other goals, but one objective amongst a host of others that would help guarantee America's place in a complex international system.[42]

Lake was equally clear on this point, and in a little noted part of a much-cited speech, was insistent that the strategy of enlargement was bound to be hedged in by what he defined as a 'host of caveats'. We have to be 'patient', he warned; 'our strategy must be pragmatic', he went on. 'Our interests in democracy and markets do not stand alone . . . other American interests at

[41] See Clinton, *A National Security Strategy Of Engagement And Enlargement*, p. 32.

[42] Governor Bill Clinton, *Democracy in America*, speech delivered at the University of Milwaukee, Wisconsin, 1 October 1992.

times will require us to befriend and even defend non-democratic states for mutually beneficial reasons.'[43] Talbott made much the same argument. In a powerful defence of the administration's policy of democracy promotion, he attacked the critics—isolationists and realists alike—for failing to understand why it was in America's interest to support democracy in certain countries. But he was equally careful to distinguish between a policy driven by ideals alone and one—Clinton's—guided by enlightened self-interest. He was equally keen to point out that 'for the United States, the attractions and advantages of supporting democracy abroad must be balanced against other strategic interests'; and, he added significantly, 'against the difficulty of sponsoring transitions that will inevitably entail a degree of disruption, if not instability'. 'Support for democracy', he concluded, was 'not an absolute imperative'.[44]

These indications of a clear willingness to compromise did not go entirely unnoticed, especially by those in the corporate sector who perhaps had most to lose if the United States attempted to sacrifice its economic relations with influential authoritarian regimes on the altar of democratic principle. But the more business leaders heard from Clinton about the supreme importance of America's role in an increasingly globalized economy, the less they tended to worry about his unalloyed commitment to democracy promotion. His many speeches on the importance of American economic power in the world, his repeated references to the need to compete and win in the global marketplace, and his upgrading of economics at all levels of the foreign policy bureaucracy could only have reassured them that there was little to fear from this most pro-business of Democratic administrations. Clinton himself certainly did not give the impression of someone willing to exchange US economic influence for some distant prospect of democratization in countries such as China or Saudi Arabia. As he stressed in one of his most important interventions outlining US foreign policy, under his leadership the main aim would be to promote American economic power and 'make trade a priority element of American security'. Naturally enough, he would support democracy and human rights where it was feasible to, but never—it was implied—to the same degree or with the same seriousness as he would back American business efforts in the international economy.[45]

Clinton's stress on the importance of economics in US foreign policy was married to an equally strong attachment to the tools of traditional statecraft. Indeed, in spite of appearances, Clinton was in many ways a most orthodox president when it came to defining American interests, and time and again he reiterated the simple but important point that what had worked before and brought the United States victory in two world wars and the cold war—namely, strong alliances and an even stronger military—would not be abandoned in his time. Anthony Lake made much the same point in two key

---

[43] Lake, *Lake Says U.S. Interests Compel Engagement Abroad*, p. 5.

[44] Talbott, 'Democracy and the National Interest', p. 52.

[45] President Bill Clinton, 'American Leadership And Global Change', *US Department of State Dispatch*, 4/9 (1 March 1993), pp. 113–118.

speeches made in 1994. Designed in large part to reassure the 'realists' that the Clinton administration was not about to unlearn the lessons of the past, Lake went out of his way to stress the centrality of 'military force' in world politics in general and American diplomacy in particular. He also made it clear that while it was in America's interest to enlarge 'the community of democracies', democracy promotion could not be made to bear all, or even most of, the weight of US national security. The world was simply too ruthless a place to abandon the traditional tools of international diplomacy. Democracy promotion was obviously important, he conceded; and a democratic world was more likely to be prosperous and peaceful than one which was not. But in the last analysis, he noted with Achesonian *gravitas*, there was no substitute for power. Power without diplomacy, he accepted, was 'dangerous'. However, 'diplomacy disconnected from power usually fails'. America would continue to negotiate from a position of strength.[46]

But perhaps the most significant indication of the administration's pragmatic approach was the manner in which it assessed the role of previous American presidents—including Woodrow Wilson, the personification of the idealistic strain in American foreign policy in the twentieth century. Wilson, it was readily accepted, was a great Democratic president. But there were others too, and while Clinton himself paid homage to Wilson, he seemed to have more time for more traditional occupants of the White House like Harry Truman and John F. Kennedy, leaders whose policies were as hard-headed as they were sometimes ruthless and whose commitment to democracy promotion never overrode their more general desire to balance the power of the Soviet Union. Moreover, though Wilson had much to recommend him, he also had his weaknesses. Hence, it would be foolish to slavishly follow his example. Lake made this argument in a key statement which revealed the administration's attitude towards democracy promotion as much as, if not more than, its attitude toward Wilson himself. Wilson, he agreed, 'had it right' when he argued that 'principles matter and that power unhinged from principle will leave us rudderless and adrift'. Wilson was also correct to insist that what happened 'within nations' was 'fundamental' to what happened 'among them'. In this sense, he was an especially important president whose 'core beliefs' about 'the value of spreading democracy to other nations' remained 'more relevant than ever'. But he was not without his faults. The most obvious was a tendency to employ 'lofty rhetoric' which suggested the US would be engaged on a mission impossible 'to make the world safe for democracy'. The consequence of this, unfortunately, was to create the impression that the nation would be playing 'too global a role', something that frightened the American people back into the very isolationism Wilson was seeking to combat. Equally misguided was his reliance on and ill-founded 'confidence in the power of morality' to reshape the international order after 1919. Though commendable at one level, this approach left America and the world without the

---

[46] See Anthony Lake, 'American Power and American Diplomacy', *U.S. Department of State Dispatch*, 5/46 (14 November 1994), pp. 766–9.

means to deter aggression and safeguard the peace. The results were catastrophic; and while it would be unfair to blame Wilson for what happened thereafter, his vain attempt to build a new world order on idealism alone contributed, albeit indirectly, to the several crises that followed. And it was only when the US had learned the lessons of its past mistakes that it could play a meaningful international role.

The implications of Lake's foray into history were obvious. The Clinton administration would be building upon the legacy of Wilson, but it would be drawing its real inspiration from those who were present at creation after 1945, and who in Lake's opinion constructed a stable world that was neither naively liberal in the Wilsonian sense nor relentlessly realist in the conservative sense. As Lake observed, 'Today it is the spirit of the post-World War II generation that we need to recapture in forging a coalition of the centre'. This would draw upon Wilson, albeit selectively, but it would also learn from realism as well. Only in this way could the US forge a foreign policy for a 'rapidly changing world' without overcommitting American resources or raising false expectations.[47]

Towards a Political Economy of Democracy Promotion

The Clinton administration's careful efforts to plot a course in foreign policy that it quite consciously regarded, and referred to as being, 'neither rigidly Wilsonian nor classically realist'[48] in character was often lost on opponents from both left and right: the former because they could see no difference between Clinton's grand strategy and those of his various predecessors, the latter because, apparently, they could see too many. But what critics also seemed to pass over in silence was the administration's rather interesting attempt to relate the politics of democracy promotion to the economics of the global market. Yet Talbott made a very direct connection between the two. In 'an increasingly interdependent world', he noted in the context of a more general effort to spell out the national interest reasons for promoting democracy, Americans had a 'growing stake in how other countries govern or misgovern themselves'. This had not always been true, but 'a combination' of factors 'technological, commercial' as well as 'political' were 'shortening distances, opening borders, and connecting far-flung cultures and economies'. This had its upside, but it also posed new dangers as narcotics, criminals, terrorists, even viruses, moved more quickly across borders. To control this required cooperation; this in turn presupposed democracy; and 'the larger and more close-knit the community of nations that choose democratic forms of government' the less risk there was from these various threats. Moreover, in a world where the market was now the only serious economic option in the international

[47] Anthony Lake, 'The Need for Engagement', *U.S. Department of State Dispatch*, 5/49 (5 December 1994), pp. 804–7.

[48] Lake, 'The Need for Engagement', p. 805.

system, the US had greater reason than ever for strengthening democracy in other countries: the two went hand in hand. Supporting political pluralism, therefore, was not just the right thing to do—though Talbott cautioned there would be circumstances where the US would not be able to get its way—but, more importantly, the economically smart thing to do as well. [49]

The belief that there was a symbiotic and positive relationship between market forms and political democracy was not, of course, shared by all commentators. The influential French critic Jacques Attali, for example, saw little relationship at all, and took the American administration to task for its lack of historical perspective and myopic belief that the market and democracy were logically or even empirically related. 'Contrary to popular belief', he argued 'the market economy and democracy—the twin pillars of Western civilization—are more likely to undermine than support one another.'[50] A similar point was made by the conservative American scholar, Irwin Stezler. The 'relationship', he believed, was 'ambiguous'. However, 'democracy', he concluded, was 'no guarantor of prosperity, nor its absence a guarantor of poverty'. The 'linkages between economic and political structures' were in fact immensely complex, and simply to assume that the market and democracy were necessary partners was quite naive.[51] A number of realists took the same line. The market, they argued, could quite easily function in the absence of political freedom—note the case of China. Democratic reform, on the other hand, need not lead to a flourishing capitalist economy—witness the example of post-communist Russia.[52]

Yet in spite of what many saw as irrefutable evidence to the contrary, the Clinton administration persisted in believing that there was a positive, rather than an ambiguous or even non-existent, connection between capitalism and democracy. In many ways, the idea seemed to run like a thread through its thinking, influencing its rhetoric and helping define its attitude towards the outside world—to such a degree that the strategy of enlargement came to be viewed not just as a stand-alone political objective but as an integrated part of the administration's larger effort to help the United States compete more effectively in the global economy. This is why Clinton found the idea so appealing. As has been pointed out, 'what Clinton liked best about Lake's enlargement policy was the way it was inextricably linked to economic renewal with its emphasis on making sure the United States remained the number one exporter'. Vice-President Al Gore was equally enthusiastic. A firm advocate of the classical liberal view that the expansion of trade and the spread of political freedom were the twin foundations of world order, Gore, it seems, felt that commerce, democracy and peace formed part of a single whole.[53]

[49]   Talbott, 'Democracy and the National Interest', pp. 48–9.

[50]   Jacques Attali, 'The Crash of Western Civilization: The Limits of Market and Democracy', *Foreign Policy*, 197 (1997), p. 58.

[51]   Irwin Stelzer, 'A Question of Linkage: Capitalism, Prosperity, Democracy', *The National Interest*, 35 (1994), pp. 29–35.

[52]   See Fareed Zakaria, 'Democracy and Tyranny', *Prospect* (December 1997), pp. 20–5.

[53]   See Douglas Brinkley, 'Democratic Enlargement: the Clinton Doctrine', especially pp. 117, 120–1.

But it was more than just market access that interested Clinton and his foreign policy advisers. In some larger sense they really did think that over time democracy could not function without the market, or the market without democracy. Competition at the ballot box and in the marketplace were in this sense twins, with democracy being the necessary political accompaniment of free enterprise, and free enterprise the only secure foundation upon which to construct and sustain democracy. It was no accident that Clinton and his advisers persistently coupled the two words together and employed the term 'market democracy' to more fully describe the policy of enlargement. They simply could not conceive of one without the other, or the strategy succeeding where either was absent. The question is: why? There are several parts to the answer.

To some degree it reflected the administration's rather heroic interpretation of the American experience. Here, democratic forms and market economics had always existed together, and the assumption was that if the two had coexisted happily in the US, there was no reason to believe they would not do so elsewhere, especially if the United States itself intervened to support and sustain nascent market democracies in other countries. This viewpoint was in turn bolstered by the administration's understanding of the end of the cold war. There were, it was true, many causes of 1989, but the most critical, it was argued, was not the Reagan military build-up—a line championed by the republicans—or simply that the Soviet economy was inefficient, but the attractiveness of Western institutions overall. But, as Talbott pointed out, the West did not win the cold war because of the market alone, but because of the market and democracy together.[54] Lake agreed, adding that that those who wanted to build a better world could not do so without introducing both forms. Democracy was essential if you wanted 'justice', and capitalism if you wished to generate the wealth and 'material goods necessary for individuals to thrive'. And while the two may have performed entirely different functions without which 'civilized societies' were bound to 'perish', neither could really exist without the other.[55]

The connection also seemed to make a good deal of sense for another, more practical, reason relating to the issue of economic restructuring in those countries where previously there had been forms of planning and social protection. How were these often painful changes to be introduced without generating deep resentment and political upheaval? The answer, it was suggested, was through the ballot box. It had, after all, worked in Poland after 1989. Here, the people voted for a government prepared to take the tough market measures that would have provoked political opposition under the old system, and there was no reason to expect that the same strategy would not work elsewhere. As Warren Christopher conceded, democracy had many advantages over the alternatives, but one was that it permitted countries to take harsh economic decisions. He noted, 'in nations undergoing economic transformation,

[54] Talbott, 'Democracy and the National Interest', pp. 54–5.
[55] Anthony Lake, *Lake Says U.S. Engagement Compel Engagement Abroad*, p. 3.

market reformers who enjoy popular legitimacy are more likely to win popular support for tough economic measures' than those who do not.[56] Another official made much the same point. Democracy, he noted, helped new reforming elites in many ways, but in particular it allowed them to 'modernize their economies, ameliorate social conditions and integrate with the outside world' by legitimizing 'painful but necessary economic choices'.[57] Moreover, once these market democracies had undergone reform and been more fully integrated into the world economy, they were also more likely to be reliable trading partners.[58]

Finally, the Clinton administration saw a more general relationship between democracy and the market. Warren Christopher put it thus. The market, he argued, was not a self-regulating economic system but one that required a framework within which to operate—and the most appropriate framework, he believed, was a democratic one in which the rule of law operated. This was not because of any moral imperative; rather it was because mature market economies demanded stability, order and certainty—and democracy was more likely to provide these than any other system. The market also needed well-defined regulations that could govern contract, protect property and facilitate competition; and again, the best guarantee of all these things was a democratic polity with clearly defined rules. From this perspective, the rule of law under democracy was essential not only to protect 'political rights but also the essential elements of free market economies'.[59] Moreover, as markets evolved they generated changes that were bound to threaten the integrity of even the most carefully constructed authoritarian regime. Again, this was not because the market was moral, but rather because it was dynamic and, in its own way, revolutionary too. Thus, as it developed, it spawned new social groups, including a more active middle class who placed increased demands upon the political system. It also generated a need for a much higher level of information; this also was likely to promote change in a progressive direction. Even more corrosive of traditional political forms was the very dynamics of globalization, which impelled all countries to operate by the same standards; and if the dominant standards being set were those defined by the West, then this was bound to lead, over time, to liberalization. Naturally, the pace of change would vary from country to country. Moreover, there was no guaranteeing that the film of history would always run in the same pluralist direction, as the events of Tiananmen Square proved only too graphically. However, according to the Clinton team there was no escaping the longer-term logic of capitalism. In the end, even the most repressive regime would have to become more open as its economy adapted and became more integrated into the world market.

[56] Warren Christopher, 'America's Fundamental Dedication To Human Rights', *U.S. Department of State Dispatch*, 6/6 (6 February 1995), p. 76.
[57] Talbott, 'Democracy and the National Interest', p. 51
[58] Bill Clinton, speech to the Los Angeles World Affairs Council, 13 August 1992.
[59] Warren Christopher, statement to the Senate Foreign Relations Committee, 14 February 1995 (USIS European Wireless File, 15 February 1995), p. 4.

Will the Real Woodrow Wilson Please Stand Up?

The concept of enlargement, therefore, was not rooted just in a larger political theory about the world at large, but in a developed political economy about the relationship between democracy and democracy promotion on the one hand, and the market and global capitalism on the other. However, sitting like Banquo at this particular feast was the ever-present historical figure of Woodrow Wilson, someone who according to critic and admirer alike—not to mention the Clinton administration—was the quintessential moral president in foreign affairs. Indeed, in the great contemporary debate about America's democratic mission, the name of Woodrow Wilson figures very prominently, and for good reason. More than anyone else, he remains the president most readily associated with the idea of democracy and democracy promotion. And while realists and liberals might disagree about nearly everything else, both seem to accept at face value the claim that Wilson was a true enlightenment figure whose ultimate goal was to make the world a more democratic place. The only difference is that, whereas realists such as Kennan and Kissinger criticize him for having such a vision, liberals do not.

This of necessity leads to the obvious question: to what extent is this portrait an accurate one? Certainly, the view of Wilson as a rather simple-minded liberal idealist is not shared by all historians of the period. In fact, whereas most contemporary commentators see Wilson as someone slightly out of touch with international realities, his biographer actually views him as being driven by a higher realism. This view has been upheld by more recent scholarship, which portrays Wilson as a rather astute war-time leader who managed to maximize US negotiating leverage at the post-war conference table.[60] Levin paints an equally complicated, less soft-focused picture of a Wilson motivated not so much by idealism but by a more fundamental desire to make the word safe for capitalism in the immediate aftermath of World War I—a view also endorsed by Lloyd Gardner.[61] Link even argues that he was inspired less by political idealism than by Christianity.[62] Nor do all historians subscribe to the view that Wilson underestimated the role of power. According to one historian of the Wilson presidency, nothing could be further from the truth. In fact, 'no other American president before or since used force more than' Woodrow Wilson. As Calhoun has observed, 'within four years, from 1914 to 1918, Wilson resorted to force twice in Mexico, in Haiti, in the Dominican Republic,

---

[60] See Arthur S. Link, *The Higher Realism of Woodrow Wilson and Other Essays* (Nashville: Vanderbilt University Press, 1971); David F. Trask, *The United States in the Supreme War Council: American War Aims and Inter-Allied Strategy, 1917–1978* (Middletown, CT: Wesleyan University Press, 1961), and David F. Trask, *The AEF and Coalition Warmaking, 1917–1918* (Lawrence: University Press of Kansas, 1993).

[61] See N. Gordon Levin, *Woodrow Wilson and World Politics: America's Response to War and Revolution* (New York: Oxford University Press, 1980) and Lloyd Gardner, *Safe for Democracy: The Anglo-American Response to Revolution, 19131923* (New York, Oxford University Press, 1984).

[62] Arthur S. Link, *Wilson*, vols. 3, 4 and 5 (Princeton: Princeton University Press, 1960–5).

in World War I, northern Russia and Siberia'.[63] This hardly conveys the impression of a staunch moral idealist and consistent advocate of the peaceful resolution of international disputes.

The search for the 'real' Woodrow Wilson should also take account of his hierarchical world-view.[64] Wilson may well have been a democrat in the formal sense, but there was always something distinctly elitist about his political vision. At heart a Burkean who worried more about threats to the established order than about representation, Wilson had little faith in the people or even, it seems, in elections. According to one commentator, 'Wilson greatly downplayed the role of elections as the proper touchstone of democracy'. In Wilson's view 'democracy was not an electoral process as much as a meritocracy' in which the best and the brightest would rule on behalf of the ignorant masses.[65] This fear of *vox populi* partly reflected a fairly profound hostility to all things French, including Rousseau and the French Revolution; but it was also shaped by his own attitude towards the Founding Fathers. Though sometimes referred to as a Jeffersonian democrat, Wilson had far more in common with the patrician views of Alexander Hamilton and James Madison—neither of whom could remotely be regarded as genuine democrats—than he did with the populist Jefferson. This did not bother Wilson, however. Good government, he believed, was always preferable to majoritarian democracy, and the form of government which worked best, in his view, was one composed of what Wilson regarded as those 'of highest and steadiest political habits'.[66]

If Wilson had a restricted concept of democracy—he once argued that American democracy had nothing in common with 'radical thought and a restless spirit'—he had forthright views about race. A Virginian by birth who was not entirely unsympathetic to the plight of the South and southern whites—he once objected to black suffrage on the grounds that the negro mind was 'dark, ignorant, uneducated and incompetent to form an enlightened opinion'—he always tended to look at the world through the prism of colour. He certainly saw nations in terms of a racial hierarchy and in 1917 informed his Secretary of State, Robert Lansing, that 'white civilization and its dominion over the world rested largely on our ability to keep this country intact'. This is one of the reasons, amongst others, that he later opposed Japan's efforts at the Paris peace talks to have a clause about racial equality attached to the Covenant of the League of Nations. Wilson's motives in opposing the Japanese move were far from straightforward. In part it 'demonstrated his determination to maintain Anglo-American control' of the international agenda. But it also reflected his own racial prejudice. As Ambrosius has pointed

[63] See Frederick Calhoun, *Power and Principle: Armed Intervention in Wilsonian Foreign Policy* (Kent: Kent State University Press, 1986).

[64] A question raised in the important intervention in the democratic peace debate by Ido Oren, 'The Subjectivity of the "Democratic Peace": Changing U.S. Perceptions of Imperial Germany', *International Security*, 20/2 (1995), pp. 147–84.

[65] Sidney Bell, *Righteous Conquest: Woodrow Wilson and the Evolution of the New Diplomacy* (Port Washington, NY: Kennikat Press, 1972), pp. 10–28.

[66] Bell, *Righteous Conquest*, p. 17.

out, 'sharing rather than challenging the racial attitude of white supremacy, the president chose to alienate the Japanese by rejecting their amendment'.[67]

Wilson was also less than enthusiastic about the idea of self-determination. As Lynch has noted, there is no reference to the idea in any of his writings or speeches before 1914; and when he did advocate it later, he did so with the greatest of reservations. It is true that he opposed certain forms of imperial control in Europe, and was in the end forced to accept the dissolution of the Austro-Hungarian empire.[68] But earlier he had actually argued for the union of the Austro-Hungarian peoples;[69] moreover, when the United States did enter the war, there is no evidence it did so in order to stimulate the dissolution Austria-Hungary. We should also not forget that Wilson did nothing for the Irish or the Chinese at Versailles; that 20 years earlier he had endorsed the brutal American takeover of the Philippines; and that he was not in favour of independence for all peoples, especially if they were brown or black. Furthermore, in spite of his suspicions of the British, he was something of an admirer of the British Empire and the British constitutional system: strange things to admire, one would have thought, for someone inspired and animated by democratic idealism. He even uttered more than a passing word of praise for pre-World War I Germany with its efficient and orderly bureaucracy. As Oren has shown, Wilson admired rather than attacked Germany under the Kaiser on the grounds that it embodied the highest form of administrative rationality. The fact that there was a limited franchise and that left-wing parties were effectively excluded from government was not something that seemed to bother him overly. The German system, he felt, was a 'shining model' that American reformers would be well advised to emulate.[70]

Finally, though Wilson may well have employed certain grand phrases like 'self-determination' and 'democracy', he did so not out of some mystical faith in reason but because he thought these broad objectives would help advance American power at a time when the world was threatened by hunger, chaos and a new ideology in the shape of Bolshevism. A new form of politics was thus essential, in his view, to build what he hoped would one day become a more viable international order. This was no simple-minded crusade for its own sake. Nor was it mere idealism. Rather, it was a recognition that the old order had collapsed and that unless the United States put itself at the vanguard of building a new one, then a great opportunity would be lost. It was also the only way in which Wilson could ever hope to mobilize a reluctant American public after the war. Dry talk of a clearly defined American national interest was all very fine in theory, but unless the notion of interest could be married to the ideal of democracy there was little chance of building a foreign policy

[67] Lloyd Ambrosius, *Woodrow Wilson and the American Diplomatic Tradition* (New York: Cambridge University Press, 1987) especially pp. 30, 77, 119–22.

[68] Allen Lynch, 'Woodrow Wilson and the Principle of "National Self-Determination": A Reconsideration', unpublished manuscript (October 1999), p. 35.

[69] See David Fromkin, 'What Is Wilsonianism?', *World Policy Journal*, 11/1 (1994), p. 108.

[70] See Oren, 'The Subjectivity of the "Democratic Peace"', p. 178.

consensus and breaking the political back of isolationism. Wilson, at least, seemed to understand this, even if his later realist critics did not.

Of course, to make these various observations is not to criticize Wilson as an historic figure, but rather to challenge those who later idealized or denigrated his role. Wilson was neither a fool nor a saint, and to portray him as if he was one or the other only serves to distort his place in history. In fact, the more one examines Wilson's ideas over time, the more one is drawn to the conclusion that there never was something so clear and unambiguous as 'Wilsonianism'. As one writer has noted, 'Wilson's connection with the doctrines ascribed to his name' remains 'tenuous at best'.[71] Indeed, it was only after his death that the term acquired meaning. Unfortunately, the meaning it acquired—either as inspiration to those who hoped the League of Nations would save the world from war or as synonym for foreign policy utopianism—inevitably tended to simplify the record. The best example of this, of course, is Carr's highly influential work on the inter-war crisis.[72] Carr does not spare what he sees as the hapless Wilson, 'the most perfect modern example of the intellectual in politics'.[73] However, in his rush to judgement, Carr ignores the real Wilson and paints instead a caricature of some faintly risible figure rooted in the nineteenth century with no understanding of the ways of the world. The fact that Wilson might have been less naive than Carr believed, or more aware of power realities, was ignored in the English historian's scorching but highly effective attack.

Conclusion: But What to Promote?

This brings us to our last question: not whether the United States should or should not engage in democracy promotion, but rather what is it exactly that America promotes? Thus far, the debate around this issue has been unnecessarily polarized between two positions rather well defined by one of the doyens of American realism, Henry Kissinger. Kissinger summed up the dilemma for Americans in the following way. The United States had a choice: either to promote its political values or simply to act as an example for others to follow. He noted,

. . . the singularities that America has ascribed to itself throughout its history have produced two contradictory attitudes towards foreign policy. The first is that America serves its values best by perfecting democracy at home, thereby acting as a beacon for the rest of mankind; the second, that America's values impose on it an obligation to crusade for them around the world.[74]

Kissinger himself was in no doubt which of those two options he preferred, and concluded by observing that in the real world of competing states it was

---

[71] Quote from Fromkin, 'What Is Wilsonianism?', p. 107.
[72] E. H. Carr, *The Twenty Years' Crisis, 1919–1939* (London: Macmillan, 1951).
[73] Carr, *The Twenty Years' Crisis*, p. 14.
[74] Henry A. Kissinger, *Diplomacy* (New York: Simon and Schuster, 1994), p. 18.

simply bad politics—and even worse diplomacy—to try and export liberal ideas to countries that did not want them and were only likely to be alienated from the United States if it tried to do so.

Kissinger poses the problem clearly and starkly, though the flaws in his argument are all too evident. Like the good realist he is, he first tries to erect what are, in effect, false barriers between domestic politics and foreign policy. He then goes on to constructs a straw man in the shape of democratic 'crusades' that no liberal president, including Clinton, has ever sought to wage. That said, he does draw our attention to a fundamental truth: that America is always exporting or projecting a story about itself, even when it is not consciously trying to do so. That is its fate or privilege given its position of influence within the wider international system. Simply being America with a dynamic economy, diverse culture and vibrant political system makes a massive impact on the rest of the world. It could not be otherwise. This leads us to the important conclusion that the success of US efforts to promote democracy may in the end depend less upon the amounts of money invested in the policy, and more on the ability of America as a nation to fulfil its promise. If it can continue to do so, then its efforts abroad are likely to be successful; if it cannot, then democracy promotion as a grand strategy will be unable to live up to the claims made for it by its supporters, namely, that it makes the world a safer and more peaceful place.[75]

---

[75] See Thomas Carothers, *Aiding Democracy Abroad: The Learning Curve* (Washington, DC: The Carnegie Endowment, 1999).

IV

US Democracy Promotion in Practice

11

Russia: Limping Along Towards American Democracy?

PETER RUTLAND

NEARLY ten years after the collapse of the Soviet Union, the political system of the newly independent Russian federation is still work in progress. Although Russia has managed to achieve formal adherence to the rules of democratic procedure, at least since 1993, the political institutions of the new Russia have not proved able to meet the severe challenges that lie before the country. At best, the political system has been paralyzed in the face of the problems demanding resolution; at worst, political power has been wielded by unscrupulous national and local leaders in order to consolidate their grip and exclude their opponents and society at large.

The newly independent states of the former Soviet Union faced three transitions in 1991: to construct a democratic political system; to build a market economy; and to realize a new national consciousness and identity as a sovereign state. It is now clear that Russia has made only partial progress with regard to the first and second of these tasks, and almost no progress at all towards the third.

The sudden collapse of the Soviet Union was immediately taken as vindication of Western values and proof of the superiority of both market economics and a democratic system of government. It was seen as a natural eastward extension of the process of popular rebellion that had ignited in Poland and spread across Central Europe. America had won the cold war, and 'market democracy'—to use President Bill Clinton's concise term—would spread from Belgrade to Bishkek. No one stopped to question the teleological assumption that events in Russia should be understood in terms of a transition from point A—a state-socialist political system with a command economy—to point B— a democratic polity with a market economy. Although the 'third wave' of democratization in the 1980s saw many countries around the world move in the direction of this 'market democracy' model, an equal number of countries obstinately refuse to conform to that pattern. Japan, India, and China all

For an earlier and much shorter version of this essay see my 'Has Democracy Failed Russia?', *The National Interest*, 38 (1994/95), pp. 3–12.

have important structural features that diverge from the paradigm towards which Russia is supposedly headed. Russia too, with its unique history and geography, is likely to fall into the category of countries with a distinctive political system.

However, back in 1991–2 few analysts were inclined to ponder the special problems that the concepts 'democracy' and 'market' might encounter in the post-Soviet landscape. On the contrary, building democracy and building a market economy were assumed to be compatible and complementary processes which could be introduced to any country on the planet. This meant that US leaders had to pretend that Russian President Boris Yeltsin was carrying out the dual role of a Russian George Washington and Adam Smith.

This chapter tests the validity of the 'transition to democracy' paradigm on two fronts. First, it will question the extent to which Russia has indeed become a democracy since 1991. Second, it will consider democratization in the context of unresolved problems of state- and nation-building in Russia, challenges which most other countries in political transition have not had to face—but which are not unique to Russia: witness the unravelling of Yugoslavia and Czechoslovakia. By implication, the chapter also raises a series of difficult questions: about the extent to which democracy can ever be promoted by the West; about the difficulties involved in consolidating democracy in countries where democracy has never been the norm; and the degree to which an 'American' model of democracy—or at least a version of it—was the best one to adopt after 1991. As we shall see, the experiment in democracy in Russia provides us with no nice, easy political lessons. Nor does it leave much room for complacency about the spread of democracy or democratization. It does, however, challenge the original Panglossian complacency which blithely assumed there were universal 'liberal' answers to the enormous challenges facing humanity in the post-cold war era. If this chapter does no more than dent that complacency, then its purpose will have been fulfilled.

1991: A Limited Revolution

A key point to bear in mind is that post-communist Russia is still on a downward path of disintegration, rather than an upward march of transition. The abrupt collapse of the Soviet state unleashed turbulent centrifugal processes which are still coursing through the political, economic, and social fabric of Russia. Yeltsin and the democratic movement managed to mobilize sufficient political force to destroy the old system, but were not able to agree among themselves on the permanent shape of the new order. The exercise of political power and economic decision-making took place in something of an institutional vacuum—a vacuum that has in part been created and sustained by those in positions of power.

The democratic opening of 1988–91 created three new political actors within Russia: a broad but shallow democratic movement, geared to election campaigns and mass protests; a ramshackle parliament with minimal legislative power, the Russian Federation Congress of People's Deputies, elected in 1990; and a president, popularly elected in June 1991. Two important constitutional pillars of the old regime were shattered during those years: the Communist Party of the Soviet Union, with its hierarchy of branches reaching down into every workplace; and the labyrinthine bureaucracy of central planning, presided over by Gosplan. Many institutions, and many segments of the ruling elite, continued to soldier on through the chaos: the managers, the bureaucrats, the military, the secret police, and regional political bosses.

These developments were already in place before the break-up of the Soviet Union in December 1991. Despite all the rhetoric of reform and dramatic crises and conflicts, not that much has changed since 1991 in terms of the deep structural features of the political system. The democratic movement has faded and fragmented, its only politically salient legacy being a relatively free media, whose room for manoeuvre has shrunk since 1992 under the twin pressures of financial stringency and political pressure.

The political scene since 1991 has been dominated by two trends: *presidentialism* and *regionalism*. Presidentialism refers to the pivotal role played by Boris Yeltsin in mediating between the old and the new political groups. Yeltsin was a Janus-like figure, simultaneously a product of the old system—for 20 years a regional party boss—and the main standard bearer of reform. Yeltsin's role as mediator between the past and the future stemmed from his personal authority rather than from the office he held; for the most part it was neither defined by law nor checked by institutional structures.

Regionalism surfaced because the loss of control by the old bureaucracies led to a shift from functional to territorial representation of political interests. This is probably good for democratic institutionalization in the long run, but it makes the task of the national leadership much more difficult in the short run.

Power is heavily concentrated in the hands of the president, with various bureaucratic and financial clans struggling to gain access to the Kremlin. Key elements of the Soviet *nomenklatura* decided to embrace capitalism during the period 1988–92, and used the privatization programme to secure their control of industrial assets in the new market economy.[1] They were joined by a small number of new, upwardly mobile young oligarchs, most of whom had close ties to the old Soviet elite. These 'winners' from the transition to market democracy are vastly outnumbered by the 'losers', such as the military, the elderly, and workers trapped in collapsed industries and isolated regions. Although the new democratic system gives the losers a chance to register their discontent, it has not provided them with the institutional opportunity to exert any influence over the people who wield real political and economic power. Counterelites who could potentially challenge the new Russian oligarchy, such as the Communist Party or army officers, were confused and discredited by the

---

[1] Fred Weir and David Kotz, *Revolution from Above: the Demise of the Soviet System* (New York: Routledge, 1997).

collapse of the Soviet system, and have not been able to gain power—that is, control over the state apparatus—through the ballot box.

The Theory and Practice of Russian Democracy

Russia has been a democracy since 1991, holding three sets of reasonably free and fair elections for both parliament and president. On these grounds alone, optimistically inclined observers would stop the argument here, and assert that Russia has made a decisive break with its communist authoritarian past. However, it is a very imperfect form of democracy that has emerged, one that has more in common with the quasi-democracies of Indonesia or the Philippines than Westminster or Washington. Most discussions of the spread of democracy to Russia share similar assumptions about the elements which constitute a democratic political system. The checklist includes:

(1) free and fair elections;
(2) separation of powers;
(3) a fair and independent judicial system;
(4) a free and inquisitive press;
(5) the widespread sharing of democratic values;
(6) respect for human rights, at least individual rights and possibly collective rights—for example, for ethnic minorities; and
(7) the presence of civil society, that is, a plurality of social organizations.

Each of these elements in the liberal democratic canon has been introduced in Russia, but in a curiously distorted form. To paraphrase Leon Trotsky, it is democracy reflected in a samovar. Russia's faltering steps down the road to democracy have been accompanied by economic disintegration, rampant crime, the collapse of public morals, rising death rates, loss of international influence, and the continuation in power of much of the old communist-era elite. Rather than question the applicability and appropriateness of their own model of democracy, Western liberals typically blame these problems on Russia's political culture or the personal qualities of its leaders. We are told that Russia has failed democracy, and not that democracy has failed Russia.

In fact, the checklist approach is rather naive in adopting a procedural conception of democracy, reducing it to a set of values and institutions. What is absent is any consideration of politics: the struggle for resources and clash of ideas between different social and political groups. A shift from authoritarianism to democracy should be accompanied by a shift in public policy away from the elite towards the citizenry. This has not occurred in Russia. The assumption was that sound policies and good government would be the natural result of the introduction of democratic institutions. Once democratic values and institutions were in place, parties would emerge more or less spontaneously to compete for the popular vote—founded if necessary by political entrepreneurs, who saw the opportunity for advancement through their creation. In reality, what has happened in Russia is the formal adherence to most of the principles of democracy as a convenient façade, behind which a self-serving elite has cynically looted the country of its assets. Bearing in mind these limitations to the checklist approach, it may be useful to examine each of the elements in turn.

1. Free and Fair Elections

Partially free elections were held to the USSR Congress of People's Deputies in 1989 and to the Congresses in the 15 constituent republics of the USSR in 1990. Communist Party General Secretary Mikhail Gorbachev declined to submit himself for popular election, instead having himself appointed president of the USSR by the Congress of People's Deputies. In June 1991 Boris Yeltsin was chosen as president of the Russian Federation in an open and competitive election, winning 57 per cent of the vote. Hence Yeltsin was seen as the legitimate voice of the Russian people, and had the authority—and audacity—to face down the hard-liners' coup when it came in August 1991. This experience shows how dangerous it can be for authoritarian regimes to toy with elections. Gorbachev introduced limited electoral choice in a bid to put pressure on conservative party officials who were blocking *perestroika*. This experiment set in train a dynamic of democratization which swiftly undermined the authority of the Communist Party, shattered the coherence of the Soviet Union, and drove Gorbachev from office.

So far, so good for the liberal democratic model. However, after the failed coup of August 1991, Yeltsin proved strangely reluctant to pursue the electoral path. In Eastern Europe, free elections were held within months of the breakdown of the socialist regime. However, Yeltsin found he could not agree with his democratic allies on the key policy issues of the day: market reform and the creation of a post-Soviet confederation of all 15 former Soviet republics. Unlike most of the democratic movement leaders, Yeltsin favoured rapid market reform and the speedy cutting of most ties with the newly independent states. Thus he chose to go it alone and introduce the reforms using his presidential powers. He delayed calling elections for a new legislature—for fear it would strengthen his political opponents—until December 1993.

One can speculate that if elections had taken place in December 1991 the democratic coalition would probably have won handsomely, and hence received a popular mandate for radical reform. However, the price liberalization of January 1992, bungled because it was not accompanied by a tight monetary policy, triggered hyperinflation—1,600 per cent in 1992—which wiped out people's savings. Within weeks, the popular legitimacy of the democrats was squandered, and little structural reform was to be achieved in return.

The crucial problem was that, even by 1999, no credible political parties worthy of the name had emerged in Russia.[2] The only party with a national

[2] John Lowenhardt (ed.), 'Party Politics in Post-Communist Russia', special issue of *Journal of Communist Studies and Transition Politics*, 14/1 (1998); Stephen Fish, 'The Advent of Multipartyism in Russia', *Post-Soviet Affairs*, 11/3 (1995), pp. 340–83.

presence and coherent organizational structure is the Communist Party of the Russian Federation, which is the shadow of the former ruling Communist Party, and whose aging supporters are driven by nostalgia for the Brezhnevite past. The communists seem most comfortable as a party of opposition, and since the 1993 confrontation between parliament and president—see below—they have repeatedly shied away from direct challenges to Yeltsin's authority.

Political parties come from one of two sources: they either grow upwards from social movements or regional groupings, or they grow downwards from parliamentary factions. During the elections of 1989 and 1990 a loose coalition of voters' clubs emerged, which came together as the Democratic Russia movement. They showed that they could win elections and bring thousands of followers on to the streets. The sole issue on which they agreed, however, was the need to dislodge the Communist Party from power. Given the postponement of elections, there was no opportunity for the fledgling parties to develop their identity through campaigning in 1992–3. Instead, their leaders had to engineer crises and confrontations around which to mobilize their followers, which added to the already highly polarized climate in Russian politics.

The top-down route of party formation was also weak. The Interregional Deputies Group, which democratic deputies formed in the USSR Supreme Soviet in 1989, never coalesced into a coherent political party. It was riven by personal jealousies and divided over how to deal with the demands of nationalists in the non-Russian republics. All decision-making power rested in the presidential apparatus, which left nothing of substance to bargain over in Parliament and provided no incentive to forge lasting political coalitions. Instead, there was an endless succession of 'taxicab parties'—so called because all their members could fit into a cab—which were used as launching pads for politicians seeking entry into government. Remarkably, this pattern of party behaviour is still characteristic of the Russian system in 1999.

Communists and nationalists aside, it was hard to differentiate between the various parties on the policy spectrum. The key distinguishing characteristic was whether or not they were part of Yeltsin's patronage network—'ours or theirs?'. The political map of Russia did not consist of a left-right spectrum, but a series of concentric circles of diminishing access, radiating outwards from the Kremlin. To the annoyance of the democrats, Yeltsin refused to personally take over the leadership of Democratic Russia, arguing that the Russian president should be 'above politics'. He instead chose to forge a new ruling elite out of old and new politicians by doling out individual jobs and favours.

The weakness of the Russian party system has its roots in the constitutional system which emerged in Russia, and which was enshrined in the new constitution adopted in December 1993. The system placed a huge agglomeration of power in the hands of the president, who is responsible for appointing and dismissing the government—subject to approval by the lower house of Parliament, the State Duma—and who has few checks on his power between elections. This 'super-presidential' system had the effect of creating a largely powerless and largely irresponsible legislature. When voters elected the parliament they were not choosing between rival parties with credible programmes, one of which would rule the country, since the voters knew that the legislature had only a marginal role in the selection of the government. Voters treated parliamentary elections as an opportunity to register a protest vote: hence the victory of Vladimir Zhirinovsky's Liberal Democratic Party of Russia in the December 1993 election, and the leading position of Gennady Zyuganov's Communist Party of the Russian Federation in the December 1995 election. As with the voters, so with the parliamentary parties: there was little incentive for them to behave responsibly, since they knew that they would not have to form a government and take on the burden of rule themselves.

When fresh elections for the State Duma were finally held in December 1993, in the wake of Yeltsin's dismissal of the old parliament, there was a frantic scramble among the democrats to come up with viable parties.[3] The election turned into an American-style media blitz, with the four leading democratic parties spending $85 million on their media campaigns. The only taxicab party which has survived as a viable entity is Grigory Yavlinsky's Yabloko, which won 7.9 per cent of the votes on the party list and 23 seats in the 1993 Duma election, and was returned as the fourth largest party in the 1995 election with 6.9 per cent of the vote and 45 seats. Yavlinsky's niche was to provide a democratic opposition to Yeltsin.

In the 1993 election it was hard to tell the parties apart on policy grounds. Everybody was in favour of stopping inflation, ending subsidies to the other republics, and so on. Dissatisfaction with Yeltsin's use of force against the Parliament meant that the four democratic parties together polled only 35 per cent of the vote in 1993. The Communists and their agrarian allies won 20 per cent. The Liberal Democratic Party topped the party list with 23 per cent, thanks to the flamboyant nationalist rhetoric of their leader, Vladimir Zhirinovsky.

Thus, Russia's first free election produced a propaganda victory for an eccentric neo-fascist whose campaign pledges included stockpiling nuclear waste on the Lithuanian border and seizing Alaska. Because of Yeltsin's reluctance to enter the electoral arena, the election had come two years too late. By the end of 1993 the voters had lost their faith in all politicians. Ironically, while competitive elections had been vital in destroying the old communist system, they had come to be seen—by Yeltsin, and by Western leaders—as an awkward obstacle in the path of building the new market democracy.

In the wake of the stunning defeat of the democratic parties in 1993, Yeltsin's aides tried to create a bloc of loyal deputies in the Parliament by offering them inducements of varying types, from posts in the government to new apartments. In the run-up to the 1995 parliamentary elections, the government tried to create two new parties to consolidate parliamentary support for the executive branch. One party, left of centre, was led by the former

[3] Stephen White, Richard Rose and Ian McAllister, *How Russia Votes* (London: Chatham House, 1996).

parliament speaker Ivan Rybkin and was imaginatively titled the 'Bloc of Ivan Rybkin'. The second was 'Our Home is Russia', led by Prime Minister Viktor Chernomyrdin.

The fragmentation of the political spectrum in Russia was amply illustrated by the outcome of the December 1995 elections. Forty-three parties ran for office, of which 39 failed to clear the 5 per cent threshold for entry into parliament on the party list. (Half of the 450 Duma seats are allotted through party list proportional representation, and half in single-member majoritarian constituencies.) Fully 50 per cent of voters supported parties that did not make it into Parliament. The party list was headed by the Communist Party, with 22 per cent support, followed by Zhirinovsky's Liberal Democrats with 11 per cent. The would-be 'party of power', Our Home is Russia, won third place, with 10 per cent support. Given that half of the votes on the party list were wasted on losing parties, the Communists ended up with 34 per cent of the seats in the lower house—and their allies, the Agrarians, won another 4 per cent.

2. Separation of Powers

If Yeltsin's first political error was the postponement of elections and subsequent lack of interest in creating a united democratic party, his second crucial mistake after August 1991 was procrastination in drawing up a new constitution. His advisers urged him to model the Russian political system around a US-style presidency, with a constitutional court policing the separation of powers between president and legislature. There were several problems with this approach, which led to the emergence in practice of a 'super-presidential' system that has little in common with the original American model.

First, Yeltsin was in no rush to create a strong legislature which could rival his authority. Despite the fact that it was the Russian congress that had propelled him to power, Yeltsin felt himself to be an independent political actor after his election in June 1991 and his pivotal role in facing down the August coup. Second, while the idea of a strong executive branch had plenty of parallels in Russia's past, the other elements of the American model—an independent constitutional court, respect for rule of law, and a powerful legislature—were totally absent from Russian history. These were not institutions that could be created overnight.   Third, there are grounds for arguing that the US-style separation of powers is less universally applicable than is often assumed—the US Founding Fathers themselves were all too aware of the uniqueness of the model they were devising. The US system takes for granted such features of society as civilian control over the military and a reasonably wide dispersion of economic power—neither of which pertained in Russia. Presidentialism in Latin America has typically resulted in deadlock between president and congress.[4] One can argue that Russian democracy would have

---

[4] Juan J. Linz and Arturo Valenzuela (eds), *The Failure of Presidential Democracy: Comparative Perspectives* (Baltimore: The Johns Hopkins University Press, 1994); Alfred Stepan and Cindy Skach, 'Constitutional Frameworks and Democratic Consolidations', *World Politics*, 46/1, pp. 1–22; Gerald Easter, 'Preference for Presidentialism,' *World Politics*, 49/2 (1997), pp. 184–211.

been better served by a parliamentary system, in which the executive and legislative branches of government are joined rather than separated. (Again, one must acknowledge that this model also has no roots in Russia's own history, but at least it would be a step away from the tradition of a strong executive.)

After the coup of August 1991, Yeltsin persuaded Congress to grant him emergency power to rule by decree for one year. He then appointed a team of young technocrats, led by Deputy Prime Minister Yegor Gaidar, to implement radical economic reform along Polish lines. The stage was thus set for two years of political confrontation between a truculent Congress and a president determined to pursue his own political and economic agenda. The rivalry between Yeltsin and Congress was not solely driven by alternative conceptions of Russia's future; it was also a straightforward struggle for power.

Unwilling to share power, Yeltsin tried to rule the country directly, with scant regard for the opinions of Congress. The presidential apparatus grew to more than 20,000 officials, and took over the former Communist Party Central Committee building in addition to the Kremlin. This hastily assembled bureaucratic Leviathan, effectively the closest Russia had to a functional replacement for the old Central Committee, operated in a very haphazard and ineffective manner—in that it differed from its communist predecessor. Through 1992 Yeltsin ruled through the issuance of thousands of decrees, not subject to legislative review, and augmented by thousands more regulations signed by government ministers.[5] Lord Acton's dictum that 'absolute power corrupts absolutely' held as true for post-communist Russia as many thought it might do for nineteenth-century England. Rule by decree became an invitation and an opportunity to corruption at the highest levels and on a massive scale.

There followed two years of political trench warfare between Yeltsin and Congress. Yeltsin used television addresses and calls for referenda to appeal directly to the people. He continued to play the anti-communist card, accusing the parliamentarians of seeking the restoration of Soviet socialism. He lured parliamentary deputies into jobs in his administration. Each side accused the other of corruption on a lavish scale. Yeltsin's half-hearted efforts to forge a coalition with centrist forces fell apart at the Seventh Congress in December 1992, which declined to renew his emergency decree powers. The Congress also forced Yeltsin to jettison radical reformer Gaidar as prime minister. He was replaced with Viktor Chernomyrdin, the dour founder of Gazprom and Minister of Oil and Gas.

In April 1993 Yeltsin turned to the populist device of a national referendum in order to beat back the Congress. While a majority of those voting in the referendum expressed their confidence in Yeltsin's rule and in his economic policies, the questions calling for new elections for President and Congress in 1993 failed to win the required majority—50 per cent of the electorate. When

---

[5] Jonathan Steele, *Eternal Russia: Yeltsin, Gorbachev and the Mirage of Democracy* (Boston: Harvard University Press, 1994).

Yeltsin summoned a Constitutional Assembly of his own choosing in June to discuss his draft constitution, Congress blocked its approval.

Yeltsin decided to break the constitutional deadlock by disbanding the parliament on 21 September 1993 and calling for fresh elections. Neither of these actions was within his legal powers. Parliamentary deputies occupied the White House—at that time the location of the parliament—and after a violent two-week standoff they were ousted by troops on 4 October. The striking television images of tanks shelling the White House would cost Yeltsin dear in the December 1993 parliamentary election.

In the wake of the October events, Yeltsin disbanded all the elected regional councils, suspended the Constitutional Court—whose members he himself had nominated—and banned eight political parties and their newspapers—although these bans were subsequently lifted. Yeltsin also dropped his pledge to hold early presidential elections—not due until 1996.

The hastily written draft constitution created a new bicameral legislature: the lower house, or State Duma, with 450 deputies; and the upper house, or Federation Council, consisting of the head of the executive and legislative branches in Russia's 89 regions—although the delegates from Chechnya never took up their seats. The constitution was approved in a referendum on the same day as the congressional elections in December 1993. (Despite initial reports that 51 per cent of voters endorsed the constitution, it was later revealed that the actual figure was 46 per cent.)

The new 1993 constitution created a lop-sided political system in which tremendous authority rested in the hands of the president while the government and parliament were deprived of real power. In practice, the parliament had almost no influence over the composition of the government. The president nominates the prime minister, and if parliament rejects the nominee in three successive votes, the president can dismiss the parliament and call fresh elections. The president has direct responsibility for the appointment of law and order ministers, and has a decisive say over the appointment of all other individual ministers.

Viktor Chernomyrdin remained as prime minister from 1992 until 1998, and during his tenure he managed to establish a *modus vivendi* with both Yeltsin and the State Duma. Still, Yeltsin had the habit of launching major government reshuffles once or twice a year in an effort to deflect attention from political and economic crises. Ministers and advisers were promoted and demoted with bewildering rapidity. Some were switched from the presidential apparatus to the government and back, some were plucked from the ranks of the hostile Duma in a bid to appease—or disorient—the opposition. The key qualification for promotion was personal loyalty to Boris Yeltsin rather than commitment to any particular political philosophy. Favourites who were seen to have betrayed Yeltsin's trust were swiftly cast aside.

By 1996 Yeltsin's personalistic leadership style had resulted in a curious patchwork of political figures and interests in his administration. Macroeconomic policy was dominated by reform-minded liberals; industrial policy by the energy lobby; and security issues by the 'party of war' which had launched the disastrous invasion of Chechnya in December 1994. Yeltsin's Kremlin became the site of Byzantine intrigue. A key role was played by Aleksandr Korzhakov, Yeltsin's bodyguard and tennis partner of long standing who became the head of presidential security. In those years Korzhakov was Yeltsin's closest confidant, and he was able to protect several networks of conservative officials, including key groups controlling the export of arms and metals. By early 1996, as the Chechen war dragged on and the economic depression entered its sixth year, Yeltsin's popularity rating fell to 8 per cent. Yet Yeltsin rejected Korzhakov's advice to cancel the 1996 presidential election—a sign to some of his democratic convictions.

In the June 1996 election Yeltsin was able to prevail over communist challenger Gennadii Zyuganov, thanks to a sophisticated media campaign financed by contributions from Russia's banking elite and from the public purse. A three-year, $10 billion lending package announced by the IMF in March was another significant boost. Yeltsin's campaign hammered home a single theme: the dire threat of a return to the communist past in the event of a Zyuganov victory. Yeltsin narrowly led Zyuganov by 35.3 per cent to 33.0 per cent in the first round, with maverick ex-general Aleksandr Lebed drawing 14.5 per cent. In the second round, Yeltsin scored 53.8 per cent to Zyuganov's 40.3 per cent. Yeltsin suffered a heart attack between the first and second round of the elections, but this fact was concealed from voters thanks to the media's loyalty to the Yeltsin camp. He underwent quintuple bypass surgery in November and physically returned to office only in January 1997.

Russia's political and financial elite, and her Western allies, breathed a huge sigh of relief upon Yeltsin's electoral victory. For some observers, the 1996 election represented the consolidation of democracy in Russia. For others, it meant the triumph of pseudo-democracy and the consolidation of an oligarchic regime. Perhaps the most positive outcome of the election was the prompt signing of a peace with Chechnya in August 1996—thanks to the intervention of Lebed, who served briefly as Security Council Secretary—and the withdrawal of Russian troops from the rebel province.

However, after the election the return to policies of market reform which the West awaited failed to materialize. Korzhakov was expelled from the Kremlin for mishandling a campaign finance scandal in June 1996, and leadership of the inner circle passed to Yeltin's daughter Tatyana Dyachenko, who served as his 'image consultant' during the campaign. After the election, representatives of the new banking elite such as Vladimir Potanin and Boris Berezovsky, associates of Dyachenko and Chubais, entered the government. The interests of the oligarchs who had bankrolled the election campaign clashed with the reform agenda of the liberal ministers. In Spring 1997 the oligarchs, in coalition with conservative regional leaders, managed to block efforts by liberals Anatolii Chubais and Boris Nemtsov to launch a new wave of market reform—the abortive 'second liberal revolution'.

Overtaken by age and infirmity, Yeltsin grew increasingly jealous of political figures who might aspire to replace him as president. Prime Minister Chernomyrdin was peremptorily dismissed in March 1998, his sin being that he was starting to break out of his low-key style and behave in too presidential a manner. He was replaced with the 35-year-old Sergei Kirienko, a political non-entity from Nizhnii Novgorod who had worked as a banker before being brought to Moscow by Nemtsov as energy minister. Kirienko was soon faced with a massive financial crisis, caused by mismanagement of the federal budget financing, by the delayed impact of the Asian financial crisis, and by the fall in world oil prices, which hit Russian export earnings. In June 1998 the IMF and World Bank came through with a $22 billion rescue package, but this failed to halt the leakage of funds as foreign investors cashed out their holdings. On 17 August Kirienko announced the suspension of payments on treasury bills and on most categories of foreign debt: in effect, a default. The rouble was allowed to float, and it crashed from six to the dollar to 20 within a week.

Kirienko resigned, and after Yeltsin's proposal to reappoint Chenomyrdin was rebuffed by the Duma, he appointed former Foreign Minister Yevgennii Primakov as prime minister. Primakov lasted until April, when he suffered the same fate as Chernomyrdin: abrupt dismissal for growing too popular and hence casting a shadow over Yeltin's authority. Primakov was replaced by the virtually unknown Interior Minister Sergei Stepashin. Stepashin in turn was fired by the capricious Yeltsin in August, to be replaced by his future successor, the equally obscure head of the Federal Security Service, Vladimir Putin. Both Primakov and Stepashin had good relations with the Duma and rising ratings in the opinion polls; in both cases their fault was to refuse to obey the whims of Yeltsin's inner circle of advisers, who came to be known as 'the Family'. The latter were increasingly concerned with staving off national and international investigations of their murky business dealings.

While the government spun through Kremlin intrigues, the parliament lacked the power to enact an effective legislative programme. The government and legislature ran on parallel tracks: less than half of the legislation was introduced by the government, but the government was predictably lax about effective implementation of such laws. (In fact, they were also increasingly ineffective when it came to implementing their own legislative initiatives.) Yeltsin was energetic in vetoing legislation, and if the parliament was able to muster a two-thirds majority to override his veto he was prone to appeal the issue to the Constitutional Court. That occurred twice in 1997, for example, with Yeltsin refusing to recognize parliamentary votes overriding his veto of bills on the return of art works seized by the Red Army during World War II, and on the structure of the federal government.

Optimists took such developments as signs of a rudimentary respect for separation of powers taking root in Russia. However, they came alongside a steady stream of thinly disguised threats from Yeltsin to dismiss parliament, sweetened with occasional offers of ministerial posts to Duma leaders, that were usually sufficient to persuade the Duma to accept his bidding. The parliament did enjoy a degree of negative power: it was able to block or delay the passage of certain legislation, such as a new code allowing free sale of land, or the law allowing production sharing for foreign investors in mining projects. There was an annual ritual over the adoption of the next year's federal budget which revealed the constitutional deadlock of the post-1993 regime. In December each year the Duma takes the government's draft budget for the next year and writes in over-optimistic revenue and spending projections, which the government reluctantly accepts. By the spring of the next year, when it is clear that the revenue targets will not be met, the government is forced to step in and 'sequester' spending, which means that they spend much less than authorized in the budget. It is government ministers—at the president's bidding—who get to decide which programmes get cut the most. Hence actual federal spending often bears scant relation to the targets laid down in the budget law: most defence spending, for example, ran at less than half the targeted level.

By late 1999, having gone through four prime ministers in 18 months, it was clear to even the most casual observer that the Russian government was in chaos from the point of view of policy formulation and implementation. The dysfunctionality of Yeltsin's presidential system was plain for all to see. Yeltsin constructed what Igor Klyamkin and Lilia Shevtsova call an 'elective monarchy'.[6] His style of rule was that of a monarch, unchallenged and absolute, but his source of legitimacy was periodic public elections. This kind of elective autocracy led to the worst of both worlds: the inflexibility of autocratic rule and the uncertainty of competitive elections. Rather than using his power to implement effective and far-sighted public policies, Yeltsin was forced every few years to devote the resources of his office to securing re-election.

Klyamkin and Shetsova argue that this contradictory and unstable political system will collapse after Yeltsin has departed the political stage, and the entire political structure of post-Soviet Russia will then have to be redesigned. The Communist Party raised the question of constitutional reform in 1998, in parallel to their abortive efforts to impeach Yeltsin—something which the constitution makes near-impossible. But no one expected any serious negotiations on constitutional reform until after the 2000 presidential elections, since all the top leaders were positioning themselves for that contest. What Russia needs is a constitutional reform which would mandate the appointment of the government from the leading party in the parliament and not at the whim of the president.

3. A Fair and Independent Judicial System

The non-emergence of an independent judiciary has been one of the weakest spots in Russia's attempted transition to democracy. The old system of political controls—'telephone law', so called because party officials would call judges to tell them the verdict—collapsed with the banning of the Communist

---

[6] Igor Klyamkin and Lilia Shevtsova, 'Eta vsesil'naya bessil'naya vlast', [This all-powerful powerless rule], *Nezavisimaya gazeta* (24 June 1998).

Party after the August 1991 coup. But politicians, Yeltsin included, continued to ignore or manipulate the judicial system as they saw fit.[7] This was evident in Yeltsin's reliance on rule by decree; in his reluctance to recognize the authority of the Constitutional Court; and in his centralization of control over the judiciary.

Liberals hoped that marketization would promote the rule of law, by creating a new class of property owners with a strong incentive to have their rights respected. In Russia's free-for-all economy, however, quite the opposite occurred. Wilful disregard of legal norms was embedded in behaviour at all levels of society, from the person in the street, through the law-enforcement agencies, to the leaders of the state. The corruption extended deep into the heart of the market reform process. It became the organizing principle of large parts of economic policy—most notably, the financing of the government deficit through short-term treasury bonds, and the loans-for-shares privatization of major oil and metals firms, both policies launched in 1995. In this environment even honest businessmen could be expected to turn to private enforcement regimes—often, organized crime—and not the courts in order to ensure contract compliance.[8]

By 1999, Western editorial page writers had belatedly come to realize that democratization and market reform had led to the rise of a deeply corrupt and self-serving elite in Russia. However, by framing the problem as one of individual venality they tended to overlook the institutional flaws—the artificial separation of powers, the lack of real political party competition—which had caused this state of affairs to arise.

4. A Free and Inquisitive Press

Russia's democratization began with *glasnost*, or the limited easing of media censorship that Gorbachev launched in 1986. Over the next decade the country acquired a combative and occasionally independent press with a core of dedicated journalists. But it is premature to talk of a completely free press in Russia. The financial constraints that followed the cutting of state subsidies, and the need to pay close to market prices for newsprint and distribution, caused a catastrophic decline in circulation.[9] Aside from scandal-sheets, only a couple of newspapers generate sufficient revenue to cover their costs—*Argumentyi i fakty* and perhaps *Komsomolskaya pravda*. The remainder are all dependent on subsidies from either a financial magnate or a local political boss. While the multiplicity of backers in Moscow ensures a rough and ready pluralism of opinions, in the provinces this is rarely the case. Most of the

---

[7] Peter Solomon, 'The Limits of Legal Order in Post-Soviet Russia,' *Post-Soviet Affairs*, 11/2 (1995), pp. 89–114.

[8] Stephen Handelman, *Comrade Criminal: Russia's New Mafia* (New Haven: Yale University Press, 1997).

[9] Floriana Fossato and Anna Kachkaeva, *Russian Media Empires*, Radio Free Europe/Radio Liberty website, 28 March 1998. [www.rferl.org]

'national' papers simply do not circulate outside Moscow, and most of the local press remains under the control of provincial political bosses.

Television is more powerful and more profitable, and thus even more closely guarded by its financial and political masters. The commercial television channel NTV is owned by Vladimir Gusinskii's Most group, while the state-owned channel ORT is closely controlled by the Kremlin—in part through the conduit of magnate Boris Berezovsky. In 1998 Moscow Mayor Yurii Luzhkov set up his own channel, TV-Center, in order to boost his presidential election chances.

Observers took heart from the fact that some media—including NTV—criticized the government's December 1994 invasion of Chechnya, seeing this as a sign of the media playing a much-needed role as a check on arbitrary authority. However, such hopes were dashed by the media's performance in the 1996 election campaign, when most of the newspapers and all the electronic outlets lined up behind Yeltsin's re-election bid, and were not above using some dirty tricks to derail Zyuganov's campaign.

5. The Widespread Sharing of Democratic Values

The presence or absence of a civic culture in Russia has been a topic of controversy among Western political scientists. Most of the research money allocated by bodies such as the US National Science Foundation has gone into opinion surveys, whose findings appear to show that democratic norms such as free speech are widely respected in Russian society.[10] Many ex-Sovietologists question the significance and durability of these findings. In most cases the questions were taken from surveys in the US, where the political context is quite different. It is well known that respondents tend to give what they suppose to be the 'right' answer, and this is even more likely to apply in Russia, where citizens are unused to opinion polls. Be that as it may, the surveys found little evidence of an 'authoritarian personality', and concur that Russians prefer to live in a democratic system than in one which denies personal freedoms, including the right to vote. However, Russians saw a growing gulf between democratic systems in the abstract, which they evaluate positively, and their actual realization in Russia, which they evaluate negatively. Initial confidence in the capacity of democratic institutions to deliver a better life has been deeply shaken by the political stagnation and economic decline that have been Russia's unhappy lot since 1991.

The surveys also found a preference among voters for strong political leadership, as evidenced by the good electoral performance of the authoritarian-inclined communists and nationalists in 1993 and 1995. The 1996 election can be taken as either a confirmation or a refutation of this potentially

---

[10] James L. Gibson, Raymond M. Duch and Kent L. Tedin, 'Democratic Values and the Transformation of the Soviet Union,' *Journal of Politics*, 54/2 (1992), pp. 329–71. See also the regular New Democracies Barometer surveys, as cited in Richard Rose and Christian Haerpfer, 'Fears and Hopes', *Transition* (World Bank), 7/5 (1996), pp. 13–14.

sinister inclination for a strong leader. Pessimists would argue that voters meekly and resignedly voted for the incumbent leader in 1996, seeing no viable alternative to Tsar Boris and fearing chaos if the sitting ruler was voted out. Optimists would note that leaders with a more authoritarian agenda, such as Gennadii Zyuganov or Aleksander Lebed, failed to dislodge the pro-reform, pro-Western Yeltsin. Thus far, Russian democratization has not produced a populist autocrat along the lines of Alberto Fujimori in Peru or Hugo Chavez in Venezuela.

6. Respect for Human Rights

There has been dramatic progress in human rights in Russia compared with communist times. Persecution of political dissidents has ended. Freedom to travel and to emigrate is enjoyed by all. Although the lack of due process in the legal system is worrying, measured in terms of human rights Russia has moved decisively towards democracy.

And yet the record still leaves cause for concern. Human rights cannot be sustained in a general climate of lawlessness. There have been a number of contract killings of investigative journalists, the most notorious being the assassination of Vladislav Listev, investigating military corruption, in 1995. The security services seem to have been given a free hand against whistle-blowers deemed to threaten national security by exposing environmental damage from military installations. Some rights guaranteed by the Russian constitution, such as the right to alternative military service, to own land, or to live where one chooses, are not implemented in law. Moscow, for example, bars non-residents from moving to the city despite a series of court rulings declaring that the Soviet-era registration system—*propiska*—is unconstitutional. Ethnic minorities have been targets of persecution, such as the periodic roundups of 'blacks'—people from the Caucasus—in Moscow.

Not all the problems stem from violations of legal norms. A new 1997 law introduced tight restrictions on the registration of religious organizations, and was perceived in the West as a grave potential threat to religious freedom, especially for evangelical Protestant groups.

In addition, the desperate economic situation of the majority of Russian citizens can itself be regarded as a violation of their human rights. With some 50 per cent of the population living at or below the poverty line, access to basic human needs of food and shelter is problematic for many. The phenomenon of wage arrears, which became widespread from 1995 on, is but one specific example of how the lack of legal rights impacts on ordinary citizens. About one-third of workers, especially state employees, are paid between one and three months in arrears; this was one of the ways in which the state sought to plug its budgetary shortfall. One slightly encouraging trend has been that the courts are increasingly willing to rule against the government in suits bought by persons with pension arrears and similar grievances; but such suits are too few in number to make a significant dent in the general pattern of disrespect for legal rights.

7. The Growth of Civil Society

Alexis de Tocqueville argued that the strength of democracy in the United States lay in the dense network of social organizations characteristic of American society. Reflecting this belief, US aid for democratization in Russia emphasized the promotion of associative behaviour, from independent trade unions to environmental action groups, in the belief that this is the best long-run foundation for democracy—although in practice the greatest amount of aid dollars went into building the institutions of a market economy.

In the 1980s some academics argued that elements of a civil society were already sprouting up under the surface of Brezhnevite stagnation. This Tocquevillian vision seemed to be coming true during the Gorbachev era, when there was an explosion of informal groups, ranging from Buddhists to body-builders, anti-Semites to amateur theatricals. These so-called 'informal' groups—*neformalye*—played an important role in the Soviet collapse, chiselling away at the mortar holding together the communist monolith.

Once *glasnost* gave way to democratization, however, these groups mostly proved unable to make the transition from the social to the political sphere. In the Baltic republics and Armenia, they helped to generate mass political movements—with a nationalist agenda—but no such pattern appeared in Russia. As political and economic disintegration accelerated, the 'informals' were left behind. Their rationale was tied to the communist regime: either fighting in opposition to it or seeking a more humane life within its interstices. Contrary to Tocquevillian expectations, the climate of the new market economy in Russia seemed rather inimical to the flourishing of civil society. Activists diverted their efforts from organization-building to earning a living or making a political career. Many of their leaders were indeed elected to regional and national legislatures, and even entered the executive branch at the both levels. The main role of the informal movement in the transition period was to provide a channel of upward mobility for a new, much younger generation of political leaders: people like Boris Nemtsov, the former physicist who became mayor of Nizhnii Novgorod and later deputy prime minister of Russia.

Thus by 1999 it was still hard to find voluntary associations which could be cited as incubators of democratic values and experience. Those which have survived have mostly done so thanks to infusions of cash from sympathetic Western governments and non-government organizations. In retrospect, the emphasis on a nascent civil society that dominated much of the academic debate in the late 1980s and early 1990s seems rather misplaced.

Summary

Scanning the checklist of features of procedural democracy, we see that Russia scores a passing grade, barely, on most of the items. Yes, the nation's political leaders are chosen through regular, competitive elections. Yes, there seems to be widespread support for democratic values, and a marked improvement in respect for human rights. On the negative side, civil society is weak and the rule of law highly deficient.

However, the atrociously poor performance of the Russian political system since 1991—as measured by the fall in GDP and popular living standards, alongside the rise in crime, corruption, and ethnic unrest—raises profound doubts about the future stability of the system. The ultimate test of a democracy is its ability to serve the interests of its people. By that test, Russian democracy has not yet proved itself. Its poor performance in part can be traced to institutional flaws in the 'super-presidential' political system which Yeltsin created. Hence no one can rule out the possibility of radical political change in Russia's immediate future, once Yeltsin leaves the stage—and such change may threaten even the limited level of democracy which Russia currently enjoys.

Democracy and the Search for the Russian Nation

In Russia, the democratic transition involved the break-up of a multinational empire. This raises profound questions about the nature of the state which most other nascent democracies did not had to face—although the cases of South Africa, India, Czechoslovakia, and Yugoslavia are in some ways comparable. Democracy presupposes agreement on the boundaries of the *demos*—the people—who are to exercise self-rule. Liberal political theory has little to say on the subject of where nation-states come from and the principles on which they should be constituted. In most cases the liberal democracies inherited nations which were already in existence.

In Russia there is still no agreement on the shape of the political community which will enjoy self-determination. Russia must choose not merely what sort of political system it desires, but also *what* Russia is as a cultural entity, and *where* it is in terms of its physical borders. Russia had never been constituted as a nation-state in the conventional sense. Less than half the population of the Russian Empire back in 1914 were ethnic Russians, and 350 years of expansion across contiguous territory made it difficult for Russians to discern where Russia ended and foreign lands began. ('Scratch a Russian, find a Tatar', as Lev Tolstoy observed.) In both the Tsarist and Soviet eras Russian ethnic identity had been channelled into language and culture and was divorced from political identity. Although ethnic Russians played a dominant political role in the Soviet state, many aspects of Russian culture were suppressed and Russians had to rule in the name of multinational socialism.

Nationalism—of the non-Russians—emerged as the crucial factor in the demise of the USSR. Gorbachev's political reforms opened up a Pandora's box of ethnic claims, suppressed for decades, which Gorbachev himself was unable to resolve. One can, however, argue that it was Russian nationalism, rather than the nationalism of the non-Russian peoples, which was ultimately responsible for the destruction of the USSR. Gorbachev's commitment to the Soviet state created an opening for Yeltsin's political comeback after his dismissal from the Politburo in 1987. Yeltsin was able to turn the institutions of the Russian Federation into a power base to rival that of Gorbachev in the federal Communist Party and government. In August 1991, the core institutions of the Soviet state—the army and the KGB—switched their loyalty to Yeltsin's Russia.[11]

The newly independent Russian Federation could not simply take over its identity from where the Soviet state left off. The Russian state abandoned the communist ideology and political structure which had been the backbone of the USSR. In consequence a huge institutional vacuum opened up at the core of the new Russian polity. President Boris Yeltsin decided to make a radical break with the communist past, scrapping the old state symbols and banning the Communist Party of the Soviet Union. But he was not sure what to put in its place—the symbols of the defunct Tsarist regime evoked archaic and controversial imagery.

Yeltsin's essential strategy was to proclaim the birth of a new Russia: neither Tsarist not Soviet, but embracing the values of the West. Theoretically, this could be seen as an effort to build a civic rather than an ethnic notion of citizenship—except that in practice the civic values of the new Russia were rather too weak to support such an identity. The essential factor in proving the legitimacy of the new Russia was recognition by the West. If Yeltsin was treated as an equal partner by world leaders, surely this was proof that Russia was at long last a normal state? This strategy of external legitimisation left unresolved the question of what the Russian state meant to Russians themselves. After his re-election in 1996 Yeltsin formally launched a national debate to try to define the essence of the 'Russian idea': an artificial exercise that produced a few mystical essays about the spiritual essence of Russia, but nothing of political utility for Yeltsin.

Having freed itself from the Soviet Union, therefore, Russia's problems in defining itself as a nation-state were far from resolved.[12] Its cohesion is threatened from within and from without, raising issues which would sorely test even a stable and well-functioning democratic political system.

The internal challenge stems from the fact that 19 per cent of Russia's population are not ethnic Russians, most of them living in 21 autonomous republics within the boundaries of the federation. Secession is not a realistic option for most of these republics, since they are surrounded by Russian territory and lack an external border with another state or the open sea. As well, in most cases the titular nationality—Yakuts in Yakutiya, for example—are outnumbered within their own republic by ethnic Russian inhabitants. The exception is Chechnya in the north Caucasus, which declared independence

---

[11] John Dunlop, *The Rise of Russia and the Fall of the Soviet Empire* (Princeton: Princeton University Press, 1993).

[12] Vera Tolz, 'The National Debate over Nation-Building in Russia,' *Prism* (Jamestown Foundation), 4/10 (15 May 1998). [www.jamestown.com]

in 1991 and successfully defended its de facto independence in its 1994–6 war with Russia, at a cost of at least 40,000 dead. Tatarstan, with its oil wealth and 5 million strong population, has also pursued the goal of national sovereignty. Tatarstan issues its own passports, refuses to allow its young men to serve in the military outside its territory, and negotiated a special financial arrangement with the federal government in 1994 which gained it exemption from most federal taxes. However, unlike Chechnya, Tatarstan is located deep in central Russia and has no external border with another country. Secession from the Russian Federation is thus not a realistic proposition for Tatarstan. Nevertheless, the ethno-territorial heterogeneity of the Russian Federation has led to the rise of a fractured federalism in Russia which makes it extremely difficult to rule Russia effectively.

The external challenge to Russia's identity and cohesion involves Russia's relations with the 14 other newly independent states that emerged from the break-up of the USSR. The Soviet collapse left 22 million ethnic Russians marooned in the states of the 'near abroad', half of them in Ukraine. Nationalists, including Alexander Solzhenitsyn, urged that these diaspora communities be brought within the boundaries of an enlarged Russia. Moscow has shrunk from such an agenda, although it is still willing to use alleged infringements of the rights of the Russian diaspora to put pressure on neighbouring states—especially Estonia and Latvia, which have been pursuing policies of rapid integration with the West.[13]

Ethnicity aside, questions of security and economics also entangled Russia with its newly independent neighbours. The economies of the ex-Soviet republics remained heavily dependent on Russia, due to the logic of geography and the economic infrastructure inherited from 70 years of Soviet planning. Kazakhstan, Turkmenistan, and Azerbaijan relied on pipelines across Russia to transport their oil to world markets. Belarus and Ukraine in turn depended on cheap energy imports from Russia—energy they could not afford to buy from other sources. Every year or two Russia would have to strike a deal with Ukraine and Belarus and write off some of their energy debts. Belarusian President Alyaksandr Lukashenka has tried to parlay these negotiations into a full-blown unification of this country with Russia. The Belarusian case illustrates, in extreme form, how the economic legacy of interdependence cast a shadow over Russia's relations with its neighbours long after the political entity of the USSR had ceased to exist.

The security dimension also remained unresolved. Russia inherited most of the military assets of the former Soviet Union. Its border guards still patrol the 'external' frontier of many of the newly independent countries—all except Ukraine, Azerbaijan, Georgia, Uzbekistan and the Baltics—and it maintains military bases in most of those countries. What military policy should a democratic Russia adopt towards its neighbours? Could it persuade Ukraine to keep

---

[13] Igor A. Zevelev, 'The Russian Quest for a New Identity: Implications for Security in Eurasia', in Sharyl Cross, Igor Zevelev, Viktor Kremenyuk, and Vagan Gevorgian (eds), *Global Security Beyond the Millennium* (New York: St. Martins, 1999), Ch. 6.

Russia's major naval asset, the Black Sea fleet, stationed in the Ukrainian port of Sevastopol? Should it stand by while Tajikistan is torn apart by civil war? Should it intervene to try to stop the ten-year conflict between Armenia and Azerbaijan? Should Russia continue to station 'peacekeepers' in the region of Abkhazia, which broke away from Georgia—with Russian assistance—in 1992? Democratization *per se* does not provide an answer to any of these questions; yet these were the very issues at the forefront of Russian politics, around which the battle lines were being drawn.

This interdependence with the ex-Soviet republics complicated and confused Russia's own search for political identity as a new and independent country. It also led the Russian nationalists and communists off on the wild-good chase of Soviet restoration. What was a political dead-end for them was a godsend for Boris Yeltsin. In March 1996 the Duma famously passed a resolution denouncing the December 1991 Belavezha accords which had terminated the Soviet Union, and hence they effectively declared the Russian state illegitimate. This was a political gift to Yeltsin, who made the threat of communist restoration the central theme of his campaign to win re-election in June 1996. This tactic was sufficient to secure Yeltsin's re-election, but it distorted the spectrum of political debate in Russia, and distorted the structure of political power.

The European empires, which had the benefit of an ocean between their homeland and their colonies, all suffered political identity crises of varying severity after the end of empire. The Russian post-imperial dilemma was even more wrenching. Russia remains a work in progress, its national identity and *raison d'être* ill-defined. Comparisons are sometimes drawn with the identity crisis of Weimar Germany, but the parallel is a little misleading. The German state and people had little problem defining who they were in 1920; it was finding a place for Germany in the international system that was a problem, after the humiliation of Versailles. In present-day Russia, both its place in the global system and its internal political identity are in doubt.

Democracy and the Disintegration of Russia?

Even taking the external national boundaries of Russia as given, the crucial issue in Russian domestic politics is state-building rather than democratization. Back in 1991, state-building was not seen as a problem. On the contrary, for Western observers Russia had inherited an over-powerful state apparatus from the Soviet Union, and dismantling rather than rebuilding state institutions was the order of the day. Unfortunately Russia had too many state institutions of the wrong sort—Gosplan, the KGB, and so forth—and not enough of the right sort—courts, civic associations, regulatory agencies—needed for the functioning of a democratic market economy.

Russia is an unwieldy giant of a country, spread over 7,000 miles with atrocious means of communication between its component parts. The collapse of the Soviet state apparatus severely weakened Moscow's ability to manage the country, and it is a misnomer to describe the resulting decentralized, unstable political system as 'democratized'. Rather, it reminds one of the periodic lapses into anarchy, such as the 'Time of Troubles' (1598–1613), which have punctuated Russian history.

In 1990–1 Yeltsin had to make concessions to provincial elites in order to overcome his political opponents in Moscow, encouraging the leaders of the ethnic republics to 'take as much sovereignty as they could swallow'. In October 1991, after he had dislodged Gorbachev, he tried to regain some of these powers, persuading Congress to suspend regional elections for one year, during which he would directly appoint regional governors. He also set up a network of presidential envoys in the provinces—a move for which he had no legal authority—which was intended to provide a functional substitute for the now banned chain of command of the Communist Party of the Soviet Union.

Within each of Russia's 21 ethnic republics and 67 regions—*oblasts* and *krais*—new and old political elites battled for power as the old order collapsed.[14] At the same time, these regional elites manœuvred for allies in Moscow. The 21 ethnically designated republics adopted their own constitutions, most of which violate the federal constitution to some extent. The growing confrontation between Yeltsin and the parliament in 1992–3 provided another opportunity for regional leaders to extract concessions from Yeltsin in return for their support. The ethnic republics were exempted from Yeltsin's direct presidential rule, and were allowed to select their own leaders. Following the lead of Tatarstan and Chechnya, they forced Yeltsin to sign a new federation treaty in March 1992, which seemed to recognize their sovereign authority over everything except military affairs. Yeltsin poured subsidies into the republics in 1992 to win them away from supporting the anti-Yeltsin coalition led by Ruslan Khasbulatov in Congress. In 1993 Yeltsin tried and failed to rein in the regions. Provincial leaders blocked his efforts to establish presidential rule through his network of plenipotentiaries, and some non-ethnic regions began electing their own governors. At the insistence of regional elites, the new constitution adopted in December 1993 included the text of the 1992 federation treaty, recognizing the sovereignty of the ethnic republics, and created an upper house in the new parliament, the Federation Council, to represent regional elites—two from each region. In 1994 Yeltsin began signing bilateral treaties with the leaders of the ethnic republics—starting with Tatarstan—laying down special terms for their contributions to and receipts from the federal budget. Russian provinces complained bitterly of the special treatment being accorded to the ethnic republics, and eventually persuaded Yeltsin to start signing bilateral treaties with them. By 1999 about half the regions had signed such treaties.

---

[14] Peter Stavrakis, Joan de Bardeleben and Larry Black (eds), *Beyond the Monolith: The Emergence of Regionalism in Post-Soviet Russia* (Baltimore: Johns Hopkins University Press, 1997); Peter Kirkow, *Russia's Provinces: Authoritarian Transformation versus Local Autonomy* (New York: St Martins, 1998).

In 1996 Yeltsin once again turned to regional leaders for support in his electoral campaign. The authority of regional governors was also boosted by the wave of gubernatorial elections in late 1996; prior to that, most of them had been directly appointed by Yeltsin. However, regional leaders are still generally unsure of the extent to which they can challenge the federal centre. Only about 10 of Russia's 89 regions are net donors to the federal budget; the others are all dependent to some degree on subsidies from Moscow. The Federation Council has slowly emerged as a possible platform for the collective expression of regional interests and a check on presidential power. It has flexed its muscles over legislation, despite being constrained by the infrequency and short duration of its meetings.

More ambitious efforts to organize the governors and present a collective challenge to the national leadership from a regional perspective were slow to develop. The provincial leaders may have been little autocrats in their own territories, but they found it difficult to agree on their common interests *vis-à-vis* the centre. One important development came in July 1997, when the Federation Council blocked Yeltsin's efforts to remove the obstreperous governor of Primorskii Krai in the Russian Far East, Yevgenny Nazdratenko. A second example of the upper chamber flexing its muscles was their refusal to endorse Yeltsin's dismissal of the then Procurator-General Yurii Skuratov in the Spring of 1999: Skuratov was investigating the affairs of business associates of 'the Family.'

The Russian Federation is not about to go the way of the Soviet Union and break up into independent states. Russians share a common sense of cultural homogeneity, and have four centuries' experience of life in a common state. Central and northern Russia and Siberia are totally dependent upon European Russia for access to the outside world, while the Russian Far East needs Moscow's support to safeguard against its potential vulnerability to China and Japan. But in the short term the political struggles between the centre and the regions have derailed the process of democratization. Yeltsin's success in establishing his grip in Moscow in the early 1990s rested in no small measure on his manipulation of these disintegrative tendencies. He thus bequeaths a most troubled legacy to his political successor, Vladimir Putin.

Conclusion

Russia faces daunting challenges in overcoming the legacy of the Soviet state and building a functioning democracy. Unlike most of Eastern Europe, Russia has not experienced a more or less clean break with the old system. Instead of a wholesale turnover of the political elite, there has been a protracted battle between the executive and the legislative branches of government, each claiming to be the true guardian of democracy. Alone among the ex-socialist countries in transition, Russia is also a former empire that has still not defined its relations with its neighbours or its character as a federal state.

Russia, moreover, is disadvantaged if one looks at its level of economic development. Very few countries with an annual national income of less than $5,000 per head have been able to operate as stable democracies. Russia is less than half way to this income target. Russia lacks the cultural traditions—such as a history of British colonial rule—which have assisted those few states like India and Botswana which have defied this trend and created stable democracies in low-income countries.

This implies that the prognosis for the future of democracy in Russia must be rather grim. However, the transition period has also seen a steadily growing interaction between Russia's economy, culture and political elite and the outside world. In that global context, there are precious few alternatives to the model of 'market democracy' in one or other of its variants. For all of the vociferous nationalist rhetoric on the 'red-brown' end of the political spectrum, the chances of a return to a rigorously centralized authoritarianism in Russia are slim. Eighty years of communist rule seem to have inoculated the Russian people and, more importantly, the Russian political elite against such illusions. The same factors that have made it difficult to run Russia as a democracy—distrust of leaders, lack of respect for the state, regional fragmentation, etc.—would make it even more unwieldy as an authoritarian regime.

The attempted adoption of a model of democracy based on the American-style separation of powers has exacerbated political feuding at national level and encouraged the fragmentation of central authority. Russia has not been well served by hasty efforts to transplant models of democracy and the market economy from abroad, as if local circumstances and conditions count for nothing. Still less did it need the 'propaganda of success' which often accompanied those efforts, and which clouded outside perceptions of the true trajectory of the Russian political system.

12

Three Frameworks in Search of a Policy: US Democracy Promotion in Asia-Pacific

TAKASHI INOGUCHI

Introduction

AMERICAN foreign policy wears many masks. As the sole superpower with the will and the ability to act globally, and as a nation required to deal with a vast array of problems occurring intermittently around the globe, the United States assumes a very different visage depending on the nature of the problems it faces. At times it looks like a guardian angel, at times like a monster. One cannot imagine any other country whose foreign policy could be characterized as 'beautiful imperialism'.[1] The liberal democratic tradition with which the United States has been endowed from its inception seems to lead American authors to portray its foreign policy as either broadly in harmony with that tradition or betraying that tradition. In the historiography of American foreign-policy literature, the argument that American foreign policy must live up—or has lived up—to such a tradition is often called idealism, while the conviction that American foreign policy must adjust—or has adjusted—to the wicked outside world is known as realism.[2]

In the last half century, while the United States has been a superpower, with or without a self-proclaimed rival, the picture has been far more complex. The United States has encountered difficulties with its promotion of democracy because at times its apparently good intentions smack of 'democratic imperialism'. To examine this difficulty, it is worth examining American foreign policy, not in terms of its intellectual origins and sources from the time of the pilgrim fathers, but in terms of major frameworks of foreign-policy thinking that govern its outlook toward the end of the twentieth century and

---

[1] David Shambaugh, *Beautiful Imperialist: China Perceives America, 1922–1990* (Princeton: Princeton University Press, 1991).
[2] George Kennan. *American Diplomacy, 1900–1950* (Chicago: University of Chicago Press, 1951).

beyond[3]—an international systemic explanation rather than a domestic explanation.[4]

In this chapter I will illustrate an understanding of American foreign policy within the three global currents determining world politics *fin de siècle* and beyond. There are two major justifications for this approach. First, the United States is involved in every corner of the globe. It is in no position to seclude itself from the rest of the world, protesting that it is the God-given land and that evil and villainy are invariably the work of outsiders. Second, to be effective, the United States must be conversant with major and often even minor currents of thinking the world over.[5]

In what follows I will first briefly introduce three major currents of global politics at the end of the twentieth century. Then I will characterize the three currents of the era in terms of geopolitical frameworks, geoeconomic foundations, and geocultural networks, starting with three works by Henry Kissinger, Francis Fukuyama, and Samuel Huntington, respectively. Third, I will illustrate how the three major currents help shape American foreign policy, citing US promotion of democracy in Asia-Pacific in the 1980s and 1990s.

Three Major Currents of Global Politics

Toward the end of the twentieth century, the framework of global politics can be seen to be modelled upon three legacies of sovereign power. Throughout much of the nineteenth and twentieth centuries, the sovereign and territorial nation-state was considered the basic unit of action power. This so-called Westphalian legacy was the dominant model during these two centuries and especially during much of the cold war period. Its essence is state sovereignty premised on the prevalence of order within and anarchy outside.[6] Toward the end of the twentieth century, however, two other legacies have made something of a comeback: the Philadelphian and what might be termed the anti-utopian. The Philadelphian legacy refers to the liberal union of American States starting in the colonial period and extending to the time of the civil war. The Philadelphian model, premised on the principle of popular sovereignty, was based on the legal procedures whereby states tried to resolve disputes

[3] Takashi Inoguchi, 'Peering into the Future by Looking Back: The Westphalian, Philadelphian, and Anti-Utopian Paradigms', *International Studies Review*, 1/2 (1999), pp. 173–94; also in Davis Bobrow (ed.), *Prospects for International Relations: Conjectures about the Next Millenium* (Malden, MA: Blackwell, 1999), pp. 173–94.

[4] Kenneth Waltz, *Man, the State and War* (New York: Columbia University Press, 1959).

[5] Takashi Inoguchi, *Global Change at the Dawn of the New Millenium: How Japan Interprets the Dialectics of the World* (London: Macmillan, forthcoming).

[6] Hendrik Spruyt, *The Sovereign State and Its Competitors* (Princeton: Princeton University Press, 1994); Stephen Krasner, 'Westphalia and All That', in Judith Goldstein and Robert Keohane (eds), *Ideas and Foreign Policy* (Ithaca: Cornell University Press, 1993), pp. 235–64; David A Lake and Donald S. Rothchild (eds), *The International Spread of Ethnic Conflict: Fear, Diffusion, and Escalation* (Princeton: Princeton University Press, 1998); Thomas Biersteker and Cynthia Weber (eds), *State Sovereignty as Social Construct* (Cambridge, UK: Cambridge University Press, 1996).

among themselves.[7] Marginalized for a considerable period of time, the model has recently seen a revival among the liberal democracies, constituting part of the third wave of democratization. This is evidenced by the number of sovereign states that incorporate into their constitutions conventions and declarations on freedom, democracy, equality, and human rights.[8] The anti-utopian legacy is, of course, very different and refers, basically, to the degeneration or collapse of former colonial states that had originally been based on the universal principles of national self-determination, human rights, and democracy. In spite of these noble ideals, many of these experiments in state creation became failed states, experiencing prolonged civil strife and prolonged hunger at home—and if they were held together at all it was through international aid and outside humanitarian intervention.[9]

These three 'legacies' are broadly speaking theorized in the work of Henry Kissinger, Francis Fukuyama, and Samuel Huntington.[10] Let us briefly deal with each in turn.

According to Kissinger, state sovereignty and foreign policy are primary; all other things are judged according to whether they facilitate the realization of adroit exercises in the balance of power, that is, the maintenance of peace. American hegemony going back to 1945 is bound to slowly diminish, he argues, so its international leadership can be enhanced only by engaging in intermittent balancing acts. His central concern is with peace achieved by the skilful manipulation of balance of power politics among the major powers. Francis Fukuyama discusses the predominantly non-violent mode of conflict resolution among global actors that share common sets of norms and values such as those of democracy and liberalism. Advocates of this theory assert that by promoting democracy everywhere, the United States can diminish the likelihood of war. States that share common values can settle their differences without resort to armed violence. It is called the 'democratic enlargement' strategy. A more passive approach counsels limiting interaction with other states to liberal democracies. Contact with non-democracies only depletes resources and should therefore be avoided.

Samuel Huntington's *Clash of Civilizations and the Remaking of World Order* focuses on regions of the world that are potentially resource-draining: the Islamic world and China. Huntington argues that many civilizations are fundamentally incompatible and that the world is rife with situations that could

[7] Daniel Deudney, 'Binding Sovereigns: Authorities, Structures, and Geopolitics in Philadelphian Systems', in Biersteker and Weber (eds), *State Sovereignty as Social Construct*, pp. 190–239; Nicholas Greenwood Onuf, *The Republican Legacy in International Thought* (Cambridge, UK: Cambridge University Press, 1998).

[8] On the statistical trends/waves of democratization, see Samuel Huntington, *The Third Wave: Democratization in the Late Twentieth Century* (Norman, Oklahoma: University of Oklahoma Press, 1993).

[9] International Federation of Red Cross and Red Crescent Societies, *World Disasters Report, 1997* (Oxford: Oxford University Press, 1998); UN High Commissioner for Refugees, *The State of the World's Refugees* (Oxford: Oxford University Press, 1998).

[10] Henry Kissinger, *Diplomacy* (New York: Simon and Schuster, 1995); Francis Fukuyama, *The End of History and The Last Man* (New York: Free Press, 1992); Samuel Huntington, *The Clash of Civilizations and the Remaking of the World Order* (New York: Simon and Schuster, 1995).

lead them to clash. As summarized by the titles of his own articles, he argues that international primacy matters, although without asserting that Western values are universal. Rather, he argues, they are 'unique'.[11] Huntington's primary perception is of the essential incompatibility of civilizations, and some combinations of religion, race, language, geography, and history, he believes, are destined to clash.

Geopolitics, Geoeconomics, Geoculture

Geopolitical Frameworks

The actors in the Westphalian framework are what are known as 'normal states', where the sovereignty of the state is the basic premise. In the Philadelphian framework, the actors are liberal democracies as politico-economic systems, and the basic premise is popular sovereignty.[12] In the anti-utopian framework, the actors are failed and failing states where sovereignty has been relinquished. Normal states are characterized as having strong state sovereignty and are especially sensitive to infringements of sovereignty and territoriality; they abhor 'interference' in the internal affairs of states. Liberal democracies are characterized by firmly entrenched popular sovereignty and broad acceptance of democratic norms and values. They downplay protectionism and state sovereignty. Failed and failing states are those that have 'hollowed-out' in terms of sovereignty and have become marginalized economically. They are vulnerable to global economic changes and prone to internal disorder and civil strife. They tend to be ripe for interference from outside, whether in the form of colonial-style domination, humanitarian relief, armed aggression, or economic penetration and exploitation.

The behavioural modalities of normal states are balancing and bandwagonning.[13] Balancing is aimed at limiting the potentially explosive assertiveness of other normal states. To deal with a very powerful normal state, other countries may also bandwagon on the assumption that, if you cannot beat them, then why not join them? The behavioural modalities of liberal democracies are binding and hiding.[14] Like-minded actors band together in order to achieve broader, stronger union. When faced with forces that jeopardize liberal democratic norms at their foundation, however, it is sometimes expedient to practice concealment. The behavioural modalities of failed and failing states are 'hollowing-out' and collapse. Failed states are no longer autonomous

---

[11] Samuel Huntington, 'Why International Primacy Matters', *International Security*, 17/4 (1993), pp. 71–81, and 'The West: Unique, Not Universal', *Foreign Affairs* 75 (1996), pp. 28–46.

[12] Bruce Russett, *Grasping the Democratic Peace* (Princeton: Princeton University Press, 1993); Michael Doyle, 'Liberalism and World Politics', *American Political Science Review*, 80/4 (1986), pp. 1156–69.

[13] Stephen Walt, *The Origins of Alliances* (Ithaca: Cornell University Press, 1987); Randall Schweller, 'New Realist Research on Alliances: Refining, Not Refuting, Waltz's Balancing Position', *American Political Science Review*, 91/4 (1997), pp. 927–35.

[14] Daniel Deudney, 'Binding Sovereigns'.

and are often the objects of pressure from without. However, these states are so amorphous that such intervention rarely makes much difference to their development over the long term.

How then should we characterize the United States? The United States is the acknowledged primary actor in global politics; and if we accept Waltz's category of normal states as those able to determine their own destiny, it is the world's only 'normal' state in the Westphalian sense. At the same it is the original Philadelphian actor that later spearheaded economic liberalization and political democratization in the second half of the twentieth century. The US also purports to lead the world. Indeed, it is the only state that can do so when marginalized segments of the global market become volatile and instability erupts in peripheral areas of the international system. Whether it does so adequately or not is a moot question; and the US has been variously criticized as intervening 'too often', 'too hastily', 'not often enough' and 'not quickly enough'. Such are the travails of being a superpower.

Geoeconomic Foundations

The geoeconomic foundations of our three frameworks are articulated, respectively, in Alexander Gerschenkron's *Economic Backwardness in Historical Perspective*, Robert Reich's *Work of Nations*, and David Landes' *Wealth and Poverty of Nations*.[15]

Gerschenkron's key concept is the national economy, which he applies to Germany and Russia in the late nineteenth century. In the late twentieth-century context, he could have extended his argument to the east Asian states; he might also have included the Napoleonic state with its strong element of state regulation, as well as the social democratic Nordic states of Europe. In all these groups the state played a key role in bringing about economic prosperity and social stability.[16] Reich focuses on a world without borders where anonymous and omnipresent speculators are constantly on the lookout for opportunities to exploit. The global future, according to Reich, will be sustained by the fortunate few who can adapt to and excel in global mega-competition. His premise is that further liberalization will lead to the 'global cornucopia'. The majority, he argues, can be rescued only through massive training schemes financed by the privileged minority. Protectionism is impossible in Reich's universe, where the United States constitutes itself as the model for the rest of

---

[15] Alexander Gerschenkron, *Economic Backwardness in Historical Perspective* (Cambridge: Harvard University Press, 1965); Robert Reich, *The Work of Nations* (New York: Knopf, 1991); David Landes, *The Wealth and Poverty of Nations: Why Some Are So Rich and Some So Poor* (New York: Norton, 1998).

[16] Robert Wade, *Governing the Market: Economic Theory and the Role of Government in East Asian Industrialization* (Princeton: Princeton University Press, 1991); Goesta Esping-Anderson, *Politics against Markets: The Social Democratic Road to Power* (Princeton: Princeton University Press, 1985); Robert Boyer, *The Regulation School: A Critical Introduction* (New York: Columbia University Press, 1990); Manfred Bienefeld, 'Is a Strong National Economy an Utopian Goal at the End of the Twentieth Century?', in Robert Boyer and Daniel Drache (eds), *States against Markets: The Limits of Globalization* (London: Routledge, 1996), pp. 415–40.

the world.[17] With Landes the main concern is economic development; the key actors in this are groups of entrepreneurs with the propensity to make the best use of technological breakthroughs. The attitudes and norms of such entrepreneurs regarding innovation and enterprise become the driving force in a favourable cultural environment. The critical variable, therefore, is the cultural orientation to invention and know-how in the context of economic development.

The mechanism that brings about transformation in Gerschenkron's view is massive input of capital and labour. The most effective systems will depend on stockholding to collect capital, state-led industrialization to guide entrepreneurs, and long working hours in exchange for permanent employment status or high wages. As Paul Krugman correctly points out, a good deal of the east Asian miracle can be explained in terms of the massive input of capital and labour.[18] The transformative mechanism according to Reich is the straightforward input of technological innovation. In the process, technology itself is endogenized in the market, in contrast to the Gerschenkron view, where technology tends to be treated as exogenous. The global market began to flourish after telecommunications devices became available to all speculators and after the Plaza Accord of 1985, dramatically amplifying opportunities for currency trading. It will further flourish as telemanufacturing and teledistribution devices are invented and come into use around the world. The transformative mechanism in Landes' view is Weberian. He portrays the inner values and attitudes that guide a population as fundamental in preparing the way for, advancing, and sustaining economic development. Certain values and attitudes cherished by a population are more conducive to invention and innovation and to enterprise and development than others.

These three mechanisms coexist in the late twentieth century. The Gerschenkron world continues to flourish in east Asia despite diminished self-confidence triggered by the recent financial crisis. The Reich world is rapidly on the rise almost everywhere. The remarkable spread of telecommunications technology around the world and the availability of instantaneous global financial services associated with that technology are the basis of this expansion. The Landes world prevails almost indefinitely because fundamental differences in the inner values and attitudes inculcated and inherited across cultures are more durable than the technology-driven, cultural-convergence thesis allows.

The Gerschenkron scheme corresponds roughly to the Kissinger world, the Reich scheme to the Fukuyama world, and the Landes scheme to the Huntington world. Geopolitics has its geoeconomic basis in each of the three frameworks.

[17] For a discussion of Robert Reich's influence on the Clinton administration, see Michael Cox, *US Foreign Policy after the Cold War: Superpower Without a Mission?* (London: Royal Institute of International Affairs, 1995), pp. 26–7.

[18] Paul Krugman, 'The Myth of Asia's Miracle', *Foreign Affairs*, 73/6 (1994), pp. 62–78.

Geocultural Networks

The Westphalian, Philadelphian, and anti-utopian frameworks each have geo-cultural networks of their own. These are depicted in the works of Benedict Anderson, Benjamin Barber, and Robert Kaplan.[19]

Benedict Anderson shows how the state radio network of Indonesia played a primary role in nation-building. Benjamin Barber describes the starkly different networking technology and strategy of the Philadelphian and anti-utopian worlds. They are symbolized by McWorld and Jihad, respectively. CNN and Samizdat (*Samoizdatel'stvo* or self-publication) symbolize another aspect of the contrast between these two different networks. Kaplan focuses on networking techniques and the strategy of the anti-utopian world. Networks nurture and cement sharing and solidarity, and are therefore self-strengthening. The rise or decline of the three frameworks depends in part on the degree to which these three networks flourish, compete, or go into decline.

In the Anderson network, the state and state-owned radio and television play key networking roles. Indonesia provides an example of how such networks are forged. Indonesia consists of 17,000-odd islands; it is a country where countless mutually unintelligible native languages are spoken. The language chosen as the national *lingua franca* for Indonesia when it became independent from the Netherlands was a somewhat artificial and very local language spoken mostly in the Malay peninsula coastal areas and the surrounding area for commercial purposes. A sort of Creole or pidgin form of Indonesian, Bahasa Indonesia can be described as a Malayo-Polynesian Esperanto. The leaders deliberately chose Bahasa Indonesia instead of Javanese, the dominant language of the island of Java, which was the origin of most of the Indonesian founding fathers. For the sake of the unity and solidarity of the Republic of Indonesia, it was decided not to impose the dominant language of the dominant population on all the rest. Efforts are made to disseminate the national language on all possible occasions through the public network Radio Indonesia. Bahasa Indonesia is the symbol and tool of nation building. Children begin to learn Bahasa Indonesia formally after they start primary school, so it is expected that in time this language will become the national standard of communication, solidifying communications throughout the diverse archipelago.

McWorld and CNN are symbols of global penetration. CNN specializes in global on-the-spot reporting calculated to provide dramatic visual effect. At the time that the Liberal Democratic Party was trounced in the June 1993 general elections in Japan, I appeared on CNN with Diet member Wakako Hironaka. I soon noted that everything was recorded live, without prepared scripts or rehearsals. CNN Tokyo's Eileen O'Connor simply appeared shortly

---

[19] Benedict Anderson, *Imagined Communities: Reflections on the Origin and Spread of Nationalism*, 2nd edn. (London: Verso, 1991); Benjamin Barber, *Jihad vs. McWorld* (New York: Times Books, 1993); Robert Kaplan, *The Ends of the Earth: A Journey to the Frontiers of Anarchy, From Togo to Turkmenistan, From Iran to Cambodia* (New York: Vintage Books, 1997).

before broadcasting time and said that she would ask certain questions. The setting was also deliberately chosen: a building of one of the Japanese television stations where CNN Tokyo has its offices where monitoring of the vote count was going on. The discussion, held against the background noise of the vote-monitoring room, was clearly calculated to give the strong visual impression that Japan was experiencing a dramatic change and that TV viewers were witness to it. Perhaps this is what the United States government wanted to see in the context of the ongoing trade negotiations and in view of Japan's limited participation in the Gulf war.

Samizdat is the symbol of dissident communication, although, today, fax and e-mail are the main devices of dissident communication. They are used for underground or subversive operations or for clandestine intelligence activities. Back in 1989, I received a fax message some weeks after the 4 June Tiananmen massacre, when anti-Chinese government demonstrations and meetings were taking place in Tokyo. The message was a call for solidarity from Chinese students at the University of Tokyo. I knew the name of one of the students, who had come to me a couple of years earlier with a letter of recommendation from Yan Jiaji, then director of the Institute of Political Science at the Chinese Academy of Social Sciences. I had known Yan through correspondence regarding the publication in Chinese of a book series in political science put out by the University of Tokyo Press, of which I was editor. In my introduction to the Chinese edition, I acknowledged the efforts of a number of colleagues, including Professor Yan Jiaji. The massacre took place before the Chinese translation started to come out, and, when it appeared in late 1990, my reference to Yan Jiaji had been deleted.

The three frameworks, as shown by the above anecdotes, display three different styles of networking featuring state-run media, private entrepreneurial networks, and personal—sometimes underground—networks, respectively.

The United States and the Promotion of Democracy in Asia-Pacific

In Asia-Pacific, the United States was directly involved in the democratization of the Philippines and Japan in the immediate post-war period. Japan was the direct target of American promotion of democracy during the US-led occupation. In the fourth quarter of the twentieth century, the US promotion of democracy generated a third global wave of democratization in the region. In the Philippines this was manifested in the US-engineered 'people power' revolution of 1986 that brought Corazon Aquino to power. In South Korea the United States also gave its blessing to the end of military rule and the adoption of democratic elections, first bringing former military leaders and eventually civilian leaders to power. In Taiwan, too, American influence favoured the abolition of the one-party rule of the Kuomintang and the emergence of opposition parties. In the 1990s, movements for protecting human rights and for promoting democracy were mounted in other countries of Asia-Pacific—most obviously China, Indonesia, and Myanmar, countries which according to Washington had poor human rights records.

In analysing US efforts to promote democracy in Asia-Pacific, it is important to grasp the historical and contextual setting of each policy thrust. In the case of the Philippines and Japan, it was occasioned by direct American occupation. The Philippines in fact was the first republic in Asia-Pacific, and Japan the only practising liberal democracy in the region for half a century. Later, American involvement in the ousting of Ferdinand Marcos from the presidency of the Philippines had a massive impact on the rest of the region. Witnessing how the US had behaved, Taiwan's Jiang Jingguo—rather grudgingly—began to experiment with democratic forms. Similarly, the South Korean military regime headed by Roh Taewoo moved to democratize politics. In all three countries democratic elections were held and democracy has been observed in practice there ever since.

In the 1990s, the targets of US promotion of human rights and democracy have been mainly China, Indonesia, and Myanmar. An array of different sanctions have been imposed at different times. However, the US has never been entirely consistent and US criticism has often been less strident where it has major commercial and security interests.

Our three frameworks of global politics coexist side by side in Asia-Pacific. We may compare, for example, China, Japan, and Cambodia as targets of US promotion of democracy. Before examining American strategy toward the three, it is important to note that the three countries do have particular preferences as to how they wish to be seen. China portrays itself primarily as a normal state in the Westphalian framework. China abhors interference in its internal affairs. Japan portrays itself as a liberal democracy in the Philadelphian framework and is bewildered when it is criticized as an abnormal semi-sovereign state, since it is content with being a semi-sovereign state as far as security is concerned. Cambodia has no choice but to follow outside advice when it is told that a fair and free election is the key to nation-building. The aim of the US promotion of democracy differs from one framework to another. In the case of China, a key component is the protection of human rights. The US government acts strongly in the Philadelphian framework; but, needless to say, all US action is based on the undeniable reality of its being the world's prime hegemonic power in the Westphalian framework.

In Japan, the US has pursued a policy designed to foster genuine political competition in a two-party system. But again, even though its purpose is Philadelphian, the reality of power always underlies US actions there. To this extent, the framework governing relations between the two countries remains very much Westphalian. Thus, if and when the US cannot get its way on many issues, it often threatens to take punitive economic sanctions. Examples include the US government's 'soft ultimatum', conditional on the pledge of achieving numerical quotas for Japanese imports of US semiconductors;

demanding that Japan allow the United States to act more freely in Japan in the case of a military emergency; and demanding that it implement drastic financial and banking-sector reforms in tandem with the US cooperative intervention in the financial market to prevent the drastic decline of the value of the Japanese yen.

In the failed state of Cambodia, United States actions have aimed at paving the way for free, multiparty elections. Here, however, it has not acted alone but more often than not delegated all the civilizing actions to international organizations or to the United Nations—and especially those members of the UN having a regional presence like France, Australia and Japan—as well as a range of non-governmental organizations.

Human Rights in China

The general prospects for progressive political change in China looked rather optimistic in the 1980s.[20] Deng Xiaoping's reform policy began in late 1978 and the general liberalization of Chinese society and economy could be observed throughout the 1980s. Intellectuals started to speak more freely. Democratic consciousness was on the rise. Even the government itself gradually shifted position on the issue of human rights in such international forums as the United Nations. To a degree it even became part of the human-rights regime.

However, the Chinese government became alarmed by the sudden development of national mourning occasioned by the death of Hu Yaopang, Secretary General of the Chinese Communist Party in the mid-1980s, reminiscent of the mourning over Zhou Enlai's death in the mid-1970s. Underlying this alarm was the growth of a nascent, indigenous, pro-democracy movement. In 1989 the pro-democracy movement became increasingly influential, to the point that it began to bring pressure to bear upon the Chinese government. The leadership group led by Deng Xiaoping, however, supported by the military and party hard-liners, struck back sharply and on 4 June ordered the actions that led to the massacre in Tiananmen Square.[21] The pictures of the newly erected Statue of Liberty rising above the thousands of students in the Square, then being torn down by agents of a 'communist' state—not to mention the image of one lone protestor facing down a tank—did more to change American images of China than any sort of military adventure or high-level diplomatic dispute. Moreover, these events were then televised around the world by CNN and other television networks. In this way, the actions taken by the government in China immediately assumed global significance, and, naturally enough, changed the character of US-China relations, possibly for ever.

---

[20] Ann Kent, *Between Freedom and Subsistence: China and Human Rights* (Hong Kong: Oxford University Press, 1993).

[21] Craig Calhoun, *Neither Gods Nor Emperor: Students and Struggles for Democracy in China* (Berkeley: University of California Press, 1997).

Even before the repression, the US had established contacts with opposition leaders, intellectuals and officials close to the group led by Zhao Ziyang in the party and government. But Tiananmen Square pushed human rights to the fore in US-China relations. Immediately after 1989 economic sanctions were imposed and the US made powerful statements in public denouncing China, even though it continued to engage in cautionary—and much-criticized—secret consultations with the Chinese government. Economic sanctions continued, but in 1991, following initiatives by the Japanese government, these were partially lifted.[22] The change from the Republican administration to the Democrat administration in 1992 did not lead to a major change in policy, in spite of President Clinton's apparent promise to take a much tougher stance on human rights. American business interests—indeed the wider foreign policy community as a whole—also began to question the wisdom of single-minded emphasis on the political dimension of the relationship, and in the end, it seems, forced the Clinton administration to adopt the policy of 'comprehensive engagement' that came to define US strategy thereafter.[23]

The strategy can be summarized thus. China, it was accepted, was far too important to be left out in the cold. Its large and expanding domestic market, its regional influence, the fact that it was a nuclear state and, moreover, a permanent member of the UN Security Council, meant that the United States would have to deal with China as serious power in its own right. It was simply too important a player to push around, and certainly far too important to allow human rights alone to determine bilateral relations between the two countries. Nor was there much chance that a policy of punishment would work. If anything it might make matters worse. The relationship between the two countries therefore had to be put on a sound, comprehensive basis. This would not ignore human rights, but would locate the issue within a wider framework. Over the long term, the best and most effective policy, it was therefore felt, was not short-term sanctions but the longer-term integration of China into the wider world system. In this way, through a gradual process of learning and adaptation, China, it was reasoned, would begin to adopt international norms and play by the international rules of the game, rules which included not only open markets and fair trade but also an acceptance of Western-style human rights.

Laying down a policy was one thing; implementing it was quite another, and not surprisingly the Clinton administration had problems in maintaining a steady course. This became only too apparent in 1994, when the United States faced a renewed threat from North Korea,[24] and two years later when there was the stand-off between China and Taiwan during which China held military exercises in the Taiwan Straits to put political pressure on the

---

[22] Tanaka Akihiko, *NitChu kankei 1972–1991* [Japanese-Chinese Relations, 1972–1991] (Tokyo: University of Tokyo Press, 1992).

[23] See for the latter Ezra Vogel (ed.), *Living With China: U.S.-China Relations in the Twentieth-first Century* (New York: W. W. Norton, 1997).

[24] See, *inter alia*, International Institute of Strategic Studies, *Strategic Survey 1996–1997* (London).

government in Taipei.[25] In both situations, the issue of human rights almost seemed to be irrelevant. Thus, when the US needed China's help to manage the crisis in North Korea, China's record in this area was not even mentioned, and was not likely to be when Washington required Chinese diplomatic support to contain Pyongyang; and when the US was forced to face down China in 1996, the big question then was not human rights but China's intimidatory tactics towards a key American ally.

A quasi-détente between China and the United States continued in November 1997 when President Jiang Zeming visited the United States. It looked as if business-as-usual was the predominant mood in Sino-US relations and as if the issue of human rights was an intense but not a priority issue.[26] After his visit, the Chinese government also threw the US a sop and released Wei Jingsheng, an intermittently jailed dissident first arrested for appealing to the communist leadership for a 'fifth modernization', that is, democratization.[27]

Clinton's visit to China in July 1998 only confirmed that human rights was an important but not a priority issue in US-Chinese relations. Prior to the visit, the release of a prominent dissident, Wan Dan, was announced, while during the visit itself Clinton's speech and the questions and answers thereafter in the auditorium at Peking University were televised live on CNN. The US government, however, also used the occasion to reassure China about Taiwan with its 'three nots' principle: not allowing Taiwan to seek independence, not allowing Taiwan to become a member of the United Nations, and not returning to a two-China policy. This was accompanied by two other initiatives: enhancing the means of preventing further nuclear proliferation, and reassuring the democratic allies of the United States—Taiwan, South Korea, and Japan—of its commitment to their security.

However, the United States stiffened its position on China's human rights practices only seven months after this 'honeymoon period'. First, the Asian financial crisis led to a major increase in the US trade deficit with China and a slightly sour note began to be sounded in discussions between the two governments. Second, the Chinese government sharpened its opposition to the US-led scheme of theatre missile defence (TMD) envisaged to be built by Japan, South Korea and Taiwan. Third, the Chinese government escalated its suppression of human rights activists and democracy movements at home. Under these pressures, America once again stepped up its political criticism, showing particular interest in human rights abuses and in the fledgling democracy movement, especially in the cultural realm and at the village level.[28] This was

[25] John W. Garver, *Face Off: China, the United States, and Taiwan's Democratization* (Berkeley: University of California Press, 1997).

[26] David E. Sanger, 'Business Leads Diplomacy in Relations with Beijing', *International Herald Tribune*, 29 October 1997, pp. 1 and 10.

[27] Kathryn Sikkink, 'The Power of Principled Ideas: Human Rights Policies in the United States and Western Europe', in Goldstein and Keohane (eds), *Ideas and Foreign Policy*, pp. 139–72.

[28] Yali Peng, 'Democracy and Chinese Political Discourse', *Modern China*, 24/4 (1998), pp. 408–44; Jing Wang, *High Culture Fever: Politics Aesthetics and Ideology in Deng's China* (Berkeley: University of California Press, 1996); Baogang He, *The Democratic Implications of Civil Society in China* (Basingstoke, England: Macmillan, 1997); Andrew Walder (ed.), *Zouping in Transition; The Process of Reform in Rural*

sustained by vigorous intelligence and research activities at all levels from the Department of State through to the academic world. Human rights simply would not go away.

Creating a Two-Party System in Japan

Japan is a liberal democracy. Yet the politics of Japan for the greater part of the postwar period was dominated by one party—the Liberal Democratic Party (LDP)—which brought political stability to Japan and ensured that Japan pursued a foreign policy acceptable to the United States. While the cold war persisted, it was an arrangement that few in the US cared or even dared to criticize. The end of the cold war, however, and the increase in economic tensions between the two countries changed all this and led America to promote a new form of more open democracy in Japan—though less for political than economic reasons. The story bears some retelling.

During the 1980s the United States began to complain about what it viewed as the closed nature of the Japanese economy. The ratio of Japan's foreign direct investment abroad to foreign direct investment in Japan was just too unfavourable.[29] Why, American critics asked themselves? Their reasoning went roughly as follows.[30] The bureaucracy, they insisted, was too strong, regulating economic activities at home and denying reasonable access to foreign capital. Consumers, they also felt, were too weak. However, if they were to assert their rights, civic groups and political parties committed to the sovereignty of the consumer were needed. One-party dominance by the LDP—the friend of bureaucracy and business but not necessarily Japanese consumers—had to be moderated by a healthy opposition that was not only strong enough in its own right but capable of actually replacing the LDP as the governing party. What was also required, it was argued, was a change in business practices—practices that hitherto had encouraged closed networks between corporations and banks, government and business. These practices also encouraged the Japanese to stick together and exclude healthy competition. So, reasoned American analysts, we should try to crack open the outer protective shell by gradually persuading Japan to adopt certain global standards and in the process get rid of the barriers that prevent normal economic intercourse between Japan and the outside world.

The United States also sought to change the way decisions were made by the Japanese government. Often these were very slow and evasive. Indeed, the

North China (Berkeley: University of California Press, 1998); Anita Chan *et al.*, *Chen Village under Mao and Deng* (Berkeley: University of California Press, 1984/1999).

[29] Nakamura Yoshiaki *et al.*, *TaiNichi chokusetsu toshi wa naze sukunaika* [Why Is Foreign Direct Investment in Japan So Low?] (Tokyo: MITI Research Institute, 1997).

[30] The following is my selective summary of what the revisionists say. See Clyde Prestowitz, *Trading Places: How We Allowed Japan to Take the Lead* (New York, Basic Books, 1988); Chalmers Johnson, *MITI and the Japanese Miracle* (Stanford: Stanford University Press, 1982); James Fallows, *Looking at the Sun: The Rise of the New East Asian Economic and Political System* (New York: Pantheon Books, 1994).

government seemed to outsiders at least like some multi-headed monster, such that it was impossible see where the ultimate decision-making authority lay. There were also too many decision-making units with veto power.[31] The American goal thus was to encourage the establishment of what it regarded as a 'normal state' where authority lines were clear. To achieve this goal, however, it had to first identify and then encourage those politicians who would challenge the old structure and lead the nation in a different way.

This new strategy of democracy promotion has to be set in the larger historical context. As we have already noted, the US was willing to live with the old order, which served its purposes well until the 1980s. The turning-point came in 1985 and 1986 when there was major liberalization of financial markets on a global scale.[32] One financial analyst called it 'the end of geography', meaning that in economic transactions, especially in financial market transactions, geographical distance had lost much of the significance it had hitherto held. The Plaza Agreement called for market-demand expansion and liberalization of the market along with measures that would lower the value of the US dollar.[33] The Japanese government took the message seriously and the Maekawa Report, submitted to Prime Minister Yasuhiro Nakasone in 1985, proposed assiduous promotion of domestic expansion of market demand and market liberalization. The former, however, advanced much more rapidly than the latter, leading to an increased trade deficit. This in turn upset the US, which now demanded liberalization of Japan's market. A series of negotiations conducted between the two countries only added to the already bad feelings on both sides, among the elite as well as the general public. Japanese public opinion was dismayed at 'Japan bashing' and certain elite spokesmen argued that Japan could, and had every right to, 'say no'. The acrimonious debates that ensued did a great deal of harm to the bilateral relationship.[34]

It was at this stage that the US now linked its economic concerns with demands for political reform within Japan itself and called, as we have seen, for bureaucratic deregulation, the overthrow of one-party dominance and an end to consumer docility. The United States government may not have been the only actor engineering the 1993 dismantling of the LDP's one-party dominance; nevertheless, it played an important part. What was critical, of course, were problems within Japan itself. Inflation worsened in the late 1980s. Political scandals mushroomed. Noboru Takeshita, prime minister and head of the largest faction of the LDP, was forced to resign and his cohorts began to wonder what strategy they might avail themselves of to avoid the same fate. Half of them broke ranks with the LDP altogether, forming a splinter party

---

[31] Inoguchi Takashi, *Nihon Keizai taikoku no seiji unei* [Japan: The Governing of an Economic Superpower] (Tokyo: Tokyo Daigaku Shuppankai, 1993).

[32] Eugene Skolnikoff, *The Elusive Transformation: Science, Technology and the Evolution of International Politics* (Princeton: Princeton University Press, 1993).

[33] Ronald I. MacKinnon and Kenichi Ohno, *Dollar and Yen: Resolving Economic Conflict between the United States and Japan* (Cambridge, MA: MIT Press, 1997).

[34] Akio Morita and Shintaro Ishihara, *No to ieru Nihon* [Japan That Can Say No] (Tokyo: Kobunsha, 1989).

headed by Ichiro Ozawa, who was portrayed favourably in former ambassador Michael Armacost's recent book.[35]

The public was also emboldened to voice their grievances and sense of injustice. The young and the ambitious rallied around the banner of Morihiro Hosokawa, former governor of Kumamoto and a member of a former aristocratic family related to the imperial family, to mobilize support for the Japan New Party which Hosokawa came to head. Meanwhile, the LDP changed prime ministers three times: Toshiki Kaifu, Sosuke Uno, and Kiichi Miyazawa. Miyazawa was defeated in a no-confidence vote on the framework for Japan–US trade negotiations. The subsequent election brought the opposition parties together to form a coalition government headed by Hosokawa. This was a brilliant victory on the part of Hosokawa and Ozawa—and some would say for the United States as well.

The political reform bills Hosokawa swiftly moved through the National Diet by the end of 1993[36] were favourably received by the public. These changed the procedure for choosing candidates for seats in the National Diet, the way political donations could be legally gathered, and the method of allocating government subsidies to political parties. Most noteworthy was the change from the multiple-member district system—wherein two to five candidates were chosen in the same district with one vote—to the single-member district system—wherein one candidate is chosen with one vote: significantly, the Anglo–American system.

The period between 1994 and 1995, under the administration of a coalition government made up of the LDP, Social Democrats, and Sakigake, was an eventful time, but the populist upsurge of the early 1990s disappeared.[37] Above all, the economy went into steady decline. The cumulative government deficit reached unprecedented heights. The tangible effects of globalization began to be felt in many sectors. Early retirement became more frequent. Once a modicum of political reform was achieved, popular attention was directed at the bureaucracy, where salaries were not negatively affected by the economic downturn, in contrast to the private sector, where white-collar workers began to feel its full force. Revelations of bureaucratic scandals and corruption in public offices filled the news. There was a succession of crises, from the North Korean 'crisis' to the tensions in the Taiwan Straits and the Kobe earthquake and the terrorist acts of Aum Shinrikyo cult members in Tokyo subways. Weighed down by continuing recession and assailed by one crisis after another, the political mood of the time became pessimistic.

Yet these were also times of important change. Indeed, Prime Minister Tomiichi Murayama, head of the Social Democratic party, achieved two major

---

[35] Michael Armacost, *Friends or Rivals? The Insider's Account of U.S.-Japanese Relations* (New York: Columbia University Press, 1996).

[36] Takashi Inoguchi, 'The Rise and Fall of "Reformist Governments": Hosokawa and Hata, 1993–1994', *Asian Journal of Political Science*, 2/2 (1994), pp. 73–88.

[37] Steven Reed, 'A Story of Three Booms: From the New Liberal Club to the Hosokawa Coalition Government', in Purnendra Jain and Takashi Inoguchi (eds), *Japanese Politics Today* (Sydney: Macmillan, 1997), pp. 108–23.

policy successes. His party changed its previous position on opposition to the Japan-US security treaty to acceptance, an action that eased the redrafting of the new Japan-US security guidelines in 19967. No less important was his statement of Japanese repentance regarding acts of war in the 1930s and 1940s. It was direct and forthright and left little room for doubt. The statement has subsequently become a very strong and standard statement of the Japanese government on that issue. Liberal Democratic Party Prime Minister Ryutaro Hashimoto completed the new security guidelines and boldly initiated reforms designed to eliminate the primacy of bureaucrats over politicians. The basic tone of Japanese politics changed completely during the 1992–1997 period.[38]

With the growth of the newly inaugurated Democratic Party headed by Naoto Kan and the Japan Communist Party making an unexpected comeback to occupy much of the space once taken up by the Social Democratic Party, one might claim that a renewal of democratic politics in Japan has been achieved with significant results. The Upper House election of 12 July 1998 seemed to confirm this observation. The governing LDP experienced a disappointing result, leading to Prime Minister Ryutaro Hashimoto's announcement that he would resign. Not only was the LDP unable to capture a simple majority in the Upper House; it also allowed three large opposition parties, the one-month-old Democratic Party, the Japan Communist Party, and the Komei Party to gain a large number of seats from the LDP. The LDP could not win one seat in its metropolitan constituencies in Tokyo, Kanagawa, Saitama, Osaka, and Kyoto. This rendered somewhat uncertain the passage of the economic recovery package that Prime Minister Hashimoto managed to announce just before his resignation. The LDP's minority status in the Upper House meant that the LDP had to get legislative cooperation from other opposition parties or members. However, these to some degree were mere details. Far more significant was the much higher voter turnout—about 58 per cent—and the unexpected advances won by the opposition. These were important signs of changed times in Japan and seemed proof of the fact that Japanese party politics had at last acquired a degree of democratic competition.

Promoting Free Elections in Cambodia

Cambodia is the ultimate anti-utopia as far as the United States is concerned.[39] After President Lyndon Johnson withdrew from politics in 1968, Richard Nixon sought to achieve 'peace with honour'. That meant massive bombing of North Vietnam and intrusion and pacification operations into the sanctuaries

---

[38] Takashi Inoguchi, 'A Step toward One-Party Predominance: Japan's General Election of 20 October 1996', *Government and Opposition*, 32/1 (1997), pp. 48–64.

[39] Judy Ledgerwood, *Propaganda, Politics and Violence in Cambodia* (Armonk, N.J: Myron E. Sharpe, 1996); William Shawcross, *Cambodia's New Deal* (Washington, DC: Carnegie Endowment for International Peace, 1994); David Chandler and Ben Kiernan (eds.), *Revolution and Its Aftermath in Kampuchea* (New Haven: Yale University Southeast Asian Studies, 1983).

of Vietnamese guerrillas, including Cambodia. The American intrusion broke the delicate bargain that Prince Sihanouk and the Vietnamese communists had struck. The consequences, as we know, were appalling in the short term and catastrophic in the long term when in 1975 the Khmer Rouge finally seized power in Cambodia.

Cambodians after 1975 experienced the most brutal of times that came to a conclusion only when Vietnam moved in and completely occupied Cambodia late in 1978. Shortly after, China invaded Vietnam—ostensibly to punish it for occupying one of China's allies. Vietnam, however, did not withdraw from Cambodia until 1985, leaving three principal actors—Cambodian communists, Royalist Conservatives and Khmer Rouge—in control of a devastated country. Into this breach was introduced the idea of achieving peace through multiparty free and fair elections conducted under the aegis of the United Nations.[40] Two major steps were necessary to bring the three antagonists together for talks. A conference convened by the Japanese government was held in Tokyo in 1990, offering as incentives the promise of official development assistance once peace had been achieved. They came and talked, setting the stage for the subsequent Geneva conference. At Geneva, terms of peace were agreed upon and preparations made for mediation by the United Nations.[41]

The United Nations Transitional Authority in Cambodia (UNTAC) occupied and ruled Cambodia until a freely elected reconciliation government was formed. The UNTAC was the most ambitious such undertaking in the history of the UN, involving an investment of $2 billion, the deployment of 16,000 troops and over 3,000 police officers, and the dispatch of 3,000 civilian officials who assumed control of key ministries. It was successful in achieving both the traditional UN functions of peacekeeping—disarmament and repatriation of refugees—as well as helping construct the basis of a functioning democratic system, including supervision and monitoring of elections, political mediation, and reconstruction of key institutions.

What was the role of the United States in all this? It is important to remember that the UNTAC emerged in the wake of the cold war and the Gulf war.[42] The latter, we should recall, was a coalition military campaign led by the United States and legitimized by various United Nations resolutions. The US role in the Gulf was direct. The US was also the dominant partner in the coalition, providing the intelligence, the leadership and the firepower that finally pushed Iraq out of Kuwait. In Cambodia, of course, the situation on the ground was quite different and the tools needed to do the job quite different

[40] For the history leading to and beyond the UNTAC, see Michael W. Doyle and Robert C. Orr (eds), *Keeping the Peace: Lessons from Multidimensional UN Operations in Cambodia and El Salvador* (Cambridge: Cambridge University Press, 1997).

[41] Larry Diamond, 'Promoting Democracy in the 1990s: Actors, Instruments, and Issues', in Axel Hadenius (ed.), *Democracy's Victory and Crisis* (Cambridge: Cambridge University Press, 1997), pp. 311–76.

[42] Lawrence Freedman and Efraim Karsh, *The Gulf Conflict: Diplomacy and War in the New World Order, 1990–1991* (London: Faber and Faber, 1993).

too. The UNTAC was a genuine multinational coalition task force whose purpose was not to fight but to foster reconciliation and help build a coalition government in Cambodia. Moreover, whereas the US role was direct in the Gulf war, in Cambodia it was indirect. Indeed, in Cambodia the United States delegated substantial power and authority to the United Nations to do the job.

Occurring at a time of great optimism in the immediate aftermath of the cold war, both the Gulf war and the UNTAC represented important, possibly brilliant, innovations of the last remaining superpower. The US approach in this period might be summed up in the following way: use force only when necessary; seek allies when large-scale involvement of US military forces is required; only deploy force legitimized through the United Nations; use force only for limited periods of time; and delegate power and authority to the United Nations when such delegation is deemed feasible and desirable. It certainly worked in the case of the Gulf; and under difficult circumstances in Cambodia it also achieved some results.

However, the problems in Cambodia were enormous and illustrated only too clearly the difficulties outsiders would have in establishing democratic forms in countries where democratic norms were virtually non-existent. Here we simply sketch in the bare details to make the point clearer than the truth.

After several years of uneasy truce between the various political parties, in 1997 a mini-*coup d'état* took place, with Hun Sen, second prime minister, ousting Ranariddh, first prime minister. The Japanese government requested that Hun Sen restore the coalition government. Hun Sen in turn requested that the Japanese government provide assistance in order to conduct free and fair multiparty elections. The Japanese government agreed to do so. Parliamentary elections were then held in July 1998 under the supervision of a United Nations team and with the financial assistance of a few countries, including Japan.[43] According to the electoral watchdog group, Committee for Free and Fair Elections in Cambodia, the Cambodian People's Party headed by Hun Sen won 41.1 per cent of the votes, the royalist Funcinpec party headed by Prince Norodom Ranariddh 32.2 per cent, and the Sam Rainsy party headed by Sam Rainsy 14.4 per cent. Although the People's Party controlled the electoral process with security forces placed at the grass-roots level, its performance improved by only 3 per cent on the 1993 UNTAC-supervised election. The major difference from the 1993 race was that the Khmer Rouge did not stand. Hun Sen then pressured the other two parties to acknowledge the results and to join a unified government. The other two parties, however, refused to accept the results because they found evidence of massive fraud. As a result, Cambodia was not admitted to the Association of South-East Asian Nations (ASEAN) at ASEAN's summit in Hanoi in December 1998. Nevertheless, the World Bank, Japan and 16 other countries held the Third Consultative Group Meeting on Cambodia on 25–6 February 1999 in Tokyo and pledged new assistance of nearly $470 million.

---

[43] 'Nihon gaiko ichio no seika—Cambodia shonenba korekara' [Japan Achieves Results in Cambodia: The Real Test Is To Come], *Mainichi shimbun* (8 November 1997).

Money alone, however, could not reconstruct what years of war and devastation had wrought on what was, after all, a traditional society. Yet the investment overall by the international community should not be underestimated. Cambodia was in its own way most fortunate. The eyes of the world were upon it. The UN decided to use it a test case. Both China and Japan for different reasons had an interest in Cambodia. And perhaps the US felt it had something to prove as well. After all, it had been its actions in the first place that led, however indirectly, to the terrible tragedy there. Hence the enormous investment of its time, effort and money. But whether this particularly unique experiment in nation-building would ever be repeated elsewhere remained an open question.

Conclusion

In my survey of Asia-Pacific I began not with a description of the region, the more obvious issue of Asian values, the impact of the financial crisis on democratic change or even a discussion of why America might promote democracy at all, but with what I term 'the three legacies': the Westphalian, the Philadelphian, and the anti-utopian. The argument I have advanced is that the three frameworks compete with each other to shape and determine the course and content of US foreign policy, both generally and towards Asia Pacific. The United States, like any country, wants to boast of, and if possible to export, what it regards as its virtues. In antimony to the old, vice-ridden states of Europe, the United States started anew and devoted itself to the ideals of freedom, democracy, and equality. To this extent it was the first new nation to develop a Philadelphian framework where binding and hiding were the key modalities, as opposed to the Westphalian where balancing and bandwagonning were the assumed norms. In many ways, the legacy of Philadelphia—with its stress on shared values, common rules, international agreements, the promotion of mutually advantageous commerce and increasing interdependence between nations—lives on and continues to shape American relations with the outside word in general and Asia-Pacific in particular.

Yet we saw that, in its dealings with China and Japan, the Westphalian framework still seems to be robust. Power remains at the heart of these relationships. But a substantial loosening of the criteria whereby a state is regarded as 'normal' in the Westphalian framework has taken place with the emergence of a series of failed or failing states. Cambodia is an excellent and tragic testimony to this. This complicates the situation for a Philadelphian actor like the United States. A Philadelphian actor must behave on the basis of universal principles and shared democratic norms and values, yet these values obviously cannot flourish where there are states in an advanced state of disintegration. The Philadelphian framework compels the United States, the founder of the framework, to act and not allow such states to 'stew in their own juice'. Global governance is expected to have a human face after all. However, translating fine ideas into practice can sometimes be very difficult. For one thing, it is very costly. America may also not have the will to act, especially if it involves the use of US troops abroad. The US may indeed have the power. But as long as the world remains a complex place—and the number of failed states keeps on rising—it would be naïve to think that it will promote democracy everywhere. It will continue to face multidimensional encounters of many kinds and more often than not it will fail to achieve what it wants; now and for the foreseeable future there will be suboptimal outcomes despite its overwhelming position of preponderance in the international system.

13

The Impasse of Third World Democratization: Africa Revisited

GEORG SØRENSEN

Introduction

WITH the end of the cold war came a period of massive and profound optimism concerning the prospects for democracy in the Third World. As the twentieth century gave way to the twenty first, things looked less bright. Are we in the early stages of a comprehensive setback for democracy in the Third World? What has been the role of Western countries in the processes of political transition? This chapter begins with an overview of achievements and shortcomings of democratization processes in the Third World. I demonstrate that many Third World countries have experienced the opening stages of a transition process to democracy. I go on to argue that a large number of them are stuck in the initial phases of a democratic transition. No comprehensive setback for democracy is likely, but there are no prospects for any substantial democratic progress either.

My discussion focuses on Africa. Although the process of democratization is by nature first and foremost a domestic, internal affair, international actors have contributed to this unfortunate outcome. My attempt to spell this out focuses on three factors: (1) the failure to appreciate the role of nationalism and political community; (2) the overemphasis on liberalism, first economic—reliance on the market—and then political—reliance on the ballot box and accountability; and (3) the emphasis on elitism, that is, the tendency to support elite-dominated democracies. Some of the problems are related to national interests. Western countries pursue their own agenda, irrespective of the broader consequences for democracy. But some of them are also related to the inability of research to properly spell out what the best policies and most appropriate measures are. Indeed, research on governance and development appears to move in odd phases that are more contradictory than cumulative. A few years ago, the emphasis was on a strong, developmental state and, in view of the east Asian success stories, it was implied that such a state was also 'soft authoritarian'. Now the emphasis is on democracy and accountability and it is implied that democracy—as defined below—creates a stronger, more developmentalist state.

In examining the travails of democracy in the Third World, this chapter is a contribution to the 'transitology' research on democratization processes. Within that general context, it aims mainly to discuss the relationship between processes of democratization and processes of state strengthening, that is, the creation of states that are more developmentalist, better capable of pursuing economic and social development. It is an underlying assumption that, without this connection between democratization and increased state strength, the development of democracy itself will be severely constrained. As for terminology, I employ the standard definition of democracy developed by Robert Dahl. Political democracy is a system of government that meets the following conditions:

(1) meaningful and extensive competition among individuals and organized groups—especially political parties—for all effective positions of government power, at regular intervals and excluding the use of force;
(2) a highly inclusive level of political participation in the selection of leaders and policies, at least through regular and fair elections, such that no major adult social group is excluded; and
(3) a level of civil and political liberties—freedom of expression, freedom of the press, freedom to form and join organizations—sufficient to ensure the integrity of political competition and participation.[1]

A reasonable operationalization of this definition is made in the index employed by Freedom House. Despite some caveats[2] and the critique by Bollen,[3] that index therefore provides us with a reasonable starting point for looking at democracy's progress.

Democracy at Century's End

The 1997 Freedom House survey of independent countries with more than one million inhabitants identified 49 countries as free. When countries with fewer than one million inhabitants were included—bringing the total number of states in the world to 191—the survey classified 79 countries as free, 59 as partly free, and another 53 as not free.[4]

Comments on an earlier draft of this paper from Jørgen Elklit and Mette Kjær are gratefully acknowledged.

[1] Larry Diamond, Juan J. Linz, and Seymour Martin Lipset (eds), *Democracy in Developing Countries. 2: Africa* (Boulder: Lynne Rienner, 1988), p. xvi. The three conditions have been reduced from the eight set out by Robert A. Dahl in *Polyarchy: Participation and Opposition* (New Haven: Yale University Press, 1971), p. 3.

[2] Georg Sørensen, *Democracy and Democratization* (Boulder: Westview Press, 1993, 1998), p.17.

[3] Kenneth Bollen, 'Liberal Democracy: Validity and Method Factors in Cross-National Measures', *American Journal of Political Science*, 37/4 (1993), pp. 1207–30.

[4] Adrian Karatnycky, 'Freedom in the World: The Annual Survey of Political Rights and Civil Liberties 1996–97', in *Freedom Review*, 28/1 (New York: Freedom House, 1997), pp. 3–12.

The question whether such numbers constitute great democratic progress is rather like the question whether the glass is half full or half empty. Yes, the glass is half full: there has been democratic progress in the past two decades. The democratic transitions began in southern Europe in the 1970s; they came to include Latin America in the early 1980s, and then eastern Europe, Africa, as well as parts of Asia in the late 1980s and early 1990s. There are more countries today than ever before with some measure of democracy. We may also note the ideological popularity of democracy. 'Never in recorded history', Robert Dahl wrote in 1989, 'have state leaders appealed so widely to democratic ideas to legitimate their rule',[5] and the trend in this direction has grown even stronger since then. Theorists who were earlier critical of democracy's potential now see it as the way forward; for example, a well-known Latin American scholar recently proclaimed that 'democracy is the only path which Latin American countries can follow to modernity'.[6] This statement is all the more remarkable when one recalls that a widespread mistrust of political democracy had been prevalent in earlier periods among the popular forces in Latin America. In Africa, the one-party system is no longer supported as the ideal framework for consensual decision-making and for the promotion of economic and social development. Finally, in eastern Europe, people no longer accept the old official position that political leadership by what was understood to be the party of the masses, the Communist Party, is infinitely more democratic than liberal democracy operating in a capitalist society. There appears to be only one major ideological opponent to the dominant idea of political democracy, and that is Islam, although the authoritarian project in China also should be mentioned.

In sum, the idea of democracy is presently very strong at the global ideological level. Very few authoritarian rulers would actively defend traditional, authoritarian modes of rule—North Korea and Iraq are possible examples. In the large majority of cases, authoritarianism is justified with reference to its supposedly positive sides of creating, for example, order, stability, growth, and welfare. The 'Tocqueville factor'—the ruling elite's loss of belief in its own right to rule—is therefore at work on a global level; very few dictators believe that they have an inherent legitimate right to be dictators. As one observer recently noted, 'to live under autocracy, or even to *be* an autocrat, seems backward, uncivilized, distasteful, not quite *comme il faut*—in a word, "uncool"'.[7]

Yet it is also clear that the glass is half empty: much of the democratic progress is only frail and shallow, a thin veil over political and social structures and institutions which have changed little since the days of authoritarianism. One scholar has reiterated a distinction made between the shallow 'electoral democracies' and the more democratically developed 'liberal democracies'.[8]

---

[5] Robert A. Dahl, *Democracy and Its Critics* (New Haven: Yale University Press, 1989), p. 313.

[6] Francisco C. Weffort, 'A America errada', *Lua Nova*, 21 (1990), p. 39.

[7] Ghia Nadia, 'How Different are Postcommunist Transitions?', *Journal of Democracy*, 7/4 (1996), pp. 15–29.

[8] Larry Diamond, 'Is the Third Wave Over?', *Journal of Democracy*, 7/3 (1996), pp. 20–38. For an earlier introduction to this, see T. Louise Brown, *The Challenge to Democracy in Nepal* (London: Routledge, 1996).

'Electoral democracies' may hold periodic elections and thus demonstrate some measure of political competition, participation, and liberty. But parts of the population are most often kept out of the political process; the military and other important sections of states power are frequently closed off from democratic control; the media may be non-free; the courts may be corrupt and ineffective; and so forth. In short, elections take place, but democracy has not developed in most other respects. Examples of 'electoral democracies' are Brazil, Burkina Faso, Congo, El Salvador, Indonesia, Kenya, Malaysia, Russia, Tanzania, Turkey, Ukraine, and Zambia.

While the number of 'electoral democracies' has increased steadily, the number of more developed 'liberal democracies' has remained almost unchanged. There were 76 'liberal democracies' in 1991 and 79 in 1996.[9] In other words, elections are held in many countries, but the process of democratization is not moving forward; at the same time, the quality of democracy has deteriorated in a number of countries with a long-term democratic experience: Venezuela, Colombia, India, and Sri Lanka. In sum, many of the current democratizations are of a restricted, elite-dominated variety: what Terry Lynn Karl has called 'frozen democracies', unwilling to carry out substantive reforms that address the lot of the poor majorities.[10] Take Latin America, where one scholar has recently emphasized how the democratic transitions are developing into a hybrid form of democratic authoritarian system which he calls 'market authoritarianism'. In this system the 'trappings of formal democracy are retained and the tenets of market economics . . . are generally followed. But in response to mounting social unrest, rule is more by decree than consent, media critical of government is bullied, and power is maintained through corruption, intimidation and, ultimately, by force'.[11]

Economic reforms have worked in Latin America in that they have brought some measure of stability and lower inflation; in that sense, the fundamental economic outlook is hopeful. But, as one observer has stressed, 'the poor cannot eat fundamentals'.[12] Income gaps are widening, the absolute number of people living in poverty is increasing, real wages have fallen, and unemployment is higher than in 1990. An authoritarian takeover by the military is not likely. But military and police forces continue to hold privileged positions in the region; spending on security exceeds total welfare spending; and political control of the military remains insufficient. Most courts are corrupt and inefficient and in many Latin American countries groups of police are a source of threat rather than a source of protection for the population.

[9] Diamond, 'Is the Third Wave Over?'.
[10] Terry Lynn Karl, 'Dilemmas of Democratization in Latin America', *Comparative Politics*, 23/1 (1990), pp. 1–21.
[11] Douglas W. Payne, 'Latin America and the Caribbean: Storm Warnings', in Roger Kaplan, Adrian Karatnycky, Jill Crawford, Charles Graybow, Christopher Kean, Thomar R. Lanser, Douglas W. Payne, Arach Puddington, Leonard R. Sussman, and George Zarycky, *Freedom in the World: The Annual Survey of Political Rights and Civil Liberties 1995-96* (New York: Freedom House, 1996), pp. 77–84.
[12] *The Economist* (30 November–6 December 1996), p. 24.

Elite domination and increasing popular despair also characterize eastern Europe and, in particular, Russia. The old communist elites, the *nomenklatura*, have not blocked economic and political reforms. Instead, they have chosen another strategy: to exploit old positions and networks in transforming themselves into the new, market-oriented economic and political elite. Instead of preventing reforms, the old elites are swimming with the tide and surfacing as owners of newly privatized companies, often acquired cheaply with the help of old friends. The old elite also continues to dominate state bureaucracies and in recent years it has regained political power with the help of newly formed non-communist parties. Why do people vote for former communists? Because the communists promise to make people rich: 'they represent success: more than any other identifiable social group in eastern Europe, they are seen to have achieved the most in the new regime'.[13] Old communists no longer represent the past; they represent the successful capitalist future. What then is the problem? Is it not the ideal situation that the forces of the past are becoming the architects of the future? The problem is that only few of the new entrepreneurs are bearers of traditional capitalist virtues such as hard work, honesty, and responsibility: instead, they form a 'corrupt business class which is intimately intertwined with a corrupt political class'. The result is a form of 'robust private entrepreneurship, an enormous grey market, and large companies—some state-owned, some privately owned—which enjoy deeply corrupt relationships with powerful politicians. Various forms of criminal mafia will dominate some parts of the region; politicians will come to "represent" various business interests, as they clearly do already, particularly in Russia'.[14]

There are some positive elements in this otherwise gloomy picture of eastern Europe. Economic and political relations with western Europe are developing rapidly. The attraction of closer cooperation with the European Union will help prevent any across-the-board deterioration of democratic conditions. In that sense eastern Europe's external environment is conducive to democracy. That is not the situation in south and east Asia. In China, economic growth rates remain high, but corruption among political and economic elites is an increasingly severe problem. Political repression of any dissident voice is swift and severe, including numerous executions. Corruption is a main problem in many other countries in the region as well, including Thailand, the Philippines, and Indonesia.

India has experimented with market oriented economic reforms in recent years and that has led to some increased economic dynamism. But benefits have not reached the 400 million Indians who are poor. The resulting popular discontent is being tapped by Hindu nationalist parties, leading to political fragmentation and bitter communal violence. India will not disintegrate, as some very weak African states have, but Indian democracy has suffered in the

---

[13] Anne Applebaum, 'Central Europe: Nice Guys Finish Last', in Kaplan *et al.*, *Freedom in the World*, pp. 14–22.

[14] Applebaum, 'Central Europe: Nice Guys Finish Last', p. 19.

process and political life in several Indian States is dominated by militant groups or even by criminal gangs, as in the case of Bihar.

The most spectacular setbacks for early and frail democratic openings have occurred in sub-Saharan Africa, where ethnic violence in some cases has led to the breakdown, not merely of embryonic democracy, but also of state authority as such, as in Rwanda and Somalia. In several cases, the fragile democratic opening has itself fuelled violent conflict, as will be discussed below. In many African countries, the new, weak parliaments tend to become merely additional participants in the old, authoritarian systems of personal rule. It should be emphasized, however, that with the exception of some African countries there has not been any comprehensive decay of democracy. This is true also on a more general level, encompassing the Third World and eastern Europe. We are not facing a general relapse into authoritarianism; the problem is rather one of democratic consolidation, as a very large number of the current transitions have run aground in the shallow waters of 'electoral democracy'. External actors bear some substantial responsibility for this unfortunate state of affairs.

The Role of Outsiders in the Democratization Process

There are two principal views on the role of outsiders in the democratization process in the Third World. The first is that democracy is basically a domestic affair and so there is very little that outsiders can do about it, one way or the other. The second view is that most weak Third World countries are the puppets of stronger states in the North; the strong therefore heavily influence not only the economic and social structures and processes of the weak but also the political. There is some truth in both views. But a longer historical perspective on the issue would be helpful. What is 'domestic' or 'internal' as opposed to 'international' or 'external' is not an historical given. Most Third World countries acquired their domestic spheres at the time of independence, of decolonization. Before that, they were part of the domestic spheres of their colonial motherlands. That experience left them with features more or less conducive to the pursuit of democracy. Liberal modernization theory normally stresses the positive legacy: some local industry and infrastructure; an education system; machinery for upholding order; an institutional structure; some basic rule of law; and a constitution which contained democratic values—Latin America, colonized by non-democratic Spain and Portugal, is of course an exception here. Radical dependency theory stresses the destructive elements of the colonial legacy: a distorted economic infrastructure, geared to the demands of the motherland; a hierarchical political system directed at control and surveillance, not at any form of democracy; and an institutional structure aimed at order and repression, not at participation and pluralism. The blend of 'constructive' and 'destructive' elements in the colonial legacy, of course, varies across countries. Robert Pinkney has provided a very helpful overview of these variations in colonial rule as seen from the perspective of democratization.[15]

The advent of decolonization is often downplayed in radical analyses, which argue that economic dependence continues exactly as before and the state institutions of the newly independent countries remain under foreign influence. This contention is profoundly misleading. Formal independence—that is, juridical sovereignty—is of the utmost importance. At the moment of independence a new political, economic, social, and cultural sphere is created which has a substantial amount of autonomy. External forces can still influence the domestic sphere, of course, but they operate under different conditions. On the one hand, there is a new need to find domestic allies—which implies some sort of bargaining situation between insiders and outsiders. On the other hand, interventions in sovereign states cannot be conducted in complete ignorance of the rules of international society. After all, the basic norm of juridical sovereignty is non-intervention, which means that acts of intervention have to be justified. So in both the domestic and the international spheres the rules of the game change in ways which provide increased autonomy to domestic actors.

After the advent of independence, external actors can either help or hinder democracy and democratization in specific countries. External actors have done both, and a debate has arisen, similar to the one about colonialism, over which impact—help or hindrance—has been dominant. The current consensus on the issue appears to be this: during the cold war, the superpowers were first and foremost looking for allies in the Third World, caring little whether their partners were democratic of not. The logic of power and national interest prevailed: 'he's a son of a bitch, but he's our son of a bitch.' That logic could lead to US support for non-democracy in Chile, Guatemala, Zaire—now Congo—and elsewhere. That the Soviet Union would support non-democracy in the Third World was less surprising given its own status as a totalitarian dictatorship.

The end of the cold war has strengthened a trend already under way in US policy for some years: to emphasize support for democratization and human rights. This goes hand in hand with a general tendency in international society to upgrade support for liberal values. Radical critics deny that this is a real change, and see it merely as a fresh tactic employed by imperialist forces whose goals remain unchanged: subordination and control of the Third World.[16] I think there is more to it, including a real intention to promote liberal values, although such policies are not conducted in a completely unselfish manner—I am not aware of any examples of national policies which have that quality. One problem in this context is that it is easier for external forces to prevent, hinder or block a democratization than to encourage, promote,

---

[15] Robert Pinkney, *Democracy in the Third World* (Buckingham: Open University Press, 1993), pp. 42–3.

[16] For example, David Moore, 'Reading Americans on Democracy in Africa: From CIA to "Good Governance"', *European Journal of Development Research*, 8/1 (1996), pp. 123–49.

preserve and protect it; the negative job is easier for outsiders than the positive one. What follows is not an attempt to analyse the support for democratization in empirical detail. Instead, I want to examine three factors which are below the surface of everyday policy implementation even though they significantly influence the ways it is conducted. The first factor is nationalism; the second is variants of liberalism; and the third is elitism. The aim of the exercise is to establish a connection between these factors and the lack of democratic progress in the Third World, as diagnosed above.

Nationalism: Promoting and Obstructing Democracy

If nationalism is a bond of loyalty among the people that constitute a nation, then some measure of nationalism is a necessary precondition for democratization. That is because the nationalist bond of loyalty is the glue which ties the people inside the state's territory together; it helps create the minimum of national unity which is at the core of the political community that is the nation. As spelled out in Rustow's classic model, national unity simply indicates that 'the vast majority of citizens in a democracy-to-be . . . have no doubt or mental reservations as to which political community they belong to'.[17] There may well be ethnic or other cleavages between groups in the population; it is only when such divisions lead to basic questioning of national unity and political community that the problem must be resolved before a transition to democracy becomes feasible. National unity was an issue in India and Pakistan and is an issue today in the Third World, in particular in Africa. The problem is also present in Russia and Bosnia. Democratization demands a settling of the national question: who are the nations that are going to democratize?

The issue will emerge elsewhere as well. For example, in China any process of democratization will have to settle the problem of Tibet's claim to autonomy. The question is also relevant for established democracies that have to confront crises concerning their national unity and political community: If these matters are not resolved in a democratic manner, the result will be the breakdown of democracy combined with repression of the minority group, or even civil war, as in the cases of Sudan, Sri Lanka, and Chechnya.

Political community was created in Europe with the help of nationalism over an extended period of time. Territory came first; the state-building elites first consolidated control over a territory and only in a later phase came the construction of a nation. This building of a national community was helped by two factors, one material the other non-material. The material factor was the welfare, security, and order provided by the state; the non-material factor was the idea of national community provided by mythology, interpretations of history, and ideology. Put differently, political community is based on two types of legitimacy: vertical legitimacy—the connection between state and

---

[17] Dankwart A. Rustow, 'Transitions to Democracy', *Comparative Politics*, 2/3 (1970), pp. 337–65 at 350.

society, the notion that the state elite and its institutions have a right to rule—and horizontal legitimacy—defining the membership and the boundaries of the political community of people.[18] The nationalism of the nation-state thus contains two different elements of nationalism which coexist in harmony: a territorially based idea of *Gesellschaft*, the association of citizens within defined borders; and the ethnic idea of *Gemeinschaft*, the community of people defined by the nation.

The European idea of the nation-state was exported to the Third World. My discussion of this will focus on Africa, the region with the most severe problems in terms of political community, even though there are also serious problems in the Balkans. African states were created from the outside by colonial powers; Resolution 1514 of the United Nations Declaration on the Granting of Independence to Colonial Countries and Peoples adopted in 1960 emphasized that 'all peoples have the right to self-determination'. But note that 'peoples' does not mean communities of people such as nations. It means the territorial entities that were the colonies. Independence meant independence for the colonial territories, upholding colonial borders. The people inside those borders were communities only in the sense that they shared a border drawn by others. Their idea of nationalism was a negative one: get rid of the colonizers. When that project succeeded, there was no positive notion of community left over. Political elites made attempts to construct such a notion, such as Nyerere's *Ujamaa* socialism, Kenyatta's *Harambee*, and Mobutu's *authenticité*.[19] There was some measure of success in a few countries, but in general the project was a huge failure: it was extremely difficult to knit together diverse ethnic groups with different languages, beliefs, and ways of living. And the state elites quickly gave up trying. What emerged instead was, in Christopher Clapham's terminology, 'monopoly states':

Confronted by weak administrative structures, fragile economies, and in some cases dangerous sources of domestic opposition, political leaders sought to entrench themselves in power by using the machinery of state to suppress or coopt any rival organization—be it an opposition party, a trades union, or even a major corporation. Rather than acknowledging the weakness of their position, and accepting the limitations on their power which this imposed, they chose to up the stakes and went for broke.[20]

It was abundantly clear that these clientelist systems lacked 'the capacity to create any sense of moral community amongst those who participate in them, let alone among those who are excluded'.[21] Therefore, political community was not created, neither in the *Gesellschaft* nor in the *Gemeinschaft* sense. The communities that prevailed were the different ethnic sub-groups which

---

[18] Cf. Kalevi J. Holsti, *The State, War, and the State of War* (Cambridge: Cambridge University Press, 1996).

[19] Liisa Laakso and Adebayo O. Olukoshi, 'The Crisis of the Post-Colonial Nation-State Project in Africa', in Liisa Laakso and Adebayo O. Olukoshi (eds), *Challenges to the Nation-State in Africa* (Uppsala: Nordic Africa Institute, 1996), pp. 7–40.

[20] Christopher Clapham, *Africa and the International System: The Politics of State Survival* (Cambridge: Cambridge University Press, 1996), p. 57.

[21] Clapham, *Africa and the International System*, p. 59.

competed for access to state power and resources, sometimes building frail alliances amongst each other.

It is extremely difficult, if not impossible, to graft democracy upon countries lacking political community. On the one hand, if an election is to be seen as legitimate, then the state must clearly be seen as legitimate; but that is rarely the case in Africa, where there is a lack of horizontal legitimacy because of the absence of both the material and the non-material factors that created legitimacy in Europe. On the other hand, political liberalization opens more, not less, conflict in society because of the lack of horizontal legitimacy.[22]

The problem has not been properly confronted by Western politicians and researchers. For several years after independence, it was believed that the general process of modernization in all spheres of society would take care of the problem. The belief was predicated on the notion that 'all good things go together'; modernization in one area would positively influence modernization in other areas. Eventually, modernization would root out the traditional, backward-looking values and attitudes. There are two problems with this view; on the one hand, it overestimates the synergetic effects of modernization; on the other hand, it downplays the extent to which the so-called 'traditional' baggage has a role to play in the building of political community.

In research, the modernization view of the 1950s and 1960s was put on the defensive by dependency theory. The latter had little to offer, however, in analysing the political community and nationalism issue in the Third World. It was more or less assumed that a severing of the ties to the old colonial master, the metropolis, would take care of the problem. In real politics, the problem was overshadowed by the priorities of bipolar competition. In much of 1980s, Western politics and research converged on the idea that a weakening of the state and a strengthening of the market would take care of the problem. That notion has not been validated by events and in the 1990s a more nuanced view has finally emerged in both politics and research, perhaps because the fragile processes of democratization have exposed the issue. At the same time, this new realism is accompanied by serious doubts as to whether a number of countries, especially in sub-Saharan Africa, are really viable entities when the issue of political community is brought in.[23]

In sum, one of most serious problems hindering the process of democratic development in many Third World countries and especially in sub-Saharan Africa is the issue of political community and nationalism. Western politics and research have neglected the problem and currently appear to have few ideas about how to confront it in a serious way.

---

[22] E.g. Clapham, *Africa and the International System*; Holsti, *The State, War, and the State of War*; Edward Mansfield and Jack Snyder, 'Democratization and War', *International Security*, 20/1 (1995), pp. 5–38.

[23] Henry Bienen and Jeffrey Herbst, 'The Relationship between Political and Economic Reform in Africa', *Comparative Politics*, 29/1 (1996), pp. 23–42; Georg Sørensen, 'Development as a Hobbesian Dilemma', *Third World Quarterly*, 17/5 (1996), p. 903–16.

The Many Versions of Liberal Democracy

Liberal democracy is a big house with many rooms. This is due to the fact that liberalism developed in opposition to the medieval, hierarchical institutions, the despotic monarchies whose claim to absolute rule rested on the assertion that they enjoyed divine support. Liberalism attacked the old system on two fronts. First, the liberals fought for the rolling back of state power and the creation of a sphere of civil society where social relations, including private business and personal life, could evolve without state interference. An important element here was support for a market economy based on respect for private property. The second element of early liberalism was the claim that state power was based not on natural or supernatural rights but on the will of the sovereign people. Ultimately, this claim would lead to demands for democracy: that is, for the creation of mechanisms of representation that assured that those who held state power enjoyed popular support. The tradition that became liberal democracy was liberal first—aimed at restricting state power over civil society—and democratic later—aimed at creating structures that would secure a popular mandate for holders of state power. Even when the focus was on democracy, the liberals had various reservations. They feared that democracy would impede the establishment of a liberal society.[24]

In the context of promoting liberal democracy in the Third World, the liberal tradition has been carried forward by Western countries in three different models of liberal democracy, drawing upon different aspects of the liberal heritage. The first model stresses the strictly liberal elements of liberal democracy, that is, a limited role for the state in an economy guided by market principles and open to international exchange. That is the version of liberal democracy behind the first generation of structural adjustment programmes (SAPs), although the view is not expressed in these terms in the World Bank publications because the bank sees itself a neutral, non-political player. The state is viewed as a problem or a constraint rather than a positive player in economic, social and political development. The SAPs aimed to minimize the role of the state in society, liberalize markets, and privatize public enterprise. While the World Bank gave a qualified 'yes' to the question of whether adjustment was paying off in sub-Saharan Africa,[25] an editorial in *Codesria Bulletin* a few years earlier was in no doubt that the liberalization 'completely undermines Africa's sovereignty, [and] creates and/or further strengthens authoritarian regimes who will have to implement an inherently anti-democratic set of socioeconomic reforms entailed in the programmes'.[26] A similar debate has taken place concerning the use of SAPs in Latin America.

[24] Goran Therborn, 'The Rule of Capital and the Rise of Democracy', *New Left Review*, 103 (1977), pp. 3–41 at 3.

[25] World Bank, *Adjustment in Africa: Reforms, Results and the Road Ahead* (Oxford: Oxford University Press, 1994), p. 131.

[26] Quoted from J.-J. B. Barya, 'The New Political Conditionalities of Aid: An Independent View from Africa', paper delivered at an EADI conference on The New Political Conditionalities of Development Assistance (Vienna, 23–4 April 1992).

There appears to be little doubt that structural adjustment has had some positive effects in a number of cases, especially in improving the conditions for agricultural production. It is equally true that the balance between market and state had tipped too much in favour of the state in a number of countries; and adjustment can play a constructive corrective role in such cases. But most of the time, the possible beneficial effects tended to be cancelled out by the short- and medium-term negative effects of rapidly increasing prices, more unemployment, cutbacks in public services, and so on. We tend to get the 'market authoritarianism' mentioned above in addressing current democracy in Latin America: political and economic systems with some of the institutions and procedures of liberal democracy, but with very little to offer the poor majority whose everyday problems of mere survival remain a low priority on the political agenda.

The second model of liberal democracy that the West has supported put a greater emphasis on the political and participatory aspects of democracy. But in many cases, perhaps especially in Africa and some parts of Asia, the focus has been on the notion of holding free and fair elections rather than on the broader political, cultural and institutional transformation connected with a process of democratization. There is no doubt than holding free and fair elections is an important element in a transition to democracy. But as an isolated event, the election should be only the tip of the democratic iceberg. If it is not closely connected with deeper rooted changes it does not mean very much. There is ample evidence of this from the African scene.[27] With the introduction of multiparty systems, swarms of political parties have been formed. They are most often separated along ethnic lines and led by individuals with no clear ideological visions but with ambitions of becoming strongmen in their own right, controlling their own political patron-client networks. Thus, 1,800 candidates from 26 political parties ran for election in Benin, a country of four million inhabitants. Fourteen candidates were on the ballot for the presidential election. Ninety-six parties requested registration in Zaire—now Congo—when liberalisation made that possible. In other words, democratic openings can easily result in tugs-of-war along ethnic lines in the fierce competition for the vacant seats of the strongmen.

In other cases, incumbent leaders have preempted the new winds of democracy and have succeeded staying in power by holding quick elections. The situation in Côte d'Ivoire provides an example. Felix Houphet-Boigny, who had been president for several decades, took the opposition by surprise in 1990 by quickly giving in to its demands for open presidential and legislative elections. In a country where there had not been opposition activity for 30 years, 26 political groups were summoned by the president and told about the forthcoming elections. Opposition requests for a delay in order to gain time for getting organized were rejected; the argument was that the demand for instant elections came from the opposition itself. As a result, the election could be

---

[27] These remarks draw on Georg Sørensen, *Democracy and Democratization* (Boulder: Westview Press, 1993, 1998).

controlled by the president's own party, which also had a large measure of control over the media. Both the president and his party scored comfortable victories at the elections.

Against this background, one may speculate whether the current pressure from Western donors for multiparty systems and political democracy in Africa can have counterproductive effects. The Western countries themselves are examples of the fact that democracy cannot be installed overnight; it is a long-term process of gradual change. When quick fixes of imposing multiparty systems, for example, are substituted for the long haul of patiently paving the way for a democratic polity, the result may be that a thin democratic coating is superimposed on a system of personal rule without major changes in the basic features of the old structure. According to Marina Ottaway, Western countries have tended to interpret democratization

very narrowly as the holding of elections, and the sooner the better. But elections, or the prospect of elections, are highly destabilizing in countries threatened with collapse . . . Elections appear to be the wrong place whence to start a process of democratization in a collapsing, conflict-ridden state. In recent years, African elections have typically been organized in a hurry, in some cases before parties had time to consolidate or armed movements had agreed to disarm. As a result, losers have found it easy to reject election results, and voters had little choice but to vote on the basis of ethnic or religious identity . . . Elections held under wrong conditions can be a real setback for democratization.[28]

The other major drawback of a democratization which focuses on elections is that there is little change for the better in the economic policies of the new regimes. A recent analysis found that

elections may actually increase the use of patronage . . . Traditional patron-client relations have often been critical in winning recent elections, indicating that the nature of African politics has not changed despite the new liberalization. Ghana, Nigeria, and Kenya have all reported massive overspending as governments sought to reward traditional supporters, notably members of particular ethnic groups and civil servants, to smooth the transition process or gain votes . . . The particular circumstances of political liberalization in Africa cause leaders' horizons to be relatively short and therefore induce particular strategies such as clientelism which may be unnecessary where democratic structures are more institutionalized.[29]

For such reasons, several scholars have stressed the need for the establishment of order, stability, and civility in the African political systems. Otherwise, democracy runs the risk of degenerating into a caricature, the direct opposite

[28] Marina Ottaway, 'Democratization in Collapsed States', in I. William Zartman (ed.), *Collapsed States: The Disintegration and Restoration of Legitimate Authority* (Boulder: Lynne Rienner, 1995), pp. 235–51 at 245. For a similar view, see Robert A. Dahl, 'Democracy and Human Rights under Different Conditions of Development', in Asbjørn Eide and Bernt Hagtvet (eds), *Human Rights in Perspective* (Oxford: Blackwell, 1992), pp. 235–52; and Jørgen Elklit, 'Is the Degree of Electoral Democracy Measurable?', in David Beetham (ed.), *Defining and Measuring Democracy* (London: Sage, 1994), pp. 89–111.

[29] Bienen and Herbst, 'The Relationship between Political and Economic Reform in Africa', pp. 38–9.

of what it claims to be in theory. According to one analysis, democracy has deteriorated in this way in Nigeria, a country of more than 100 million people. Corruption among politicians has swelled due to the country's income from the export of oil, creating a political climate 'in which the democratic control of the government was regarded by politicians of all parties as a license to plunder the state'.[30] Recent developments tell a similar story. The Nigerian military annulled the 1993 elections and took over once again. The military remains in power by feeding on revenues from the country's oil and gas reserves and through violent repression and rampant corruption.

Given the problems with the 'market model' and the 'election model' of democracy, a third model is currently gaining ground in Western theory and practice. It takes a broader view of the political and economic issues at stake in that it combines ideas about a state that is democratic in the sense of being responsive, legitimate, and under the rule of law, with ideas about a strong, developmentalist state, better capable of promoting economic and social development. This is a fresh turn in Western thinking; many observers used to see strong, developmentalist states as basically undemocratic, citing the experience of the authoritarian developmentalist states in east Asia—South Korea and Taiwan—as empirical evidence. The tone of this debate was set by Chalmers Johnson's emphasis on the need for 'soft authoritarianism', which could provide political stability and order; the idea is that political pluralism which might challenge the goals of the developmental elite must be avoided. Japan showed the way in this respect, in displaying 'an extremely strong and comparatively unsupervised state administration, single-party rule for more than three decades, and a set of economic priorities that seems unattainable under true political pluralism during such a long period'.[31]

Yet is was never quite clear that authoritarianism was a necessary element in a developmentalist state.[32] And comparative analysis could quickly reveal that the special conditions surrounding a 'soft authoritarian' developmentalist state in east Asia were not present elsewhere, least of all in Africa. In other words, any attempt to make a general claim on the basis of the east Asian experience that authoritarianism will invariably help create a strong developmentalist state must be rejected. The different variants of 'soft' and 'hard' authoritarianism found in Africa, Latin America, and south Asia have all failed to help generate a developmentalist state.[33]

Against this background, more recent thinking among both scholars and practitioners in the West focuses on the combination of the merits of a strong, developmentalist state and a more democratic, responsive state. This comes to

---

[30] Robert H. Jackson and Carl Rosberg, 'Democracy in Tropical Africa: Democracy Versus Autocracy in African Politics', *Journal of International Affairs*, 38/2 (1985), p. 301.

[31] Chalmers Johnson, 'Political Institutions and Economic Performance: The Government Business Relationship in Japan, South Korea, and Taiwan', in Fred C. Deyo (ed.), *The Political Economy of New Asian Industrialism* (Ithaca: Cornell University Press, 1987), pp. 136–65 at 137.

[32] Clive Hamilton, 'Can the Rest of Asia Emulate the NICs?', *Third World Quarterly*, 9/4 (1987), pp. 1225–56; H. Baeg Im, 'The Rise of Bureaucratic Authoritarianism in South Korea', *World Politics*, 39/2 (1987), pp. 231–58.

[33] Sørensen, *Democracy and Democratization*.

the fore, for example, in the recent work by Merilee Grindle. According to her analysis, a strong state in the developmentalist sense has the following capacities: institutional capacity; technical capacity; administrative capacity; and political capacity, where the latter includes legitimate authority and responsive and representative government.[34] A similar view, in most respects, emerges in the most recent World Bank report on the state in a changing world:[35] the bottom line of the analysis is that the state needs to be effective as well as responsive, that is, developmentalist and democratic.

I believe that this time Western sources must at least be credited for getting the analysis right: it is necessary to push state effectiveness and democratic responsiveness simultaneously. Finding powerful ways of doing so, however, is no easy task. The current agenda of 'good governance' appears to have several deficiencies in this respect, because it continues to scratch the institutional surface and not address the underlying problems.[36] And in the short and medium run, the 'effectiveness' part of good governance—cutbacks in public employment, controls on expenditure, and so forth—can work against the 'legitimacy' part of more responsive government. According to one observer, the alternative to governance is to

look at the roots of legitimacy—the acknowledged right to command—both of states and institutions, without the fallacious assumption that certain institutions will always be seen as legitimate. The fundamental arbiter of state power is the strong identity of the citizen with the state. Without a strong sense of loyalty from followers, a leader's actions, goals and policies are not supported unless they are to the direct, clear and personal benefit of the follower . . . Throughout much of Africa, the level of aggregation into groups willing to give some amount of disinterested support to a leader is far lower than that of the whole state.[37]

In one sense, this takes us back to the problems addressed above about nationalism and political community. At the same time, we are able to find cases where good governance programmes have worked much better than in Senegal, the case addressed by Kenny.[38] I return to this issue below.

In sum, liberal democracy is no simple, straightforward entity. Three different models of liberal democracy have been pushed by the West in the Third World: the liberal market model, the election model, and the strong/responsive state model. The two former models contain serious weaknesses; the latter is attractive, but rather difficult to establish in practice, especially in the short and medium run.

[34] Merilee Grindle, *Challenging the State: Crisis and Innovation in Latin America and Africa* (Cambridge: Cambridge University Press, 1996).

[35] World Bank, *World Development Report 1997: The State in a Changing World* (New York: Oxford University Press, 1997).

[36] Mette Kjær, 'The World Bank and Civil Service Reform in Africa', paper delivered at a conference on Africa and Globalisation (University of Central Lancashire, 24–6 April 1998).

[37] Charles Kenny, 'Senegal and the Entropy Theory of Development', *European Journal of Development Research* 10/1 (1998), pp. 160–89.

[38] Kenny, 'Senegal and the Entropy of Development'.

Support for Elite-Dominated Democracy?

The final item I want to address is more straightforwardly political than the others. It rests on a distinction between elite-dominated and mass-dominated democracies.[39] Elite-dominated democracies are systems in which traditional rulers remain in control, even if pressured from below, and successfully use strategies of either compromise or force—or some mix of the two—to retain at least part of their power. Mass-dominated democracies are systems in which mass actors have gained the upper hand over traditional ruling classes; they push for reforms from below, attacking the power and privilege of the elites.

During the cold war, support for traditional rulers took priority even over democracy. In the early 1960s in the Dominican Republic, a democratically elected government under Juán Bosch set out to promote economic development through nationalist economic policies that went against some American interests in the country. When Bosch faced the prospect of a military coup, Washington decided to opt for the authoritarian military dictatorship. John F. Kennedy set forth the alternatives as follows: 'There are three possibilities in descending order of preference; a decent democratic regime, a continuation of the Trujillo regime [a military dictatorship], or a Castro regime. We ought to aim at the first, but we can't really renounce the second until we are sure we can avoid the third.'[40] Thus, fearing that the Bosch regime would develop into a Castro regime, the United States found it safest to back a military dictatorship. Even in sub-Saharan Africa, an area of less strategic importance during the cold war, the United States has been charged with pursuing similar policies. Sean Kelly has analysed 'how the United States put Mobutu in power, protected him from his enemies, helped him become one of the richest men in the world, and lived to regret it'.[41] America's support for Mobutu is often explained by his willing assistance in facilitating American support for the non-Marxist side in the Angolan civil war, but Kelly's analysis makes clear that a number of additional factors were involved in the long-term relationship between the US and Mobutu, a relationship heavily influenced by the CIA.

The charge put forward by some observers is that the United States follows basically the same policies today, after the end of the cold war, albeit with a new twist: the elites must support the basic rules of a liberal democratic game. The most thorough investigation making this point has been done by William Robinson, who contends that

All over the world, the United States is now promoting its version of 'democracy' as a way to relieve pressure from subordinate groups for more fundamental political, social and economic change . . . The promotion of 'low-intensity democracy' is aimed not only

---

[39] Terry Lynn Karl, 'Dilemmas of Democratization in Latin America', *Comparative Politics*, 23/1 (1990), pp. 1–21.

[40] Quoted from Michael W. Doyle, 'Kant, Liberal Legacies and Foreign Affairs, Part 2', *Philosophy and Public Affairs*, 12/4 (1983), pp. 323–54 at 335.

[41] Sean Kelly, *America's Tyrant: The CIA and Mobutu of Zaire* (Washington: The American University Press, 1993), p. iii.

at mitigating the social and political tensions produced by elite-based and undemocratic status quos, but also at suppressing popular and mass aspirations for more thoroughgoing democratization of social life . . .[42]

A similar charge has been put forward against France in context of that country's policies in francophone Africa.[43]

Yet before finding the US, France, and perhaps other Western countries guilty of narrow support for elite-dominated democracies, the broader context of the issue must be considered. First, the distinction between elite-domination and mass-domination is less straightforward than it seems. Some administrations may have the support of both substantial factions of elites and of a majority in the population—for example, Cardoso in Brazil, Mandela in South Africa—and such broad support may even be reflected in their policies. Second, democracy introduces a degree of uncertainty into the political process. It opens channels for popular pressure on the rulers. Even elite-dominated democracies may be pushed in the direction of more effective reform measures and in that sense become more responsiveness to mass needs, as demonstrated, for example, by the travails of democracy in Costa Rica.[44] Third, some of the measures backed by Western countries—for example, increasing the economic and administrative discipline on state elites in Africa—square poorly with the notion of unremitting support for those same elites. After all, the whole idea behind structural adjustment was that the political interests of the state elites were 'the source of the mismanagement of the African economies, and any rectification therefore required that economic management be taken out of their hands and placed in those of the "market"'.[45]

Taking this into consideration, I believe we end up with a soft version of the elite-support thesis. Western countries are likely to support administrations that (1) are liberal on economic policies, including support for economic openness toward the world market; (2) respect private property, including setting up an effective system of commercial law; and (3) exercise leadership that is oriented towards cooperation with the leading Western countries. In that sense there is an elitist orientation in Western support for democracy in the Third World. And although domestic forces are more important for the outcome, this support has helped sustain what Karl terms 'frozen democracies', that is, restricted, elite-dominated systems, unwilling to transgress the narrow limitations imposed on them by elite factions who engineered the transition to democracy in the first place.[46] They are unwilling to carry out substantive reforms that address the lot of poor citizens. Both Latin America and Asia have a number of administrations that correspond to this description.

[42] William I. Robinson, *Promoting Polyarchy: Globalization, US Intervention, and Hegemony* (Cambridge: Cambridge University Press, 1996), p. 6.
[43] Celestin Monga, 'Eight Problems with African Politics', *Journal of Democracy*, 8/3 (1997), pp. 156–70.
[44] Cf. Sørensen, *Democracy and Democratization*.
[45] Clapham, *Africa and the International System*, p. 812.
[46] Karl, 'Dilemmas of Democratization in Latin America'.

In Africa, however, the question of elite support is especially complex because civil society is so weak that the above notion of 'mass-dominated democracy' is not really meaningful. Given the problems with quick elections discussed above, Western donors have increasingly supported the strengthening of civil society in Africa by giving aid to various non-government organizations, human rights groups, the emerging independent press, and the like. Seen from this perspective, Western policies can hardly be classified as driven by a notion of support for 'elite-dominated' democracy. At the same time, a recent analysis has debated the soundness of this support for 'a mosaic of small clubs and associations trying to protect their interests, and thus harnessing the excessive power and authoritarian tendencies of the state'.[47] The major reason for being sceptical is that such civil society organisations do not have sufficient strength to be able to organize countervailing centres of power. In other words, many Western donors appear to be 'doing the right thing' in Africa by strengthening groups in civil society. But the overall outcome is not democracy, because these small organizations are not strong enough to challenge existing—mostly authoritarian—state power in any meaningful way.

The problem emphasises the extraordinary difficulties of promoting democracy in an African setting. On the one hand, there is a need to support groups that are democratic in the sense of being participatory, bottom-up organizations in local areas. On the other hand, there is a need to create strong organizations that can effectively challenge incumbent state elites. These problems emerge because the societal preconditions for democracy are highly unfavourable in the large majority of the countries.

And Now the Good News . . .

I have painted a rather bleak picture of the current democratizations in the Third World. Furthermore, I have pointed to the lack of political community, the various models of democracy promoted by the West, and the notion of elitism as underlying elements which help explain the lack of sustained democratic progress—elements which donor countries have not adequately addressed. There are some positive factors which have not been given much attention above. In a number of Third World countries—generally those at the higher levels of socioeconomic development—both political and economic reforms are doing reasonably well. Yet the most encouraging signs are likely to be found in those countries that have achieved political and economic success despite being beset by some of the problems mentioned above, including a high potential for ethnic conflict because of many ethnic groups in the population and a rather low level of economic development at the time of independence. If we can explain why these countries have been successful in spite

---

[47] Marina Ottaway, 'African Democratisation and the Leninist Option', *The Journal of Modern African Studies*, 35/1 (1997), pp. 1–17 at 12.

of the adverse conditions they faced, we may have some indications about how to get around the problems discussed above.

Two obvious candidates for further scrutiny in this respect are Mauritius and Botswana. On independence in 1968, Mauritius was a poor sugar economy with deep ethnic cleavages in the population; Botswana was a cattle economy with a population divided into eleven tribes that had the good fortune of discovering diamonds in its soil (although several other African countries have had rich mineral deposits and still been unable to convert that potential into broader development). How could Mauritius and Botswana succeed economically and even be able simultaneously to establish functioning political democracies? A recent analysis is helpful in providing an answer to that question. Carroll and Carroll identify the following factors behind the political and economic success of the two countries: (1) talented political leaders who were personally committed to democratic government and to economic development; (2) the creation of a competent, politically independent state bureaucracy with personnel policies based largely on merit, but with a composition that is reasonably representative of their societies; and (3) the development of a public realm that is capable of imposing at least modest checks on the actions of the state, and that is characterized by a balance between universalistic and particularistic norms and by a pragmatic recognition of the important representative role of tribal or ethnic organizations and institutions.[48]

These are interesting and convincing answers to the question posed above; yet it is also clear that such answers begs new questions. Where do talented leaders committed to democratic government and economic development come from? As indicated by Carroll and Carroll, it is reasonable to assume that success cultivates success: once a competent leadership has been established and has demonstrated a decent track record, chances are good that capable leadership will continue. But what about that crucial initial phase, where success is by no means secure and leadership might well turn out to be narrow-minded, egoistic, and self-serving? What is it that brings forward the Mandelas and the Musevenis instead of the Mobutus and the Mois? If it is not pure coincidence then the question merits further research. The hopeful answer—that such leadership is more or less automatically created by holding elections— has not been confirmed by events. It should also be emphasized that good and honest leaders are not enough, especially if they are committed to bad policies. Julius Nyerere of Tanzania was an honest man who did much good for the country, but his policies of a state-led economy and a basically non-democratic polity had disastrous results.

As for the second factor—a good bureaucracy—it is clear that early decisions were made in both Botswana and Mauritius not to sacrifice competence for 'nativization' of the public service, and to base recruitment on merit. At the same time, however, Carroll and Carroll stress that the Weberian ideal of an

---

[48] Barbara Wake Carroll and Terrance Carroll, 'State and Ethnicity in Botswana and Mauritius: A Democratic Route to Development?', *The Journal of Development Studies*, 33/4 (1997), pp. 464-86 at 470.

impartial public service probably should be abandoned when it comes to developing countries with many different ethnic groups in the population. In the two countries examined, care has been taken to make the bureaucracy representative of subgroups in society without sacrificing merit. Such a representative bureaucracy 'is more likely to consider a wide range of views and interests in making decisions. Indeed, the simple existence of a representative bureaucracy is often taken by the public as evidence that the state is responsive and legitimate'.[49]

The third factor concerns the need for a civil society to constrain the state. In many poor Third World countries, there is no civil society in the traditional Western sense of the term. At very low levels of development, there is no business class, no middle class, not even a well-defined class of peasants. Partly as a consequence of this, there are few autonomous, strong secondary organizations based on universal membership criteria. According to a recent analysis by Goran Hyden, 'the prime contemporary challenge is how to restore a civic public realm. The trend of postindependence politics in most African countries has been to disintegrate the civic public realm inherited from the colonial powers and replace it with rivalling communal or primordial realms, all following their own informal rules'.[50] Yet the good news from Botswana and Mauritius is that these communal and primordial realms can act as at least 'a modest check on the power of the state'.[51] In other words, under favourable circumstances traditional social forces can perform some of those functions that we would normally expect to demand the presence of a more fully developed civil society. That is, ethnically divided societies can sustain democracy even though their civil societies have been weak, and ethnic divisions continue to exist.

Perhaps the main message from the experience of these countries is the importance of competent leadership and some measure of institutional innovation. None of the countries may live up to the highest demands of liberal democratic procedures and institutions, but they should be credited with substantial democratic success. Current developments in Uganda appear to suggest another encouraging case of the combination of competent leadership and institutional innovation. Under Yoweri Museveni an institutional and political reconstruction of the state is under way which promises to respect basic democratic features—political control is vested in elected bodies after a process of basically free elections. Yet political democracy is far from complete: a multiparty system is not allowed because of fears that it will recreate the ethnic divisions that drove Uganda to civil war and state failure. A referendum around 2000 is expected to decide whether or not this system will continue.[52]

The lesson for outsiders appears to be that support for competent leadership and some measure of institutional innovation, which may compromise the

---

[49] Carroll and Carroll, 'State and Ethnicity in Botswana and Mauritius', p. 473.
[50] Goran Hyden (ed.), *Governance and Politics in Africa* (Boulder: Lynne Rienner, 1992), p. 23.
[51] Carroll and Carroll, 'State and Ethnicity in Botswana and Mauritius', p. 479.
[52] Mette Kjær and Palle Svensson, 'Rekonstruktion i Uganda', *Politica*, 29/2 (1997), pp. 164–80.

ideal of a 'perfect' political democracy, is the way ahead. One must hope that narrow interests will not prevent moving in this direction. In any case, outsiders can probably only be facilitators; they cannot on their own produce the necessary conditions for democracy and development. In other words, democracy and development cannot be taught; it can only be learnt.[53] The learning process will, however, continue to be heavily dependent on the lessons and recommendations that Western countries have to offer.

Conclusion

The process of democratization does not fare well in many Third World countries. We are not facing a general relapse into authoritarianism. The problem is rather one of democratic consolidation; a very large number of the current transitions have run aground in the shallow waters of 'electoral democracy' where there may be elections, but even so, large parts of the population remain outside of the political process; the media are not free and the military and other parts of the state apparatus are outside democratic control. This is an indication of the prevalence of 'frozen democracies', unwilling to carry out substantial reforms that address the lot of the poor majorities.

I have pointed to various factors which help explain the situation. External actors bear some substantial responsibility for this state of affairs. The problem of the lack of political community in many developing countries has not been sufficiently confronted by Western decision-makers and analysts. Furthermore, the promotion of the 'market model' and the 'election model' of democracy combined with support for elite-dominated democracy has yielded limited results. Even if it is true that democracy cannot be taught but only learnt, Western countries would do well to rethink some of the practices in support of democracy. Such a process is under way now, under the label of 'good governance'. Especially, more support for competent leaders and institutional innovation appears to promise better results in terms of both democracy and development. At the same time, conditions for democracy in several countries in Africa are so highly adverse that there appear to be no readily available blueprints for the creation of both fast and sustainable democratic progress. It may be necessary to try to develop models of democracy which remain based on the core liberal elements of participation, competition, and political and civil liberties, while also better addressing the special problems of weak states with fragile political communities.

[53] Cf. Christopher Clapham, 'Governmentality and Economic Policy in Sub-Saharan Africa', *Third World Quarterly*, 17/4 (1996), pp. 809–24 at 823.

14

Promoting Capitalist Polyarchy: The Case of Latin America

WILLIAM ROBINSON

SOCIAL change is driven by contradictions that make the continuation of an existing set of social arrangements impossible. Over the past 30 years the world economy has experienced dramatic crises and restructuring as globalization has unfolded. Structural changes have had a profound transformative effect on the social and political fabric of each nation, on international relations, and on the global system as a whole. By the 1980s it had become clear to dominant groups, and especially to emergent transnational elites and their organic intellectuals, that the old methods of political domination were no longer workable. Elite rule required renovation in the face of the global integration of social life and the mass mobilization of people whose way of life was becoming fundamentally altered by capitalist globalization. Sweeping changes in the mode of social control were necessary if the global order was to hold together.

The shift in US policy that took place in the 1980s from promoting authoritarianism and dictatorship in much of the Third World to promoting polyarchy has been one factor, more reactive than proactive, in this scenario. Elsewhere I have argued that, at the level of theoretical generalization, the shift to promoting polyarchy may be conceived, in the Gramscian sense, as signalling new forms of transnational control accompanying the rise of global capitalism. Specifically, behind this shift is an effort to replace coercive means of social control with consensual ones within a highly stratified global system, in which the United States plays a leadership role on behalf of an emergent *transnational* hegemonic configuration. At the practical level, this shift has involved the development of new organs of the US state and new modalities of engagement abroad conducted under the rubric of 'democracy promotion'.[1]

---

[1] See William I. Robinson, *Promoting Polyarchy: Globalization, US Intervention, and Hegemony* (Cambridge and New York: Cambridge University Press, 1996); William I. Robinson, 'Globalization, the World System, and "Democracy Promotion" in US Foreign Policy', *Theory and Society*, 25 (1996), pp. 616–65.

Latin America provides a good illustration of these processes. Authoritarianism there as the predominant mode of social control faced an intractable crisis by the late 1970s. The region's authoritarian regimes were besieged by mass popular movements demanding not only democracy and human rights but also fundamental change in the social order. These movements threatened to bring down the whole elite-based order along with the dictatorships, as actually happened in Nicaragua in 1979, and threatened to happen in Haiti, El Salvador, Guatemala, and elsewhere. This threat from below, combined with the inability of the authoritarian regimes to manage the dislocations and adjustments of globalization, generated intra-elite conflicts that unravelled the ruling power blocs.

The crisis of elite rule was resolved through transitions to polyarchy that took place in almost every country in Latin America during the 1980s and early 1990s. What transpired in these contested transitions was an effort by transnational dominant groups to reconstitute the hemispheric order through a change in the mode of political domination, from coercive to more consensually-based systems of social control. At stake was what type of a social order—the emergent global capitalist order or some popular alternative—would emerge in the wake of authoritarianism. Transnationalized fractions of local elites in Latin America, with the structural power of the global economy behind them, as well as the direct political and military intervention of the United States and other transnational forces, were able to gain a controlling influence over democratization movements and steer the break-up of authoritarianism into polyarchic outcomes.

In this chapter, I will examine these transitions in light of the shift in US policy. I will discuss what US policymakers mean by 'democracy promotion', draw out the relationship between capitalist globalization and promoting polyarchy, and examine some instances of US polyarchy promotion in Latin America. I will also focus on the antinomy in promoting capitalist polyarchy, and in particular the contradiction between simultaneously promoting a consensual-based political system and promoting an exclusionary socioeconomic system. The dilemmas of the new polyarchic regimes in Latin America are symptomatic of the social contradictions of emergent global society.

Making the World Safe for Capitalism

Projects of domination are always unstable. The terror that the privileged few have of the dispossessed many has been expressed in diverse pathologies throughout the ages founded on fantastic and often delusional discourses aimed at rationalizing domination and inequality as part of the drive to secure social order. Earlier colonial and racial theories that naturalized social inequalities have been replaced more recently by arguments of 'cultural difference' and a 'clash of civilizations' that purport to explain current global stratification.[2] It is in this context that we must see a discourse of 'democracy promotion' that portrays those political agents at the centre of power and privilege in global society as the highest representatives of freedom and democracy in the world.

What US policymakers mean by 'democracy promotion' is the promotion of polyarchy. Polyarchy refers to a system in which a small group actually rules and mass participation in decision-making is confined to leadership choice in elections carefully managed by competing elites. This polyarchic or 'institutional' definition developed in US academic circles closely tied to the policy-making community in the post-World War II years of US world power and built on the early twentieth century elitism theorists of Gaetano Mosca and Vilfredo Pareto. This redefinition of the classical concept as rule, or power (*cratos*) of the people (*demos*), started with Joseph Schumpeter's 1942 call for 'another theory of democracy' and culminated in Robert Dahl's 1971 study, titled *Polyarchy*.[3] Democracy, however, is an essentially contested concept, and the polyarchic conception competes with concepts of popular democracy. Popular democracy is seen as an emancipatory project of both form and content that links the distinct spheres of the social totality, in which the construction of a democratic political order enjoys a theoretically internal relation to the construction of a democratic socioeconomic order, and democratic participation is a tool for changing unjust social and economic structures. The polyarchic definition of democracy had achieved, in the Gramscian sense, hegemony among scholars, journalists, and policymakers, not just in the United States but in international public discourse in general. It is the conception that informed the 1980s 'transitions to democracy' or 'democratization' literature on Latin America and the 1990s 'consolidating democracy' literature. Smith's claim that 'academics across the political spectrum have come to something of a consensus as to what they mean by the word *democracy*'[4] indicates the hegemony that the polyarchic definition of an essentially contested concept, and one that is necessarily value- and theory-laden, has achieved. As a result of this hegemony, sets of assumptions that set *a priori* limits on the intellectual as well as political agenda are left unproblematized.

---

[2] See for example Samuel Huntington, *The Clash of Civilizations and the Remaking of World Order* (New York: Simon and Schuster, 1996); and for a wide-ranging analysis and critique, Kenan Malik, *The Meaning of Race: Race, History and Culture in Western Society* (New York: New York University Press, 1996).

[3] Joseph A. Schumpeter, *Capitalism, Socialism and Democracy* (New York: Harper and Row, 1942), especially Chs 21 and 22; Robert A. Dahl, *Polyarchy: Participation and Opposition* (New Haven: Yale University Press, 1971).

[4] Tony Smith, *America's Mission: The United States and the Worldwide Struggle for Democracy in the Twentieth Century* (Princeton: Princeton University Press, 1994), p. 13. John Markoff notes that the meaning of democracy is historically determined—it shifts over time—and democracy is defined and redefined by historical social struggles. This is crucial, but Markoff's phrase 'really existing democracy' is not satisfying because it ignores the contemporary dispute over the meaning of a highly contested concept and denies that this dispute is itself part of the social struggle to establish that meaning. Moreover, it can be argued that 'really existing democracy' is no more genuine democracy than 'really existing socialism' was genuine socialism. See 'Really Existing Democracy: Learning From Latin America in the Late 1990s', *New Left Review*, 223 (1997), pp. 48–68.

What concerns us are three interwoven propositions. First, the polyarchic definition, resting on the theoretical model of pluralism and of structural-functionalist sociology, isolates explicitly the political from the social and economic spheres and situates democracy within the bounds of the former—and even at that, it limits democratic participation to voting in elections—in contrast to the popular definition. This separation is crucial to 'democracy promotion' and I will return to this issue below. Second, behind essentially contested concepts are *contested social orders*. Mass movements for democratization around the world are movements seeking fundamental social change, including but encompassing much more than reforms leading to contested elections and other institutional structures of polyarchy. Third, the contradiction between popular democracy and polyarchy is a contradiction between distinct class and group protagonists and their opposing projects for organizing society.

The emergence of polyarchy promotion is in contrast to prior periods in US foreign policy history and to the general practice of capitalist world powers, in which military dictatorships or authoritarian client regimes, and before them colonial states, were sustained as the best guarantor of social control and of stability.[5] As mass popular movements in the Third World spread in the latter part of the twentieth century against repressive political systems and exploitative socioeconomic orders, support for authoritarianism became an increasingly ineffective means of assuring stability and confronting mass demands for popular social change. A crisis of elite rule began to coalesce in the 1970s at the world systemic level. American state managers and organic intellectuals in the extended policymaking community reflected on the best means to resolve this crisis. In the early 1980s their long-running debate over whether authoritarianism or polyarchy was the better means of achieving order was decisively resolved in favour of the latter.

Seen in structural perspective, the shift to promoting polyarchy corresponds to the emergence of the global economy since the 1970s. Globalization redefined the basis for international relations and class formation, created new sets of actors which became transnational in character, and generated new pressures for political change in global society. New modes of social control constitute a political exigency of macroeconomic restructuring on a world scale, in the context of the transnationalization of the economy, political processes, social classes and civil societies. Specifically, transnational capital has emerged as the agent of globalization.[6] At the apex of the global economy

---

[5] On authoritarianism as the principal colonial and post-colonial mode of domination, see Thomas Y. Clives, *The Rise of the Authoritarian State In Peripheral Societies* (New York: Monthly Review Press, 1984). This study reminds us of the centrality of analysing the historical and structural basis for the development of political systems in the mediation of class relations.

[6] There has been an explosion of literature in the 1990s on globalization, including a number of important works on transnational class formation. In addition to Robinson, *Promoting Polyarchy*, see Leslie Sklair, *Sociology of the Global System*, 2nd edn. (Baltimore: Johns Hopkins University Press, 1995), which discusses the formation of a 'transnational capitalist class'. Roger Burbach and William I. Robinson, 'The Fin de Siècle Debate: Globalization as Epochal Shift', *Science and Society*, 63/1 (1999), pp. 10–39, also provides empirical discussion on the emergence of transnational fractions in

is a transnational managerial elite, based in the centres of world capitalism, which controls the levers of global policymaking and which responds to transnational capital as the hegemonic fraction of capital on a world scale. The agenda of this transnational elite is to promote the economic and political conditions around the world for the unfettered activity of transnational capital. The economic component includes international economic integration processes, the establishment of the World Trade Organization, negotiations over the Multilateral Agreement on Investment, and so on, all of which are intended to convert the world into a single unified field for global capitalism. It also embraces 'neoliberalism' or what Robert Cox has termed 'hyperliberalism',[7] involving the elimination of state intervention in the economy and the regulation of individual nation states over the activities of capital in their territories. The neoliberal 'structural adjustment' programmes sweeping the South seek to achieve the macroeconomic equilibrium and liberalization required by transnationally mobile capital and to integrate each nation and region into new globalized circuits of accumulation.[8]

If this economic component is to make the world available to capital, the political component is to 'make the world safe for capital'. This requires developing social control systems and political institutions most propitious for achieving a stable world environment. Interaction and economic integration on a world scale are obstructed by authoritarian or dictatorial political arrangements, which are unable to manage the expansion of social intercourse associated with the global economy. The turn to promoting polyarchy in US foreign policy is an effort to modernize political systems in each country incorporated into global structures so that they operate through consensual, rather than through direct, coercive domination. The demands, grievances and aspirations of the popular classes tend to become neutralized less through direct repression than through ideological mechanisms, political co-optation and disorganization, and the limits imposed by the global economy. While mediating inter-class relations, polyarchy is also a more propitious institutional arrangement for the resolution of conflicts among dominant groups. With its mechanisms for intra-elite compromise and accommodation and for hegemonic incorporation of popular majorities, polyarchy is better equipped in the new global environment to legitimize the political authority of dominant groups and to achieve a minimally stable environment, under the conflict-ridden and fluid conditions of emergent global society, for global capitalism to operate.

the South. On the emergence of transnational groups in the North, see among several important works: Robert Cox, *Production, Power, and World Order: Social Forces in the Making of History* (New York: Columbia University Press, 1987); Stephen Gill, *American Hegemony and the Trilateral Commission* (Cambridge and New York: Cambridge University Press, 1990); Kees van der Pijl, *Transnational Classes and International Relations* (London: Routledge, 1998).

    [7] Cox, *Production, Power, and World Order*.
    [8] These issues are discussed more broadly in William I. Robinson, 'Globalisation: Nine Theses of our Epoch', *Race and Class*, 38/2 (1996), pp. 13–31; William I. Robinson, 'A Case Study of Globalisation Processes in the Third World: A Transnational Agenda in Nicaragua,' *Global Society*, 11/1 (1997), pp. 61–91.

The shift to global capitalism thus requires concomitant shifts in the global polity, in particular, the rationalization of domination. It is in this context that promoting polyarchy is a political counterpart to the project of promoting capitalist globalization, and that 'democracy promotion' and the promotion of free markets through neoliberal restructuring has become a singular process in US foreign policy. Opening up the markets and resources of the world for capital, assuring investment opportunities, and seeking to create the general social and political conditions for international capital accumulation have always been at the core of the foreign policies of capitalist powers. What theoretical or empirical basis is there to claim now that promoting polyarchy has any different function? Even if some academics posit an autonomous state guided by moral or ideological concerns, US state managers are under no such illusions. The forefather of modern polyarchy promotion, Woodrow Wilson, made quite clear that US state policy in the international arena was to serve private capital. 'Since trade ignores national boundaries, and the manufacturer insists on having the world as a market, the flag of his nation must follow him, and the doors of the nations which are closed against him must be battered down', he stated. 'Concessions obtained by financiers must be safeguarded by ministers of state, even if the sovereignty of unwilling nations be outraged in the process. Colonies must be obtained or planted, in order that no useful corner of the world may be overlooked or left unused.'[9]

Wilson was the first to 'promote democracy' and he did so in order to secure the best conditions for international capital accumulation. The difference in the age of globalization is that the US state promotes polyarchy not to stabilize the old interstate system of Wilson's day but to stabilize a new transnational capitalist historic bloc. It is the logic of global accumulation, rather than national accumulation, that guides the political and economic behaviour of the transnational ruling bloc. As this transnational bloc emerged in the 1980s and 1990s it carried out a 'passive revolution' in the Gramscian sense, involving modifications made from above in global social and economic structure through the agency of state apparatuses. The ruling groups coopted potential leaders of subaltern social groups through the strategy of 'assimilating and domesticating potentially dangerous ideas by adjusting them to the policies of the dominant coalition'.[10] The 'dangerous idea' to be assimilated and domesticated was that of popular democracy and the policies of the dominant coalition were neoliberalism and polyarchy. The transitions to polyarchy have not been illusions of reform; they constitute real political reform. Clives predicted

[9] Cited in Michael Parenti, *Against Empire* (San Francisco: City Lights Books, 1995), p. 40. Transnational corporate executives are also aware of the relationship between 'democracy' and profits. As reported by the World Trade Organization, business executives in the vast majority of countries believe 'democracy' would 'lower the cost of doing business' and improve the climate for profit making. World Trade Organization, *Annual Report* (1997), p. 314, as cited in Craig N. Murphy, 'Inequality, Turmoil, and Democracy: Global Political-Economic Visions at the End of the Century', *New Political Economy*, 4/2 (1999), pp. 289–304.

[10] Roger Simon, *Gramsci's Political Thought* (London: Lawrence and Wishart, 1982), pp. 48–9, as cited and discussed by Mark Neufeld, 'Democratization in/of Foreign Policy: Critical Reflections on the Canadian Case', forthcoming in *Studies in Political Economy*, 58 (1999), pp. 97–119.

in the 1980s that core countries would promote political reform—democracy—and social reform—a redistributive social democracy—in the periphery in order to undercut revolutionary pressures there. He was right only in part. Polyarchy was promoted as 'pre-emptive reform', in the words of Henry Kissinger and Cyrus Vance, in reaction to mass popular movements.[11] But transnational elites have promoted neoliberalism, not social democracy, and this has brought an end, at least temporarily, to redistributive projects.[12]

Promoting the Transnational Agenda in Latin America

The promotion of polyarchy by the US in Latin America has involved two phases. In the first phase, the United States launched 'democracy promotion' and other forms of intervention during mass struggles against authoritarian regimes and for popular democratization in order to seek polyarchic outcomes to transitions. The challenge of 'pre-emptive reform' was to remove dictatorships *and* to pre-empt more fundamental change. American intervention synchronized political aid programmes with covert and direct military operations, economic aid or sanctions, formal diplomacy, government-to-government programmes, and so on. The objective was to suppress popular democracy and to liaise with and help place in power local contingents of the transnational elite. Local transnational fractions swept to power in country after country and set out to integrate their respective nation-states into the new global order. In the second phase, US policy has aimed to 'consolidate democracy' through broad 'democratic aid' and other government-to-government and multilateral programmes. These programmes sought to train the new elites in the procedures of polyarchy, to inculcate a polyarchic political culture, and to strengthen a polyarchic institutional environment as a complement to economic restructuring under the superintendence of the international financial agencies.

When US policymakers and organic intellectuals speak of 'helping democratic forces', they mean assisting these transnational fractions of local dominant groups in their struggles to establish social order and hegemony in the local environment. These elites are assisted in opposition to popular sectors *and also* in opposition to the far right, to authoritarian-oriented elites, 'crony' capitalists, and other dominant strata opposed to the transnational project. The transitions from authoritarianism to polyarchy in Latin America afforded transnational elites the opportunity to reorganize state institutions and create a more favourable institutional framework for a deepening of neoliberal adjustment. Without a single exception in Latin America, the new polyarchic regimes, staffed by state managers tied to the transnational elite, have pursued

[11] See Henry Kissinger and Cyrus Vance, 'Bipartisan Objectives for American Foreign Policy', *Foreign Affairs*, 66/5 (1988), p. 119.

[12] See Thomas Y. Clives, 'Restructuring of the World Economy and its Political Implications for the Third World', in Arthur MacEwan and William K. Tabb, *Instability and Change in the World Economy* (New York: Monthly Review Press, 1989), pp. 331–48.

profound neoliberal transformation. The new elites have set out to modernize the state and society without any fundamental deconcentration of property and wealth, and without any class redistribution of political and economic power.[13] They have implemented a transnational model of development based on a rearticulation to world markets, new economic activities linked to global accumulation, the contraction of domestic markets, and the provision of cheap labour and abundant natural resources to transnational capital as the region's 'comparative advantage' in the global economy.[14]

The cases of Chile, Nicaragua, Haiti, Panama, and Mexico demonstrate these patterns.[15] In Chile, the United States, after orchestrating the 1973 overthrow of the Allende Government, provided consistent support for the military dictatorship of Augusto Pinochet until 1985, when it abruptly shifted support to the elite opposition and began to promote a transition. From 1985 on, the US applied a myriad of carrot-and-stick pressures on the regime to open up and to transfer power to civilian elites. Simultaneous to these pressures, it implemented political aid programmes through the Agency for International Development and the National Endowment for Democracy to help organize and guide the coalition that ran against Pinochet in the 1988 plebiscite and against the dictatorship's candidates in the 1990 general elections. Political intervention by the US played a key role in achieving unity among a splintered elite opposition, in eclipsing the popular opposition, and in assuring elite hegemony over the anti-dictatorial movement between 1985 and 1987, when this hegemony was in dispute. It also played an important role between 1987 and 1990 in consolidating a reconstituted elite and in placing a 'transnational kernel', committed to the process begun under Pinochet of far-reaching neoliberal restructuring and integration into the global economy, to a position of leadership among the new civilian authorities.

In Nicaragua, the United States supported the Somoza family dictatorship for nearly five decades. Foreign capital poured into Central America in the 1960s and 1970s, integrating the region into the global economy and laying the structural basis for the social upheavals of the 1980s. The Sandinista government which came to power in the 1979 revolution became the target of a massive US destabilization campaign. In 1987, the objective of this campaign changed dramatically, from a military overthrow of the Sandinistas by an externally-based counter-revolutionary movement seeking an authoritarian restoration, to new forms of political intervention in support of an internal

---

[13] The emergence of this fraction in Latin America is discussed in detail in William I. Robinson, 'Maldevelopment in Central America: Globalization and Social Change', *Development and Change*, 29 (1988), pp. 467–97.

[14] For detailed discussion on this new model of development and its social implications, see Duncan Green, *Silent Revolution: The Rise of Market Economics in Latin America* (London: Cassell, 1995); William I. Robinson, 'Latin America and Global Capitalism', *Race and Class*, 40/2/3 (1998/99), pp. 111–31. For a devastating historical critique of the liberalism and neoliberalism that informs this model, see Frederic F. Clairmont, *The Rise and Fall of Economic Liberalism* (Goa, India: The Other Indian Press, 1996).

[15] The following discussion on Chile, Nicaragua, and Haiti, is summarized from Robinson, *Promoting Polyarchy*.

'moderate' opposition. This opposition, organized and trained through large-scale US political aid programmes, operated through peaceful (non-coercive) means in civil society to undermine Sandinista hegemony. These were the same elite civilian groups that had opposed the Somoza dictatorship in its final years but had not been able to gain hegemony over the anti-dictatorial movement and to thus prevent a Sandinista victory. The shift from hard-line destabilization to polyarchy promotion culminated in the 1990 electoral defeat of the Sandinistas, a conservative restoration and the installation of a polyarchic political system, the reinsertion of Nicaragua into the global economy, and far-reaching neoliberal restructuring.

In Haiti, the US sustained the Duvalier dictatorship at the same time as it promoted a development model in the 1960s and 1970s which inserted the country into the emergent global economy as an export-assembly platform. This model helped uproot the rural peasantry—a class which had constituted the backbone of the social order for nearly two centuries—and hastened a mass movement against the dictatorship. In early 1986 a popular uprising brought down the Duvalier regime. In Chile elites had gained enough hegemony over the anti-dictatorial movement to secure a polyarchic outcome, and in Nicaragua the Sandinistas led popular sectors in a revolutionary outcome. In Haiti, however, neither elite nor popular forces could gain any decisive hegemony. The elite was fragmentary and wedded to authoritarianism, and a small 'transnational kernel' poorly-organized. Popular forces had no unifying political organization, programme or leadership which could facilitate a bid for power. Haiti became submerged in a national power vacuum and a cauldron of turmoil in 1986–90. During this period, the US introduced a massive 'democracy promotion' programme to marginalize popular sectors and cultivate a polyarchic elite and place it in power through US-organized elections. The liberation theologist Jean-Bertrand Aristide defeated Marc Bazin, who had been carefully groomed in US political aid programmes, in the 1990 elections. This was an upset for the US programme, but Aristide was overthrown in a 1991 military *coup d'état*. The United States did not obstruct the coup and subsequently provided tacit support for the consolidation of the military dictatorship. The return of Aristide to office as a lame-duck president through a US invasion in September 1994—after the military interlude had crushed the project of popular democracy and after Aristide had committed to a structural adjustment programme drafted by the World Bank—underscored a complex ongoing and open-ended scenario in Haiti whereby the conditions for a stable polyarchic system continued to elude US strategists yet neither elite nor popular forces could achieve any hegemonic order.

In Panama, as in Nicaragua, military aggression was combined with political intervention to achieve a polyarchic outcome. In 1903 the United States orchestrated the country's independence from Colombia and brought to power a tiny white oligarchic elite—in an overwhelmingly black country—that would support its plans to build the canal. This elite was sustained in power by US support and numerous direct US interventions until it was displaced, but only partially, by the 1968 coup that brought Omar Torrijos to power. Manuel Noriega, a CIA asset and close US ally, came to power with US support following Torrijos' death in 1981, opening a period of crisis and instability. Washington continued its support for the Noriega regime, despite its practice of electoral fraud and mass repression, until a combination of conjunctural geopolitical concerns and the shift to promoting polyarchy and neoliberalism as part of the broader world-wide strategy led to a decision to overthrow Noriega. The destabilization campaign included economic sanctions, coercive diplomacy, psychological operations, and finally a direct invasion. The campaign also involved a multimillion dollar political intervention programme to create a 'democratic opposition' by bringing together 'modernizing' groups from within the old oligarchy tied to international banking and trade. Through the invasion this 'modernized' sector within the old oligarchy was placed in power—literally. Despite ongoing social conflict and an internally divided elite, neoliberal reform proceeded apace in the 1990s.[16]

In Mexico, the ruling Institutional Revolutionary Party (PRI) became racked by a power struggle in the 1980s. The 'dinosaurs', the old bourgeoisie and state bureaucrats tied to Mexico's corporatist-import substitution model of national capitalism, were unable to prevent the rise of the 'technocrats', the transnational fraction of the Mexican elite that captured the party, and the state, with the election of Carlos Salinas de Gortari in 1988. This transnationalized fraction has implemented sweeping neoliberal structural adjustment, thoroughly transforming the Mexican economy and integrating the country into global capitalism. However, the struggle between the national and transnational fractions was not fully resolved and became violent in the early 1990s. Intra-elite conflict, combined with the widespread mobilization of popular classes and armed insurrections by the Zapatistas in Chiapas and other guerrilla groups in the States of Guerrero and Oaxaca, made stability elusive and threatened the whole transnational project for the country. There has been a disjuncture between the economic dimension of the transnational project and the political dimension: an incomplete transition to polyarchy has lagged far behind neoliberalism. American policymakers wanted to see a functioning bipartisan system based on the PRI and the rightist and neoliberal National Advancement Party (PAN), which houses an important wing of the country's transnational fraction. However, too much pressure on the PRI could open up space for popular classes. The US strategy has therefore been to provide strong and consistent support for an authoritarian state even while prodding it to complete a transition to fully functioning polyarchy. This has included support for the Mexican state's brutal counter-insurgency program.[17] The Mexican case underscores that the US objective is to promote polyarchy and

---

[16] See for example John Dinges, *Our Man in Panama* (New York: Random House, 1991); Philip Wheaton, *Panama Invaded* (Trenton: The Red Sea Press, 1992); John Weeks and Phil Gunson, *Panama: Made in the USA* (London: Latin America Bureau, 1991).

[17] On Mexico, see, among other sources, 'The Wars Within: Counterinsurgency in Chiapas and Columbia', *NACLA Report on the Americas*, 31/5 (1998); 'Contesting Mexico', *NACLA Report on the Americas*, 30/4 (1997); Tom Barry, *Zapata's Revenge* (Boston: South End, 1995).

oppose authoritarianism only when doing so does not unacceptably jeopardize elite rule itself. Indeed, the United States provided support in the 1980s and 1990s for mass repression in *all* of these cases discussed, and in other countries as well, such as in El Salvador, Guatemala, Bolivia, and Colombia. A policy of conditional promotion of polyarchy is perfectly compatible, and in fact regularly includes, the promotion of repression.

Power, Polyarchy and the Global System

We should recall when we speak of democracy that at issue is *power*. Power, in the Weberian definition, is the ability to achieve one's will even in the face of resistance by others. Power as exercised by social groups and classes is the ability to meet objective interests, to determine social behaviour, and hence shape social structure in defence of these interests. Some have argued that polyarchy is more responsive to popular majorities who have greater opportunities to advance their demands. If this hypothesis is valid, the argument could be made that popular majorities have more relative power now in the new polyarchies, even if power in absolute terms is still highly concentrated among elites. But what evidence do we have that this is so in Latin America? Whether popular majorities have more influence under the new polyarchies is to ask if they have been able to influence social structures in their interests to a greater extent. This is how we operationalize the theoretical proposition for empirical examination. What is most striking about the new polyarchies is the extent to which elites have been insulated from popular pressures and demands. Globalizing elites have been able to achieve social outcomes in the interests of transnational capital and against the objective interests as well as the actual subjective demands of popular classes.

In many countries in Latin America the neoliberal project has advanced despite systematic and organized mass opposition. The challenge for those promoting the new order is how elected regimes can push through unpopular neoliberal programs—how the wishes of the electorate can be subverted within the institutional framework of polyarchy.[18] Numerous Latin American polyarchic regimes, such as Alberto Fujimori's in Peru, Carlos Menem's in Argentina, Fernando Collor de Mello's in Brazil, and Carlos Andres Perez's in Venezuela, among others, were elected in the late 1980s and 1990s on explicit

---

[18] Much of the 'democratic consolidation' literature explores in this regard the types of 'political engineering' required to ensure economic reform in the face of mass opposition. Some of the literature has focused on the need to build up strong executives and to weaken legislatures more susceptible to popular pressure in order to insulate governments from democratic pressure. See for example George Philip, 'The New Economic Liberalism and Democracy in Latin America', *Third World Quarterly*, 14/3 (1993), pp. 555–71. Others argue than parliamentary government can best do the trick. See Juan Linz and Arturo Valenzuela (eds), *The Failure of Presidential Democracy* (Baltimore: Johns Hopkins, 1994). What the literature has in common is its normative system-maintenance bias and the search for the institutional organization of polyarchy most propitious for achieving order by absorbing popular discontent. 'Success in governing' becomes the ability not to *meet*, but to *diffuse*, mass demands on the political system.

anti-neoliberal platforms, only to perform U-turns on coming to power and implement sweeping austerity. In the face of mass protest these regimes had to govern by executive fiat, violating constitutional norms and individual civil rights. As Duncan Green has pointed out, Argentina's Menem issued as many decrees during 1989–92 as were announced by all of his civilian predecessors since 1922. In Bolivia, the elected government declared a state of siege to suppress opposition to structural adjustment. In Colombia, the government used anti-terrorist legislation to defuse opposition to privatization. In Peru, Fujimori simply dissolved the legislature and seized emergency powers in his 1992 'self-coup'. In most cases, these 'U-turn specialists', as Green has called them, were thrown out by electorates—impeached in the cases of Perez and Collar de Mello—that then voted for new anti-neoliberal candidates who in turn repeated the U-turn.[19]

The transnational elite has demonstrated a remarkable ability to utilize the structural power of transnational capital over individual countries as a sledgehammer against popular grassroots movements for fundamental change in social structure. In Haiti and Nicaragua mass popular movements were impotent to change the social structure, even when they gained access to the state, due to the ability of the global economy and the transnational elite to dictate the internal conditions in these countries. In Honduras and in Venezuela anti-neoliberal blocs elected their own candidates in the early 1990s; but these candidates soon found it impossible to resist the pressures of transnational forces. The assumption of pluralist theory that informs much discussion of US 'democracy promotion' is that the act of voting is a free act through which the will (power) of voters is exercised. But voting against the dominant project by electing to office candidates who oppose that project has not given electorates the ability to change that project. Local technocratic elites operate increasingly through transnational networks that bypass the formal channels of government and other social institutions subject to popular influence. John Markoff notes that 'as power passes upwards to supranational structures, including financial networks . . . it is far from obvious that ordinary people have more effective control over the institutions that shape their lives'.[20] Here we see the limits that the global system places on the ability of popular majorities to actually utilize polyarchy to have their will prevail. The 'twin dimensions' of polyarchy, 'political inclusiveness'—the popular vote—and 'political contestation'—the ability of popular majorities to run their own candidates and to even place them in power—do not translate into the exercise of power by popular classes understood as the ability to shape social structures in their interests.

Argentine sociologist Carlos Vilas notes that, under prevailing conditions of socioeconomic exclusion, personal autonomy is not possible for the poor

---

[19] For these details on discussion on this issue, see Green, *Silent Revolution*, especially p. 161.

[20] See Markoff, 'Really Existing Democracy: Learning From Latin America in the Late 1990s', p. 66. For a detailed case study of insulated technocratic decision-making in the Andean polyarchies, see Catherine M. Conaghan and James M. Malloy, *Unsettling Statescraft: Democracy and Neoliberalism in the Central Andes* (Pittsburgh: University of Pittsburgh Press, 1994).

majority and 'patron-client relations of domination and subordination tend to substitute for impersonal institutional loyalties'.[21] Subordinate groups manage their survival in non-democratic power structures and social networks by developing direct, non-mediated political relationships with power holders. The impoverished appear to support strongmen and authoritarian solutions and also exhibit political apathy and electoral abstentionism. 'Poverty is usually accompanied by a feeling of powerlessness which in turn is reinforced by the objective insecurity pervading everyday life in poor neighborhoods', notes Vilas. 'In this setting, voting may harbour quite a different meaning from that discussed in conventional political theory . . . Here, voting is an ingredient of an overall system of tradeoffs between the haves and the have-nots, an instrument to achieve specific resources like schooling, jobs, personal security, land titles, and the like.'[22]

These pervasive authoritarian power relations housed within the formal structures of polyarchy help explain voting patterns of subordinate classes, shaped by the structures of socioeconomic exclusion and class domination, and the electoral reproduction of neoliberal regimes. More generally, embedded in the social order are what David Held terms conditions of 'nautonomy' generated by the asymmetric production and distribution of life chances that negate autonomy and severely circumscribe the real possibilities of political participation.[23] It is the structural power of global capitalism to impose discipline through the market that—usually—makes unnecessary the all-pervasive coercive forms of political authority exercised by authoritarian regimes. But here the concept of coercion is not limited to physical coercion such as military and police force. Economic coercion as the threat of deprivation and loss, the threat of poverty and hunger and so on, forces people to make certain decisions and take certain actions, such that apparently 'free' choices are made by groups that have in fact been coerced by structures, and by other groups that control those structures, into making particular choices.

Socioeconomic power, therefore, translates into political power: the political and the socioeconomic spheres cannot be separated. It cannot be said that any real power has gone to broad majorities in Latin America. But elite theorists *don't* claim that power has gone to the majority: *this is the whole point.* Elitism theories claim that democracy rests exclusively on process and that the political sphere can and should be separated from the economic sphere, so that there is no contradiction between a 'democratic' process and an anti-democratic social order characterized by sharp social inequalities and minority monopolization of society's material and cultural resources. Diamond, Linz, and Lipset articulate this theoretical view: 'We use the term democracy in this study to signify a political system, separate and apart from the economic and social system . . . Indeed, a distinctive aspect of our approach is to

---

[21] Carlos M. Vilas, 'Inequality and the Dismantling of Citizenship in Latin America', *NACLA Report on the Americas*, 31/1 (1997), pp. 57–63 at 60.

[22] Vilas, 'Inequality and the Dismantling of Citizenship in Latin America', p. 62.

[23] David Held, *Democracy and the Global Order: From the Modern State to Cosmopolitan Governance* (Cambridge: Polity Press, 1995).

insist that issues of so-called economic and social democracy be separated from the question of governmental structure.'[24]

However, even though 'democratization' theorists claim to separate the political from the socioeconomic, they do not really do so. A central argument in the literature, and one that directly mirrors US policy, is that polyarchy requires free-market capitalism and that promoting polyarchy is complementary to and supportive of promoting free-market capitalism. The institutional definition of 'democracy' thus claims to separate the political from the economic and yet it simultaneously connects the two in its actual construct. I have discussed this logically fatal contradiction in democratization theory elsewhere[25] and it is worth reiterating here. When global capitalism is the concern, the political is expected to be linked to the social and the economic and 'normal society' is capitalist society.[26] But when economic inequalities and social justice are the concern, the political is expected to be separated from the social and the economic. By making this separation, such issues as socioeconomic exclusion, who exercises power, who controls the material and cultural resources of society, and so forth, become irrelevant to the discussion of democracy. What is relevant is simply political contestation among elite factions through procedurally free elections. This separation of the socioeconomic from the political sphere is an ideological construct because it appears in the mind of the intellectual and the policymaker but not in reality. This type of social science becomes to a large extent the legitimisation of political practices—such as promoting polyarchy—and the social interests served by those practices. But this antinomy in theory reflects the antinomy in the practice itself.

The Antinomy of Promoting Capitalist Polyarchy

Transitions to polyarchy have been accompanied by a dramatic sharpening of inequalities, social polarization, and a growth in poverty—a consequence of polarizing processes inherent in capital accumulation liberated from the constraints of developmental and interventionist states and the countervailing powers of popular classes. Between 1980 and 1995, some 94 million new people in Latin America joined the ranks of the poor, as the number of people living in poverty went from 136 million to 196 million, and then to 230 million in 1995: an increase from 41 per cent to 44 per cent, and then to 48 per cent, respectively, of the total population.[27] Moreover, inequality in Latin

---

[24] Larry Diamond, Juan J. Linz, and Seymour Martin Lipset, *Democracy in Developing Countries: Latin America* (Boulder: Lynne Rienner, 1989), p. xvi. See also 'Economic Reform and Democracy', special issue of *Journal of Democracy*, 5/4 (1994). The unproblematized assumption here is that transitions to free-market capitalism are desirable and that polyarchy is an institutional framework to facilitate these transitions.

[25] See Robinson, *Promoting Polyarchy*, pp. 48–56.

[26] See for example Larry Diamond and Mark F. Plattner (eds), *The Global Resurgence of Democracy* (Baltimore: Johns Hopkins University Press, 1993).

[27] See Comision Economica para America Latina (CEPAL), *Panorama Social de America Latina* (Santiago, Chile: CEPAL/United Nations, various annual reports).

America, while historically high in comparison with other regions, increased throughout the 1980s and 1990s, as income became more and more concentrated among a privileged 20 per cent of the population.[28] Added to income polarization has been the dramatic deterioration of social conditions as a result of neoliberal policies and a frightening escalation of deprivation indicators. An explosion of the informal sector, mass unemployment and underemployment, homelessness, the spread of hunger and malnutrition, and the reappearance in epidemic proportions of such diseases as malaria, tuberculosis, and cholera, have accompanied the transitions to polyarchy and the integration of Latin America into the global economy.[29] These trends are not peculiar to Latin America and are part of a broader pattern of growing inequalities, deprivation, and poverty amidst plenty under global capitalism.

The world-wide inequality in the distribution of wealth and power is a form of permanent structural violence against the world's majority. This structural violence generates collective protest, which calls forth state repression. This repression transforms, on a regular ongoing basis, structural violence into direct violence. The structural violence of the socioeconomic system and violations of human rights are different moments of the same social relations of domination. State repression employed by the 'new democracies' has been used throughout Latin America to repress protest against neoliberal structural adjustment and has claimed thousands of lives—see Table 14.1. Almost every

Table 14.1 Sample of Anti-Neoliberal Uprisings in Selected Latin America Countries, 1980–1994

Country and date(s)	Action	Severity	Precipitating event
Argentina			
1982–5	Marches, strikes, looting	Hundreds arrested	Prices hikes, austerity policies
1985	General strike, violence/looting	Over 100 wounded	Government anti-inflation measures
1989	Food riots and looting	14 dead, 80 wounded, thousands arrested	Outbreak of hyper-inflation
1993	Riots	4 dead, 50 wounded	Government cutbacks
Bolivia			
1983–93	General strikes, street violence, looting	c. 10 killed, 1,500 arrested	Numerous neoliberal adjustments
Brazil			
1983	Riots over food prices, looting, political protest	2 killed	Removal of price subsidies

[28] See for example World Bank, *Poverty and Income Distribution in Latin America: The Story of the 1980s* (Washington, DC: World Bank, 1997), and *World Development Report*, various years.
[29] See for example discussion in Robinson, 'Latin America and Global Capitalism'.

Country and date(s)	Action	Severity	Precipitating event
1986–7	Violence, looting general strike	Scores injured 30 arrested	Renewed austerity
1992	Wave of looting, hunger riots in north-east	(N/A)	Inflation/death of 38 children from starvation in north-east
Dominican Republic			
1984	Demonstrations/riots attacked by troops	100 killed 500 wounded	Devaluation, price rises after IMF agreement
1990	Strikes, riots	12 killed, 100 injured, 5,000 arrested	Price rises/other austerity measures
Ecuador			
1982–7	General strikes street violence and protests	7 killed, 50 wounded, 500 arrested	Price increases, removal of subsidies
1991	Four days of riots	1 killed, 30 wounded	Public transport fare increase
Guatemala			
1985	Riots, looting, protests and strikes, university militarized	2–10 killed 1,000 arrested	Increase in bus fares, bread and milk prices
Mexico			
1986	Frequent street protests	Injuries, deaths and arrests	1985 earthquake and austerity
1994	Mayan indian guerrilla uprising, land invasions	At least 107 dead, wounded and arrested	Reversal of agrarian reform and NAFTA
Nicaragua			
1990	Strikes and rioting	6 dead, 150 injured	New government's proposals for mass layoffs, austerity, reversal of Sandinista reforms
Peru			
1991	Strikes, riots, demonstrations,	Several killed and disappeared by army	Incoming President Fujimori's 'Fujishock' austerity programme
Venezuela			
1989	Riots, looting	300–1,500 killed (depending on source)	Public transport fare increase as part of IMF package
1991	Demonstrations	7 killed	Privatizations, fuel price rises

Source: Duncan Green, *Silent Revolution: The Rise of Market Economics in Latin America* (London: Cassell, 1995); John Walton and David Seddon, *Free Markets and Food Riots: The Politics of Global Adjustment* (Oxford: Blackwell, 1994).

Latin American country has experienced waves of spontaneous uprisings generally triggered by austerity measures, the formation in the shantytowns of urban poor movements of political protest, and a resurgence of mass peasant movements and land invasions, all outside of the formal institutions of the political system, and almost always involving violent clashes between states and paramilitary forces and protesters.

Social relations in daily life in Latin America are violent and ordered on authoritarian hierarchies. Human rights violations are still systematic and widespread, as the annual reports by the various human rights monitoring groups make clear. The new victims are now as much the social and economic outcasts as they are political dissidents. The following are examples of what 'social cleansing' of the poor and undesirable has involved: the infamous mass murder of street children in Guatemala, Brazil, and elsewhere by police and by death squads hired by affluent businessmen and local politicians; the death of thousands of poor people—the vast majority as they await trial—in countless prison uprisings in penitentiary systems unfit for human habitation; such grizzly scandals as the round-up and the execution by security forces in Colombia in 1995 of homeless individuals and their delivery to a private medical school as specimens for medical students to practice autopsies; the burning alive of an indigenous leader in Brasilia in early 1997 by upper-class teenagers for apparent amusement—they were acquitted of homicide; and so on. None of these cases is an anomaly: they are all manifestations of the social power of a minority wielded against the outcast in a socioeconomic system which by its very nature violates the human rights of a majority of society's members. When the very right to life is denied by the social order, discussion of democracy becomes philistine.[30]

These uprisings highlight the relationship between the violation of socio-economic rights and the violation of 'traditional' human rights. Social polarization brought about by neoliberalism has generated mass conflict that the neoliberal states have not been able to control without resorting to human rights violations. In the end, the imperative of social order makes itself felt in coercive domination. Hegemony, Gramsci reminds us, is consensus protected by the 'armor of coercion'. Polyarchy does not mean an end to direct coercion but a more selective application than under a dictatorship and that such repression becomes 'legalized' (legitimized) by civilian authorities, elections, and a constitution. In the long run, the US state cannot promote polyarchy and also promote global capital accumulation and the class interests embedded therein. This has already become clear in Colombia and Mexico. Even though the United States has attempted to promote polyarchy in these countries, the need to save the state from popular and insurrectionary sectors has

---

[30] On these cases, and for general discussion, see for example 'The Face of Human Rights in the '90s', special issue of *Latinamerica Press*, 27/10 (1995); Nancy Scheper-Hughes and Daniel Hoffman, 'Kids Out of Place,' *NACLA Report on the Americas*, 27/6 (1994), pp. 29–35; 'Pope's Visit raises hopes, frustrations', *Latinamerica Press*, 29/37 (9 October 1997), p. 1; and 'Prisons bursting at seams', *Latinamerica Press*, 30/10 (19 March 1995), p. 4; Steven Dudley, 'Walking Through the Nightscape of Bogota', *NACLA Report on the Americas*, 32/2 (1998), pp. 10–14.

led it into an ever deeper alignment with local authoritarian political forces and paramilitary groups who have been strengthened by US support.[31]

Latin America's polyarchic regimes face growing crises of legitimacy and governability. The transnational model of accumulation being implemented since the 1980s does not require an inclusionary social base and is inherently polarizing.[32] This is a fundamental structural contradiction between global capitalism and the effort to maintain polyarchic political systems that require the hegemonic incorporation of a sufficiently broad social base. Global capitalism generates social conditions and political tensions—inequality, polarization, impoverishment, marginality—conducive to a breakdown of polyarchy. The same market that generates an affinity between capitalism and polyarchy largely because the market replaces coercive systems of social control also creates and recreates the socioeconomic conditions that make impossible genuine democracy.

It is not clear what the future holds. We will not assume there will be a reversion to outright dictatorship. The changed correlation of class and social forces brought about by capitalist globalization helps to explain the continued survival of the new polyarchies. The fragmentation and weakening of the popular classes through restructuring and marginalization, along with the neoliberal culture of individualism and consumerism, contribute to the social control of the dispersed and atomized victims of global capitalism. Popular oppositional forces have not articulated an alternative to the current order, whether of a democratic socialist or of a redistributional character. This lack of an organized alternative provides space for the dominant project. On the other hand, there has been an upsurge from within civil society of struggle by popular social movements of the indigenous, women, shantytown dwellers, trade unionists, peasants, environmentalists, and so on, and this raises the issue of the prospects for popular democracy. The dominant groups have managed to gain control over and reshape political society; but they have not been able to establish their hegemony in civil society, underscoring the problematic nature of domination despite the transitions to polyarchy. Popular social movements, in their struggle to win the power necessary for the effective transformation of the social order, have discovered that democratization and social emancipation are not separable. Their demands for social and economic justice are not compatible with global capitalism and their demands cannot be met within the constraints set by the polyarchic political systems promoted by the United States and the transnational elite. The problem of order and control has not been resolved.

---

[31] See 'The Wars Within: Counterinsurgency in Chiapas and Columbia', *NACLA Report on the Americas*, 31/5 (1998). Highly revealing in this regard was the 1995 Mexico peso crisis and the US bailout. As the crisis was brewing, Goldman Sachs and Merrill Lynch told the Mexican government that it needed to do something about the Zapatista uprising, and an internal Chase Manhattan Bank memo declared, 'The [Mexican] government will need to eliminate the Zapatistas to demonstrate their effective control of the national territory and security policy'. Within days of President Clinton's announcement of a bailout plan the Mexican army initiated combat operations against the Zapatistas. See Medea Benjamin and Keven Danaher, 'Killing Mexican Peasants to Restore Investor Confidence', *Global Exchange*, 3 (1995), p. 1.

[32] For detailed discussion, see Robinson, 'Latin America and Global Capitalism'.

15

American Power, Neo-liberal Economic Globalization, and Low-Intensity Democracy: An Unstable Trinity

BARRY K. GILLS

Introduction

WE are all in favour of democracy. Democracy is a good thing. It is good that the United States now seeks to promote democracy in the world. It is hard to disagree with any of these propositions. However, the relationships among the power and interests of the United States of America, the policy of neoliberal economic globalization and the prospects for democratization in developing countries may not be positive. On the contrary, there may be a deep-seated antagonism between the extension of American power through accelerated and intensified neoliberal economic globalization and the realization of social progress through meaningful democratization. The economic policies pursued by the US tend to pre-configure the political, narrowing the range of regime type to a form called 'low-intensity democracy',[1] which itself is a political form not necessarily conducive to real economic progress for the majority. Low-intensity democracy has, however, emerged as a characteristic political form of the post-cold war era, in which formal electoral democracy is promoted, but the transformatory capacity of democracy is limited in order to facilitate neoliberal economic policies.

The ambitious pursuit of accelerated economic liberalization, including not only trade but also finance, can have destabilizing effects not conducive to democratization. Indeed, it can even be argued that 'the democracy we are encouraging in many poor parts of the world is an integral part of a transformation toward new forms of authoritarianism', given that 'If a society is not

---

[1] See Barry Gills, Joel Rocamora, and Richard Wilson (eds), *Low Intensity Democracy: Political Power in the New World Order* (London: Pluto, 1993); Barry Gills and Joel Rocamora, 'Low Intensity Democracy', *Third World Quarterly*, 13/3 (1992), pp. 501–23; and Barry K. Gills, 'Whither Democracy? Globalization and the "New Hellenism"', in Caroline Thomas and Peter Wilkin (eds.), *Globalization and the South*, (London: Macmillan, 1997), pp. 60–75.

in reasonable health, democracy can be not only risky but disastrous'.[2] Such unstable relationships among the influence of American power, neoliberal economic policies, and low-intensity democracy can be found today in many parts of the developing world.

Rather than promoting an ideal world of justice and democracy, neoliberal economic globalization (NLEG) is facilitating the emergence of an *historic malaise* in global capitalism, perhaps even an 'historic reversal' of capitalist civilization when judged in terms of social progress. Increasing inequality, social polarization, and the concentration of wealth in a few hands accompany this formal democracy. This 'New Hellenism' might be better understood through an historical analogy with the long death agony of democracy in classical Graeco-Roman civilization, in which democracy was slowly stripped of its meaningful substance through a process of concentration of economic power and increased exploitation of labour.[3] The historic malaise of global capitalism is now so pronounced that someone like George Soros could recently predict that, if left unchecked, the global crisis of 1997–9 would bring the complete disintegration of the system.[4]

Although US foreign policy has long made rhetorical claims to democracy as a universal value and goal, American power was deeply compromised with authoritarian and dictatorial governments around the world. The relationship between domestic capitalism and democracy may have been fairly positive in the US, but the relationships among US capitalism, US power and democracy abroad have been contradictory.[5] President Bill Clinton was the champion of a new US foreign policy which emphasized the global benefits of democracy and free trade. When visiting the states of Central America in March 1999, Clinton delivered an unexpected apology for US-sponsored terror and repression during the past four decades, which he called a 'dark and painful period'. He pledged that the US 'must not repeat' such a mistake. For the past decade Central American states have been formal and 'low-intensity' democracies, but the people of the region are still mired in the same miseries of extreme debt, poverty and inequality. The same elites remain in power. For example, Arena, the far-right party in El Salvador associated with the death squads of the Reagan period, has held power throughout the period of low-intensity democracy and was easily re-elected to power in the same month that Clinton delivered his historic apology. Meanwhile, as the president promised 'springtimes of renewal', a billion dollars of disaster aid for the region was being held up in the US Congress, US trade policies threatened local grain producers while

[2] Robert D. Kaplan, 'Was Democracy Just a Moment?', *The Atlantic Monthly* (December 1997), pp. 55–80 at 55–6, 58.

[3] Kaplan, 'Was Democracy Just a Moment?'; Barry Keith Gills, 'Adonde va la democracia? La globalizacion y el "nuevo helenismo"', *Politica Internacional*, Revista de la Academia Diplomatica del Peru, 42 (1995), pp. 7–20.

[4] George Soros, *The Crisis of Global Capitalism: Open Society Endangered* (London: Little, Brown, and Co., 1998).

[5] For a historical discussion of the relationship between capitalism and democracy from a Marxist perspective, see Ellen M. Wood, *Democracy Against Capitalism* (Cambridge University Press, 1995), particularly Ch. 9, where she discusses the separation of politics and economics under capitalism.

protecting US markets, and tens of thousands of Central American refugees who fled from the US-sponsored wars and terrorism of the 1980s were being threatened with deportation.[6] Such are the vicissitudes of globalization and democracy where the pursuit of power and national interest remain the primary concerns.

Re-Strategizing, Re-Articulating, and Re-Deploying American Power

The post-cold war era has already been dubbed the 'era of globalization'. With the collapse of the Soviet Union the emphasis in international relations turned swiftly toward accelerated economic liberalization. American power has been instrumental in consolidating this agenda. Moreover, the continuation and further extension of American power in this new era may be dependent on the success of 'globalization'. The quest for the global hegemony of the ideas of neoliberal economic globalization is connected to the quest for the continuation of American hegemonic power in the global system. By establishing 'hegemonic globalization',[7] American power may retain its centrality, even in a disputably 'post-hegemonic' world order.[8]

The US may or may not be 'hegemonic', but American power certainly remains central to the global system—economically, militarily, and politically. The fundamental desire of American policymakers to preserve and extend US centrality is a hallmark of post-cold war US foreign policy, and this should alert us to a basic continuity between the cold war era and the present situation.[9] The Clinton White House's 'National Security Strategy of Engagement and Enlargement' released in February 1996 focuses on three interrelated US goals: enhancing security—by means of military forces; bolstering US economic interests—through 'our work to open foreign markets and spur global economic growth'; and promoting democracy abroad. As the following excerpts from that document reveal, Clinton's philosophy combined Kantian and neoliberal elements:

Secure nations are more likely to support free trade and maintain democratic structures. Free market nations with growing economies and strong and open trade ties are more

---

[6] 'American reckoning', *Guardian* (13 March 1999).

[7] I am indebted to Thanh Duong for this formulation and would like to acknowledge his assistance in preparing this essay.

[8] See Alfredo G. A. Valladao, *The Twenty-First Century will be American* (London, NY: Verso, 1996). Valladao discusses the construction of a 'universal democratic empire' and the 'imperialism of freedom'. Valladao argues that 'The victory of World-America has rushed the poor countries, the newly industrialized countries (NICs) and even some highly developed states into jostling for integration with Washington's democratic empire. Governments everywhere are privatizing, deregulating, liberalizing the exchange of goods and capital flows, accepting the values of free enterprise, fighting for more foreign investment; committing themselves, for good or ill, to the path of individual freedom and democratic institutions. All are hoping to establish a direct connection with that great dynamo of the world economy, the American market' (pp. 190–1).

[9] See Michael Cox, *US Foreign Policy after the Cold War: Superpower Without a Mission?* (London: Pinter/The Royal Institute of International Affairs, 1995).

likely to feel secure . . . and democratic states are less likely to threaten our interests and more likely to co-operate with the United States to meet security threats and promote free trade and sustainable development . . . It is therefore in our interest that democracy be at once the foundation and the purpose of the international structures we build . . . Promoting democracy does more than foster our ideals. It enhances our interests . . . Democracies create free markets that offer economic opportunity, make for reliable trading partners and are less likely to wage war on one another . . . Our national security strategy is therefore based on enlarging the community of market democracies while deterring and limiting a range of threats to our nation, our allies and our interests. The more that democracy and political and economic liberalization take hold in the world, particularly in countries of strategic importance to us, the safer our nation is likely to be and the more our people are likely to prosper.[10]

The White House's comprehensive national strategy documents of 1996 and 1997 both placed great emphasis on enhancing access to foreign markets by US companies. They were also explicit about the integral relationships among foreign market opening, the ambitious US export strategy and the creation of US jobs and prosperity. This in turn was related overtly to the promotion of democracy, through the intention of giving 'democratic nations the fullest benefits of the integration into foreign markets'[11] which drove the agenda of the North American Free Trade Area (NAFTA), the Free Trade Area of the Americas (FTAA), the Uruguay Round process (the World Trade Organization, WTO) and the Multilateral Agreement on Investment (MAI) initiative. The 1996 statement was summarized under 'Promoting Democracy' thus: 'the core of our strategy is to help democracy and free-markets expand and survive.'

However, in pursuit of this unitary concept of 'democracy = free market', the US involved itself in what may more often than not be a set of contradictory social alliances. As the 1996 statement noted, 'Private firms are natural allies in our efforts to strengthen market economies'. On the other hand, 'our goal of strengthening democracy and civil society has a natural ally in labor unions, human rights groups, environmental advocates . . .'. In practice, the interests of these two sets of actors might be antagonistic. They might act at cross-purposes in relation not only to the economy but to the wider process of democratization.

Nevertheless, NLEG has emerged as the central aspect of the *re-strategization* of post-cold war US foreign policy. Re-strategizing is essential in the absence of a visible and 'common enemy'. The 'search for enemies' in the post-cold war environment must of necessity take on new appearances, ranging from narcotics barons and pariah leaderships to hysterical images of alien cultures or civilizations. Nevertheless, this should not obscure the basic continuity of American interests and their global ambition. The American 'grand strategy' post-World War II consisted of consolidating a world order in which capitalist values and American economic interests could flourish—always an extremely

---

[10] White House, 'National Security Strategy of Engagement and Enlargement' (February 1996), pp. 2–7. http://www.fas.org/spp/military/docops/national/1996stra.htm

[11] White House, 'A National Security Strategy for a New Century' (May 1997), p. 25. http://www.whitehouse.gov/WH/EOP/NSC/Strategy/

ambitious agenda requiring tremendous commitment of resources.[12] Today, as then, the real ideological enemy remains essentially any form of political or economic system that is resistant to the extension of American economic interests, whether nationalism, socialism, or the 'fundamentalism' of alien value systems.[13] Re-strategizing entails the search for new methods of pursuing the extension of American power and economic interests in the absence of the rhetorical framework of cold-war anti-communist ideology.

Re-articulation follows from re-strategizing. Having identified NLEG as central to the US foreign policy agenda, the emphasis shifts to foreign economic policy and relegates military security to a supplementary role. This brings a tendency to increase the use of economic means of intervention, whether sanctions, lending, trade or aid policy. These means of intervention grow more effective as more countries become increasingly liberalized and therefore more dependent on external economic linkages. In this environment, political linkages with foreign elites may be more instrumental to the realization of foreign policy goals than the threat of military force or traditional means of intervention. In this sense, therefore, re-articulation means arranging, consolidating or extending political alliances between American power interests and external elites, capturing them from 'within' and therefore seeming to stay within the bounds of international respect for national sovereignty while pre-configuring their economic policies in a neoliberal form. This is the essence of the international diplomacy of low-intensity democracy.

Re-deploying American power in the era of neoliberal globalization therefore calls for an ambitious programme of action simultaneously conducted on many levels of political reality. Not only does the United States itself move in the direction of neoliberalism—in the process creating future problems for its own democracy—but it encourages this tendency in all possible partners, whether in bilateral, regional, or multilateral global relationships.

The Post-Cold War US 'Multi-Level' Strategy

US post-cold war global policies involve a multi-level strategy of *global imbrication* of US influence. The US realizes that the tendencies of globalization and the diffusion of industrialization produce effects that could undermine its global centrality. The melée of competition may produce profound change in the global social formation, leading to regional regroupings of states and to global 'fragmentation' into antagonistic groupings. These patterns are fundamentally beyond any one state's control, but nevertheless the US fears losing control. Either a division of the world into rival bloc formations or the formation of a global 'anti-hegemonic' coalition, involving Europe, Asia and other

---

[12] Gabriel and Joyce Kolko, *The Limits to Power: The World and United States Foreign Policy, 1945–1954* (New York: Harper and Row, 1972).

[13] See Noam Chomsky, 'The Struggle for Democracy in the New World Order', in Rocamora, and Wilson (eds), *Low Intensity Democracy*, pp. 80–99, and Noam Chomsky, *Deterring Democracy* (London: Verso Press, 1991).

regions, is something that the US logically seeks to deter. American strategic policy is designed to neutralize these antagonisms.[14] In order to neutralize potential antagonistic developments, the US has to get 'inside' the new global, regional, and even national formations and work from within. The 'imbrication' strategy, therefore, potentially reaches everywhere and touches every level of international diplomacy, including bilateral, regional, and global.

Let us briefly review some of the implications at these three levels.

Bilateral

Using direct pressure on economic partners, the US presses—often quite aggressively—for increased market access, acceleration of economic liberalization, privatization, deregulation, and economic reforms in other 'sovereign' states, particularly the most successful exporters, as in east Asia. Whilst advancing the interests of US capital in gaining increased global market share, this bilateralism also has a tendency to weaken the target state's capacity for economic intervention and protection. It may also place the domestic firms or financial institutions of the partner state at a disadvantage *vis-à-vis* US and other core country competition. Unions in the target country may also be weakened by the effect of such 'reforms'. In extreme cases, the US Congress has recourse to special retaliatory legislation such as the notorious Super 301, to intimidate bilateral partners into making economic concessions, couched in the language of 'reform'.

This process of bilateral pressure for economic liberalization has occurred simultaneously with the ongoing processes of democratization in Latin America, Africa and Asia. Although there has been a turn away from military and civilian dictatorships in many countries in all three of these continents since the 1980s, their economic restructuring processes have been under pressure to turn away from nationalist paradigms towards a universal neoliberal paradigm. This simultaneity of economic liberalization and democratization creates particular problems of transition for all of these societies and generally exacerbates the problem of maintaining social and political stability.

Regional

Seeking to prevent regional groupings from becoming antagonistic to US interests and centrality, the multi-level strategy has a particular emphasis on imbrication within regional economic associations. The most conspicuous of these arrangements has been the NAFTA agreement between the US, Canada, and Mexico, which has involved the US in a common market approach with

---

[14] See 'US Strategy Plan Calls for Ensuring No Rivals Develop', *New York Times* (8 March 1992), which leaked elements from a Defense Department draft outlining the goal of preventing any major rival from emerging in western Europe, Asia, or the former Soviet Union's territory. The document argued that in order to maintain its central position of power, the US 'must sufficiently account for the interests of the advanced industrial nations to discourage them from challenging our leadership or seeking to overturn the established political and economic order'.

a Third World country for the first time. Given that the western hemisphere has been a primary area of US influence for many decades, it is logical that the US has made its most substantial regional imbrication efforts here. The economic integration agenda in the western hemisphere extends to plans for FTAA, involving some 34 'democratic countries' of the Americas, where US centrality is virtually assured. This would supersede or incorporate recent regional regroupings such as MERCOSUR in South America. The US trade relationship with Asia has emerged as a priority not only because of friction over the trade deficit, but also because of the quantity of trade with Asia. Strategic imbrication in the Asian regional regrouping process, principally through Asia Pacific Economic Cooperation (APEC), allows the US to influence the restructuring process, and deflect or constrain the ability of Japan to exercise its potential leadership of the region. This approach complements the US bilateral diplomacy of pressure for economic liberalization in key economies of east Asia. Thus, 'anti-hegemonic coalition' ideas such as those voiced by Prime Minister Mahathir of Malaysia are deflected and 'open regionalism' and support for the liberal international trading system are reinforced. This has applied to US relations with the European Union (EU) for some time, where 'fortress Europe' has been vilified and open regionalism encouraged. The US launched a 'New Transatlantic Agenda' in December 1995 to bring about further reduction in trade barriers and create a 'US-EU Transatlantic Marketplace', although incidents such as the 'banana war' in 1998–9 reveal continued and deeply embedded trade tensions. Although the US cannot gain direct entrance into the EU or prevent its rapid eastward expansion, it has its position in NATO and the Organization for Security and Cooperation in Europe (OSCE) in the security field as an indirect means of imbrication of its influence. American membership in the OECD and WTO are also avenues for imbrication strategy in the EU arena. Deflecting an independent security policy by the EU, such as potentially exists through the Western European Union (WEU), has logically been very important to US European policy.

Global

American multi-level global strategy includes a continued emphasis on multilateral diplomacy in international organizations with global scope or membership. The IMF has emerged as one of the most powerful political agencies on earth, capable of far-reaching intervention into domestic economies, despite the formal barrier of state sovereignty. The US has jealously guarded its premier position in the IMF in order to uphold the neoliberal economic orthodoxy by which it 'disciplines' some three score developing countries.[15] Although the Asian crisis and its 'global contagion' called into question the

---

[15] See Robert Wade's analysis of Japan's challenge to Anglo-American economic orthodoxy, 'Japan, the World Bank, and the Art of Paradigm Maintenance: "The East Asian Miracle" in Political Perspective', *New Left Review*, 217 (1996), pp. 3–36; and R. Wade and F. Veneroso, 'The Asian Crisis: The High Debt Model versus the Wall Street-Treasury-IMF Complex', *New Left Review*, 228 (1998), pp. 3–34.

orthodox policies of the IMF more than at any previous time, the response of the Group of Seven (G–7) to these criticisms was merely to establish a financial stability commission to coordinate policy in the future, whilst simultaneously rejecting the idea of establishing fixed trading bands for the largest currencies in an effort to curtail financial speculation and enhance currency stability.[16] In terms of trade liberalization, the WTO—successor to the GATT— has further extended and consolidated the liberalization trend in the world economy. The WTO expands the process of liberalization to new sectors, such as services, agriculture, and domestic procurement policies, while also undermining old-fashioned industrial policies with the code on subsidies and countervailing measures.[17] Yet further extensions of liberalization are planned through the negotiations for the MAI—defeated in the short term by global mobilization of opposition through the Internet—and proposals to give the WTO more binding and punitive powers against transgressions of its rules. The WTO, unlike the IMF, poses the possibility, however, that the transparency and universality of the rules will be applied equally to the US as well as to other member states. Beyond such universal organizations—including the UN apparatus—the US maintains centrality in the G–7, where it simultaneously emphasizes 'sound fundamentals' as the solution to global currency instability, campaigns for punitive economic sanctions against transgressors— such as India, following its explosion of a nuclear device, or the EU in the banana trade dispute—and endorses 'democracy' in cases of popular rebellion such as Indonesia or Nigeria, both of which have suffered tremendously from the rapaciousness of alliances between domestic authoritarian rulers and foreign multinational corporations.

Global Capitalism and Social Restructuring

The origins of the US pursuit of NLEG go much deeper than the changing policies of US presidents. They are embedded in the logic of the development of the global capitalist system itself. For much of the post-World War II era, American and western European capitalism rested on the foundation of a domestic compromise with labour allowing higher wages and expansion of social expenditure. The democratic regimes in the West had allowed wages, welfare spending and union power to rise in the postwar era, producing an era of mass prosperity but gradually narrowing the freedom of manoeuvre for private corporations and, in their view, threatening long-term growth and profits. Eventually 'core capital' began to react negatively to the increase in costs of production in the core, which were perceived to have reached unacceptably high levels. By the onset of the 1970s the West and the global

---

[16] 'Forum to help prevent crises agreed', 'Currency zone split remains', *Financial Times* (22 February 1999).

[17] For example, the WTO ruled that key government support programmes to the aerospace industry in Brazil and Canada constitute 'illegal subsidies'. *Financial Times* (22 February 1999).

capitalist system were increasingly beset by periodic recession and growing structural problems. As Keynesianism gave way to monetarism, a systemic reorganization of global capitalism was set in motion.

Two key strategies were pursued by core capital to improve the conditions for capital accumulation on national and global scales: *deindustrialization* of the core through relocation of production sites abroad, and *disinvestment* in manufacturing production through so-called 'financialization' of capital. Both have contributed to what we now call 'globalization', by which the West exported its crisis adjustment on to the rest of the world and in the process more tightly integrated the global capitalist system. Both have a systemic relationship to 'downsizing' and 'flexibilization' of labour in the core and the diffusion of industrial production to the developing countries.

The tendency toward 'deindustrialization' of the core, and the concomitant increase in the role of services, information technology, and finance in core economic structures, can be understood as occurring through three modalities. These are the *new international division of labour* (NIDL), *maquiladorization*, and *neoliberal economic globalization* (NLEG). These three modalities are not separate successive stages of a linear chronology of recent capitalist development. Rather, they are only partially or weakly sequential. Although NIDL may have characterized the initial stage of the adjustment of core capital to the 'crisis' in the 1960s, it was also accompanied quite early on by export processing zones (EPZs) or *maquila* enclaves for multinational corporations located in developing countries from east Asia to Central America. Neoliberal economic globalization, which has steadily intensified since the 1980s, has overlapped with a continuation of both NIDL patterns and *maquiladorization*, but extends to finance, requiring its full liberalization, and undermines alternative national systems of industrial regulation.

The new international division of labour, through foreign direct investments, brings reorganization of the international division of labour, allowing a larger role for industrial production in developing countries. As such, NIDL was a major factor in the onset of a new wave of industrialization in a number of peripheral economies, from Brazil and Mexico to Taiwan and South Korea. It engendered a proletarianization process in the periphery that extended not only to light but also to heavy industries and brought into being large and often militant and unionized working class movements. However, such industrialization was not associated with democracy, especially in east Asia.

Maquiladorization added new tiers of relocation of production sites, particularly in east Asian EPZs and the *maquila* enclaves of Mexico, Central America and the Caribbean region. However, it is marked by the intensification of the exploitation of labour and concentration of labour-intensive production into controlled sites in which union activities are more restricted. Its higher element of foreign direct investment and foreign ownership and control can make it less compatible with national economic development goals than conventional NIDL. Its relationship to democracy is ambiguous at best when judged from Mexican and Central American experience.

Neoliberal economic globalization is characterized less by its proletarianizing tendency than by its capacity to stimulate polarization among different sectors of society and different segments of the workforce. It is deployed not only *vis-à-vis* labour, but also *vis-à-vis* the national states themselves. It weakens both organized labour and the interventionist or developmentalist state, thus threatening the social compromises on which postwar global capitalism was reconstituted and which underpinned national social cohesion and national development in both core and developing countries.

Neoliberal economic globalization has four defining characteristic tendencies: (1) to protect the interests of private capital and expand the process of capital accumulation on both national and global scales; (2) to homogenize state forms and state policies to render them instrumental to the protection of private capital and the expansion of capital accumulation on both national and global scales; (3) to create and expand a new tier of transnationalized institutional authority above the nation state with the purpose of re-articulating states to the end of facilitating national and global capital accumulation; and (4) to exclude dissident social forces from the arena of state policymaking, in order to insulate the neoliberal state from the societies and social forces over which it presides, thus to 'socialize risk' on behalf of private capital. [18]

It is important to recognize that these trends are not solely the outcome of US power or pursuit of US corporate interests alone. They are part of a global logic of capitalist development and industrialization, to which the US and its companies must respond and in which the US is certainly a major actor as the largest single bloc of capital, with the most multinational corporations. Moreover, the US actively promotes all three processes as it pursues its fundamental policy of extension of American power through the extension of US economic interests. Historically, the strongest economic power tends to favour a liberal trade doctrine, as it has the most to gain from free access to others' markets.

The ever-increasing global mobility of capital is not only an expression of core capital's response to the policies of the welfare state, the social democratic compromise with labour in the core countries, and the Keynesian emphasis on sustaining full employment, but at the same time is the creation of a new global problematic of 'expansion and competition'. The exacerbation of the expansion and competition syndrome has become a constant feature of the global system. As the industrialization process becomes more globally diffused, industrial over-capacity gives rise to drastic industrial restructuring on the one hand and to the flight from production and the 'financialisation' of capital on the other. These tendencies are accompanied by a demand for deregulation and liberalization of finance, corporate mergers and acquisitions

---

[18] Louise Amoore, Richard Dodgson, Barry K. Gills, Paul Langley, Don Marshall, and Iain Watson, 'Overturning "Globalisation": Resisting the Teleological, Reclaiming the "Political"', *New Political Economy*, 2/1 (1997), pp. 179–95 (special issue on 'Globalisation and the Politics of Resistance', ed. Barry K. Gills), and in Barry K. Gills (ed.), *Globalization and the Politics of Resistance* (Basingstoke: Macmillan, and New York: St Martin's Press, 2000), pp. 12–28. See also the special issue on NLEG of *Millennium: Journal of International Studies*, 24/3 (1995).

in both industrial and financial service sectors, and, often, downsizing and flexibilization of the workforce in order to boost short-term profitability.

It is an intrinsic aspect of the global logic of expansion and competition that industrialization is further diffused throughout the world. American capital needs the diffusion of industrialization, despite the fact that this intensifies international competition. Attempts to cut costs of production and boost profit levels by the international relocation of manufacturing production sites and the exploitation of low-cost labour produced the 'global factory' system, uniting the industrial production of workers in the periphery with consumption by the population of core countries. However, as high-skill and high-paid jobs in industries in the core decline and are replaced by flexibilized, low-skill and low-paid jobs, the aggregate consumption power of the core population may decline also, so that low-paid workers in the US, for example, consume the products of even lower-paid workers in the periphery. Over the long term, this pattern may aggravate the tendency to low growth in the global economy. Lower aggregate growth further exacerbates the global systemic problem of intensifying international competition. Corporations fight over slices of a limited pie rather than of an ever growing pie. The global economy is hampered by a structurally embedded recessionary tendency.

In short, all ad hoc or 'anarchic' efforts to escape or overcome the expansion and competition problem through increasing the mobility of capital and increasing the exploitation of labour exacerbate the global problem. Nevertheless, it is precisely this same tendency which US foreign economic policy, both economic and 'democratic', seeks to further promote. Recent evidence that premature or inappropriate economic liberalization, particularly in the area of finance, has actually been seriously destabilizing has increased to such a degree that 'global crisis' discourse has now entered the media mainstream.[19] The ferocity and persistence of the most recent global crisis caught many by surprise, but these events should be understood in a long-term framework that stresses a culmination of NLEG rather than a short-term analysis of capital market turbulence.

When this underlying industrial situation is combined with a shortage of liquidity in world capital markets—which Klaus Schwab, President of the World Economic Forum, predicted by 2000 and which the global financial crisis of 1997–9 has demonstrated is a real possibility—and a growing problem of 'underconsumption' brought about by falling real wages and high structural unemployment, we arrive at the recipe for global depression and potential systemic disaster. Only the 'great American market' props up a tottering international economic system. By no coincidence, NLEG gives way to 'global

---

[19] See William Greider, *One World Ready or Not: The Manic Logic of Global Capitalism* (Harmondsworth: Penguin, 1997); John Gray, *False Dawn: The Delusion of Global Capitalism* (London: Granta Books, 1998); George Soros, *The Crisis of Global Capitalism: Open Society Endangered* (London: Little, Brown, and Co. 1998); 'Global Contagion: A Narrative', *New York Times* (17 February 1999). For the argument that premature or inappropriate financial liberalization was responsible for the recent Asian crisis, see S. Radelet and J. Sachs, 'The East Asian Financial Crisis: Diagnosis, Remedies, Prospects', *Brookings Papers on Economic Activity*, I (1998), pp. 1–90.

crisis'. Low-intensity democracy is not the solution to this crisis, but an intrinsic aspect of its cause and development. The US has made 'hegemonic globalization' its primary goal and identified it with vital national interests such as prosperity and security. Having extended NLEG to the globe, the US now also seeks to universalize 'democracy' as the corresponding political form of this global economic system. The unstable trinity of American power, NLEG, and low-intensity democracy is now entering a critical phase.

American Power, NLEG, and 'Wild Capitalism'

American power has been closely associated with the expansion of NLEG. The triumph of 'market ideology' represents a redistribution of resources from labour to capital on both national and global scales. In NLEG, the political process is represented as being a mere 'transmission mechanism' moving from 'capital logic' to society and the state. By making choices appear to be purely technical, NLEG therefore obscures the political nature of the strategic choices that must be made by any society as it responds to pressures for globalization. The emergent teleology of globalization is therefore economistic, ahistorical, and above all apolitical.

The danger in the further extension of NLEG rests in its threat to destabilize society, undermining existing and potential democracies and the complex but often fragile social compromises on which they rest. Neoliberal economic globalization confronts the democratization process, which is nowhere a completed historical process, with the threat of growing social polarization, conflict, and delegitimization. As such, NLEG is likely to constitute, in the long run, a politically retrogressive force, though couched in the language of the economically progressive. Historically, the removal of regulatory and protective measures designed to provide social stability and enhance social justice represents a tendency to return to the norms prevalent in pre-unionized, pre-welfare state, and pre-democratic capitalism. Without adequate corrective measures, historical experience indicates that 'wild' or 'savage' capitalism will produce a few 'winners' and many 'losers', thus exacerbating inequality, marginalization, poverty, and disempowerment for vulnerable groups in society. Such a situation, again as the history of capitalism amply demonstrates, is not conducive to social peace, human progress, or meaningful democratization.

Wild or savage capitalism is as unacceptable as the boom and bust cycle and the extremes of exploitation and conflict with which it is so clearly historically associated. The flaws in the market system certainly require prudent and continuous social intervention to sustain a just and prosperous society.[20]

Although it is a central tenet of economic liberalism that the market is the most efficient organizer of economic resources, the history of the twentieth

[20] See John Kenneth Galbraith, 'Preface' in special issue of *New Political Economy* on 'Globalisation and the Politics of Resistance', ed. Barry Gills, 2/1 (1997), pp. 5–9; and John Kenneth Galbraith, 'The Social Left and the Market System', in Gills (ed.), *Globalization and the Politics of Resistance*, pp. ix–xiv.

century is replete with necessary recourse to the state, precisely to overcome the instability engendered by market capitalism or to correct market failure. It is interesting that in the wake of the most recent 'global crisis', Mr Stiglitz of the World Bank made it something of a personal crusade to preach a revisionist economic doctrine which rehabilitated the notion of the state as a stabilizer, and the necessity of the 'social safety net' for social cohesion.[21]

Neoliberal economic globalization, and its association with low-intensity democracy, makes new social struggles for meaningful democracy both inevitable and historically necessary. Neoliberal economic globalization is a potent force in contemporary history, and has given rise to the idea that 'globalization' is an external and inexorable force that all must adapt to or suffer the adverse consequences. The idea that no one is in political control of the forces of economic globalization is a new mythology, part of the ideology of neoliberal globalization and its retreat from the state.[22] Everyone must indeed respond to the further extension of NLEG: individuals, households, companies, and states. The question is *how* they respond, in what way and by what means? This crucial question has direct implications for the future of democracy.

Democracy and the Politics of Globalization: *Trasformismo* vs. *Reformismo*

Democracy should be defined in a broad sense. It must include a formal democratic political system, a legitimate civilian government, and the rule of law. However, a formal electoral system alone is not enough to constitute democracy. The democratization process is above all a socially *inclusive* political process. It should, therefore, bring about significant changes in the composition of state power, allowing the inclusion of a broad spectrum of social forces, giving them direct and indirect access to state policymaking processes. This should include organized labour as well as other new and old social move-

---

[21] The IMF internal review of the east Asian crisis reform programmes also recognises that adjustment of the programmes toward a focus on social safety nets was necessary 'to contain the effects of the downturn on the most vulnerable parts of society' and in future the emphasis should be on an 'orderly and well-sequenced liberalization process', while the new international financial architecture should possibly include a 'social building bloc' including 'appropriate social safety nets, core labour standards, consensus-building in countries, and common social goals'. S. Sugisaki (Deputy Managing Director of the IMF), 'Economic Crisis and Recovery in Asia and its Implications for the International Financial System' (IMF: 5 March 1999), http://www.imf.org/external/np/speeches/1999/030599.htm

This view on the importance of proper sequencing of financial liberalisation reforms was endorsed by Michel Camdessus, though he stresses continued liberalisation and opening in order to 'reap the benefits of globalization': Michel Camdessus (Managing Director of the IMF), 'Bolstering Market Access of Developing Countries in a Globalized World' (IMF: 6 July 1998), http://www.imf.org/external/np/speeches/1998/070698.htm

[22] On the idea of the myth of globalization, see Ian Robert Douglas, 'Globalisation and the End of the State?', *New Political Economy*, 2/1 (1997), pp. 165–77, and in Gills (ed.), *Globalisation and the Politics of Resistance*, pp. 110–32; and Amoore *et al.*, 'Overturning "Globalisation"'.

ments. The process of inclusion hinges on decreasing social and economic inequality, polarization and marginalization.

The debate over globalization often focuses on the role of state power in relation to changing world economic conditions and new technologies. Two key aspects of this debate are the degree of manoeuvrability of the national state, and the degree to which national economies remain primary arenas of economic and social change.[23] A preference for global market forces over national sources of economic change signifies very different political conclusions and thus very different implications for democracy. A focus on the determining role of transnational capital and technologies, accompanied by global trends of hyper-mobility, deregulation and liberalization, often results in pessimistic political conclusions toward state manoeuvrability outside the NLEG paradigm.[24] A focus on the continued importance and viability of the national economy, however, may generate far less pessimistic political conclusions concerning the prospects for state manoeuvrability, and by implication for democracy.[25]

I summarize these two positions by recourse to the Gramscian concepts *trasformismo* and *reformismo*. The politics of *trasformismo* is a politics of preserving the status quo and therefore an *exclusionary* process, relying on cooptive strategies. The politics of *reformismo*, in contrast, is a politics of directly challenging the status quo and therefore depends on decisively changing the balance of forces in favour of the *inclusion* and empowerment of social forces. In *trasformismo*, 'opposition' political programmes converge to conservative ones until there ceases to be any meaningful difference between the 'alternative' and the elite position. In *reformismo* the hegemony of the conservative ruling bloc is rejected along with cooptive strategies, and the alternative posed is a progressive social programme aimed at actively reducing polarization, marginalization, disempowerment and poverty.

The quest for preservation of American power and its global centrality by means of NLEG generates a tendency to promote the politics of *trasformismo* and to obstruct the politics of *reformismo*. Thus, American power and its NLEG strategy align with the forces of *trasformismo*, while the forces of democratization must embrace *reformismo* and a political will to resist NLEG in all its various manifestations. By asserting NLEG, the US encourages the reorganization of production in such a way as to weaken organized labour, dissident social forces, and the national state.

However, it is the paradox of neoliberal globalization that while NLEG weakens labour and other dissenting social forces, it also stimulates the

---

[23] See for example John Zysman, 'The Myth of a "Global" Economy: Enduring National Foundations and Emerging Regional Realities', *New Political Economy*, 1/2 (1996), pp. 157–84.; and Robert Boyer and Daniel Drache (eds), *States Against Markets: The Limits of Globalization* (London: Routledge, 1996).

[24] See for example Philip G. Cerny, *The Changing Architecture of Politics: Structure, Agency and the Future of the State* (London and Newbury Park, CA: Sage, 1990).

[25] See for example Boyer and Drache (eds), *States Against Markets*; Linda Weiss, 'Globalization and the Myth of the Powerless State', *New Left Review*, 225 (1997), pp. 3–27.

activation or mobilization of these social forces into active resistance. These dissident social forces are called into action by the destabilizing effects of NLEG. American sponsorship of NLEG is therefore a politically contradictory process, simultaneously stimulating and repressing the mobilization of dissident social forces. Such a form of power can only intensify social conflict and strain the framework of the formal 'low-intensity democracy' which has been constructed around the world.

Illustrations of the contradictory nature of NLEG can be found from cases in the Americas, Asia, and Africa. In Mexico, the conclusion of NAFTA immediately brought the emergence of the Zapatistas, a critical social movement locally situated in Chiapas but dedicated to the mobilization of a broad social coalition for the democratization of Mexican society. When the ensuing peso crisis threatened to cripple Mexico, the US bailed out the authoritarian PRI government with massive financial assistance. The austerity effects of the peso crisis brought further social resistance, spreading even to the middle classes. The anti-NAFTA movement had already mobilized a new coalition of social forces across North America, furthering the creation of new solidarities between Canadian, US, and Mexican social forces. Whilst the US government and major corporations supporting the NAFTA agreement have pursued the logic of NLEG and the politics of *trasformismo* with the conservative Mexican elite, the same process has stimulated the mobilization of new dissident social forces dedicated to the politics of *reformismo* and creating new forms of trans-border solidarity.

In South Korea, US bilateral pressure for accelerated economic liberalization accompanied the transition to low-intensity democracy.[26] The state and conservative elite have pursued the politics of *trasformismo* and the economics of NLEG. The inability of the Kim Young Sam government in the mid-1990s to discipline the great business empires, the *chaebol*, led to formal adoption of the *segyehwa chong chaek*, or 'globalization policy', which accelerated the economic liberalization schedule, including financial liberalization. Following Mexico's lead, South Korea hastened to join the OECD. However, the government's attempt to promote NLEG by railroading legislation on the flexibilization of labour through the National Assembly in December 1996 led directly to a confrontation with organized labour. The ensuing national strike was remarkable for its longevity—two months—and the degree of organizational coherence. Above all, the national strike succeeded in winning over most of the population—some 80 per cent at the peak—to support its basic position. This was because the unions were able to represent the general public interest in resisting flexibilization of labour and in favour of restoring the impetus towards democratization.[27]

[26] See Barry Gills, 'Korean Capitalism and Democracy', in Rocamora and Wilson (eds.), *Low Intensity Democracy*, pp. 226–57; and B. K. Gills, 'Economic Liberalisation and Reform in South Korea in the 1990s: A "Coming of Age" or a Case of "Graduation Blues"?', *Third World Quarterly*, 17/4, pp. 667–88.

[27] Personal Interview with Kwon Young Kil, General Secretary of KCTU and leader of the national strike (Seoul: August 1997).

The national strike paved the way for the social legitimization of labour and its future political inclusion. However, the situation was dramatically affected by the 'IMF crisis' which surfaced in late 1997. The failure of reform during the tenure of Kim Young Sam led to a national financial debacle and the necessity for an unprecedented IMF bailout exceeding $50 billion. The US reportedly played a key role behind the scenes in formulating the 'reform' requirements stipulated in the South Korean IMF agreement. While a new government under President Kim Dae Jung was inaugurated in February 1998, austerity and unemployment rapidly increased. The reform-minded President Kim Dae Jung promised to implement the IMF agreement, restructure the *chaebol*, and discipline organized labour. The flexibilization of labour was immediately re-introduced alongside emergency legislation to liberalize foreign investment. By exacerbating recession through IMF austerity policies in his first six months in office, President Kim Dae Jung may have undermined his own efforts to end the political exclusion of labour and incorporate the unions into a new tripartite framework with government and business, modelled on similar arrangements in Mexico.[28] President Kim hoped to use neoliberal economic policy as a tool to discipline the *chaebol* but they have once again proved remarkably resistant to change. The further pursuit of neoliberal economic policies by the new government may jeopardize its ability to form a new polit-ical alliance with a broad range of social movements.

In the case of South Africa, while the struggle for democratization mobilized domestic social forces, combining the strength of organized labour with that of a range of other social movements,[29] the subsequent reform record of the democratic regime led by Nelson Mandela proved to be disappointing, leaving much of the status quo intact, while pursuing economic liberalization.[30] The South African model may be in a similar category to Zimbabwe, where the promise of liberation soon became the practice of liberalization.[31] The failure of the government to deliver meaningful reform for the impoverished major-ity of non-whites leaves the underlying structural problems of inequality and disempowerment unresolved. As one commentator put it,

Democratic South Africa . . . has become one of the most violent places on earth that are not war zones . . . There are ten private-security guards for every policeman. The cur-rency has substantially declined, educated people continue to flee, and international drug cartels have made the country a new transshipment center. Real unemployment is

---

[28] B. K. Gills and D. S. Gills, 'Globalization as Strategic Choice', paper prepared for the conference on South Korea and Globalization, Columbia University, East Asian Institute, Center for Korean Research (New York: 22–3 May 1998), and in Samuel S. Kim (ed.), *Globalisation and South Korea* (Cambridge and New York: Cambridge University Press, 2000); Barry K. Gills and Dong-Sook S. Gills, 'South Korea and Globalization: The Rise to Globalism?', *Asian Perspective*, 23/4 (1999), pp. 199-28 (special issue on 'G;lobalization in East Asia', ed. Samuel S. Kim).

[29] See: Glenn Adler, 'Global Restructuring and Labour: The Case of the South African Trade Union Movement', in James Mittleman (ed.), *Globalization: Critical Reflections* (Boulder, CO: Lynne Reinner, 1996), pp. 117–43.

[30] See John Pilger, special report on South Africa, *Guardian* (May 1998).

[31] See Sandra J. Maclean, Fahimul Quadir and Timothy M. Shaw, 'Structural Adjustment and the Response of Civil Society in Bangladesh and Zimbabwe: A Comparative Analysis', *New Political Economy*, 2/1 (1997), pp. 149–64, and in Barry K. Gills (ed.), *Globalization and the Politics of Resistance*.

about 33 percent, and is probably much higher among youths. Jobs cannot be created without the co-operation of foreign investors, but assuaging their fear could require the kind of union-busting and police actions that democracy will not permit.[32]

The struggle against apartheid did generate a solidarity movement within the United States, as citizens opposed the link between corporations and repressive regimes and campaigned for corporate disinvestment. Its example spread to other cases such as Nigeria, as well as Indonesia and Burma. However, US corporations organized a counter-movement to block municipal and state legislation in support of economic sanctions against dictatorial regimes like Nigeria. 'USA engage' enrols some 600 major US corporations, who argue that such sanctions are illegal—undermining Federal government authority to make foreign policy—and undermine US business interests. In the case of Nigeria, the Clinton administration intervened to stop a proposed sanctions law by the state of Maryland. Similar counterattacks by corporations are occurring against the sanctions movements on Burma.[33] President Clinton's summit tour of Africa in the first half of 1998 focused on further extension of US bilateral economic relations in the region and consolidation of the neoliberal paradigm for Africa.

Conclusion: The Politics of Globalization: Resistance and Democratization

The unstable trinity of American power, NLEG and low-intensity democracy is entering a critical historical phase in the context of mounting global crisis tendencies that threaten everyone. Therefore, political resistance to NLEG is both an historical inevitability and a necessity if the life chances of the majority are to be protected or enhanced and democracy given its true meaning. The US pursuit of NLEG promotes a politics of *trasformismo*, and attempts to weaken labour, dissident social forces, and the national state. At the same time, NLEG stimulates the mobilization of dissident social forces seeking to practice the politics of *reformismo* and reinvigorate the impetus to democratization in the interests of the majority. In response to the globalization of economic power, political bridges are needed between local, national, regional, and global arenas of resistance, political solidarity, and democratization struggles.

By promoting NLEG, the US may find that it pits itself against the interests of the working majority and the impoverished many, and will therefore face

---

[32] Kaplan, 'Was Democracy Just a Moment?', p. 69.

[33] The National Foreign Trade Council, representing 550 US manufacturing companies, filed suit against Massachusetts, claiming the State's new selective purchasing law infringes the US federal government's right to make foreign policy. This backlash in favour of NLEG may spread to the WTO and the EU, where there are threats of a suit against the Massachusetts Burma Law. For more information on these issues, contact Russell Mokhiber, editor of *Corporate Crime Reporter* (Washington, DC) at russell–essential.org, and Robert Weissman, editor of *Multinational Monitor* (Washington, DC) at rob–essential.org. See the 'Focus on the Corporation' columns posted at the Multinational Monitor web site at www.essential.org/monitor

their political resistance. American power and its strategic role in constructing NLEG presents a formidable challenge to resistance and democratization movements around the globe. The key element needed in the new politics of *reformismo* must be to strategize, articulate, and deploy a coherent practice of resistance to NLEG that can 'unify' local, national, regional and global dissident social forces wherever possible. This need not require the substitution of new 'grand strategies' for old and discredited projects of universal emancipation. The key objective is for social forces to reassert political control over private capital in the interests of society, rather than allowing existing political elites to capitulate to the growing social power of private capital. Society must not retreat from politics and engagement with state power, but rather seek to reinvigorate mass politics and re-articulate state power through this means.

Some are optimistic about the future of resistance movements to neoliberal globalization precisely on the basis of the broad popular appeal of these movements and the struggles recently won by grassroots movements in countries as diverse as India, Mexico, Nepal, and Costa Rica.[34] Others are optimistic about the prospects for new types of cross-border solidarity among labour unions and between them and other social movements, nationally and regionally.[35] The issues on which these movements campaign may seem diverse, including regional and national land reform and social justice, resistance to structural adjustment campaigns, and the struggle for national and international labour rights, but all are a product of the same phenomenon: market-driven economic liberalization and its destabilizing effects on society.[36]

In the quest for new types of global solidarities in resistance to NLEG, the union movements and social movements of the North have much to learn from their counterparts in the South and much to gain from working with them. The leadership role in emergent global solidarity movements should be shared between Northern and Southern representatives and between men and women. Resistance to NLEG will very probably continue to come predominantly from within national civil society, national union movements, and national social movements. However, the success of all these increasingly depends on their ability to transcend old forms of organization and develop new linkages with international social forces sharing similar goals and interests. Resistance from within civil society from the base of unions and social movements working within broad social coalitions will be an indispensable part of the new politics of resistance to NLEG, but internationalism will increasingly become an indispensable aspect of the strategy of national movements.

---

[34] Patrick Bond and Mzwanele Mayekiso, 'Toward the Integration of Urban Social Movements at the World Scale', *Journal of World-Systems Research*, 2/2 (1996), pp. 1–10.

[35] See various contributions in the special issue on global labour movements, Bradley Nash Jr (ed.), *Journal of World-Systems Research*, 4/1 (1998).

[36] See Peter Waterman, *Globalisation, Social Movements and the New Internationalisms* (London: Mansell/Cassell, 1998); and Peter Waterman, 'Social Movements, Local Places, and Globalized Spaces: Implications for Globalization from Below', in Gills (ed.), *Globalization and the Politics of Resistance*, pp. 135–49.

Through such actions a new global consciousness is being constructed 'from the bottom up' and an incipient global civil society is emerging. Such movements and the new practices of global solidarity will form the basis of new democratic and progressive movements for social change at local, national, regional and global scales. The hope of the twenty-first century must be that a new social praxis will constitute the basis of new sources of popular knowledge and epistemology for the achievement of a new democratic global civilization.[37]

[37] For a fuller elaboration on the new politics of globalization see: Barry K. Gills, 'Overturning Globalisation: Rethinking the Politics of Resistance', in J. Hersh and J. Schmidt (eds.), *Globalisation and Social Change* (London: Routledge, 2000), and Barry K. Gills, 'Globalisation and the Politics of Resistance' in Gills (ed.), *Globalisation and the Politics of Resistance*, pp. 3–11.

INDEX